Under the Editorship of

LEONARD CARMICHAEL

SECRETARY, SMITHSONIAN INSTITUTION;
FORMERLY PRESIDENT, TUFTS COLLEGE,
AND DIRECTOR, TUFTS RESEARCH LABORATORY
OF SENSORY PSYCHOLOGY AND PHYSIOLOGY

COUNSELING
AND
PSYCHOTHERAPY

NEWER CONCEPTS IN PRACTICE

BY

Carl R. Rogers, Ph.D.

PROFESSOR OF PSYCHOLOGY, UNIVERSITY OF CHICAGO
FORMERLY DIRECTOR, ROCHESTER GUIDANCE CENTER

HOUGHTON MIFFLIN COMPANY
BOSTON · NEW YORK · CHICAGO · DALLAS · ATLANTA · SAN FRANCISCO

The Riverside Press

CAMBRIDGE · MASSACHUSETTS

PRINTED IN THE U.S.A.

∾ EDITOR'S INTRODUCTION ∾

IT IS not always that an author and an editor know each other personally. In the case of the present book, however, the unusual has happened. As editor it is my pleasure to be able to say that through direct observation and through the reports of many mutual professional acquaintances I can attest that Dr. Carl R. Rogers is not only an effective professor of clinical psychology but also an experienced, wise, and gifted counselor. The present book, therefore, is theoretical only in the best sense of the word. It is, to be sure, a well integrated and reasoned account of the place and techniques of counseling and psychotherapy, but it is more than this for it is at the same time a truly practical book written by one who has had long and successful experience as a counselor and psychotherapist.

This volume is intended primarily for college and professional students who are learning how to guide others, but it will be valuable also to professional workers, experienced counselors, and even to those who are already convinced that they themselves have found the secret talisman of this difficult art. The extensive use of case material and the actual reporting of many interviews in the book make it especially helpful to the prospective professional worker, teacher, or student.

The approach to counseling today, Dr. Rogers points out, is not that of providing a service by means of which specific problems may be solved. Rather, it is a technique by means of which human individuals may be taught to adopt as their own those habits of mind and of emotion that will make them able to solve their own problems as they arise. The proper aim of the counselor is the production of a new attitude in the individual being counseled. This attitude should give the client himself increasingly clear insight into his own problems and help him to gain in integration in his own personality.

Then, at later periods in his life, he may be able to solve new problems.

The chapter entitled "Releasing Expression" possibly shows the positive and constructive point of view of the book at its best. Here a sane and reasonable technique is proposed and described by means of which a client finds emotional release from feelings hitherto repressed and at the same time comes to have increasing awareness of the part that these very feelings are playing in producing the problems and confusions which disturb him.

Throughout the book the author develops a point of view which gives emphasis to the significance of insight in the client. The word "insight" has been used much in recent psychological writings in an almost mystical way. In these pages the word insight is given practical and scientific definition. Insight here means the self-perception of new meaning in an individual's own experience such that relationships of cause and effect gain new significance. Thus behavior symptoms which have previously puzzled, alarmed, or morbidly depressed the client are often eliminated.

Dr. Rogers here offers a reasoned and persuasive exposition of a new and difficult field. It will assist those who would learn to be counselors and psychotherapists to produce real and lasting changes in those whom they advise. When the interview periods are over as described in this book, the individual who has been counseled may well say to his counselor: "I am now able to handle my problems by myself. I am working toward my new goal, which I understand. I am enjoying becoming independent of your help. I feel confident that I am going to be able to solve new problems when they arise in my life. In the future I shall try to meet my problems realistically and not avoid them in the unfortunate ways that I have attempted to sidestep them in the past."

LEONARD CARMICHAEL

~ PREFACE ~

THE steadily increasing interest in the individual and his adjustment is perhaps one of the outstanding phenomena of our times. Even the mass struggles and mass programs of wartime have served to emphasize as a part of our war aims the basic concept of the significance of the individual and his right to the elements of a satisfying adjustment.

In the period of the 1920's the interest in the adjustment of the individual was primarily analytical and diagnostic. In social work it was the period of the flowering of the case history; in psychology there was a lush tropical growth of tests; in educational guidance both records and tests grew apace; in psychiatry multi-syllabled diagnostic labels blossomed into elaborate diagnostic formulations. Never had so much been known about the individual. As time has gone on, however, these groups, and others with similar interests, have given more consideration to the dynamic processes through which adjustment is improved. The balance has definitely shifted from diagnosis to therapy, from understanding the individual to an interest in the processes through which he may find help. Today the professional worker who is concerned with the adjustment of the individual wants to know how he may become more effective in therapeutic ways in assisting the individual to readjust.

The writer has lived through and been a part of this shift in thinking and interest. An initial interest in diagnosis has become subordinate to a much stronger interest in the process of counseling and therapy. During a period of years in child-guidance work, as director of a child-guidance clinic, as counselor on student and family problems, he has developed a viewpoint regarding these treatment processes in which whatever is orginal is so blended with the thinking of others as to defy separation. Hence, while the present book represents his own

viewpoint, it has also drawn, both consciously and unconsciously, from the experience of many groups. For the better
orientation of the reader, and to express his own sense of obligation, the writer would like to indicate some of these groups to
whom he feels indebted, and some of the professional relationships which have had a significant part in shaping the concepts
which underlie this volume.

Experience in the short-lived Institute for Child Guidance
in New York City provided a stimulating situation in which a
range of viewpoints extending from ultra-psychoanalytic to
ultra-statistical challenged every worker to select and develop his own orientation.

Twelve years of association with a growing and changing
staff in the field of clinical psychology and child guidance
helped in the formulation of a treatment viewpoint. Most
of the members of that staff will recognize in this volume concepts and practices which they have had a part in formulating.
The close relationships with social workers and psychiatrists,
both those on the clinic staff and those outside, have enriched
the viewpoints here expressed.

Particularly stimulating has been the thinking that has come
from the Philadelphia Child Guidance Clinic and the Pennsyl-
vania School of Social Work. Through the writings from this
source, and through working with staff members who have had
training in these organizations, the writer has greatly profited.

The challenge of student counseling has been a fresh field
in which to test and amplify, with a most promising group, the
concepts of counseling which originated in the child-guidance
field.

The writer owes a special debt to the searching and discriminating questions of graduate students — clinical psychologists in training — who in developing their own counseling and
therapeutic skills have raised basic issues for consideration and
have assisted in clarifying the principles and practices of counseling.

Another contribution has been made by a research program
in which counseling and therapeutic interviews have been

phonographically recorded. These phonographic accounts, and the typescripts which have been made from them, have exposed the processes of counseling and therapy to an objective and microscopic examination which has illuminated the principles and problems of counseling in significant ways which thus far have been only partially utilized. This procedure holds much promise for the future.

Finally, and most deeply, the author is indebted to the multitude of individuals whom it has been his privilege to try to help. Children in trouble, disturbed parents, discouraged students, unhappy husbands and wives — all have contributed, the failures as well as the successes, to the learnings about the treatment process. In and through their struggles for growth and mature development has come an increasing certainty that we have too little, rather than too much, faith in the growth capacities of the individual.

Out of such a background comes this book, which attempts to state the author's conviction that counseling may be a knowable, predictable, understandable process, a process which can be learned, tested, refined, and improved. It is presented with the hope that it will lead counselors and therapists, both in the field and in training, to undertake further investigation, in theory and in practice, which will enable us to deepen and perfect our knowledge of ways of enabling the individual to develop a more satisfying adjustment.

CARL R. ROGERS

COLUMBUS, OHIO

Contents

PART I. AN OVERVIEW

PART I

An Overview

CHAPTER I

The Place of Counseling

THERE are a great many professional individuals who spend a large portion of their time in interviewing, bringing about a constructive change of attitude on the part of their clients through individual and face-to-face contacts. Whether such an individual calls himself a psychologist, a college counselor, a marital adviser, a psychiatrist, a social worker, a high-school guidance counselor, an industrial personnel worker, or by some other name, his approach to the attitudes of his client is of concern to us in this book. If in his work he deals with individuals who are maladjusted, or perplexed, or failing, or delinquent, and if they leave their interviews with him somewhat better adjusted to their problems, facing the realities of life more constructively, then his techniques and methods are of interest to us.

There are various names which may be attached to such interviewing processes. They may be termed treatment interviews, which is a simple and descriptive term. Most frequently they are termed counseling, a word in increasingly common use, particularly in educational circles. Or such contacts, with their curative and remedial aim, may be classed as psychotherapy, the term most frequently used by social workers, psychologists, and psychiatrists in clinics. These terms will be used more or less interchangeably in these chapters, and will be so used because they all seem to refer to the same basic method — a series of direct contacts with the individual which aims to offer him assistance in changing his attitudes and behavior. There has been a tendency to use the term counseling for more casual and superficial interviews, and to reserve the term psychotherapy for more intensive and long-continued contacts directed toward deeper reorganization of the personality. While there may be some reason for this distinction, it is also plain that the most intensive and successful counseling is indistinguishable from intensive and successful psychotherapy. Consequently, both terms will be employed, as they are in common use by workers in the field.

The Use of Counseling Techniques

To what extent are such counseling and psychotherapeutic measures used in dealing with adjustment problems? While no statistical answer can be given, a descriptive answer may indicate the importance of counseling as a process.

Child-Guidance Clinics. In child-guidance clinics we find psychotherapy a highly developed tool, used in discriminating fashion with children, especially adolescents, who present adjustment problems, and with the parents of these children. Over a period of years there has been a very rapid growth of clinical thinking in regard to such psychotherapy, and we may fairly say that the techniques of psychotherapy have been more adequately developed in the child-guidance field than in any other.

One or two examples may make plain the extent to which such an approach is used in child-guidance clinics. An analysis of one year's work in the Rochester (New York) Guidance Center, of which the writer was formerly the director, gives the following information. Of the 850 cases accepted during the year 1939,

> 62 per cent were seen for 1 to 4 contacts, accounting for 42 per cent of the total clinic contacts.
>
> 30 per cent were seen for 5 to 9 contacts, accounting for 23 per cent of the total clinic contacts.
>
> 8 per cent were seen for from 10 to 80 contacts, accounting for 35 per cent of the total clinic contacts.

When a child was seen four times or less by the psychologist, it is plain that the contacts were largely diagnostic and that a very limited amount of counseling could be accomplished. For the group in which there were five to nine contacts with child and parent, counseling often formed a significant aspect of treatment, though other means of altering behavior were also used in most cases. In the group seen for intensive treatment, with more than ten contacts per case, it is plain that psychotherapy constituted one of the most important approaches to the treatment of the problem. These contacts in some cases were with the child alone, in others with the child and the parent. Generally the psychologist carried on the treatment of the child, and the social worker counseled the parent, though this was by no means always true. It is worth pointing out that while only 8 per cent of the cases coming to the clinic were selected for such intensive treatment, the work with these individuals made up one third of the clinic effort.

From the Judge Baker Guidance Center come figures which throw further light on the extent to which counseling and psychotherapy form a part of child-guidance work. Out of 1334 cases studied by this clinic under its directors, William Healy and Augusta Bronner, 400 cases were accepted for treatment. The others were given diagnostic study only, and the responsibility for carrying out the treatment was turned back to the agency referring the case. Of the 400 treatment cases, 111 of the children were seen by the psychiatrist for one or two contacts, 210 for three to nine interviews, and 79 for ten to one hundred interviews. The number and distribution of the interviews with parents is quite similar, with eighty-three of the parents being seen (usually by the case worker) for from ten to one hundred or more interviews.[1]

From both these reports one may summarize by saying that the use of psychotherapy in child-guidance clinics is definitely limited to a minority of the cases, selected because of their appropriateness for this type of therapy. The treatment interviews with this selected group, however, constitute a major part of the work of the clinic. Such a statement would be true

[1] Healy, William, and Bronner, A. F. *Treatment and What Happened Afterward*, pp. 14, 43, 46. Boston: Judge Baker Guidance Center, 1939.

of most of the clinics in the country carrying on work with maladjusted children.

Student Counseling. In working with the adjustment problems of high-school and college students, we find counseling used as the most frequent method of meeting individual problems. In fact, it may be said that the nearer the client group is to mature adulthood, the more prominent will counseling and psychotherapy appear as the method of approach to the problems presented. The reason for this will be considered later.

In dealing with problems of personal and emotional adjustment, at either the high-school or the college level, we find advisers using counseling techniques almost entirely. For problems of educational and vocational guidance, various psychometric tests are utilized, but counseling nearly always forms an important part of the process, and should, according to experts in the field, have even more place in such work.

It is evident to anyone acquainted with secondary schools and colleges that guidance programs which make use of counseling are steadily on the increase. As schools more and more become organized around the concept of individual growth and development, services which assist the student in making the best adjustment to his situation necessarily increase. As administrators realize more clearly the tremendous economic waste involved in mass methods of education, they seek for practical solutions. As they calculate the cost of fitting square pegs into round holes, of trying to educate students whose energies are taken up with unsolved problems, they look for ways of preventing this waste. In imposing certain uniform standards upon the group, they become increasingly aware of the fact that though standards may be uniform, students are not. Out of such experience comes an increasing demand for programs designed to understand the individual and to aid him in meeting his problems. Consequently, most of our colleges and a great many of our secondary schools have some type of adjustment service for students, although these resources range from highly superficial arrangements, which operate in name only, to carefully organized bureaus and departments, which offer various levels of counseling service to meet varying degrees of student need.

Mental Hygiene Services for Adults. There are relatively few clinical organizations which serve the maladjusted adult. Much of the counseling of adults is done on a private basis by psychiatrists and psychologists. There has been, however, in recent years, a development of advisory and counseling services in the field of marital adjustment. These organizations give counseling help to those about to be married, and to married couples who are finding it difficult to make the necessary adjustments in marriage.

In such services, although physical examinations, legal advice, and other elements may enter to some extent into the service, the basic tool of the worker is the counseling process. In assisting those who come for premarital advice, the counseling may be limited to one or two contacts.[2] In dealing with well-established marital difficulties, effective treatment may demand many interviews.[3] The demand for such help far outruns the resources, as any clergyman can testify. While the type of help offered is related to marriage problems, there is no reason to suppose that the effective counseling processes are any different from those used in the field of student guidance, or in work with parents of maladjusted children.

Social Work. The case worker in the field of social work is prepared to offer to her clients not only some of the elements which have traditionally been thought of as part of social work — financial relief, help in getting work, medical aid, and the like — but in addition, and perhaps most important of all, counseling help. While the term counseling is very little used

---

[2] Mudd, E. H., *et al.* "Premarital Counseling in the Philadelphia Marriage Counsel," *Mental Hygiene*, vol. XXV (January, 1941), pp. 98–119.

[3] Mowrer, Harriet R. *Personality Adjustment and Domestic Discord.* New York: American Book Company, 1935. 220 pp.

in case-work circles, it is used here precisely to emphasize the fact that in giving the client an opportunity to release his feelings, to find new solutions to his adjustment problems, the case worker is utilizing the same process as that used by the other professional individuals described. Social work is the only profession which offers any large amount of such therapeutic help to the maladjusted adult. It is, however, in spite of case workers' efforts to the contrary, largely limited to the portion of the population which is in financial need. In their work with children in institutions and foster homes, and in their co-operative work in child-guidance clinics, social workers also make use of their psychotherapeutic skills. As a professional group they have contributed much to our understanding of the process.

Industrial Personnel Work. Until recently, counseling had little part in personnel work in industry. The interviewing of employees or applicants in order to get information was an important function, but counseling, in which there was a planned effort to use interviewing contacts to improve attitudes, was almost unheard of. Now, however, one of the most outstanding studies in industrial relations, made in the plants of the Western Electric Company,[4] promises to change this situation. This study shows conclusively that the social aspect of an industrial plant has more importance to the individual than its productive organization. It shows that satisfying adjustments in the social and emotional realm play a much more significant rôle in industrial production than alterations in wages and hours. Out of this exhaustive research, which began as a study of working conditions as they affected output, came one outstanding recommendation — the establishment of a suitable counseling program to assist workers in solving their personal problems. Nothing else, the investigators felt, would do so much for industrial morale. Such a program has been organized, with one counselor for each three hundred

[4] Roethlisberger, F. J., and Dickson, W. J. *Management and the Worker.* Cambridge, Massachusetts: Harvard University Press, 1939.

employees, and is proving the correctness of the study. We shall have occasion to refer to it a number of times throughout this book. Its significance for us at this point is that it indicates that for the industrial concern which desires maximum production, maximum harmony in industrial relationships, maximum development for the individual worker, counseling is a process of the utmost importance.

In War Efforts. Although most of the statements made about student and industrial counseling apply with equal force to any military organization, whether in training or in combat, there has been very little use of a counseling approach in the vast war program which has been inaugurated in this country. The failure to utilize such a tool is due in part, no doubt, to the usual cultural lag in translating new discoveries into effective working programs. It may also be caused in part by the tendency of the military mind to think in terms of a mass, rather than an individualized, approach. Yet there are many reasons to suppose that our growing knowledge of psychotherapy could be effectively used in the military program.

Military morale, like industrial morale, rests to an important degree on satisfactory adjustments and satisfying human relationships, and in this field counseling has proved itself useful. Thousands of draftees and recruits find themselves facing new situations which are difficult for them to meet — new adjustments to authority, new social groupings, the necessity for revising vocational plans, and uncertainties regarding the future. Many of them can assimilate these problems, can create without aid a new orientation to their situation. But many are unable to do so and become the disgruntled, the neurotic, the malcontent, the inefficient members of the group. Their destructive influence on morale is costly. Counseling could do much to help such individuals face their difficulties, assimilate them, and find integrating purposes which they might wholeheartedly follow.

In addition to these usual strains, which are faced by every man going into the service, there are the special psychological stresses which are peculiar to certain types of military training. Pilots, parachutists, or other individuals training for especially hazardous aspects of service often develop unmanageable fear and states of panic which so interfere with normal learning progress that they are eventually "washed out" of such training courses. An opportunity to talk out and assimilate unreasonable fears, to achieve again a measure of self-confidence, might reclaim many of these individuals and enable them to complete their preparation. How many of the costly failures in such training régimes are due to emotional and adjustment factors which sound counseling would overcome, we cannot be sure, but the number is large in the opinion of those closely associated with the work.

The need for a counseling program exists not only while the individual is in the military forces, but perhaps even more when the inevitable period of demobilization, with all of its readjustments, arrives. He must face, at that time, the pressing problems of finding a job, of rebuilding family relationships, of becoming self-supporting, of developing new social bonds. The experience of the last war indicated that in this situation, most of all, the individual needs a type of counseling which can help him to become more independent, can help him to leave the ordered life of the army where responsibility can always be comfortably left to "the one higher up," and undertake again the decisions, the choices, the responsibilities of adult life.

These are types of counseling service which might be, but to date have not been, put into operation in the military services. The one use which has been made of counseling, in the past war as well as during the present struggle, is the readjustment of that vast number of men who become psychological casualties. The development of neurotic and evasion mechanisms among officers and men in wartime has come to be recognized as one of the outstanding problems of modern warfare. The psychological organization of the individual recoils in the face of the terrific stresses which are a part of the present war, with its two added strains in the shape of mechanized warfare and the "war of nerves." Psychological counseling has much to offer in the reorientation and cure of many of these victims of mankind's war against itself.

One further word might be said as to the place of effective counseling in a military program. Under the pressure of a war psychology, many of the characteristics of a democratic society are temporarily laid aside. There is always the risk that those characteristics may be permanently gone, that the dictatorial structure which a democratic group adopts in time of crisis may prove to be unchangeable. An effective counseling program, with its interest focused on the individual, with its purpose the more adequate development of the individual, would be a force in preserving the concept of personal integrity, and a significant symbol of the value which democracy puts on the fundamental importance and worth of each citizen.

The techniques of counseling, it may be seen from this brief survey, occupy an important place in many of the programs at present being carried on and give promise of fulfilling even more important functions in the future, particularly in education, in industry, and in such national efforts as are typified by our military-training program. A type of approach so widely used, and of increasing significance, deserves our closest study.

PSYCHOTHERAPY IN RELATION TO OTHER TYPES OF TREATMENT

Important as counseling may be, it should be clearly understood that it is not the only approach to the treatment of the problems of the individual. It is not a panacea for all maladjustments. It is not the appropriate approach for all problem children, nor to all problem parents. It is not to be used indiscriminately with all students, nor all draftees, nor all workers in an industrial plant. It is one method, albeit a significant method, of dealing with the multitude of adjustment problems which cause the individual to become a less useful, less efficient member of his social group.

At various points in our later discussion we shall have occasion to point out the limits of any type of psychotherapy as a treatment approach. It may be well to mention here certain broad differences between a counseling approach and other avenues of treatment.

Preventive Measures. Emphasis needs to be placed upon the fact that certain administrative policies may and do prevent maladjustment. The regulations regarding employment and management of workers in an industrial plant, the policies regarding grade placement and promotion in a school, may, for example, be so planned as to prevent much maladjustment. While such policies are not, strictly speaking, treatment, they have the same importance that preventive medicine has in the field of health. It is perhaps more important that we should know how to prevent typhoid than that we should know how to treat the disease when it occurs. It is perhaps more important that we should know how to prevent maladjustment in our schools, colleges, homes, and industries than that we should know how to treat such maladjustments when they do develop. Consequently, for any total overview of the treatment of maladjusted individuals, we must recognize the great importance of all administrative policies which affect human relationships and human strivings, no matter what the institutions in which these policies are formulated. We have sufficient knowledge of healthy psychological growth to make it possible to devise for a school, an industry, or any other organization a set of administrative policies which would promote adjustment, and another set which would produce warped and maladjusted personalities with an abnormally high proportion of behavior problems, neurotic personalities, and the like. Hence, if we are interested in treatment, we must also be interested in those organizational procedures which can prevent the development of problems.

If the question is raised whether we might not substitute preventive measures entirely for remedial measures, the answer runs parallel to the answer in the medical field. Most of our hard-won knowledge of effective preventive policies grows out of tested experience in treating the maladjusted individual. Out of our dealings with the problem child has come a recognition of the necessity of better reading instruction in the early grades to prevent the costly and far-reaching effects of a reading disability. Out of our work with maladjusted students has come our knowledge of the psychological and social waste, as well as the economic loss, involved in wrong vocational choices, and the consequent emphasis upon broader programs of preventive guidance and education about vocations. Out of contacts with disgruntled and nonproductive industrial and commercial workers, and the knowledge gained from these contacts, have come plant policies which pay as much attention to the psychological needs of the worker as to the financial opportunities of the corporation. In short, we need to develop more adequate techniques of treatment for the individual if we are to devise more effective preventive programs for the group.

Environmental Treatment. The methods of assisting those individuals who find themselves in difficulty — the behavior problems, the failing, the emotionally disturbed, the neurotic, the delinquent, the maritally unhappy — may be divided into two major groups. The first of these is the treatment of the problem individual through the manipulation of his environment. The forms which such treatment may take are legion. It may include every possible means by which the individual's surroundings, physical and psychological, are made more conducive to satisfying adjustment. For one individual this may mean placement in a rest home, for another a change of school, for another a transfer from one industrial department to another, while for a child it may mean removal from his own home and placement in a foster home or institution. The therapeutic changes in environment may be gross transplantations like those cited above, or subtle changes which vary the environment slightly but significantly. The child may be placed in a remedial reading group once a week, the worker may be assigned to a new machine in order to separate him from a friction-creating co-worker, the adult may be given a committee task which he will find satisfying.

If such changes are soundly planned and skillfully executed, they can be extremely effective in altering the attitudes, behavior, and adjustment of the individual. In a previous volume [5] the writer has endeavored to analyze and describe the ways in which manipulation of the physical and social environment may be most effectively used in the treatment of the maladjusted child. That material will not be repeated here. Suffice it to say that the reader should be aware of this whole area of treatment through indirect or environmental means if he is properly to understand and evaluate the more direct counseling process.

It may be noted that all such treatment assumes a socially defined and desirable goal. Thus, a delinquent boy is placed in a foster home (1) because society insists that it will not tolerate his behavior, and (2) because, in view of the facts of the particular case, foster-home placement seems to be the most efficient means of altering his attitudes and behavior. Whether the boy would have chosen such placement, whether he is aware that over a period of time it will definitely affect his attitudes — these are not questions of primary importance. Doubtless this is a sound basis for treatment in many instances. It will at once be seen, however, that it has little application to the individual who has attained a reasonable degree of adult maturity. Only in the case of the criminal, the psychotic, the defective, or the individual who is for other reasons incapable of taking responsibility for himself can we freely use such manipulative measures with adults. The fact that environmental treatment is based upon a socially accepted goal and upon some type of authority — parental, institutional, or legal — to direct the individual toward that goal is not always fully recognized. This fact tends to limit the area of its effective use.

Direct Treatment. The second major category of treatment

[5] Rogers, Carl R. *The Clinical Treatment of the Problem Child*, chaps. IV to IX. inclusive. Boston: Houghton Mifflin Company, 1939.

techniques is composed of those by which the maladjusted individual is directly influenced in an effort to help him gain a more satisfying relationship to his situation. In this category belong the treatment interviews, the counseling and psychotherapeutic methods, with which this book concerns itself. They constitute the most frequently used and most important method of direct treatment. They will, of course, be discussed in the chapters which follow.

Another group of direct therapies, each of which bears some relationship to the others and to the counseling process, might be described as the expressive therapies, since catharsis of feelings and attitudes plays a highly significant part in each one. This group would include play therapy, group therapy, art therapy, psychodramatics, and other similar techniques. Each of these has come to play a helpful rôle in the treatment of personal problems. Most of these techniques had their origin in work with children, but there is no doubt that progress is being made in adapting them to the adult as well. In each case a basic element of treatment is the full expression of feelings either through such nonverbal media as clay, dolls, drawings, and the like, or through verbal means, in which feelings are projected onto others, as in spontaneous or guided dramatic productions. It is likely that the principles which explain successful counseling also explain much successful treatment through these expressive methods. Consequently, there will be occasion for frequent reference to them, though the reader is referred elsewhere for a complete account of these new and interesting developments.

Up to this point there has been no mention of medical treatment — the alteration of attitudes and behavior through glandular medication, operations, or dietary or other measures. Such treatment is beyond the scope of this work, but its place in the total treatment field should be recognized. The individual's behavior, outlook on life, and ability to cope with adjustment problems may be directly affected by medical measures.

It becomes evident, then, that if we look upon the whole

field of readjustment techniques with a proper perspective, we see counseling as important but as by no means the only approach to the individual who finds himself out of harmony with his life situation. We need this perspective if we are to avoid the pitfalls which so often lie across the path of the over-enthusiastic. While we shall devote our attention exclusively to counseling and psychotherapy throughout the remainder of this volume, we should keep in mind the fact that counseling is but one of a number of avenues through which we may help the maladjusted person to develop a more satisfying life.

THE PURPOSE OF THIS BOOK

Although a great deal of counseling is being carried on, although members of several professions regard it as one of their major functions, it is a process to which very little adequate study has been given. We know much less about the outcomes of counseling of students, for example, than we do about the results of foster-home placement for children. The process of counseling has been much less adequately described than the methods of play therapy, although the latter is applicable only to a relatively small group of clients. We have much less understanding of what makes counseling effective or ineffective than we do of other approaches.

So vast is our ignorance on this whole subject that it is evident that we are by no means professionally ready to develop a definitive or final account of any aspect of psychotherapy. What is needed, it would seem, are some hypothetical formulations, based on counseling experience, which may then be put to the test. Scientific advance can be made only as we have hypotheses which may be experimentally tried, tested, and improved. The field of counseling has not been rich in fruitful hypotheses. It has rather been a field where good intentions and a desire to be of assistance have been accepted as substitutes for the careful formulation of the principles involved.

It is precisely in this area that the present volume is intended to serve a definite purpose. It endeavors to formulate a definite and understandable series of hypotheses in regard to counseling which may be tested and explored. For the student it aims to provide a consistent framework for thinking about counseling, with illustrative, analyzed examples of procedure. For the research worker its purpose is to provide a consistent set of hypotheses as to what constitutes effective psychotherapy, hypotheses which may be experimentally verified or disproved. For the worker in the field it may provide a challenge to formulate some alternative or more accurate set of hypotheses for himself.

Because of its purpose, the book does not attempt to present all viewpoints in the field of psychotherapy. It has seemed wiser to work toward clarification in the field of counseling by presenting one viewpoint adequately rather than to increase the confusion through description of a hodgepodge of conflicting views. Consequently this volume presents a method and a theory of counseling which has evolved out of more than a dozen years of work in the child guidance field, which has been influenced by experience in the fields of student counseling and marital guidance, and which has drawn freely upon the experience and thinking of others in these fields. It is a viewpoint which has been enhanced and clarified by the results of a research program in which many counseling interviews, both single interviews and series of interviews, were electrically recorded on phonograph records for research analysis.[6] This proved to be such a rewarding approach that many vaguely formulated ideas became crystallized as a result of the program. From these various sources definite principles and hypotheses have been developed which, it is hoped, offer a basis for further advance.

[6] Certain aspects of this program have been described in the following articles:

Covner, Bernard J., "Studies in the Phonographic Recordings of Verbal Material: I, The Use of Phonographic Recordings in Counseling Practice and Research; II, A Transcribing Device." *Journal of Consulting Psychology*, vol. VI (March–April, 1942), pp. 105–113 and vol. VI (May–June, 1942), pp. 149–153.

Rogers, Carl R., "The Use of Electrically Recorded Interviews in Improving Psychotherapeutic Techniques," *American Journal of Orthopsychiatry*, vol. XII (July, 1942), pp. 429–434.

The Basic Hypothesis. In closing this introductory chapter, it may be well to state at once the basic hypothesis which it is the purpose of the remaining chapters to explain, define, amplify, and clarify. This hypothesis may be very briefly put as follows: *Effective counseling consists of a definitely structured, permissive relationship which allows the client to gain an understanding of himself to a degree which enables him to take positive steps in the light of his new orientation.* This hypothesis has a natural corollary, that all the techniques used should aim toward developing this free and permissive relationship, this understanding of self in the counseling and other relationships, and this tendency toward positive, self-initiated action.

Since it is the purpose of the remaining chapters to give meaning to this statement, it will not be discussed here, but we will proceed in the following sections to give it specific content. The reader may wish to return to it from time to time to see whether it has gained new significance for him.

Old and New Viewpoints in Counseling and Psychotherapy

To GIVE orientation and perspective in regard to the whole field of counseling, it may be well to present a brief sketch of some of the techniques which have preceded present-day counseling, and also a hasty overview of the newer concepts which will be more fully described in the remaining portions of this book.   If we can see outworn and discarded techniques as the background out of which recent therapeutic approaches have developed, we shall have a deeper understanding of present points of view and an increased ability to criticize them in a constructive fashion, which will further their improvement. Consequently, the present chapter endeavors to provide something of a bird's-eye view of the past and present in counseling, before we proceed to the more detailed ground view of some of the counseling processes.

In making this brief survey, the focus of attention will be upon counseling processes used, not upon the theoretical formulations of various schools of thought.   There is no attempt to provide a history of the various "isms" which have both stimulated and plagued psychotherapeutic thinking.   To give such a history would in all probability align the reader with one or another camp, clouding the deeper consideration of the methods and techniques actually employed.   It is the latter problem with which we are most concerned.

Psychotherapy is not a new concept, even though the term itself is relatively recent.   Throughout the centuries individuals have, in a variety of ways, used face-to-face situations in an endeavor to alter the behavior and change the attitudes of a maladjusted person toward a more constructive outcome. We may examine some of the ways in which these direct-contact situations have been used to bring about better adjustment.

SOME OLDER METHODS

Methods in Disrepute. One of the oldest techniques is that of ordering and forbidding. A brief illustration will be sufficient. For a number of years the writer was connected with a social agency whose history began previous to 1900. It is interesting to look over some of the early records of that agency. Each card contains a description of a situation, often one of extreme social and individual maladjustment. Then, in many instances, the description is followed with this statement: "Parents warned and advised." It is obvious from the satisfied tone of these records that the workers felt that they had done their duty. They had brought to bear on the individual the personal forces which they had supposed would be therapeutic. It will be recognized by all that this method has been discarded and is now only a museum piece in psychotherapy. It is worth noting that it has been laid aside, not because of its lack of humanitarian feeling, but because it has proved ineffective. Such orders and threats are not techniques which basically alter human behavior. Indeed, they alter superficial behavior only when they are backed by coercive forces which find little place in a democratic society.

A second approach with historical interest we might label exhortation. In this class should be placed the use of pledges and promises. It was generally the procedure to get the individual "worked up" to a point where he would sign a pledge to stop drinking, or would promise to work hard, to stop stealing, to support his wife, to get "A" in his studies, or to achieve some other praiseworthy goal. He would thus supposedly bind himself to his good intentions. Such a method has been used both with groups and with individuals. Psychologically, it might be described as creating a temporary emotional upsurge and then trying to "peg" the individual at that high level of good intention. There is no doubt that this method has been almost completely dropped. The reason is not far to seek. It is well recognized even by the layman that the most common sequel to such a technique is a relapse. Exhortation and pledges and promises are not successful in bringing about a real change.

A third approach has been the use of suggestion, in the sense of reassurance and encouragement. To this approach belong such procedures as that of Coué and his notions of autosuggestion. Here also should be included the many techniques of reassurance used by counselors and clinicians the world over. The client is told in a variety of ways, "You're getting better," "You're doing well," "You're improving," all in the hope that it will strengthen his motivation in these directions. Shaffer [1] has well pointed out that such suggestion is essentially repressive. It denies the problem which exists, and it denies the feeling which the individual has about the problem. It is not unusual for a clinician or counselor to make so many statements of approval and reassurance that the subject does not feel free to bring his less acceptable impulses to the clinical situation. While this approach is still used by many counselors, there is no doubt that faith in it has steadily declined.

Catharsis. Another psychotherapeutic approach of ancient lineage is the technique of confession or catharsis. The confessional has been used by the Catholic Church throughout many centuries. It has allowed the individual to talk out his problems to an individual who provides a certain defined type of acceptance. Both the Church and individuals outside the Church have found this method helpful. Psychoanalysis has taken this concept of catharsis and has made much deeper use of it. We have learned that catharsis not only frees the individual from those conscious fears and guilt feelings of which he is aware, but that, continued, it can bring to light more deeply buried attitudes which also exert their influence on

[1] Shaffer, L. F. *The Psychology of Adjustment*, pp. 480–481. Boston: Houghton Mifflin Company, 1936.

behavior.   In recent years we have learned new ways of using this old approach.   The whole technique of play therapy is based on the fundamental principles of catharsis; the use of finger paints and psychodramatics and puppet shows all have a relationship to this old and well-established category of psychotherapy.   This is a method of approach which has definitely not been discarded, but which has been developed and more widely used.

The Use of Advice.   One commonly used type of psychotherapy is advice and persuasion.   Possibly it might be called intervention.   In this type of approach the counselor selects the goal to be achieved and intervenes in the client's life to make sure that he moves in that direction.   We find extreme examples of it in certain radio "experts" who, after listening to a complex human problem for three or four minutes, advise the individual as to exactly what he should do.   While every trained counselor is well aware of the viciousness of such an approach, it is nevertheless surprising how frequently this technique is used in actual practice.   Often the counselor is unaware of how much advice he gives or the extent to which he does intervene in the life of the client.   In any complete record of counseling such phrases as "If I were you ——," "I would suggest ——," "I think that you should ——," occur very frequently.   Perhaps an example of this tendency to give advice should be included here.   The following excerpt is from a phonographically recorded interview.   It is typical of the way in which positive advice enters into the counseling interview.

During the interview the student (who has been requested to take Psychology 411, a study-habits course) tells the counselor about his part-time job and the counselor asks a number of questions about it.   The conversation continues:

Counselor.   Well, I really believe that you ought to spend just all the time you can find on the books.   Unless you were in great danger of starving to death, it doesn't seem to me to be advisable for you to work.   If you don't make — what grades do you have to make this quarter, to stay in school?

Subject. I don't know exactly, about a two, or two point one, average.

Counselor. Well, if you really want to stay in school, you are going to have to buckle down and do some high-powered studying, and I don't see how you can do it if you spend that much time working. I think that time is needed for studying. But that's just the way it looks to me. You should know your own situation better than anybody else. I'm just sort of an outsider looking in and I'm making my comparison with — oh, my own experience and the students that I've known — the students that I've assisted in 411 courses. I know — I've been able to follow some of the students through, from the time they were in 411 until some of them graduated. Some of them do graduate and some of them don't, in any college class. But generally speaking, in order to graduate, unless a person has an unusual amount of intelligence — so-called natural intelligence so that they don't have to study — unless you happen to be one of those people, it does mean spending a lot of time on the books. (*Pause.*) You live at your fraternity house?

In reading the above excerpt, certain points should be noted. It is instructive to observe how strongly the advice is given and the fact that it is coupled with a veiled threat about staying in school. It is also significant that the counselor apologizes in effect for giving such strong advice. We find such phrases as "but that's just the way it looks to me." Nearly always the counselor has some feeling that it is not sound for him to impose his own solution of the problem upon the client. It is also worth noting in this excerpt that the counselor changes the subject at the end in order to avoid getting the resistance which he would probably receive from the student.

Following is another account of treatment of a student problem which involves even stronger advice and persuasion. This account is given in the counselor's own terms.

Emotional Problem: Part of the treatment was centered around catharsis. Frank seemed to get relief in talking out his problems to an interested and sympathetic listener. He told me of numerous occasions where he had been miserable and unhappy because he never had learned how to meet people (more of this under Clinical Data). My first step was to have him state that this personality trait was undesirable for life adjustment and that steps should be taken to correct it. My question was: "Do you want to remedy this defect in an otherwise pleasant personality?" He answered in the affirmative. I outlined the following steps for rehabilitating him socially: (1) Register in the Social Skills Course of the Y.M.C.A. (2) Attend meetings of the Cosmopolitan Club, where he could use his knowledge of world events. (3) Participate in the Y.M.C.A. mixed-group activities. (Letters were sent to the appropriate officer of each group to insure a personalized reception.)

Scholastic Problem: My job was to dissuade him from continuing in pre-business and in having him accept a substitute program of general education. First I pointed out the standard of competition in the professional School of Business. This made no dent in his armor. He still maintained that his D + average would come up to a C this year. Knowing his dislike of courses involving math, I showed him the courses as catalogued in the professional business curriculum: statistics, finance, money and banking, theoretical economics, insurance accounting, and so on. (With silent apologies to my friends who teach these courses) I told the student that these courses were "highly theoretical and abstract" and considered "very dry." On the other hand, courses in general education were practical and interesting; no economics or math prerequisites were necessary. I described some of the interesting features of the Orientation Courses. He finally agreed to think it over. I outlined this plan of action: (1) see the counselor in the general education unit for further information (I arranged an appointment); (2) discuss the matter with his folks; (3) secure transfer blanks from the Registrar's Office.[2]

Note in this account how completely the counselor directs the thinking. It is very plain that at all times the counselor knows exactly what the goal of the student should be. In trying to persuade the student to reach this goal, both straightforward, honest reasons are given and also one frankly dishonest reason. In short, any suggestion that gets the student to the goal is considered appropriate.

This method of dealing with individuals is widespread and common in college counseling and in clinical work. We shall have occasion later on (Chapter V) to analyze its character-

[2] Sarbin, T. R. "The Case Record in Psychological Counseling," *Journal of Applied Psychology*, vol. 24 (1940), p. 195.

istics and implications more thoroughly. It is sufficient here to remark that the tendency to use such advising and persuading techniques seems to be on the decline. It has two major weaknesses. The individual who has a good deal of independence necessarily rejects such suggestions in order to retain his own integrity. On the other hand, the person who already has a tendency to be dependent and to allow others to make his decisions is driven deeper into his dependency. This technique of suggesting and advising, while it may at times help in the solution of the immediate problem, does not necessarily make for the growth of the client.

The Place of Intellectualized Interpretation. There is one further psychotherapeutic approach which deserves mention before passing on to newer emphases. It might be termed the attempt to change individual attitudes by means of explanation and intellectual interpretation. In general, this approach grew out of a better understanding of human behavior. As clinical counselors learned to understand more adequately the factors which underlie behavior and the causes of specific behavior patterns, they tended to make more and more adequate diagnoses of individual situations. Then came the natural mistake of assuming that treatment was merely diagnosis in reverse, that all that was needed to help the individual was to explain to him the causes of his behavior. Thus clinicians endeavored to explain to parents that their child's problems were due to their own feelings of rejection toward him, or that their shortcoming was in their own starved emotional life and consequent overindulgence of the child. The college counselor explained to the student that his lack of self-confidence apparently was caused by continued unfavorable comparison with his older brother. There was a naïve faith that this intellectual explanation of the difficulty would result in changed attitudes and feelings. An interesting example of this approach is quoted here from one of our phonographic recordings of student counseling. The counselor is talking with a gifted high-school student who has shown many evidences of social maladjustment and who has talked freely about his many intellectual and artistic interests. Toward the end of the second interview the counselor endeavors to interpret Sam's behavior as a compensatory mechanism.

> *S.* Well, I'll tell you. I think I'm worried because I think I'm developing a superiority complex or something. I really don't feel very superior, but I don't know —— What is a superiority complex, anyhow? Is that when you think you are better than anybody on God's green earth or something?
>
> *C.* It seems that you are really worried about people. You really feel that people don't think you are so hot, and you resent them because they look down on you. And you use these other things that perhaps build up your confidence in yourself and you are really not quite sure that they do.
>
> *S.* (*Silence and long pause.*)
>
> *C.* Sam, you have built up these intellectual habits, your atheism and your love of art, your love for unusual books and many other things like that, and you believe in them, yet you are not quite sure of them, are you?
>
> *S.* I'm very sure, darn it.
>
> *C.* Well, perhaps I didn't make myself perfectly clear. You are sure of them intellectually, you have worked them all out, and you know your arguments, but you are rather worried about yourself for believing them and for being different from other people.
>
> *S.* Oh, I don't know — I'm not worried.

There is no doubt that the counselor's interpretation in this case is fundamentally correct. That does not make it any more acceptable to the student. If Sam could recognize that he had developed his overintellectualized pursuits to compensate for the social lack he feels, it is doubtful that he would need counseling.

The use of intellectual interpretation formed a significant part of classical psychoanalysis. Interpretation of dreams as showing buried hostilities, repressed incestuous or other sexual desires, or a desire for punishment was very common. Often in practice these interpretations were rejected by the client. It is only more recently that stress has been laid on the other half of the equation. Interpretation, no matter how accurate, has value only to the extent that it is accepted and assimilated by the client. To trace symptoms back to a childhood cause, or to explain the way in which symptoms are easing intolerable life situations, may have no effect, or an adverse effect, on therapy, unless the client can accept these interpretations. Hence we find, in child-guidance work, in psychoanalysis, and in counseling, less stress placed upon the verbal and intellectual interpretation of causes or meanings of the subject's behavior. It has come to be recognized that we do not change the client's behavior very effectively simply by giving him an intellectual picture of its patterning, no matter how accurate.

Basic Assumptions. All but one of these approaches to the maladjusted individual have two basic assumptions in common. They assume that the counselor is the one most competent to decide what are to be the goals of the individual, and what are the values by which the situation is to be judged. This is true of such approaches as ordering and forbidding, suggestion and personal influence, even of interpretation. Of those mentioned, all but catharsis [3] imply a goal chosen by the counselor. With this exception, all of these earlier approaches have deeply ingrained in them the idea, "The counselor knows best." A second basic notion is that, by searching, the counselor can discover techniques which will get the client to the counselor-chosen goal in the most efficient manner. These techniques are consequently considered the best counseling methods.

A NEWER PSYCHOTHERAPY

Over against these methods of psychotherapy is a newer approach which has been growing up in the field of child and adult guidance. It represents in a number of ways, which will be indicated, a fundamentally different viewpoint. These newer concepts have their roots in many diverse sources. It would be difficult to name them all. The thinking of Otto

[3] Perhaps this explains the fact that catharsis is the only one of these approaches which has been developed, extended, and improved.

Rank, as it has been modified by such individuals as Taft, Allen, Robinson, and other workers into "relationship therapy," is one important point of origin. Modern Freudian analysis, which has at last become sufficiently secure to criticize Freud's therapeutic procedures and to improve upon them, is another source. Many individuals have played a part in this, of whom Horney is perhaps the best known. The rapid development of play therapy has commanded the interest of workers from various professional fields and has done much to contribute to a new and more valid viewpoint toward psychotherapy. The beginnings of experimentation in the field of group therapy, with its attempt to translate the principles of individual counseling into therapeutic group processes, has also done much to stimulate and clarify thinking about treatment.[4] It is perhaps significant that most of the impulses toward the development and refinement of this newer approach have come from the practical field — from the practice of treatment in clinics, schools, and agencies — rather than from any academic source. This may help to explain the fact that while the sources are diverse, and the individuals who have made significant contributions come from differing disciplines and backgrounds, there is discernible a sizable core of agreement, a body of similar practice growing out of common elements of viewpoint.

Its Character. This newer approach differs from the older one in that it has a genuinely different goal. It aims directly toward the greater independence and integration of the individual rather than hoping that such results will accrue if the counselor assists in solving the problem. The individual and not the problem is the focus. The aim is not to solve one particular problem, but to assist the individual to *grow*, so that he can cope with the present problem and with later problems in a better-integrated fashion. If he can gain enough integration to handle one problem in more independent, more responsible,

[4] The selected bibliography (pages 439–445) endeavors to list the more significant contributions to present-day thinking in regard to therapy.

less confused, better-organized ways, then he will also handle new problems in that manner.

If this seems a little vague, it may be made more specific by enumerating several of the ways in which this newer approach differs from the old. In the first place, it relies much more heavily on the individual drive toward growth, health, and adjustment. Therapy is not a matter of doing something *to* the individual, or of inducing him to do something about himself. It is instead a matter of freeing him for normal growth and development, of removing obstacles so that he can again move forward.

In the second place, this newer therapy places greater stress upon the emotional elements, the feeling aspects of the situation, than upon the intellectual aspects. It is finally making effective the long-standing knowledge that most maladjustments are not failures in *knowing*, but that knowledge is ineffective because it is blocked by the emotional satisfactions which the individual achieves through his present maladjustments. The boy who steals knows that it is wrong and inadvisable. The parent who nags and condemns and rejects knows that such behavior is unfortunate in other parents. The student who cuts class is intellectually aware of the reasons against doing so. The student who gets low grades in spite of good ability frequently fails because of the emotional satisfactions of one sort and another which that failure brings to him. This newer therapy endeavors to work as directly as possible in the realm of feeling and emotion rather than attempting to achieve emotional reorganization through an intellectual approach.

In the third place, this newer therapy places greater stress upon the immediate situation than upon the individual's past. The significant emotional patterns of the individual, those which serve a purpose in his psychological economy, those which he needs to consider seriously, show up just as well in his present adjustment, and even in the counseling hour, as they do in his past history. For purposes of research, for understanding of the genetics of human behavior, past history is very important.

For therapy to take place, it is not necessarily important. Consequently, there is much less stress on history for history's sake than formerly. Curiously enough, when there is no probing for the "facts" of the history, a better picture of the dynamic development of the individual often emerges through the therapeutic contacts.

One further general characteristic of this newer viewpoint should be mentioned. For the first time this approach lays stress upon the therapeutic relationship itself as a growth experience. In all the other approaches mentioned, the individual is expected to grow and change and make better decisions after he leaves the interview hour. In the newer practice, the therapeutic contact is itself a growth experience. Here the individual learns to understand himself, to make significant independent choices, to relate himself successfully to another person in a more adult fashion. In some respects this may be the most important aspect of the approach we shall describe. The discussion here is somewhat parallel to the discussion in education as to whether school work is a preparation for life, or whether it *is* life. Certainly this type of therapy is not a preparation for change, it *is* change.

CHARACTERISTIC STEPS IN THE THERAPEUTIC PROCESS

There is nothing so difficult to put into words as a point of view. If the foregoing seems vague and unsatisfactory, let us turn to the process of therapy itself. What happens? What goes on during a period of contacts? What does the counselor do? The client? The sections which follow attempt to state, briefly and in somewhat oversimplified form, the different steps in the process, as the writer has seen them occur many times, and to illustrate them with excerpts from clinical records. Although these different aspects of therapy are described separately and placed in a specific order, it should be emphasized that they are not discrete events. The processes mingle and shade into one another. They occur only approximately in the order given here.

I. The individual comes for help. Rightly recognized, this is one of the most significant steps in therapy. The individual has, as it were, taken himself in hand, and taken a responsible action of the first importance. He may wish to deny that this is an independent action. But if it is nurtured, it can lead directly toward therapy. It may as well be mentioned here that events insignificant in themselves often provide in therapy just as satisfactory a ground for self-understanding, for responsible action, as more important occasions. This may be made clear by an example from the record of Arthur, a boy who had been sent into a remedial course (Psychology 411) which automatically exposed him to counseling. Within the first three minutes of the first interview this exchange took place (phonographic recording):

    C. I don't think that I know very much how you happened to come in — I mean, I don't know whether someone suggested you come to see me or whether you had some things on your mind that you were disturbed about and wanted some help with.
    S. I talked with Miss G. at the Arts office and she suggested that I take the course. Then my instructor told me I would see you, so I came.
    C. That's how you came to take the course, because it was suggested to you.
    S. Mm-hm.
    C. So I suppose that's why you came in to see me, too. I mean that ——
    S. Yeh.
    C. Well, now, one thing that I think I'd like to have straight at the outset is this; if there is anything that I can do to help you work through some of the things that may be bothering you, I'll be very glad to do so. And on the other hand, I don't want you to think that you have to come to see me, or that it is part of what you must do for the course, or anything of that kind. Sometimes a person has difficulty with their school work or sometimes with other things. They can work it through better if they talk it over with someone else and try to get at the bottom of it, but I think that should be up to them, and I just want to make it plain at the very start that if you wish to see me, perhaps I can save this time once a week and you can come in and talk things over — but you don't have to. Now I don't know — you

might tell me a little bit more about how you happened to take 411 — I believe because Miss G. suggested it to you.

S. Yes, Miss G. suggested it to me. She didn't think my study habits were good. If they were good, they didn't seem to be very beneficial on my grades and everything. So she thought that maybe if I'd get in this, I'd learn better study habits and make better use of time and concentration, and so forth.

C. So that — your purpose in taking it is to satisfy Miss G.

S. That's right. No, it isn't that. It's for my own improvement.

C. I see.

S. Dust off my study methods and habits and better use of time and how to concentrate.

C. Mm-hm.

S. I'm just taking —— She suggested it to me and I'm taking it for my own benefit.

C. I see. So that you got into it partly because she suggested it, but part of it was your own desire to get into something like that, is that it?

S. I thought I needed it, so I signed up. (*Laughs.*)

C. Well, now, I'm more interested in why you thought you needed it than why Miss G. thought you needed it. Why did *you* think you needed it?

Note in this opening of the first interview the complete dependence of the student in his initial statements. He takes no responsibility for taking the course or for coming to the counselor. When this attitude is recognized and clarified, he gradually veers over to a statement in which the responsibility is shared ("She suggested it to me and I'm taking it for my own benefit"), and finally takes full responsibility for his actions ("I thought I needed it, so I signed up"). It is difficult to overemphasize the difference this makes in counseling. If it is implicit that the counselor or some third person is responsible for the student's being present in the counseling situation, then suggestion or advice are almost the only avenues of approach open. If the client himself accepts responsibility for bringing himself, he also accepts the responsibility for working upon his problems.

II. The helping situation is usually defined. From the first the client is made aware of the fact that the counselor does not have the answers, but that the counseling situation does provide a place where the client can, with assistance, work out his own solutions to his problems. Sometimes this is done in rather general terms, which in other instances the situation is most plainly defined in terms of concrete issues, such as responsibility for appointments, or responsibility for steps to be taken and decisions to be made.

In the interview with Arthur, quoted above, we find an example of one way in which the situation is defined by the counselor, when it is explained that Arthur is under no compulsion, but may make use of the situation if he wishes. Obviously this type of intellectual explanation is not enough. The whole conduct of the interviews must reinforce this idea until the client feels that it is a situation in which he is free to work out the solutions that he needs.

Another example may be given from a first interview with a mother, Mrs. L. (from whose record there will be further quotations later on). This mother and her ten-year-old son had come to the clinic because of the mother's vehement complaints about the boy. After two diagnostic contacts the situation was put up to the mother as a difficulty in their relationships, and she was asked whether she and her boy would like to work through this problem. She had tentatively and somewhat fearfully agreed and she came in for the first contact with the psychologist who was to act as therapist. Here is the counselor's account (not phonographic) of a portion of this first treatment interview.

> As it was nearing the end of the hour, and I wanted to get something toward the settling up of the hour, I said, "How does your husband feel about your coming up here to work the problem through with us?" And she laughed slightly and said, "Well, he's sort of indifferent about it. But he did say something to the effect that he didn't want to be experimented on, or something — didn't want to be treated like white rats."
> And I said, "And you feel, too, perhaps, that is what will happen." "Well, I just don't know what will be done." And I assured her that she needn't feel that we were going to do anything at all strange or peculiar; that it would be a matter of her

talking things through with me, and Jim with Mr. A., to see
if we could think things through together to see how they both
felt about the situation and to think out some of the relationships between them and other members of the family, and get a
view of the interrelationships within the family.

At that she said, "Well, perhaps Marjorie too — maybe there
is something a little funny about her. Maybe she is mixed up
in it too."

Note that the counselor makes it plain that it is her task
to provide a place and an atmosphere in which problems can
be thought through and relationships recognized more clearly.
She does not imply in any way that it is her responsibility to
give the answers. The fact that this is understood by the
mother is indicated by the fact that she then feels free to bring
in a new aspect of the problem — the sister — and to suggest
that she will wish to work on that, too.

Still another example may be given to illustrate how the
situation is often defined in terms of actual responsibilities,
no matter how minor they may be. In a first counseling interview with a student, some verbal explanations of the situation
were given early in the contact, but toward the end of the
interview this exchange took place (phonographic recording):

> *S.* I think maybe the next time I come in to see you, it will
> be something different. Maybe I'll have a little bit better idea
> what to talk about by then.
> *C.* Would you like to come in next Friday at this time?
> *S.* Yes, it's all right with me.
> *C.* It's up to you.
> *S.* It's up to me?
> *C.* I'm here. I'd be glad to do anything I can do for you.
> *S.* All right, sir, I think I'll be there.
> *C.* All right.

In this brief excerpt, much has happened. The student
makes a somewhat independent statement, showing that he
plans at least to share the responsibility for the use of the
next hour. The counselor encourages this by putting the decision about the appointment up to the student. The student,

feeling this is the usual meaningless gesture, leaves the responsibility with the counselor by saying, "Yes, it's all right with me." When the counselor shows that the counseling situation really belongs to the client, the student's surprise is clearly indicated in the phonographic record as he says, "It's up to *me?*" His whole tone changes as he then responds in a firm and decisive manner, "All right, sir, I think I'll be there" — genuinely accepting the responsibility for the first time.

Thus, through words, actions, or both, the client is helped to feel that the counseling hour is his — to use, to take responsibility for, an opportunity freely to be himself. With children words are of less use, and the situation must be defined almost entirely in terms of freedoms and responsibilities, but the underlying dynamics seem much the same.

III. The counselor encourages free expression of feelings in regard to the problem. To some extent this is brought about by the counselor's friendly, interested, receptive attitude. To some extent it is due to improved skill in treatment interviewing. Little by little we have learned to keep from blocking the flow of hostility and anxiety, the feelings of concern and the feelings of guilt, the ambivalences and the indecisions which come out freely if we have succeeded in making the client feel that the hour is truly his, to use as he wishes. I suppose that it is here that counselors have exercised the most imagination and have most rapidly improved their techniques of catharsis. This can be illustrated by brief excerpts from two contacts, one with the mother, Mrs. L., and one with her ten-year-old son, Jim. These are both from the first therapeutic contacts with mother and child.

During this first hour the mother spends a full half-hour telling with feeling example after example of Jim's bad behavior. She tells of his quarrels with his sister, of his refusal to dress, of his annoying manner of humming at the table, of his bad behavior in school, of his failure to help at home, and the like. Each of her comments has been highly critical of the boy. A brief segment toward the end of this tirade is given below (not phonographic).

I said, "What things have you tried in helping him to do more as you would like?" "Well, last year," she said, "we put him in a special school, and I've tried rewarding him for things, and I've tried knocking off his allowance for things that he does that he shouldn't do, but by the time the day is over his allowance is practically all used up. I've put him in a room alone and I've ignored him until I've just felt frantic, nearly ready to scream." And I said, "Perhaps sometimes you do actually ——" And she said (very quickly), "Yes, sometimes I do actually scream about it. I used to think I had a lot of patience with him, but I don't any more. The other day my sister-in-law came over for a meal and Jim was whistling during dinner. I told him not to, but he kept right on. Finally he did quit. Later my sister-in-law said she would have knocked him right off the chair if he had done that when she told him to quit. But I've found it just doesn't do any good to get after him that way." I said, "You feel that it wouldn't do any good to use as strong measures as she said."

She replied, "No. And his table manners, that's another thing that's terrible. He eats most of the time with his fingers, even though he has a nice sterling silver knife, fork, and spoon of his own. And maybe he will pick up a piece of bread and eat a piece, eat a hole right out of the middle of it, or stick his finger clear down through the whole stack of slices of bread. And wouldn't you think a boy of his age would know better than to do that?" And I said, "That makes you both feel pretty terrible, you and your husband, too."

She replied, "Yes, of course. And sometimes he can be just as good as gold. For instance, yesterday he was good all day, and in the evening he told his daddy that he had been a good boy."

Note the fact that the counselor's sole aim is not to impede this flow of hostile and critical feeling. There is no attempt to persuade the mother that her boy is bright, essentially normal, pathetically eager for affection, though all of that is true. The counselor's whole function at this stage is to encourage free expression.

What this means in terms of a child is best shown by listening in on a portion of Jim's contact with a second psychologist during that same hour. This is Jim's first play-therapy contact. He indulges in some preliminary play and then makes a clay image which he identifies as his father. A great deal of dramatic play with this figure goes on, most of it centered around the struggle of Jim in getting his father out of bed and the father's resistance to this (the reverse of the home situation, as might be guessed). Jim played both parts in different voices and the following is from the phonographic recording, with *F.* and *J.* inserted to indicate which voice is being used.

> *F.* "I want you to stay and help me." *J.* "I ain't goin' to. I want to make somethin' of it." *F.* "Oh, ya do, do you?" *J.* "Yeah, I want to make somethin' of it!" *F.* "O.K., come on, make somethin' of it!" *J.* "All right you! (*Striking him and knocking head off.*) He won't get back on in a hurry. Huh, I'll take a piece of ya off, that'll fix him. There. I'll make you weak, that'll fix him. Now don't you go to sleep on me again! (*Very short pause.*) Oh, say, what did you do, go to sleep? Hah, hah!" *F.* "I didn't go to sleep." *J.* "Well, you must have done *somethin'!* I'm gettin' tired of your impudence. Get up, get up, get up (*shouting*), come on, dad, get up."

A few moments later he pretends that someone is holding his father up in the air to torture him. His play follows:

> *J.* "Let's git that guy for making his kid hold him all day. (*Short pause.*) They got 'im." *F.* "Hey, let me down." *J.* "Not till you promise to let your boy go for all day." *F.* "No, I won't." *J.* "All right, then, you're going to have to balance up high, see, and you are going to like it, and you'll do it." *F.* "Help, you guys, I'm fallin'. Help!!" (*Short pause as he drops clay and crushes it.*) *J.* "That's all, folks. (*Pause.*) He ain't there. He fell off a cliff in a car."

These two excerpts may make plain how deep and how violent are the feelings spontaneously expressed if the counselor does not block them. The counselor has more than a negative function in this process, perhaps best described as a separate aspect of therapy.

IV. The counselor accepts, recognizes, and clarifies these negative feelings. Here is a subtle point which seems to be very difficult for students to grasp. If the counselor is to accept these feelings, he must be prepared to respond, not to the intellectual content of what the person is saying, but to the feeling which underlies it. Sometimes the feelings are deep ambivalences, sometimes they are feelings of hostility, sometimes they are feelings of inadequacy. Whatever they are, the counselor endeavors, by what he says and by what he does, to create an atmosphere in which the client can come to recognize that he has these negative feelings and can accept them as a part of himself, instead of projecting them on others or hiding them behind defense mechanisms. Frequently the counselor verbally clarifies these feelings, not trying to interpret their cause or argue in regard to their utility — simply recognizing that they exist, and that he accepts them. Thus, such phrases as "You feel pretty bitter about this," "You want to correct this fault, but still you don't want to," "What you are saying sounds as though you feel pretty guilty," seem to crop out rather frequently in this type of therapy, and nearly always, if they are accurate portrayals of feeling, allow the individual to go forward in a freer fashion.

Sufficient examples of this type of help have already been given. In the excerpt from the case of Arthur (page 31), almost every statement of the counselor, with the exception of the long explanation, is an attempt to verbalize and clarify the feeling the student has been expressing about coming in. In the first fragment from the case of Mrs. L. (page 33), the counselor makes no attempt to combat the mother's implied fear of being treated "like white rats"; she merely recognizes and accepts that fear. In the second excerpt from this case (page 36), there are further examples of this aspect of therapy. The counselor accepts the mother's frantic feeling, her hopelessness, her annoyance, and her despair without criticism, without argument, without undue sympathy, accepting those feelings merely as a fact, and verbalizing them in somewhat clearer form than the mother has put them. The counselor is, it will be noted, alert to the feeling, not the content, of the mother's complaints. Thus, when the mother wails about Jim's table manners, there is no attempt to respond in terms of table etiquette, but in terms of the mother's obvious feeling about it. Note, however, that the counselor does not go beyond what the mother has already expressed. This is highly important, since real damage can be done by going too far and too fast, and verbalizing attitudes of which the client is not yet conscious. The aim is to accept completely and to recognize those feelings which the client has been able to express.

V. When the individual's negative feelings have been quite fully expressed, they are followed by the faint and tentative expressions of the positive impulses which make for growth. There is nothing which gives more surprise to the student who is learning this type of therapy for the first time than to find that this positive expression is one of the most certain and predictable aspects of the whole process. The more violent and deep the negative expressions (provided they are accepted and recognized), the more certain are the positive expressions of love, of social impulses, of fundamental self-respect, of desire to be mature.

This is plainly shown in the interview with Mrs. L. (page 36) to which reference has just been made. After all her antagonistic feeling has been fully accepted, it is inevitable that she should slowly work through to the positive feeling which comes out so suddenly in her statement, "And sometimes he can be just as good as gold."

With Jim, her son, it is a longer time before the positive feelings break through. For three contacts (spaced a week apart) he keeps up his aggressive play, torturing, beating, and killing father images and Satan images (sometimes called "dad"). During the latter part of the third hour his dramatic play continues and becomes a dream, then not a dream.

> "No, it wasn't any dream. I meant it. Now that will be a warning to you (*beating the clay image*). Now that will teach you not to be funny with your kids! Then the guy wakes up and finds it is all a dream, and he says, 'It's about time I got out of these dreams.'" Then Jim ceased playing with the clay, and wandered about the room a bit. He took a newspaper clipping out of his pocket, showing a picture to the psychologist and saying, "Chamberlain looked like such a nice man, so I cut out his picture and carried it with me."

This was his first statement of positive feeling toward anyone. Following it there was never more than a mild expression of hostility, and the change in the therapeutic situation was roughly paralleled by the change in the home.

VI. The counselor accepts and recognizes the positive feelings which are expressed, in the same manner in which he has accepted and recognized the negative feeling. These positive feelings are not accepted with approbation or praise. Moralistic values do not enter into this type of therapy. The positive feelings are accepted as no more and no less a part of the personality than the negative feelings. It is this acceptance of both the mature and the immature impulses, of the aggressive and the social attitudes, of the guilt feelings and the positive expressions, which gives the individual an opportunity for the first time in his life to understand himself as he is. He has no need to be defensive about his negative feelings. He is given no opportunity to overvalue his positive feelings. And in this type of situation, insight and self-understanding come bubbling through spontaneously. Unless one has thus watched insight develop, it is difficult to believe that individuals can recognize themselves and their patterns so effectively.

VII. This insight, this understanding of the self and acceptance of the self, is the next important aspect of the whole process. It provides the basis on which the individual can go ahead to new levels of integration. One graduate student says with genuine feeling: "I'm really just a spoiled brat, but I do want to be normal. I wouldn't let anyone else say that of me, but it's true." A husband says: "I know now why I feel mean toward my wife when she's sick, even though I don't want to feel that way. It's because my mother predicted when I married her that I'd always be saddled with a sick wife." A student says, "I see now why I hated that prof — he criticized me just like my dad did." Mrs. L., the mother whose remarks have already been quoted, makes this surprising statement about her relationship with her boy, after she has worked through most of her hostile feelings and some positive feelings during a number of therapeutic contacts. This is the counselor's account:

One of the things that she brought up was that he seems to want attention, but that the methods he uses get negative attention. After we had talked a little bit about that she said, "Perhaps what would do him most good would be for him to have some affection and love and consideration entirely apart from any correcting. Now, I guess that we've been so busy correcting him that we haven't had time to do anything else." Her expression of that indicated that she really felt that a change of program might do some good. And I said, "That is a very good observation on your part and nobody needs to tell you that that is what you feel really has happened." She said, "No, I know that's what has happened."

VIII. Intermingled with this process of insight — and it should again be emphasized that the steps outlined are not mutually exclusive, nor do they proceed in a rigid order — is a process of clarification of possible decisions, possible courses of action. Often this is infused with a somewhat hopeless attitude. Essentially the individual seems to be saying: "This is what I am, and I see that much more clearly. But how can I reorganize myself in any different fashion?" The counselor's function here is to help clarify the different choices which might be made, and to recognize the feeling of fear and the lack of courage to go ahead which the individual is experiencing. It is not his function to urge a certain course of action or to give advice.

IX. Then comes one of the fascinating aspects of such therapy, the initiation of minute, but highly significant, positive actions. An extremely withdrawn high-school boy, who has expressed his fear and hatred of others and has also come to recognize his deeply buried desire to have friends, spends a whole hour giving all the reasons why he would be too terrified to accept a social invitation he has had. He even leaves the office saying he will probably not go. He is not urged. It is sympathetically recognized that such action would take a great deal of courage, and that while he wishes he had such fortitude, he may not be able to take such a step. He goes to the party, and is enormously helped in his self-confidence.

To give still another illustration from the record of Mrs. L., the following positive forward step followed immediately the outstanding statement of insight quoted above. Again this is the psychologist's account:

> I said, "Then giving him attention and affection when he is not demanding it in any way would perhaps do him a lot of good." Then she said, "Now you may not believe this, but as old as he is he still believes in Santa Claus, at least he did last year. Of course he may be trying to pull the wool over my eyes, but I don't think so. Last year he was away taller than any of the other kids who went up to talk to Santa in the stores. Now this year I've just *got* to tell him the truth. But I'm so afraid he will tell Marjorie. I was wondering if maybe I could tell him about it and it would be our secret between us. I would let him know that he is a big boy now and mustn't tell Marjorie. That it's *our* secret and he's a big boy and he can help me keep things. And also, if I can get her to go to bed early enough — she's such a little wiggle worm, but if I can get her to go to bed — perhaps he can help me with some of the Christmas things. And then on Christmas Eve — that's when we have our Christmas — I'll send the other children over to grandmother's house while we get ready and Jim can stay at the house and help me to get the things ready." The way she spoke it seemed that she felt it would be quite a pleasure to have Jim help. (She seemed really more enthusiastic about it than about anything so far.) So I said, "It will be quite a bit of pleasure, won't it, to think that you have a ten-year-old boy who can help with the Christmas work." With a sparkle in her eyes she replied that it would be fun for him to be able to help her, and that she felt it would do him a lot of good. I replied that I thought so too and that it would certainly be something to try.

One can only comment here that once insight is achieved the actions that are taken are likely to be admirably suited to the new insight. Thus, having achieved better emotional understanding of the relationship between herself and her boy, Mrs. L. translates that insight into action which shows how much she has gained. Her plan gives Jim her special affection in a very adroit way, helps him to be more mature, avoids making the younger sister jealous — in short, it shows that she can now carry out with genuine motivation the type of behavior which will solve her problem. If such behavior had been suggested to her after the diagnosis of the case, she would almost certainly have rejected the suggestion or carried it out in such a way as to cause it to be a failure. When it grows out of her own insightful drive to be a better, more mature mother, it will be successful.

X. The remaining steps need not hold us long. Once the individual has achieved considerable insight and has fearfully and tentatively attempted some positive actions, the remaining aspects are elements of further growth. There is, first of all, a development of further insight — more complete and accurate self-understanding as the individual gains courage to see more deeply into his own actions.

XI. There is increasingly integrated positive action on the part of the client. There is less fear about making choices, and more confidence in self-directed action. The counselor and client are now working together in a new sense. The personal relationship between them is at its strongest. Very often the client wants for the first time to know something of the clinician as a person and expresses a friendly and genuine interest which is very distinctive. Actions are brought into the discussion for consideration, but there is no longer the dependence and fear which were noticeable earlier. As an example, this excerpt is taken from the record of one of the closing interviews with a mother who has successfully gained insight:

> Mrs. J. says, "I don't know what you have done to us, to Patty and me, but everything's all right. I couldn't have wanted a nicer little girl, I should say for the past three weeks. Oh, yesterday she had sort of an off day. She didn't want to come when I'd call her, that is, not right away. She was a little bit down, but she wasn't ugly. I don't know if I can make you see what I mean, but there's a difference in her naughtiness. It's not as if she, well, is ugly, especially to me." C. responded, "I know what you mean, I think. It is that she doesn't refuse just to hurt you." Mrs. J. nodded and said, "That's it. It's a more natural sort of thing."

As is often true in this type of therapy, certain of the behavior symptoms remain, but the mother has a totally different feeling about them and about her ability to handle them.

XII. There is a feeling of decreasing need for help, and a recognition on the part of the client that the relationship must end. Often there are apologies for having taken so much of the counselor's time. The counselor helps to clarify this feeling as he has done before, by accepting and recognizing the fact that the client is now handling his situation with increased assurance and that he will not wish to continue the contacts much longer. As at the first, there is neither compulsion on the client to leave, nor attempt on the part of the counselor to hold the client.

During this aspect of therapy there are likely to be expressions of personal feeling. Often the client makes some such statement as "I shall miss coming; I have enjoyed these contacts so much." The counselor can reciprocate these feelings. There is no doubt that we do become emotionally involved, to a certain healthy extent, when personal growth takes place under our very eyes. A time limit is set for the contacts, and they are brought to a reluctant but healthy close. Sometimes, in the last contact, the client brings up a number of old problems or new ones, as though in a gesture to retain the relationship, but the atmosphere is very different from that in the first contacts, when those problems were real.

These seem to be the essential elements of the therapeutic process as it is being carried on in a variety of organizations and with a variety of problems — with parents and their children, even very young children; in situations demanding marital counseling; in situations of maladjustment and neurotic behavior among students; in situations of difficult vocational choice; in short, in most instances where the individual finds himself facing a serious problem of adjustment.

It will be readily recognized that the analysis given above might be differently organized. In a process with so many subtleties, any attempt to break it down into steps or elements contains much that is subjective and approximate, rather than objective and exact. Yet as a whole the therapy that has been described is an orderly, consistent process — even a predictable process in its major outlines. It is very different from an approach which is diffuse, opportunistic, stressing the notion that "every case is different." It is a process which has sufficient unity to provide suitable hypotheses for experimental tests.

A Significant Research Corroboration

The foregoing description is corroborated in an interesting fashion by a study of intensive treatment counseling being made by a former colleague of the writer's, Miss Virginia Lewis. Since it corroborates at a number of points the description which has been given of the therapeutic process, a brief account may be in order here.

Miss Lewis made an exhaustive analysis of six cases of adolescent girls who were referred because of serious behavior, personality, and delinquency problems. These girls came in for interviewing contacts during periods ranging from a few months to nearly four years. The average number of contacts was more than thirty. Very complete records were kept, giving an almost verbatim account of these contacts. This complete recording made it possible to study and classify all the items of counselor and counselee conversation — some twelve thousand in all. The treatment period was divided into deciles, in order to make the cases comparable, even though the length of treatment varied. Certain of the findings may be cited in support of the description of therapy just given.[5]

It was found that those items which were classified as "Explanation of psychologist's rôle" were most frequent in the first and second deciles of treatment. Compare this with the description given of the counselor's techniques in defining the helping situation (see II, page 32).

Those elements of the girl's conversation which were devoted to a survey and exploration of her adjustment problems constituted approximately 50 per cent of the client items. Such items made up a large part of the conversation during the first decile, reached their peak during the second decile,

---

[5] Lewis, Virginia W. *Changing the Behavior of Adolescent Girls — A Description of Process.* Ph. D. thesis, Teachers College, Columbia Univ., 1942. To be published.

and steadily declined during the remainder of the contacts. This fact offers something of a parallel to the account given (see III, IV, V, pages 35, 37, 39) of the counselor's efforts to permit the freest expression of all attitudes relating to the individual's problems. It was also found by Miss Lewis that statements of the counselor classified as encouraging the girl to state the problem more fully were frequent during the early deciles, and reached their peak during the fifth decile of treatment.

During the fifth to the eighth deciles there was a sharp and striking rise in the number of statements by the girl in which she sees the relationship between various aspects of the information she has given. This seems to bear a very close resemblance to the process which the writer described as the development of insight and self-understanding (see VI, VII, page 40). This verbal expression of relationships which the girl has come to perceive rises to a peak in the eighth decile, falling off in the ninth and tenth decile.

It is replaced in importance by conversations which have to do with planning — new steps, new decisions, plans for future actions. This type of item is prominent only in the later deciles, rising rapidly to a peak in the final decile. It is scarcely necessary to point out that it seems to corroborate objectively the steps which were described earlier in the chapter as clarification of decisions and the taking of positive actions (see VIII, IX, page 41). Closely allied to this is the similar increase in statements by the girl telling of results of planned actions she has taken. This category too is most frequent in the last decile.

Only toward the end of the contacts are there any significant number of remarks by the girl which can be classified as desire for detachment from the psychologist. These indications that help is no longer needed never form a large percentage of the items. They occur only in the ninth and tenth deciles, more frequently in the latter. The parallel to the description given (see XII, page 44) is plain.

Conversation which is classified as purely friendly conversation between the girl and the psychologist occupies a small fraction of the time in all deciles, but it rises sharply during the final tenth of treatment. This typical phenomenon has already been commented upon (see XI, XII, pages 43, 44).

This study, while using different methods and different terminology, would seem to give a picture of therapy strikingly similar to the more subjective description which this chapter contains. Certainly it justifies further investigation of the hypothesis that skillfully conducted treatment interviews are not a hodgepodge of discrete elements, but that taken as a whole they represent a complex chain in which one element tends to follow another. In the remaining portion of the book we shall give more detailed attention to these varied elements.

PART II

Initial Problems Faced by the Counselor

When Is Counseling Indicated?

WHATEVER the type of counseling being carried on, or whatever the setting in which the counselor does his work, many of his most important decisions, which may decide his eventual success or failure in helping the individual, are made during the first contact. Far too often these decisions are made quite unconsciously by the counselor, or are made on the basis of a "clinical hunch" rather than upon any more solid foundation. It is the purpose of this chapter to examine the issues which face the counselor at the time the client arrives — the decision as to what type of therapeutic approach is possible and the question as to what elements of the situation constitute the focus of therapy — and to assist in formulating these issues more clearly, so that the approach to the client and his difficulties can be made in terms of observed realities rather than on a fumbling or completely intuitive basis.

The Client Arrives. A great deal of attention has been paid to the enormous variety of problems, symptoms, and causes which the clinician or counselor will find exemplified in the individuals who come to him. Too little attention has been paid to the variety of attitudes toward help which the individual may have, and the influence which these attitudes should have upon therapeutic procedure. Let us look at a few of these client attitudes toward help.

Here is a lad brought to the child-guidance clinic by the court officer. He is surly and uncooperative. He obviously regards the psychologist as an adjunct of the court, and is resistant to any friendly approach. By every gesture and inflection he makes it plain that he does not want the help that is offered and finds himself in the clinic against his will. Is counseling possible in such a case? At the other extreme we find the young woman who has come to the office of the college counselor, clearly under great stress, confident that here is a source of help and insistent that she must talk to the counselor at once. Her strong desire for help is unmistakable. A quite different attitude is encountered in the child who is brought to the clinic for help by his mother. He may be resistant to the clinic because he is resistant to his mother. He may be relatively neutral about the whole procedure. He may be fearful of it because of its similarity to a doctor's office. It is rather rare, however, that such a child is genuinely seeking help for himself. He comes because his parent wishes it. Still another type of clinical contact is illustrated by the student who comes to the counselor because he is sent by the dean, either because of failing grades or of some other academic problem. Such a student may be in need of assistance and may have some recognition of this fact. He is likely to submit himself passively to the counselor, quite willing to be helped, but with no notion of taking the initiative in the process.

Such are some of the shadings of attitudes toward clinical and counseling help. The counselor may be identified with everything which the individual is fighting or may be regarded as the answer to all problems and the solution to all difficulties. The individual may wish treatment and find it relatively easy to seek it, or his attitude may be represented by the client who later confessed how, after deciding to seek help, he walked up and down past the door time after time before he could muster the courage to come in. When we realize that these varying attitudes toward counseling help may be associated with all types of problems and with all types of individuals, we begin to see the situation in its true complexity. The individual with deep-seated emotional conflicts, the hardened delinquent, the youngster who is annoying his parent, the student who is concerned with having chosen the wrong vocation, the worker who is unhappy on his job — all are part of the total picture which we must consider. Likewise we must recognize the differing capacities and qualities which the individuals possess — the stable and the unstable, the mentally defective, the average and the superior intellect. Bearing in mind all these major variables and the unique individual situations, defying classification, in which they occur, we may well ask whether principles can be found which would enable the counselor to make his initial decisions about the case with more clarity.

What Type of Treatment Is Indicated? Ideally, the counselor would prefer to put aside any decision regarding the appropriate treatment approach until he is thoroughly familiar with the client and his problems. Actually this is impossible. Often the initiation of a diagnostic study of the individual effectively bars the road to satisfactory counseling. What is needed is careful thinking about treatment from the moment the client arrives, or even before his arrival if there is previous information regarding him in the form of a case history or a school report. The counselor must be continually asking himself certain crucial questions, the answers to which will determine whether one or another type of treatment is preferable. We shall take up some of these significant questions, considering the implications for treatment of the various answers which may be found.

Some Basic Questions

Is the Client under Stress? One of the first observations which the wise clinician will make is the extent to which the client is in a state of tension or stress. Counseling can be of help only when there is a certain amount of psychological distress arising out of a condition of disequilibrium. These stresses may be almost entirely psychic in origin, growing out of conflicts of desire. The socially maladjusted student wishes to be more social and at the same time wishes to protect himself from the risks of humiliation and inferiority which he feels when he ventures into social activities. Another individual may be torn between strong sex desires, on the one hand, and

strong guilt feelings, on the other.   More often these stresses
are caused, at least in part, by the demands of the environment
coming into conflict with the needs of the individual.   Marriage,
for example, makes fresh demands on the young person to
adapt himself in mature ways, and he may find these demands
in conflict with his own desire to be dependent, or with his own
need to regard sex as taboo, or with his need to be dominant
and superior.   The environmental demands, in other instances,
may be imposed by a social group.   The delinquent from a
gang neighborhood may have little or no inner conflict over his
activities, but stress and tension are created when the community imposes its standards, which are in conflict with his
own.   The student may have no psychic struggle over his
inadequate work until the college creates psychological stress
by its punitive threats.   We have for too long, largely because
of the classical Freudian tradition, looked upon conflict as
internal and psychic, failing to recognize that in all conflict
there is a large cultural component, and that in many instances
conflict is created by some new cultural demand which opposes
an individual need.

Environmental treatment may be employed successfully
even in the absence of such tensions.   For example, a delinquent gang may, by the provision of better leadership and
better recreational opportunities, be slowly weaned away from
delinquent activities to good citizenship without ever experiencing acutely the difference between their own original standards
and those of the community.   This is not true of counseling and
psychotherapy.   It can be effective only when there is a conflict of desires or demands which creates tension and calls for
some type of solution.   Basically the most accurate statement
of this situation would seem to be that, before counseling can
be effective, the tensions created by these conflicting desires
and demands must be more painful to the individual than the
pain and stress of finding a solution to the conflict.

This statement needs to be tested and might be subjected to
experimental investigation.   A number of clinical experiences
would seem to support it.   For example, it has been interesting

to study the treatment process in cases where the individual is temporarily released from the conflict-creating situation. A sixteen-year-old girl becomes delinquent largely because of her need for affection and social acceptance, this need in turn arising primarily out of her rejection by her mother. She is placed in a school for delinquent girls, where the psychologist undertakes therapeutic contacts. Anne makes progress in these interviews, yet she never is able completely to face the reality of her mother's rejection. She makes excuses for the fact that her mother does not write, does not visit her. She worries over the fact that an accident must have occurred to keep her mother away. She fears that her mother must be ill. "If something happened to my mother, I wouldn't have anyone." The counselor responded, "You don't feel that there is anyone else who cares for you?" Anne replied, "Well, yes, but the others don't love me the way my mother does." She continues to maintain this fantasy of a loving mother and only partially faces the actual fact that she is neglected and left severely alone. It seems more than likely that had therapy been initiated while she was living at home, the basic conflict could have been more deeply and thoroughly faced, because the mother's actions would have continually re-created and reinforced the feeling of deprivation.

Another instance which raises this same question is the case of a superior boy of fifteen who is a problem because of a compulsive desire to steal women's underclothing, which has brought him into conflict with the law on several occasions. A teacher sends him to the clinician for help. He is obviously under much stress, but the ambivalence of his desire for assistance is equally obvious. Through a series of contacts he reiterates his genuine wish for help and at the same time finds it impossible to talk frankly of his feelings in any situation. The clinician's interpretation of this therapeutic failure is that the painfulness of recognizing all his sexual feelings as his own, of bringing to light his deeply repressed attitudes, is greater than the distress of living with his problem and running the risk of embarrassment and arrest. His desire to be normal, to be free of this distressing behavior, is not strong enough to counterbalance the deeply upsetting pain of facing his own "wicked" impulses. One cannot help speculating in such a case as to the elements which might change that balance. It seems likely that actual arrest and fear of incarceration might make the distress of living with his neurosis so great that he would be accessible to psychotherapy. Further study is needed of this problem of the balance in conflict which may make counseling possible in one instance, impossible in another.

An example in which the issues are less dramatic, but in which the changing balance can be rather clearly seen, may be cited from one of the cases which is phonographically recorded.

Arthur is a college student of twenty, in his third year of college. He is sent to a counselor for help as part of the procedure in the study-habits course which has been previously mentioned. In his first interview he makes it plain that he has a serious problem of unsolved vocational choice ahead of him, but that the problem he is really concerned about is that of raising his grades. At one point in the interview he sums up what he wants to accomplish in the interviews, saying, "That's my job. To decide what I want to do is one thing, and to get better grades — that's one *sure* thing." In the second and third interviews he continues to keep the contacts centered around the more superficial problem of grades, and in the fourth interview he frankly states that he is afraid of the more comprehensive problem of vocational choice. A recorded excerpt will illustrate this. Arthur talks about how important attitudes are — if you think you are going to flunk, you will grow to dislike a subject, and vice versa. The conversation continues:

> *C.* Sometimes you feel that way about your courses, and sometimes you don't.
> *S.* Yeah, that's right. Sometimes it looks like everything is against you and other times everything is pulling for you, but I like all of my studies this quarter, so that should be in my behalf or something.
> *C.* Perhaps that makes it a little easier to put off the problems you'll meet at the end of the quarter.

S. Yeah. I believe it would. (*Pause and laugh.*) At the end of the quarter I'm going to have the problem of what to take next quarter and all that.

C. You don't like to think about that, though, do you?

S. No, boy! (*Laugh.*) I don't like to think about that until I come to it. Oh, I've been thinking, when I had some free time, trying to figure out what to take next quarter and all that, but oh, I don't know, it's a kind of material you want to put off.

C. You want to put it off if you can?

S. That's right.

C. That's one of the things that ——

S. You shouldn't do, I know.

C. No; well, you feel that people would disapprove of it. That's one of the reasons why you feel two ways about coming in for an appointment like this, because here there's always a risk you might get to thinking about some of those problems that you'd rather put off.

S. Well, that might be, I doubt it.

C. It is a lot more comfortable to put them off, isn't it?

S. Yeah, that's right. But people — (*pause*) and it would be better for you if you wouldn't put them off, that's one sure thing.

C. But it takes a lot of courage sometimes, to really think them through ahead of time. (*Very long pause.*)

S. About this question of studying, do you think — ah, what do you think is the best way to study for a midterm? Do you think you ought to make an outline of the material you've had and then go through that outline and the parts you don't know, or ... (He continues in this vein.)

This is not an unusual situation, but it is unusual for the client to make such a frank statement of his attitude. He suffers to some degree from conflicts involved in vocational choice. He even knows that pressures are approaching which will make some solution necessary. Yet until the whole conflict is heightened by social demands, he cannot face it in the counseling situation. When the counselor helps him to recognize clearly that he is evading this vocational problem, there is a long pause, in which undoubtedly he is making his decision. What that decision is he makes very evident in his next remark in which he changes the subject, completely avoids any future vocational issue, and concentrates during the remainder of the interview on the details of obtaining better grades.

Several excerpts from the following interview indicate how pressures operate to reopen the question and make him at least partially accessible to counseling help on his problem. He opens the interview by telling of some favorable results on quizzes.

> *C.* You feel that things are going pretty well.
>
> *S.* M-hm. And yesterday morning I went over and saw Miss G. in the Dean's office and I got my schedule for next quarter and she wants me to take another quarter in fine arts and then she thought sociology would be good for me and appreciation of literature. I didn't know what to take, and I thought that I would go over and ask her. She told me that any time I was in doubt to come over and see her, so — that is what she advised.

This statement is eloquent, indeed. Arthur seems to have dodged his conflict completely. He makes it plain that he is doing what he is told, taking no responsibility for the decision himself. He also makes it plain that if the present counselor will not solve his problems for him, he can find counselors who will. He goes on to describe in some detail the courses he will take, mentioning that he wondered about taking a mathematics course.

> *S.* I know it would have helped me in physics, but since I've had both quarters of that and they're both over, why, I don't see that it would be any benefit.
>
> *C.* So that you're doing quite a lot of thinking about your course yourself as well as getting advice from others, aren't you?
>
> *S.* M-hm. I don't know, I told you, I think last week, that I was all in a muddle about this what to take next quarter, but I think I'll take fine arts because he said I'm showing so much improvement in my work, and I like it, and I think it teaches you detail, it teaches you to express yourself, it teaches you to use your hands, and — I don't know, I think it will help me a lot.
>
> *C.* That interests me because now you are saying that *you* think you should take fine arts, and that to me means something, where the fact that Miss G. or somebody else thinks you should take fine arts — well, that's interesting, it's worth getting, but I think the real decision is yours.
>
> *S.* Sure. I know I want to take that because I — well, I like it and I'm getting along all right in this first course in it.

Here the client gives some indication that he is, in some slight degree, taking the responsible choice into his own hands. After some further discussion of the pros and cons of the courses selected, he tells how the conflict was definitely brought to a head by the demands of his college situation.

C. It interests me that last week you felt you were going to put off those questions just as long as you could, but this week you ——

S. Oh, I got inspiration this week. (*Laugh.*) I thought — I saw some kids with their schedule cards and they were freshmen, I guess ——

C. You saw what?

S. I saw some kids with their schedule cards ——

C. Oh, yeah.

S. — and I guess they were freshmen, and I said, "Hey, when are those schedule cards due?" They said, "Oh, you have to have them in by Friday," so I thought, "Well, Arthur M., you get to work." (*Both laugh.*) So I went over and saw Miss G. right away.

He goes on to discuss further the question of whether he has selected the right courses, showing both sides of his ambivalent attitude toward making up his own mind. The interview continues:

C. Do I gather that your schedule for next quarter is now pretty well set?

S. M-hm. Yeah. If I get the chance, I'm going home and work out the time schedule so I'll have my time and classes and everything and then I'll forget all about my schedule until it comes up (*laugh*) next quarter. I was kind of relieved ——

C. You don't like to think of it even after you get it made up, hm?

S. It isn't that. I'm just going to forget it and start working on something else. It's kind of a relief to have the thing made out. I saw a lot of boys sitting over there. They had a book, and they had pencils, and they were scratching their heads (*laugh*) and they would write something out and then they would scratch it — (*laugh*) — oh gosh!

C. This whole business of deciding what direction we are taking and what we are going to do and all is a pretty tough job, isn't it?

S. That's right. (*Pause.*) I still wish I knew definitely what I intend to do. I mean what vocation to follow.

C. You've been doing some thinking about that too, have you?

S. I have, m-hm, but I still don't know which way to go.

C. Do you want to tell me a little of what you have been thinking about along that line?

S. Oh, I don't know — my uncle from the very first, he said I should go into music and he's been arguing that every time he sees me — he asks me why I don't get into music, and oh, what I had in mind at first was optometry, and — then I thought optometry. And I talked to several boys down home that are taking osteopathy and they said that would be a wonderful field to go into, so — but right now my three main things are music, osteopathy, and optometry. I mean, that's the three I'm working on.

From this point on Arthur began to explore his vocational problem and to work on it constructively. After several more contacts, he arrived at a satisfactory course of action, choosing a primary goal for himself, but also setting his plans with certain alternatives in mind, in case he failed to reach his first choice.

Although the excerpts from these interviews illustrate several principles of counseling, the point to be observed here is that effective counseling in regard to vocational choice became possible only when the pressure of circumstance became so strong that the discomfort of facing the problem was more than outweighed by the discomfort of not facing it. Although Arthur evaded the immediate issue by placing the responsibility almost entirely on Miss G.'s shoulders, nevertheless the conflict was heightened to a point where he determined to seek help in making his own decision on the basic question of vocational choice.

These illustrations may help to put in concrete form one of the questions which the counselor must ask himself from the very beginning of his contact with the client. Is this individual under psychological stress and tension which would make a solution to his problems more satisfying than his present state? Is this psychological discomfort sufficiently great to overbalance the distress of bringing out into the open the intimate attitudes, the repressed feelings, which may enter into the creation of the problem?

Is the Client Able to Cope with His Situation? It is sometimes forgotten that any type of psychotherapy depends for its results on the assumption that if the individual is helped to reorient himself, to reorganize his attitudes in new patterns, he can meet his life adjustments more normally and with less strain, and can find healthy satisfactions in a socially approved manner. A moment's reflection will reveal the fact that some individuals are so weighed down by unfortunate circumstances or so weakened by personal inadequacies that no reorganization of attitudes would enable them to meet life on a normal basis. Here is a delinquent boy, living in a so-called "delinquency area," where social forces encourage delinquent acts, residing in a home where he is rejected in favor of a younger brother, attending a school which makes no allowance for his retarded mentality, but continually makes him conscious of his failures. No amount of counseling or psychotherapy is likely to be successful in such a case. The strength of the destructive factors is such that a mere reorganization of the boy's attitudes is insufficient to make normal satisfactions possible. Even if he could achieve a high degree of insight into his situation, there are few elements of his life over which he could exercise control. This is a case in which environmental treatment must be the primary approach. Counseling can play only a secondary rôle.

Or let us consider the situation of a mother who is harming her daughter through her oversolicitous attitude. This mother is deeply introverted and neurotic. She has a number of serious physical difficulties which make her an invalid and greatly restrict her activities. She has few friends, and any real social life would be almost out of the question, because of her combined physical and psychological handicaps. She gains little satisfaction from her relationship with her husband, partly because of her poor health, partly because of deeper incompatibilities. Her one major interest is her only daughter. Even this thumbnail sketch will make plain the inevitability of her oversolicitous attitude toward the girl. It should also suffice to indicate that any type of psychotherapy is foredoomed to failure. It is unlikely that she could gain any true insight into the rôle she is playing, but even if she were able, it is quite certain that she could not act upon it. In order to free her daughter, to allow her to become independent, this mother would have to relinquish her one source of genuine satisfaction in life. This she would find herself unable to do. The situation is too heavily weighted with adverse factors to allow insight and self-understanding to become operative.

An illuminating failure in psychotherapy which illustrates this point is the experimental psychoanalysis of eleven criminals by Healy and Alexander in 1931–32.[1] Although these offenders — older adolescents and young adults — were chosen for analysis because psychological conflict seemed to play an important part in their behavior, the practical results of the analyses were distinctly disappointing. Considerable insight was gained by the individuals, and light was shed upon some of the psychological origins of crime, but delinquency was by no means checked. In commenting upon this experiment later, Healy recognized that without better economic and social conditions, the insight gained from psychoanalysis in such cases is ineffective.[2] With our present knowledge, it is plain that such individuals were not suitable candidates for treatment which emphasized psychotherapy alone. The weight of factors making for maladjustment was too great. Instability of a deep-seated sort, delinquent associations, lack of employment, lack of socially approved skills, added up to a total which in a number of instances more than outweighed the partial reorientation which the individual had achieved.

In short, the counselor must, at the outset of his contacts with the client, evaluate the strength or capacity of the indi-

[1] Alexander, Franz, and Healy, William. *Roots of Crime*. New York: Alfred A. Knopf, 1935. 305 pp.

[2] Healy, William. "Psychoanalysis of Older Offenders," *American Journal of Orthopsychiatry*, vol. 5 (January, 1935), pp. 27–28.

vidual to take action altering his life course, and must also judge whether the situation is to some extent changeable, whether alternative satisfactions and alternative ways of dealing with the situation are possible.

The author, in a previous volume, pointed out that the basic capacities and assets of the individual might be estimated by careful rating of certain component factors which help to determine adjustment.[3] Such elements as the constitutional stability, the hereditary background, the physical and mental equipment of the individual, enter into such an evaluation. The type of social experience, too, has had its molding effect, and the emotional components of the family situation are especially important in judging the basic assets of the younger person. The economic, cultural, and educational factors, both positive or negative, which have entered into the experience of this person are also important. Whether the counselor makes a careful and objective evaluation of the client's basic strengths by means of this component-factor method, or whether the situation is so clear that a subjective estimate is sufficient, it should be recognized that this judgment is a significant one. If the assets of the individual are too meager, counseling as a major avenue of approach is likely to be futile.

Corroboration of this viewpoint is given in a study carried on under the author's supervision.[4] In testing the accuracy of clinical prognoses on two hundred cases, one of the incidental findings was that psychotherapy was more likely to be planned for those children with a higher component-factor rating, drastic environmental treatment for those whose component-factor rating was low. For the whole group of two hundred cases, the average component-factor rating was calculated. This figure is the average of the various ratings of the basic factors in the child's adjustment. It expresses, in a crude way, the

[3] Rogers, Carl R. *The Clinical Treatment of the Problem Child*, chap. III, "The Component-Factor Method of Diagnosis." Boston: Houghton Mifflin Company, 1939.

[4] Bennett, C. C., and Rogers, C. R. "Predicting the Outcomes of Treatment," *American Journal of Orthopsychiatry*, vol. 11 (April, 1941), pp. 210-221. This article gives the major findings of the study, but the data presented here are from unpublished material growing out of the same research.

total assets for adjustment which the child possesses. For the two hundred cases, this figure was 1.88 on a seven-point scale on which 3.00 was considered the average for the general population. In comparison with the total group, the twenty-nine children for whom intensive treatment interviewing was recommended had an average component-factor rating of 2.17, while the group for whom institutional care was recommended averaged 1.64, and the children for whom foster-home care was deemed best averaged 1.62. These are statistically significant differences, the comparison with the first group yielding critical ratios of 3.4 and 3.6, respectively. Since the more detailed ratings on each factor may be of interest, they are included in Table 1. It will be seen that the group selected for psychotherapy is definitely superior to the other two groups in hereditary assets and in mental capacity. These children are more fortunately situated from the point of view of socio-economic status and neighborhood environment. They have had slightly more favorable experiences in the social realm and in education. There is no observed difference in the physical assets of the three groups. The group selected for direct treatment comes from a more favorable family background than the institution group. There is no sharp difference in respect to self-insight, though the direct-treatment group is superior to the institution group in this respect.

This study gives evidence that in actual clinical practice the group for whom intensive counseling is recommended tends to be more favorably situated with respect to fundamental factors of adjustment than groups for whom environmental treatment is planned. Or we may state the findings in reverse fashion, and say that psychotherapy is less likely to be employed in those instances where there is a heavy weight of destructive factors.

Evidence such as this indicates the necessity of making some judgment as to the ability of the client to cope with his situation before regarding him as capable of receiving help through counseling. The significance of such a decision is sometimes clouded by the fact that most students, or most employed

TABLE I. COMPONENT-FACTOR RATINGS OF SEVERAL TREATMENT GROUPS

Component Factor	Treatment Plan		
	Direct Treatment (N = 29)	Institutional Placement (N = 51)	Foster Home Placement (N = 76)
Hereditary factor: Consideration of inheritable traits and predispositions, both negative and positive, present in the ancestry. Degree of physical and emotional stability in family, etc.	2.61 *	1.78	1.88
Physical factor: Consideration of negative health factors — long illnesses, instabilities, glandular disorders, etc. — and positive factors.	2.41	2.49	2.41
Mentality factor: Capacities and abilities, general and special.	2.90	1.47	1.96
Family influences: Emotional tone of family experience, rejection, oversolicitude, friction, etc., *versus* security and normality.	1.52	1.49	.95
Economic and cultural influences: Degree of financial security, cultural opportunity, neighborhood and community influence.	2.55	1.31	1.14
Social factor: Degree and satisfactoriness of social experience with own age group and adults.	1.66	1.36	1.25
Educational factor: Degree of healthy educational stimulation and consistent philosophy of control.	2.31	2.00	1.87
Self-insight: Degree of understanding of self and problems, and ability to be responsible and self-critical.	1.38	1.06	1.36
Average total rating: General balance of destructive and constructive forces in child's experience.	2.17 σ = .73	1.64 σ = .55	1.62 σ = .64

* The ratings are in terms of a 7-point scale from zero to 6, with 3.0 representing the hypothetical average of the general population.

workers, for example, do have, from the very nature of their situation, some capacity to deal effectively with their situation. Simple as such a decision may be in many of these cases, we should recognize it as a decision, in order that in the case of the highly unstable individual, or of the person who is completely hemmed in by adverse circumstances, we shall not expect counseling to achieve the impossible.

Can the Client Take Help?   Another basic question which the counselor must ask is frequently phrased, "Does the individual want help?"   This is oversimplifying the matter.   Counseling has, to be sure, other things being equal, the greatest likelihood of success when the client wants help and consciously recognizes this fact.   When this need for help is strong, the client is apt to go quickly into significant material, and if the counselor is an alert listener who can keep himself from blocking the flow of expression, rapid progress may be made.   An example of this strong desire for assistance, consciously felt by the individual, may make the situation more concrete.

Paul, a college student, comes to the counselor without appointment and says that he is feeling desperate.   He feels he is under much tension, he cannot face social groups, his hands sweat, and so on.   An appointment is given for the following day and the student comes in for his first interview.   This initial interview commences as follows (phonographic recording):

> *C.* Well, now, yesterday I sent you off before we really got started talking.   This will be a good time when we can talk things over.   Do you want to tell me what's on your mind?
> *S.* Yes.   I told you that I experience — uh — excessive tension whenever — uh — my personality to any degree was concerned, that is, whenever I — uh — when any issue was at stake, even if small, it's — uh — exceedingly gotten worse, and as I told you it's become quite unbearable, and I really have to do something about it, because I'll make a perfect flop of my college career.   I can't waste my father's money.
> *C.* You really feel it's interfering a lot with your college career?
> *S.* Tremendously, oh, tremendously.   I'm — uh — in some subjects I'm failing which I wouldn't fail, I'm sure of, if I wasn't feeling this way, and I'm so despondent and I haven't got any morale at all.   (*Pause.*)   As examples, I can't get up, I told you I couldn't get up to a blackboard and illustrate problems which

I knew very well, and when I was called I was so tense that I couldn't think straightly and — uh — it seems all out of proportions — this tension.

C. In what way?

S. I said I couldn't even go into a restaurant without feeling tense, which seems very queer, but I — uh — that's the problem I'm confronted with nevertheless. (*Pause.*)

C. You feel you've gotten to a point where you've just got to do something.

S. Yes, I have to, definitely. It's been going on, I should say — I can recall I was twelve years old, the first time, when I was asked to read a — a composition that I did. I was rather proud of it, and when I got in front of the class, why — uh — my hands started shaking like anything, and I had to sit down. I was extremely humiliated, too.

C. You felt very much humiliated.

S. Very much so.

C. In what way?

S. In the fact that I felt abnormal, because everybody else could do it and I couldn't.

Undoubtedly counseling gets off to its most comfortable start when, as in this excerpt, the individual is under stress, eager for help, and able to talk about his problems. However, an examination of various counseling cases carried on in a variety of circumstances bears convincing testimony to the fact that psychotherapy may be successful in many instances where there is no conscious desire for help. Jim, the small boy cited in Chapter II, who found such release in attacking the clay image of his father and who eventually came to more positive expressions of feeling, certainly had no conscious desire for assistance, nor probably any real recognition of the fact that he was receiving help. His situation could be paralleled by that of an eighteen-year-old girl, brought to the clinic by her mother because she wished to put a check to the daughter's plans for marriage. This girl had no recognition of any need for help, yet as contacts continued, she was able to take a very constructive type of help, and eventually decided quite independently that her proposed marriage had been more in the nature of a threat to her parents than a real plan for a lifetime partnership. Likewise, instances might be cited of individuals who are coerced into the counseling situation by someone with authority and who, in spite of initial resistance to any kind of help, end by taking assistance of a sort they can use. It seems clear that we need to analyze more adequately the situations which make it possible for a person to accept counseling help.

Assuming that the client is experiencing some conflict or stress, there would seem to be two other conditions which must be met in order that he may make constructive use of the counseling situation. In the first place, there must be the physical opportunity for interviewing to take place. Such a statement may seem superfluous; actually it deserves some thought. Frequently, in situations where the client is coerced into counseling contacts (not by the counselor, of course), it is this fact of being in the situation which gives a genuine therapeutic process its start. Thus, it is frequently possible for a child who is held in a detention home or institution to make use of counseling help in gaining insight into himself and his situation, while such an individual might be quite inaccessible to counseling if he were free to decide for himself whether he wished such contacts. (Counseling in this type of situation raises many questions, which are discussed in the following chapter, as to the dangers of mixing an authoritative with a counseling rôle.)

It is not enough that there should be a physical opportunity for interviewing. The client must also be able to express in some fashion the conflicting desires which have created his problem. This expression may be through the media of play materials, or through symbolism of other sorts, but psychotherapy is powerless to deal with problem-creating forces which are not in some way brought into the therapeutic relationship. Whether or not the individual can express his feelings is as much a test of the counselor's skill in creating a therapeutic atmosphere as it is a quality of the client, but it must be taken into account in making a decision regarding the possibilities of counseling with a particular individual.

A first contact with twelve-year-old Sally will indicate some of the difficulties and some of the possibilities which exist when

an individual is forced into a counseling situation. Sally's
mother (whom we shall meet in the following chapter) brought
her to the clinic because she was failing in school in spite of
superior intelligence, and in addition was a constant source of
friction in the home, particularly with her sister. Sally rebuffed
all attempts of her parents and others to "reach" her, and with-
drew into her own private world. She was resistant about coming to the clinic for diagnostic contacts, and this attitude
seemed magnified when, some months later, arrangements were
made for both the mother and Sally to come for treatment contacts, the mother working with one clinician, Sally with another. The following is the counselor's account of the first part
of the first treatment interview.

As we were getting seated I said, "It was pretty slippery, I
expect, coming here today. Driving must be pretty bad." No
reply. "You live in B——, don't you?" A grunt to signify
yes. She sat in the chair with her legs crossed, her mouth rather
tightly shut, and looked at me most of the time — not avoiding
my glance.

After a very brief pause I said, "You are probably sort of
wondering why you are here and probably not wanting very much
to be here." No reply. After that first remark I made a few
more statements to the effect that I knew nothing about her or
her family, except that it had seemed that her mother had felt
she might be helped to be happier and could do better the things
she was really able to do. No reply.

I went on to say, "We can't explain just why it is, but it seems
to be that it helps people to get straightened out on things and
to feel better about them if they talk them over with someone.
Now, I can't or wouldn't want to tell you what you *ought* to do or
how you ought to feel about things." Sally mumbled, "What
do you mean?"

I continued, "Well, of course, most people who come up here
to talk with us come of their own accord — when they feel that
they want to get some help with something which may be bothering them. You may feel a little different because it was your
mother who did the deciding that it would be well to come. But
it does seem that talking with someone seems to help a person
get straightened out in his thinking and helps him to feel better
toward other people and maybe even toward himself. We don't
always feel exactly comfortable toward ourselves. My only

aim is to be a listener to whatever you may have to say about how you feel about anything at all and so perhaps help you to be happier in general."

The paragraph just finished was not said all at once but with pauses between thoughts and with an effort on my part to look as friendly and unsevere as possible. She sat looking at me most of the time, chewing on a gold heart she was wearing on a chain, or fiddling with her hair.

After a pause I continued, "You feel it is pretty hard to talk to a person — to put into words how you feel about things." No reply. After another pause I said, "Now I don't have any sort of notion of the whole thing — you and your family and all. Let's see, do you have sisters?"

Sally responded to this question and to other specific questions with polite answers, containing a minimum of information. After a little conversation of this kind, there was another pause. The record continues:

Then I said, "Would you want to talk about how you feel about any of the things about yourself — your family, or school, or anything?" "How do you mean?" A further statement on my part of how it does seem to make people feel better to talk to a person who won't be telling them what to do or what they ought to do. And I added, "It's sort of hard for you to see how it would help."

Her reply was, "Maybe it would help some people, but I don't think ——" (sort of mumble implying it wouldn't help her). "You think it might help some people but it doesn't seem much use to you." No reply.

After a pause while we both just sat (probably forty-five to sixty seconds) I said, "Do you girls usually get along pretty well as a family? Let's see, what are your sisters' names?"

Again there was a short period of questions and answers. Sally named the members of her family, making one complete sentence in regard to their quarreling, her first in the interview. After a dozen questions, mostly answered in monosyllables, silence fell again. Quoting from the record:

After quite a pause I said again, "As I said before, it does seem to help sometimes to talk things over — but also most folks come because they want to. Students sometimes come because they feel they aren't doing as well in school as they would like and want help. But you probably came just because your mother wants you to and not because *you* wanted to." No reply of any sort.

I continued, "If you could say how you feel about coming here — what you say will make no difference to anyone — and you could say whatever you feel. It won't make any difference as to how I feel, for my only thought is to help." Brief pause. "How might you say you feel about coming up here?"

Sally replied, "I didn't want to — would rather not." I nodded, as she paused, and said it was perfectly all right that she felt that way — that it was to be expected — that it was not her own idea to come. She added, in a fairly pleasant tone, "I didn't really want to — but I'll come." "But at the same time you feel it is not your choice." No reply.

After some pause I asked, "Are there any things you often think about, or problems, or anything — you would like to talk about?" "Well, about the only thing I think much about is grades in school." I nodded and said, "They sometimes sort of worry you." "Yes, and I think about what it would be like to be put back with the younger kids." "You feel it wouldn't be a very pleasant thing to have happen." Pause. Then I said, because it occurred to me that I was not quite sure of her meaning, "That has happened, or just might?" "Oh, it might, but I don't think it will. I get C's and D's and I think I'll get by. It is only the F's I worry about. But I don't think I'll get that."

From this point on, Sally gradually became freer, talked of her school grades, of her hatred of school, of her own future plans of becoming a housewife. This excerpt illustrates admirably the fact that even the highly resistant individual, forced into a situation which he expects to fight, can gradually be enabled to accept help. It is probably not a coincidence that the turning point of this skillfully handled contact comes when Sally is able to express her resistance to coming and finds that this feeling is also accepted by the counselor. Following this, her hostility decreases, and she is better able to make use of the situation. It might be mentioned that in the second contact she again showed equally strong resistance and inability to talk throughout most of the hour, but by the same type of approach the counselor very slowly worked through to a constructive type of relationship.

Sally illustrates the fact that, although a conscious desire for help is valuable, counseling progress can be made even in the face of much resistance to help, if there is an opportunity for interviews and if the client can to some degree find ways of expressing conflicts that are real to him.

With the fully independent adult, the opportunity for contacts is not likely to exist unless there is a real desire for assistance. Two studies made at the Smith College School of Social Work confirm this statement.[5] Investigation of cases in two child-guidance clinics showed that when parents brought their children unwillingly to the clinic, simply because school or court authorities advised them to do so, little treatment progress was likely to be made. On the other hand, if the parent wished help for his child, or, best of all, if the parent wanted treatment for the child and for himself, treatment was likely to be successful. It was possible to judge these parental attitudes during the first interview.

Is the Client Independent of Family Control?   Still another question which the counselor will need to consider in planning the focus of therapeutic work, particularly with the child or adolescent, is the nature of the client's tie to his family. As long as the child is emotionally dependent on his parents, subject to parental control, and living in his own home, counseling of the child alone is very often unsuccessful, and may even increase his difficulties. We must recall again the fact that one of the assumptions regarding the outcome of counseling is that the individual has the capacity and the opportunity to take some effective action in regard to his situation, once a degree of insight is achieved. This assumption is not often justified in the case of a child. Effective psychotherapy with a youngster usually involves treatment of the parent also, in order that the parent and child may jointly make those changes which will improve adjustment. Otherwise therapy with the child may

5 Mills, Harriet J. "The Prognostic Value of the First Interview," *Smith College Studies in Social Work*, vol. 8, no. 1 (September, 1937), pp. 1–33.

Ritterskampf, Louise. "The First Interview as a Guide to Treatment," *Smith College Studies in Social Work*, vol. 8, no. 1 (September, 1937), pp. 34–84.

simply succeed in setting him in basic opposition to his parent and in increasing his problem. Treatment of the child alone also runs the risk of making the parent jealous and antagonistic as he finds that the therapist has a close relationship with the youngster. This occurs even when the parent intellectually wishes the child to have therapeutic help.

The picture is quite different when the dependent individual finds himself out of the sphere of parental care and control. Every college counselor knows of students who are as dependent as the average child of ten — individuals who have never selected their own clothes, have never made their own decisions, have never been responsible for their own actions, and rely completely upon their parents. Such students, spatially removed from home by college attendance, are decidedly accessible to counseling help. The conflict between their desire to be dependent and the demands for independent living which the college places upon them creates a tension which must be solved.

Thus we might say that for a counseling procedure to be effective with a younger person, it is usually necessary that the child or adolescent should be emotionally or spatially free of family control. The only exceptions to this are those instances, rarer than is supposed, where the child's problem is not in any way tied up with the parent-child relationships. Thus we may give counseling as well as tutoring help to a child whose whole problem is a reading disability. Perhaps the same is true of the adolescent making a vocational choice, but here again, unless there is a considerable degree of emotional independence of the family, counseling is likely to be rather futile.

Is the Client of Suitable Age, Intelligence, and Stability? Although our information is meager, there is reason to suppose that counseling is a more appropriate and successful procedure with certain age levels and certain intelligence levels than with others. Evidence has already been cited to show that in actual clinical selection of cases for direct-interview treatment, there is a tendency to select a group with essentially normal inteliectual ability. It is probably rare that an individual of border-line level or below is selected for psychotherapy.

The Healy and Bronner study of treatment, previously cited, gives the most striking information yet available along this line. It will be recalled that this research dealt with the treatment outcomes of four hundred cases selected for intensive therapeutic work. There was found to be a very striking relationship between intelligence and outcome. Of the children with I.Q.'s from 70 to 79, 66 per cent had unfavorable later careers, with problems unresolved or becoming worse; of those with I.Q.'s of 80 to 89, 23 per cent were failures; of those with I.Q.'s from 90 to 109, 21 per cent were failures, and of the superior group, with I.Q.'s over 110, only 10 per cent had unfavorable later careers.[6] The authors wisely make the comment that this material should be interpreted with caution, and that unfavorable outcomes may be owing to the concomitant circumstances which so often accompany low intelligence rather than to the low intelligence itself. In any event, their findings would lead us to consider the individual of low intelligence with some care before deciding upon counseling as the best treatment approach.

Age is a still more uncertain factor. It seems clear that the older individual is not likely to be able to reorient himself, nor to reorganize his life as effectively as the younger individual. Chronological age is, however, a poor measure of the person's elasticity, and perhaps all that can be said is that careful consideration should be given to this question when the client is beyond the age of fifty. The lower age limit is equally elusive. Psychotherapy, in the form of play therapy, is certainly effective with children as young as four. Counseling, in which the approach is entirely verbal, would not often be utilized below the age of ten. Between four and ten or twelve, some use of play techniques would almost certainly be advisable, since verbalization of significant feelings is not easy for the child at this age.

[6] Healy, William, and Bronner, A. F. *Treatment and What Happened Afterward*, p. 34.

Another element for consideration, implied in the earlier discussion, is the stability of the individual. Both clinical experience and a certain amount of research evidence indicate that the highly unstable individual, particularly when such instability seems to have an organic or hereditary basis, is not a good risk for psychotherapy, or indeed for any type of treatment approach developed to date. In the Healy and Bronner study just mentioned, there is material which bears on this point. Of those individuals diagnosed as definitely or probably of abnormal personality — a group which includes "psychopathic personalities," "constitutional inferiors," and brain-damage cases — seven had favorable after-careers, thirty-seven had unfavorable later histories. While this seems convincing, additional evidence from the same study shows how subtle the dividing line may be. Of the nine cases showing definitely psychotic symptoms, or some psychotic characteristics, all responded favorably to treatment. Of the seventeen classed as extremely neurotic or "peculiar," fifteen responded favorably and only two had unsuccessful later careers. The satisfactory interpretation of this seemingly contradictory material will no doubt have to await further studies. It may well be that organic instability is more prominent in the first group than in the second and third, but the information is not adequate to make this point clear.

Additional evidence is obtained from a further study made under the author's direction in the Rochester Guidance Center, a study based on the follow-up of the two hundred cases previously mentioned.[7] In an endeavor to investigate the significance of various types and syndromes of symptoms, the problems of the children were carefully classified. It was found that the problem of "hyperactivity" carried with it the likelihood of unsuccessful treatment outcome. For purposes of the study this category was defined as follows: "Hyperactivity — 'nervousness' — includes those types of behavior suggestive of a physiological basis, but where accurate medical diagnosis

[7] Bennett, C. C., and Rogers, C. R. "The Clinical Significance of Problem Syndromes," *American Journal of Orthopsychiatry*, vol. 11 (April, 1941), pp. 222–229.

may or may not have been made." Excessive activity and restlessness, nervous mannerisms and tics, erratic and uncontrolled behavior, were among the types of symptoms classified in this category. Children who presented this sort of problem were especially likely to present other serious problems of behavior and attitude. They also responded less well to treatment, including psychotherapy. Interestingly enough, after two years of treatment, the hyperactivity itself often had disappeared, but nearly two thirds of the group still showed serious problems of some sort. While the categories of this study are by no means identical with those of the Healy and Bronner study, the two researches seem to have some interesting parallels which suggest the importance of this factor of instability, if it can be adequately defined.

Tentative Criteria

Having discussed the various elements and questions which the counselor should consider in his first contacts with the client, we may attempt to make them more definite and precise by casting them in the form of criteria. In the three sections which follow, an effort has been made to state the criteria which indicate that direct counseling and psychotherapy is, or is not, advisable as a focus of treatment in a particular case. It should be stressed that these are tentative criteria, and that one of the reasons for stating them in as definite a manner as possible is to encourage their modification or verification through an experimental approach.

Conditions Indicating Counseling or Psychotherapy. From the material given in the previous portions of this chapter, it would seem that direct counseling treatment of the individual, involving planned and continued contacts, is advisable provided all of the following conditions exist:

    1. The individual is under a degree of tension, arising from incompatible personal desires or from the conflict of social and environmental demands with individual needs. The

tension and stress so created are greater than the stress involved in expressing his feelings about his problems.

2. The individual has some capacity to cope with life. He possesses adequate ability and stability to exercise some control over the elements of his situation. The circumstances with which he is faced are not so adverse or so unchangeable as to make it impossible for him to control or alter them.

3. There is an opportunity for the individual to express his conflicting tensions in planned contacts with the counselor.

4. He is able to express these tensions and conflicts either verbally or through other media. A conscious desire for help is advantageous, but not entirely necessary.

5. He is reasonably independent, either emotionally or spatially, of close family control.

6. He is reasonably free from excessive instabilities, particularly of an organic nature.

7. He possesses adequate intelligence for coping with his life situation, with an intelligence rating of dull-normal or above.

8. He is of suitable age — old enough to deal somewhat independently with life, young enough to retain some elasticity of adjustment. In terms of chronological age this might mean roughly from ten to sixty.

Conditions Indicating Direct Therapy with Child and Parent. It will be evident that the factors which make it wise to initiate therapeutic contacts with parent and child separately are similar to, but not identical with, those which make direct counseling of the individual advisable. These factors are stated here, with particular emphasis upon those points where the criteria are different.

Direct therapy with parent and child, by different counselors, seems advisable when the following conditions are all met:

1. The child's problems are based, to an important extent, in the parent-child relationship.

2. The child is not yet emotionally or spatially independent of his family.

3. Either the parent or the child (nearly always the former) feels a need of help, thus creating an opportunity of working with the situation.

4. The parent is relatively treatable, which means that

   a. he has some satisfactions, outside of the parent-child relationship, in social or marital relationships or in personal achievements;

   b. he is reasonably stable;

   c. he possesses dull-normal intelligence or better;

   d. he is young enough to retain some elasticity of adjustment.

5. The child is relatively treatable, which means that

   a. he is reasonably free from organic instabilities;

   b. he has dull-normal intelligence or better;

   c. he is old enough to express his attitudes through play materials or in other ways in the counseling situation. Ordinarily this means a chronological age of four or more.

Conditions Indicating Environmental or Indirect Treatment. We need to have clearly in mind not only those conditions which indicate that a counseling approach is definitely preferable, but also those factors which argue in favor of an indirect approach. There follows an attempt to list these criteria. Unlike the previous lists, the presence of *any one* of these conditions is probably sufficient to justify focusing effort upon environmental measures rather than upon any sort of psychotherapy.

1. The component factors of the individual's adjustment situation are so adverse that, even with changed attitudes and insight, he could not cope with it. Destructive experiences in the family or social group, or a destructive environment, added to his own inadequacies in health, abilities, and competencies, make adjustment very unlikely unless the environmental setting is changed.

2. The individual is inaccessible to counseling, in that reason-

able opportunity and effort fail to discover any means by which he can express his feelings and problems. (An example would be the highly withdrawn individual in the incipient stages of a schizophrenic psychosis, who cannot express his obviously conflicting attitudes.)

3. Effective environmental treatment is simpler and more efficient than a direct therapeutic approach. This condition probably prevails only when the problem-creating situation is almost entirely environmental — an inadequate school curriculum, an unfortunate place of residence, an irritable and incompetent foreman, or some other factor in the environment being responsible for the problem.

4. The individual is too young or too old, too dull, or too unstable, for a direct type of therapy. (See the previous sections for more exact definitions of these conditions.)

Some comments in regard to these summarized criteria may be in order. It will be obvious that they are not to be applied blindly or mechanically. They are intended as guides to intelligent thinking, not as substitutes for such thinking. They do not cover all the situations which arise. For example, they are designed to help determine the primary focus of treatment, but they do not attempt to indicate secondary emphases. Thus, some counseling may be indicated as a secondary measure, even when the primary focus should clearly be environmental, or some indirect treatment may be wise when the major reliance is placed upon psychotherapy. In short, these criteria are not intended to do more than to clarify, and to bring more sharply into the focus of thought, those decisions which are already being made on some sort of basis.

It will be seen that, by the criteria given above, some groups tend to be designated as suitable or unsuitable for counseling treatment. Thus, maladjusted students of college level are nearly always good candidates for counseling help because in most instances they are able to alter some aspects of their life situation, are almost always of suitable age and intelligence, tend to have at least a minimum of stability and to be partially free of home control. In general these statements apply also to those individuals who are maladjusted in their marriage relationships. On the other hand, the incipient psychotic, who is beginning to lose contact with reality, is often unable to take counseling help, either because he is so withdrawn that he cannot express his tensions and conflicts or because he has no longer sufficient stability to exercise control over his life situation. Mentally defective individuals are also poor candidates for counseling, since they fail rather obviously to measure up to the criteria set forth. Nor is the type of counseling described suitable for the well-adjusted individual who feels no uncomfortable strain in his life adjustment. This last fact is sometimes overlooked in setting up institutional programs of counseling, and it is supposed that a counseling experience is necessary for everyone. On the contrary, counseling is a process which is of help primarily to those who are suffering from definite tensions and maladjustments.

These comments are intended to make plain the fact that individuals differ in the extent to which they meet the tentative criteria proposed. It should be understood, however, that there are always exceptions to any generalized statement, and that careful consideration should be given to each case of maladjustment in order to determine whether the emphasis of treatment should be upon counseling or upon some other type of treatment approach.

What of the Case History?

Some readers will regard it as odd that we should discuss the various conditions which influence the choice of treatment approach and dictate the focus of therapy, without any discussion of the complete case history on the basis of which (they suppose) the decisions will be made. This omission has been purposeful, but before leaving the topic entirely, some attention should be given to the question.

As a matter of fact, a careful consideration of the place of the case history in modern clinical and counseling work is long over-due. That it has lost some of the importance formerly given to it is plain, but its present status is less clear. Let us examine the situation as it is relevant to the present discussion.

The complete case history, with its wealth of material regarding the development of the individual and his attitudes, with its comprehensive picture of his social setting and the cultural forces which have influenced him, is highly significant for a complete and satisfactory diagnosis. Let us make no mistake about that. For a full understanding of the significant life forces and life patterns, a complete case history is our best method of approach.

But the plain fact is that at times the gathering of a suitable case history definitely interferes with the treatment process. Consequently we are sometimes faced with the unpleasant choice as to whether we prefer to have a complete and accurate diagnostic picture of the individual, or whether we wish him to make progress in the solving of his problems. Let us see how this dilemma arises.

When the counselor assumes the information-getting attitude which is necessary for the assembling of a good case history, the client cannot help feeling that the responsibility for the solution of his problems is being taken over by the counselor. When the counselor says, in effect, "I should like to have you tell me about your problems and yourself, your background and your development, your education and your medical history, your family experiences and your social environment," he also definitely implies the additional assurance, "and then I can tell you how to solve your problems." If the treatment which is indicated is environmental, this mind-set on the part of the client does no harm. It may, in fact, make him feel more ready to accept environmental changes because they have been based on thorough knowledge. If, however, the treatment is to be in the nature of counseling or psychotherapy, this mind-set makes treatment more difficult. The client has given, in response to tactful questioning, all the information he knows how to give. In return he expects to receive the solutions to his problems. Any effort to get him to take the responsibility for his own situation, to try to find the type of adjustment which is realistic and within his own powers, must necessarily be interpreted by him as a deliberate refusal on the part of the counselor to tell him the answers. It is much simpler for the counselor to undertake treatment which builds up the client's independence and moves in the direction of mature growth, if he has not been a party to any case-history-taking experience.

It is for this reason that the criteria which have been given in this chapter deal primarily with elements which may be judged without an elaborate case history as a guide. Preliminary judgments, based on a first contact, can be made in most cases on all the criteria indicating the advisability of counseling. The degree of tension is nearly always a matter which can be decided by close observation. Whether the client's tension is sufficient to more than balance the distress of talking out his problems is a more subtle question, and will often be answered completely only as the counseling gets under way. Whether opportunities for counseling contacts are feasible, whether the client is relatively independent of his family — these matters are usually clear after a first contact. Likewise, the questions regarding suitable age, intelligence, and stability are often answered simply by careful observation by the counselor. The question of whether the individual is sufficiently able to express his conflicts may or may not be answered at the outset, and several interviews may be required. The criterion most likely to cause difficulty is the question of whether the client has some capacity for controlling or changing his life situation. In many instances the answer may be obvious. The average adult, the typical high-school or college student has, in nearly every case, some capacity for dealing effectively with his life-adjustment situation. With some individuals, however, handicapped in fundamental ways by their own inadequacies or the destructive quality of their environment, this decision may be a very difficult one. In such instances it is wise to undertake a thorough diagnostic study before making any decision as to what type of treatment is most likely to be profitable.   In such cases, to initiate psychotherapy without a diagnostic study may only plunge the client further into hopelessness as his own lacks are brought into greater prominence by his increasing insight.   Consequently, even though the diagnostic study may interfere somewhat with a counseling process, it is definitely advisable here.

We may summarize these comments by saying that in a great many instances counseling treatment may begin at once, in the first contact, without a diagnostic study, and that this procedure is entirely justified if the counselor is alert to the crucial aspects of the picture as they are revealed during the initial interview.   In other cases an exhaustive diagnostic study may be advisable before choosing the most promising focus of treatment effort.   In all of this the fact should be kept clearly in mind that it is the client's mature development which is important, and that the tools of clinical work are to be chosen with that fundamental fact in mind.   If the counselor makes a complete case study, it should be because that is the way in which he is most likely to be able to assist the client in reaching a normal adjustment.   If he refrains from making such a study, it should be for precisely the same reason, that in this instance he can most readily promote the client's growth by proceeding at once to treatment, avoiding the unfortunate implications of the full-case-history study.

This whole dilemma has been stated in its sharpest terms. Actually it is not a question of whether the counselor will have information regarding the client or remain ignorant.   It is a question of whether he puts the information-getting process ahead of every other consideration.   In a true counseling process, the individual is much more likely to reveal the genuinely dynamic forces in his experience, the crucial patterns of his life behavior, than in a more formal history-taking process.   Thus the counselor gradually becomes aware of the important sequences of dynamic events, even though there may be large gaps in his knowledge of the superficial and outward events in the client's life.

SUMMARY

Whether the client comes of his own accord or is sent, the counselor necessarily begins to formulate, from his first knowledge of the individual, certain decisions in regard to the most promising treatment approach.   If we analyze the elements of these decisions with care, we find that we can build up criteria by means of which these choices may be made more intelligently.   Often these decisions may be made on evidence obtained during an initial contact with the client, without a complete diagnosis, and without assembling a complete case history.   In this chapter we have discussed the criteria which indicate counseling as the best approach, the criteria which indicate separate therapy with parent and child, and those conditions which contraindicate direct therapy and point toward the wisdom of a primary emphasis upon environmental treatment.

The Creation of a Counseling Relationship

MUCH well-intentioned counseling is unsuccessful because a satisfactory counseling relationship is never established. Frequently counselors and therapists have no clear-cut notion of the relationship which should exist, and as a consequence their therapeutic efforts are vague and uncertain in direction and outcome. Much more adequate attention needs to be paid to the subtle interrelationship which grows up between the therapist and the client, the counselor and the counselee.

COUNSELING AS A UNIQUE RELATIONSHIP

Perhaps the best way to begin the discussion is by explaining what the counseling relationship is not. In speaking of therapy at its best, we may make a number of negative statements. The therapeutic relationship is not, for example, a parent-child relationship, with its deep affectional ties, its characteristic dependence on the one hand and the acceptance of an authoritative and responsible rôle on the other. The parent-child bond has an undertone of permanence and complete devotion which is not a part of the best counseling.

Likewise, the therapeutic relationship is not the relationship of friend to friend. In such a bond the outstanding characteristic is complete mutuality — mutual understanding, give and take. Neither is the counseling relationship a typical teacher-pupil relationship, with its implications of superior and inferior status, its assumption that one is to teach and the other to learn, its complete reliance upon intellectual processes. Nor is therapy based on a physician-patient relationship, with its characteristics of expert diagnosis and authoritative advice on the part of the physician, submissive acceptance and dependence on the part of the patient. The list might be extended. For instance, the counseling relationship is not the relationship between two co-workers, although it partakes of certain elements of this. It is not the relationship of leader and follower, nor of priest and parishioner.

In short, the counseling relationship represents a quality of social bond which differs from any the client has heretofore experienced. Often considerable portions of the first contacts are given over to various attempts to understand and try out this different type of human relationship. The counselor needs to recognize this if he is to handle the situation effectively.

Although the therapeutic relationship is thus described as being different from most of our ordinary life relationships, this does not mean that counseling as it exists always meets this description. Sometimes by error, sometimes by design, therapists and counselors pattern their attitudes toward their clients in one of these familiar forms. Probably Freudian psychoanalysis has most consistently stressed the attitude that the analyst adopts a parent rôle. One writer says of such an analyst: "He becomes immediately a surrogate for one of the real parents. Thus he becomes the parent or father confessor to whom everything may really be told without fear of punishment or recrimination, the father who will understand and show no amazement or emotional resentment at even the usually most unspeakable emotional facts." [1] We may wish later to consider whether this playing of the parental rôle is one of the elements which makes Freudian analysis so notoriously long.

Other counselors definitely plan to play a teacher rôle; still others stress the fact that they are friends of their counselees. In fact, any of the typical relationships which exist in real life may be found exemplified in counseling relationships. Such examples, however, do not typify psychotherapy at its best.

[1] Brown, J. F. *Psychodynamics of Abnormal Behavior*, p. 290. New York: McGraw-Hill Book Company, 1940.

Basic Aspects of a Therapeutic Relationship

After this description of the therapeutic relationship in negative terms, how may we characterize it in definite and positive terminology? How shall we say what it is, rather than what it is not? There would seem to be at least four definite qualities which characterize the most helpful counseling atmosphere. We shall describe these in terms of the situation which the counselor endeavors to create.

First is a warmth and responsiveness on the part of the counselor which makes rapport possible, and which gradually develops into a deeper emotional relationship. From the counselor's point of view, however, this is a definitely controlled relationship, an affectional bond with defined limits. It expresses itself in a genuine interest in the client and an acceptance of him as a person. The counselor frankly recognizes that he becomes to some extent emotionally involved in this relationship. He does not pretend to be superhuman and above the possibility of such involvement. He is sufficiently sensitive to the needs of the client, however, to control his own identification in order to serve best the person he is helping. On the one hand he avoids the viewpoint expressed in the following description of the analyst: "The patient becomes emotionally involved with the analyst and the analyst attempts to view the patient with the minimal amount of emotion. The analyst must appear psychologically strong, very just, and very understanding of human frailty." [2] The good counselor will recognize that the attitude just described would make him a hopeless prig. He will do better to face openly the fact that to some extent he is himself emotionally involved, but that this involvement must be strictly limited for the good of the patient. Thus he avoids the other extreme, which might be illustrated from a first therapeutic interview with a rejected and deprived eight-year-old girl.

In the midst of the girl's rather aimless and inhibited play the counselor said, "Esther, would you like to know something?"

[2] Brown, J. F. *Psychodynamics of Abnormal Behavior*, p. 290.

Esther showed her interest, and the counselor said, "I like you."
Esther seemed pleased by this. She looked out of the window,
noticed some men walking in the distance, and said, "Know where
my uncle works?"

Here the counselor is attempting to force upon the child an
affectional relationship for which the youngster is not ready,
and which, in all probability, the counselor is not able to make
good.[3]   It is the wiser course if the therapist, avoiding the ex-
tremes of aloofness and overinvolvement, creates a bond characterized by warmth, interest, responsiveness, and a clearly
and definitely limited degree of emotional attachment.   We
shall speak later of the ways in which those limits are set in the
interview situation.

The second quality of the counseling relationship is its permissiveness in regard to expression of feeling.   By the counselor's acceptance of his statements, by the complete lack of
any moralistic or judgmental attitude, by the understanding
attitude which pervades the counseling interview, the client
comes to recognize that all feelings and attitudes may be expressed.   No attitude is too aggressive, no feeling too guilty
or shameful, to bring into the relationship. Hatred for a father,
feelings of conflict over sexual urges, remorse over past acts, dislike of coming for help, antagonism and resentment toward the
therapist, all may be expressed.   In this respect the therapeutic relationship differs markedly from the other relationships of ordinary life.   It offers a place where the client may
bring into the situation, as rapidly as his inhibitions will allow him, all the forbidden impulses and unspoken attitudes
which complicate his life.

While there is this complete freedom to express feelings, there
are definite limits to action in the therapeutic interview, helping
to give it a structure which the client can use in gaining insight
into himself.   These therapeutic limits are a third and an important aspect of the counseling situation.   Take, for example,

[3] Supportive therapy, in which the therapist becomes, for all practical purposes, the
mother, father, uncle, or aunt of the child is possible, and if entered into with full
realization of the time-consuming responsibilities, can be successful. See the article
by Axelrode (Bibliography, p. 441) for discussion of this topic.

the matter of time. The client is free to keep an appointment or to break it, to come on time or to come late, to use the hour in idle talk in order to avoid his real problems, or to use it constructively. There is the limitation, however, that he is not free to control the counselor and gain more time, no matter by what subterfuge. Not infrequently the counselee waits until the last moments of the counseling hour to bring up some matter of vital importance, thus implicitly demanding more time. The small child is more direct about it and announces that he will stay two hours instead of one. The counselor is most wise, however, who holds to the essential time limits that have been set. The client can make much more effective use of a well-structured situation. There are also other limits. With the small child in the play-therapy situation, there is complete freedom to express any type of feeling, but certain broad limits to action. He may smash clay figures, break dolls, shout, spill water, but he may not throw blocks through the window, nor carry his destructive activities out into the hall or into other offices. He may tear to pieces an image of the therapist, but he may not attack the therapist personally. In short, the most complete freedom is given for the person to express his feelings and to face himself. There is not, however, freedom to harm others by carrying all his impulses into action. It is often fascinating to see the child exploring all the aspects of the therapeutic situation, to find where the limits are. We make a great mistake if we suppose that the limits are a hindrance to therapy. They are, with both adult and child, one of the vital elements which make the therapeutic situation a microcosm in which the client can meet all the basic aspects which characterize life as a whole, face them openly, and adapt himself to them.

A fourth characteristic of the counseling relationship is its freedom from any type of pressure or coercion. The skillful counselor refrains from intruding his own wishes, his own reactions or biases, into the therapeutic situations. The hour is the client's hour, not the counselor's. Advice, suggestion, pressure to follow one course of action rather than another — these are out of place in therapy. As we shall see in our further discus-

sion of the therapeutic process, this is not a mere negative restraint, a wooden refusal to influence the client.   It is the positive ground for personality growth and development, for conscious choice, and for self-directed integration.   It is in this type
of soil that growth can take place.   No doubt it is in this fourth
characteristic that the therapeutic relationship differs most
sharply from the usual relationships of everyday life in the
family, the school, and the working world.

We have spoken of this relationship as the counselor sees it,
and as he tries to foster it in counseling situations.   From the
client's point of view, while he may not be conscious of all these
elements at the outset, he does respond to the atmosphere of
freedom from all moral approval or disapproval.   He finds that
he does not need his customary psychological defenses to justify
his behavior.   He finds neither blame nor oversympathetic in-
dulgence and praise.   He finds that the counselor gives him
neither undue support nor unwelcome antagonism.   Consequently the client can, often for the first time in his life, be genuinely himself, dropping those defensive mechanisms and over-
compensations which enable him to face the world in general.
In the therapeutic relationship he can evaluate his impulses and
his actions, his conflicts and his choices, his past patterns and
present problems, much more truly because, on the one hand,
he is freed from the necessity of defending himself from attack,
and, on the other hand, is protected from a too complacent dependence.   That the individual does respond to these elements
of the counseling situation will be evident in the discussion of
the closing phases of therapy, during which the counselee often
verbalizes the manner in which the counseling atmosphere has
been a unique experience for him.

STRUCTURING THE COUNSELING RELATIONSHIP IN PRACTICE

Since the therapeutic relationship is so definitely distinct
from other life relationships, we may well ask how the client
becomes acquainted with its structure and how he comes to
recognize its true qualities.   To some extent, the structure of

the situation becomes defined by what does not happen. Moral judgments are not made; pressure to follow certain courses of action is not felt. Other elements, such as the responsiveness of the counselor, are experienced rather than verbalized. Yet the counselor often helps to hasten the structuring of the situation, by defining it to the client in one way or another. Although research in the field of therapy is only in its infancy, there are some data indicating that this structuring can be shown to be present. Porter,[4] in developing a measure of counseling-interview procedures, analyzed the part played by the counselor in nineteen phonographically recorded interviews. He divided the various counseling procedures into those which define the interview situation, those which bring out and develop the problem situation, those which develop insight and understanding, and those which sponsor or foster client activity. It is interesting to note from his data that if one groups his interviews according to their position in the series, there is a sharp difference between these groups in the extent to which the interview situation is defined. In first interviews, an average of more than six counselor statements per interview are concerned with the definition of the relationship. In the middle interviews (fourth, fifth, and sixth), there is an average of but one counselor comment per interview defining the situation. In closing interviews there are almost no comments of this sort.

Lewis,[5] in her very detailed analysis of both counselor and counselee items in six treatment cases, arrives at the same sort of finding. In the first decile of therapeutic contacts — a measure adopted to make the cases comparable — there is the greatest amount of material explaining the counselor's rôle. In the following deciles, there is a tendency for this type of item to drop out.

In a Student Counseling Situation. Some examples may serve to illustrate the variety of ways in which the unique fea-

[4] Porter, E. H. *The Development and Evaluation of a Measure of Counseling Interview Procedures.* Columbus, Ohio: Ohio State University, 1941 (unpublished thesis).

[5] From an unpublished research study made by Virginia W. Lewis at Teachers College, Columbia University. See Chapter II, p. 45, for a more complete description.

tures of the counseling relationship are more clearly defined in the interview situation, so that the counselee may use them to his own advantage.

Paul, a student from whose record we have quoted in the preceding chapter, is a boy who has suffered from a variety of fears and tensions. He becomes very tense in any kind of social situation, is afraid to recite in class, and feels abnormal. In his first interview he tells of these problems, and the conversation proceeds as follows (phonographic recording):

C. Now you're hoping that you can get some help in getting rid of these tensions?

S. Yes, I must, because I'll be a failure if I don't. Oh, I might also say that my parents, I think, have a lot to do with this. For one thing, I — in my opinion they're extremely unsociable. That's my opinion. And I, I, uh, I really don't — didn't like the idea. It made — I don't know, I guess that had a bearing on my inferiority complex — I believe, too, that it got worse because my people moved around quite a bit when I was in school.

C. You feel both those things hindered your own social development, is that it?

S. Yes, definitely.

C. And you do feel, I take it, that this thing bothers you most in a social situation?

S. Yes, whenever I'm with people.

C. You wouldn't be bothered if you were a hermit?

S. (*Laugh.*) No, but I don't want to be.

C. I understand.

(*Pause.*)

C. Well, now, I'll explain a little bit some of the ways in which perhaps you can get some help out of this. I think, that if, if you can think through this thing and talk it out more fully, get at the different aspects of it and all, then between the two of us perhaps we could see some way out of it. It isn't — I'm not the kind of person and I don't think yours is the kind of problem where I could say, "Well, now, do thus and so and everything will be all right."

S. No, I can see that right now — a very deep-seated problem.

C. It's only just a matter of your working through the thing and some help I can present ——

S. M-hm.

C. So that I think it might be a good thing if you just go on telling me more about it, why you feel so concerned about it at the present time, for example, why it's worse now than it was a few months ago.

In terms of what goes on in this interview to define the counseling relationship, it will be noted first of all that the pause comes at a significant point. The student has briefly stated his problem, and it has been accepted. He then waits for the counselor to do something — to advise, to take the lead in questions, to indicate in some way that he has taken over the responsibility for handling the client's problem. This is a very common attitude on the part of individuals coming for help. It is at this point that the counselor introduces a brief and partial explanation of the counseling situation, leaving the responsibility with the student, but nevertheless making plain that it is a joint enterprise, mentioning the fact that the problem will not be solved for him, but giving him a way of proceeding. It will be obvious to anyone who has dealt with people disturbed by their own maladjustments that such a brief explanation will not be completely assimilated or understood by the client. Nonetheless it helps to lay a groundwork for understanding, which is reinforced by the fact that the counselor's actions are in accord with this verbal description.

In Treatment of Parents. In dealing with a parent who has brought his child for help, the problem of defining the counseling relationship is sometimes more difficult than in the type of situation just described. In focusing the complaint on the child, the parent is protecting himself against criticism, and usually he is sufficiently defensive to deny that he is directly involved or in need of help. Here is a point which needs to be handled tactfully, with a basic understanding of what therapy has to offer. Therapy can help only the person in the therapeutic situation. It has no miraculous way of reaching out to a third party. Thus it may be of help in assisting the client to handle his own relationship with his child, his employer, or his spouse, but it has no way of helping or changing these other individuals directly. Consequently in defining the counseling situation to a parent, it must gradually be made clear that the help which may be obtained is help for the parent himself in his own handling of the parent-child relationships. This definition of the situation is not accomplished at once or through one statement, but it needs to be made clear if the counseling is to be effective. Examples of the way in which the relationship is verbally defined have already been given (Chapter II, pages 31, 33). In another case a mother comes to the clinic in regard to her four-year-old daughter. She tells of the child's stubbornness and negativism, and gives a picture of struggle which she herself describes as "war from morning till night."

> C. said that from the description that had come of Patty it sounded as if there was quite a bit of difficulty. Mrs. J. agreed and said something had to be done. C. agreed, saying, "But most of it will probably have to be done by you. How do you get Patty to go to bed, to do anything?" Mrs. J. said that usually she bribed her because no other means would work. C. described how children and their mothers come in, one to see one person, the other to see another, to work together on their common difficulty on which they could not get along. C. said that she did not know, that we never knew, how much might be done, because there were so many variables in each situation. The greatest part of the work, however, is carried by the mother and what she does in relation to what her child does at home. Mrs. J. nodded and said that's exactly what she wanted, that she knew she simply had to do something. For example, she cannot go back to her home to visit, because her child is so bad that she wouldn't want her folks to see her. She laughed and said, "Not many mothers will say as much, but I know my youngster's bad."

In this brief excerpt the focus of the treatment relationship is placed squarely on what the mother can do in relation to her child, and this definition of the situation is made even more clear as time goes on by the manner in which the mother's comments are handled, not in terms of the child, but in terms of those strengths which the mother has to deal with the situation that exists between them.

In Play Therapy. While to some, play therapy may seem to be a very different sort of experience from the counseling of students or therapy with parents or adults, in structure it appears to be very similar, and what we have said about the definition of the therapeutic relationship applies equally well to the play situation. The most noticeable difference is that in play therapy the relationship is defined much more through actions than through words. The therapist's friendly interest in and affection for the child are made plain through a host of minor actions. The permissiveness of the relationship is gradually defined as the child tries bolder and bolder activities and learns that they are accepted. Often after any new aggressive action, such as spilling water, making a loud noise, or "hurting" a doll, the child glances up with a guilty look, expecting some sort of punishment or reproof. When this is not forthcoming, he slowly learns that this is a new type of situation, with many permissive aspects not at all characteristic of his usual experiences. The fact that it is his time, to be used as he wishes, without pressure, direction, or coercion, is also learned through experiencing this freedom, rather than through verbal definition. It is only in the setting of limits that words play much part. The child learns that there is a time limit to the experience, that there is a limit to the affection involved, since the therapist sees other children on a similar basis, and that there is a limit to the types of destructiveness allowed. Since this problem of setting the limits of the therapy situation raises a number of questions, in relation to both child and adult clients, it will be discussed in somewhat more detail.

THE MATTER OF LIMITS

It may seem to some that the notion of setting certain definite limits to the therapeutic situation is an artificial or unnecessary procedure. Nothing could be farther from the truth. Every counseling situation has some sort of limit, as many an amateur therapist has discovered to his sorrow. He wishes to be of help to the child in a counseling situation, wishes to make plain his

interest in the youngster.   If the child asks for gifts, shall he
give them to him?   At what point shall he stop?   If the child
seeks physical affection, shall he give it?   Indefinitely?   If the
child wishes the counselor to intercede for him with parent or
school, shall he do it?   How many times?   One maladjusted
youngster wished to observe the counselor at the toilet.
Should it be permitted?   In short, in any therapeutic situation,
whether with child or adult, demands are made, desires expressed, toward which the counselor must take some attitude.
The amateur or untrained counselor, bolstered by good intentions, anxious not to hurt the client, has a tendency to accede
to these requests, to do almost anything which the client feels
will help, until the demands upon time or affection or responsibility grow too great for the counselor to bear.   Then his affection and desire to help turn to avoidance and dislike.   He
blames the client and rejects him.   The net result is that the
client feels that one more person has betrayed him, that one
more person who claimed to wish to help has actually failed in
time of stress.   He may be definitely and sometimes permanently hurt by this bungled attempt at counseling.

Every counseling situation has, then, its limits.   The only
question is whether these limits are clearly defined, understood,
and helpfully used, or whether the client, in a moment of great
need, suddenly finds limits erected as barriers against him.   It
should be obvious that the former is the preferable procedure.
Let us see some of the common forms which such limits take.

Limitation of Responsibility.   One of the limits which the
counselor must formulate clearly is the extent to which he will
take responsibility for the problems and actions of the client.
On the basis of the hypothesis expressed in Chapter I, it is plain
that responsibility is most helpfully left with the client.   One
of the commonest problems in psychotherapy, and one of the
issues most helpful in stimulating growth, if handled constructively, is the client's insistence that the counselor take over
his problem.   Mrs. D, for example, has come in for help with
her twelve-year-old daughter, who does not adjust well to her

sister, is failing in school, dawdles and daydreams, and "cannot be reached" by anything her mother may say. Following a diagnostic study Mrs. D decides to come in with her daughter for treatment help, and the following conversations take place during the mother's first interview with the therapist (phonographic recording).

> The mother repeats her complaints, stressing the fact that Sally does not put her mind on her work. She continues:
>
> S. The other girls in the family are just grand, I mean, just so normal and adjusted. They have their ups and downs, their gloom and their glory, you know, but nothing out of the ordinary, and just so easy to get along with, and do better than average work in school, and they're just fine. But Sally ——
>
> C. But Sally ——
>
> S. Little devil! Drives me crazy! So, if there's anything you'd like to ask me, I'll answer to the best of my ability.
>
> C. Well, now, why don't we consider this interview and those that may follow as a time when we can talk it over rather than my asking questions and getting information. In other words, you probably feel, as you said, that you've told us everything about Sally and the other children, but this can be a little bit different; in other words, this is just a place where you and I can talk over your problems.

In this excerpt the mother definitely endeavors to put the lead, and by implication the responsibility, in the hands of the counselor. She will answer questions while he solves the problem. However, the brief explanation given of the relationship is sufficient to start her on a constructive discussion of Sally's difficulties and her own attitudes toward them. Toward the end of the interview, however, the question of responsibility arises again. The mother has been stressing the fact that Sally can never amount to much if she does not complete high school. The phonographic recording continues:

> C. You feel then that the future is pretty dark for Sally? (*Pause.*)
>
> S. Well, but she might be the type that can sort of slip through.
>
> C. But you sort of doubt it, don't you?
>
> S. No, I don't doubt it, but — but — naturally you like to have your children more than get through life.

C. Yes, you'd like that in Sally, but you don't believe it's possible?

S. Yes, I do, if you can find the thing that will make her realize that she must put her attention on things.

C. Do you think *we* could do it?

S. Well, oh, I can't do it. I've tried for years, and the teachers down at the high school have tried, and you people were suggested to us, and we thought, well, you've studied the subject and you ought to be — if there is a point of contact there, you ought to find it. I have studied a little psychology and doo-dads of this and that the way people will, but I can't seem to get through to her, and the teachers at school can't.

C. And you probably feel that *you've* tried everything that you can?

S. Yes.

C. That it's up to us ——

S. Yeah, mm-hm. That I'd like to leave it in your hands, because — ah — and if you can't find anything that's bothering her or that's the underlying factor or something, why, then we'll just have to let her pull through as best she can.

C. And if we don't find anything that we can help, then ——

S. Then we'll make the best of what we've got.

C. Then we're back where we started.

S. Yes.

C. Here's Sally and nothing can be done for her ——

S. Well, I don't know, I wouldn't say — you like to exaggerate everything (*laugh*) put a dark cloud over it. No, I wouldn't make it quite as bad as you seem to feel.

Here is an excellent example of the persistence which the client may show in placing the solution of the problem upon the counselor. Toward the end of the excerpt, however, it is poorly handled by the counselor, who was not an experienced therapist. Instead of helping the mother to realize that she cannot leave it in the counselor's hands, no matter how much she would like to, and that the counselor cannot accept that responsibility no matter how willing he is to help, he allows the issue to become one of whether or not it is possible to find a cause of Sally's behavior. Consequently the therapeutic process goes temporarily astray. Had he used this opportunity to point out that the help he could give would be help to the mother in thinking through her relationship to Sally's problems and the ways she could handle this relationship more constructively, a profitable therapeutic issue would have been raised. The mother would have recognized that this treatment situation could only be used to gain help for herself in relation to Sally, just as she expected Sally to gain from the treatment relationship with another counselor. She could then have accepted therapy on this basis and could have moved ahead through consideration of her own rôle in the problem. (Or she might have rejected therapy on this basis, which is highly unlikely, but more constructive than continuing it on a false basis.)

It may be well to indicate by illustration the consequences of failing to set limits of responsibility to the counseling situation. A highly intelligent freshman, twenty-one years of age, came to his teacher's attention because of coming late to class, missing class, doing poor work in spite of his good ability. The teacher, who also endeavored to act as his counselor, reminded him several times of class obligations he had failed to meet, and finally gave him an appointment for an interview. Dick missed this appointment for a counseling contact, and when the counselor reminded him of his failure to appear, he asked if he might come in at once. The counselor granted his request, and he talked of his problems for three hours. He again missed class following this interview, and on the occasion of a casual contact, while returning some books, sat down again to talk. The counselor's record continues:

> After talking nonessentials for a little while, he launched forth into his problems of procrastination, absent-mindedness, and so on. When I asked what he was going to do about them, he announced that that was my job, that I must have done it for lots of people before him and that I would certainly enjoy seeing someone else come out of a mess such as he was in. When I demurred, he said that of course I didn't have to bother if I didn't want, but that he had hoped I had meant it when I said that I was there to help wherever help was needed.... When I told him flatly that I couldn't think for him, that he would have to do that for himself, he reminded me he had failed at self-reform

all these years, that he had hoped I would be interested, etc.... The debate ended in a draw.

It is obvious that this is very poor counseling. How did the counselor get into a situation where such a debate could arise? The answer lies primarily in a complete failure to define either in words or actions the limits of the counselor's responsibility. The counselor took responsibility for the student's class obligations, for his missing of an appointment, and agreed to help wherever help was needed. The boy accepted this, dominated the situation by setting the time for appointments and the length of the appointment, and capped the climax by demanding that the counselor solve all his problems. The counselor was put on the defensive, wished he had not gone so far, and entered into a debate as to how much responsibility he should accept, instead of helping the boy to realize his desire for complete dependence, a pattern already exhibited in his response to class situations. It is not surprising that in the following contact the boy even wanted the counselor to act as his secretary.

> He came in all excited. Did I know anyone who could take his beliefs down in shorthand and then write them up for him for tomorrow's paper? Could I take dictation? Well, then, would I listen to him while he explained his theories?

The student now feels he is in complete command of the situation. It is no longer in any sense therapeutic. It has merely become a new arena in which he may put into effect his customary patterns. If suitable limits had been set, it could have become a situation in which he would have endeavored to follow out his usual patterns and would have been helped to become conscious of them, but would not have succeeded in either his dependence or his domination.

Limitation of Time. One element in this case which deserves separate mention is the limitation of time. The limits of the counseling hour have been discussed by some writers as though they had some mystic significance. The end of the hour may be regarded as a separation which is symbolic of every separation and which has its relationship to the trauma of separation at birth. While these theories may have an element of truth, it is doubtful that we gain through such speculative reasoning. The time limits of the therapeutic situation, like any of the other limits, are of assistance in furnishing the counseling situation with all the aspects of the life situation. The time limit sets up an arbitrary human limit, to which the client must make adjustment. While it may be a microscopic issue compared to the issues in real life, yet it allows opportunity for all the feelings and patterns with which he responds to the larger issues. The client may feel resentful and may fight the limit and the therapist. He may feel hurt, regarding the limit as evidence of rejection by the therapist. He may attempt, as in the case just cited, to set aside any such limits and dominate the situation. He may get revenge by coming late for the next appointment or by missing it altogether. Though he may react to it in any of the ways which are natural to his personality makeup in real life, there is one important difference. In the therapeutic situation the therapist does not debate the point nor react to the client's behavior on an emotionally determined basis. The therapist endeavors merely to clarify for the individual the feelings behind his reactions. We shall see this more clearly in a later chapter.

Experience would indicate that therapy is most likely to go forward if the time limits are rather definitely understood and adhered to. They are not kept with brutal finality. Counseling is a human relationship, not a mechanical device. It might better be said that the limits are kept with a warm understanding of the client's need to break them.

A typical example of a child's reaction to the time limit of a therapy situation may be given from the case of Teddy, a seven-year-old boy who was being held in an observation home for study at the request of the Children's Court because of his unmanageableness and violently destructive temper tantrums. His mother had taken him to court because she could not control him. The excerpts below are from the second and third therapeutic contacts, though the psychologist had other casual

contacts with him in the detention home. He is playing a game
in which he demands that the psychologist count the number of
times he clicks the trigger of a toy gun. When he observes that
she is making notes, he wishes her to count all the time.

C. You want me to give all my attention to you, don't you?
S. Yes. (*Continues with his game.*)
C. I can't count all the time when I'm writing.
S. Why do it?
C. It makes you angry when I have to do it.
S. No, not me. (*Pause.*) What time is it?
C. Ten minutes after. You have ten minutes more. You
may leave any time if you want to leave before the half-hour is up.
S. (*Very decidedly.*) No. (*Starts to shoot at two soldiers which
he places on the floor.*) Is the time up?
C. No, you have ten more minutes.

While no positive interpretation can be given of such a brief
excerpt, the following does not seem unreasonable. Teddy
first makes a positive response, indicating his desire for the
therapist's affection. When he learns that her interest in him
does not allow him to control her, he becomes angry. He does
not dare to express this anger openly, even though given the
opportunity. It is at this point that he thinks about leaving,
which would be an indirect way of showing hostility. The
counselor does not urge him either to go or stay. The time is
his to use or not as he wishes. It is this manner of giving freedom within specified limits which proves so helpful. By the
handling of this small incident, Teddy comes to face more adequately the fact that the desire for affection and the resentment
toward the object of his affection, the desire to go and the
desire to leave, are all part of himself and must be handled
within himself. His shooting of the soldiers suggests some of
the annoyance he feels. He continues the hour in aggressive
fashion, asking once if the time is up. When the counselor
finally says that the time is up, Teddy says, "No, it isn't," but
he puts away the toys and leaves, saying in response to the
counselor's query that he would like to come back the following
day.

On the following day he spent the first ten minutes in rather aggressive play with the soldiers and a balloon, threatening to break the latter close to the counselor's head.

C. You like to scare me.

S. I can't bust that. (*He holds out the blown balloon.*) Tie this. Tie this for me.

C. (*Tying it.*) You like to tell me what to do.

S. (*Uses the balloon as a ball, bouncing it roughly against the wall all around the office.*) How many minutes are there left?

C. You have twenty minutes more, but you may go now if you want to. You may leave any time you want to. (*Teddy knocks a book off the desk while hitting the balloon.*) We have to be careful not to bother anything else in the room, don't we?

S. Where will we put the balloon when we get done?

C. I think we can find room for it in the bookcase so you can find it when you come again.

S. (*Coming to C. and holding up two fingers.*) I'll stay two hours today, can't I?

C. The rule is that you can stay half an hour each day.

S. Who makes that rule?

C. It is just the rule we made when you started to come. You were to come for one half-hour each day. You like to stay longer, though?

S. Yes. (*Plays with the balloon.*) How many more minutes?

C. Fifteen.

(*Throughout the remainder of the period Teddy inquires seven more times as to how many minutes remain. When there is only one more minute, he races the cars very fast, but when the time is up he puts the cars away and runs down the stairs.*)

To some it may appear that such discussion of time is futile or meaningless. Actually it helps to structure the situation so that the client can make use of it. The only criticism of the material above is that the counselor was somewhat fearful of taking responsibility for placing the limit. Her statement that "we made the rule" would have been much more helpful to Teddy if it had been "I made the rule" or "It's one of the rules we have here." Such a statement puts a definite, understood limitation upon the relationship, a limitation to which the child can respond. He does not like it, but he finds that he can accept it.

Limits of Aggressive Action. Another limitation of the relationship, which applies only in play therapy with younger clients, is the limitation upon damage to others or their property. Although the child is allowed the fullest freedom to act out his hostilities in a given framework — a certain room, with certain materials — this is not an indiscriminate freedom. Various illustrations might be given. "We can make all the noise we want here, but not out in the hall." "You may play with any of the things on that shelf, and do anything you wish with them, but we don't play with the books and things on this shelf." The simple statement, "I know you feel very angry with me this morning," is usually enough to prevent an attack on the therapist, since the need for attack is lessened when the feeling is recognized. Occasionally, however, it may be necessary to express the limit verbally. "You may feel as mad at me as you like, but you may not hit me." Beginning therapists have no confidence that the child, particularly the maladjusted problem child, will accept these limits. Again they underestimate the value of a clearly defined, well-structured situation. The only instances the author knows in which limits have been openly and completely defied (they are nearly always explored and tried out) are those where the therapeutic relationship has been very badly handled.

One type of problem which comes up in this matter of putting a limit to destructiveness is well illustrated by Jessie Taft's story of a little girl who persisted in hanging farther and farther out of the window to test out the situation to the utmost. Dr. Taft was rightly reluctant to put a limit to this activity, which did not directly affect the rights of others. When she made it plain that the responsibility rested with the child and that she might fall if she wanted to, the youngster became cautious.[6] As a matter of common sense, the office situation should be such that there are few opportunities for genuinely dangerous activities. Both the child and the therapist can deal more constructively with symbolic representations of aggression.

[6] Taft, Jessie. *The Dynamics of Therapy*, p. 60. New York: The Macmillan Company, 1933.

The Limitation of Affection.   One of the most important limitations of the therapeutic situation is the limitation upon the
degree of affection which the therapist shows.   While this issue
is most sharply defined in working with children, it occurs and
should be recognized in dealing with clients of every age.   It
may come to a focus in a request for gifts.   It is certainly
involved in the desire to be dependent upon the counselor,
which has already been illustrated.   It may come to an issue
in regard to the client's desire to continue the relationship,
socially, outside the counseling hour.   It may come to a head
in regard to other children who have appointments with the
clinician.   Let us illustrate with some examples.

A counselor working in a detention home is counseling Dorothy, an adolescent girl.   During an early interview the girl
expresses a wish for a valentine to send to her mother.   The
counselor buys one and gives it to her.   At the next interview
Dorothy tactfully expresses a wish for candy, which is also purchased for her.   A little later there is another request for candy,
which is again purchased.   In the next interview the demands
increase.   Dorothy wishes a special sort of candy and a certain
type of paper.   All this may seem harmless enough.   It is not
the method of handling which most advances therapy, however.
Of course Dorothy likes someone who gives her presents.   But
can she face the fact that this affection has limits?   Can she
learn to accept affection which is not proved every day by gifts?
Can she realize that denial of gifts does not necessarily mean
rejection?   Therapy, it cannot be stressed enough, is not
merely being "nice" to a person in trouble.   It is helping that
person to gain insight into himself, to adjust to human relationships, with their positive and negative aspects, in a healthy
fashion.

Compare the handling of this matter of gifts for Dorothy
with the following excerpt from Dr. Taft's handling of a similar
situation with Jackie, aged seven, a seriously rejected child,
to whom gifts, consequently, mean a great deal.   During the
fourth interview, Jack finds a magnet and asks that he be
allowed to take it home.   Dr. Taft refuses, telling him that

other children play with it here.   After playing for a while he
says:

    J. If I bring something down, can I take the magnet home?
    T. What do you mean, Jack?
    J. If I left one of my toys here, could I take this?
    T. What toy would you bring me?
    J. Well, I just can't think.   I'll have to go home and see.   I
don't see why I can't take this magnet home.   What can I take
home?
    T. Only what you draw or cut out.
    J. I don't like that.
    T. No, Jackie, I'm sure you don't.
    J. What else can I take?   Can I take the little bench?
    T. No, nothing else.   Just the drawings and the cutouts.   It's
the rule.   (*Jack looks very displeased.*)   That makes you mad,
doesn't it?
    J. Yes, it does.
    T. Well, maybe sometime you will forgive me.
    J. But why can't I take it?
    T. Because that's the way it is, Jack.   (*He begins to throw him-
self around the room rather roughly, slamming the toys, and finally
lifts the stool in the air as if he were about to throw it violently on the
floor.*)   You *do* feel like doing something bad, don't you, Jack?
(*He runs over and begins to throw the pillows.*)   I think you'd like
to shake me that way, Jack.   (*He will not assent to that.   He
throws himself around the room almost as if he were tempted to have
a temper tantrum, but does not quite let go.   He lifts the stool in the
air, but brings it down quite gently.*)[7]

It is almost always the rejected child who desires gifts, and
the therapist will do well to recognize that no amount of giving
can ever satisfy such a child.   The constructive possibility is
that he may learn that both affection and denial can be a part
of one relationship and that the relationship can be a satisfying
one, even with its limitations.   This is the type of learning
which has gone on in the above excerpt.   Gradually the child
learns to accept the therapeutic relationship not for what it is
not, but realistically for what it is.   If the above incident is genuinely understood, it will help to explain why Jack, following

   [7] Taft, Jessie. *The Dynamics of Therapy*, pp. 155–156.   Reprinted by permission of
The Macmillan Company.

therapy, was able to build up a satisfying relationship with a foster mother, which he would probably have been unable to do previous to therapy.

One more example may still further indicate the need of setting a clearly defined limit to the affectional aspects of the treatment situation. Charles, an eleven-year-old boy, was referred for clinical help because of a reading disability. The causative elements seemed to be primarily the fact that he had missed an important part of the first grade because of illness and that his more favored younger sister had succeeded in schoolwork where he had failed. The school's efforts at remedial reading had been a failure, but in individual contacts with the psychologist at the clinic, rapid progress was made. Gradually these contacts brought out deeper and deeper material — the loss of his grandfather, who had been very close to him, and then the loss of his favorite brother through marriage. As the contacts deepened, his relationship with the counselor became more obviously affectionate, and his interest in improving his reading declined. Then the psychologist gave a talk at Charles's school. Charles showed resentment when he heard of this, resentment which the psychologist tried to explain away rather than merely accepting as natural. Then, with mounting resentment, Charles said, "How come I tell you so much and you tell me so little?" Instead of accepting her rôle as a therapist and recognizing and clarifying this resentment, the psychologist replied that she was willing to tell him about herself. What did he wish to know about her? His reply was the completely genuine one of a child who would like to have limitless attention and affection. He said, "I want to know all about you." The psychologist gave considerable information about herself, and the more she gave, particularly such information as indicated that she had other close personal relationships, the more antagonistic the boy became. Following this interview, his situation outside the clinic became worse. He failed in school and showed a much poorer attitude. His mother (at his request?) finally terminated the clinic contacts.

Had the psychologist in this instance been willing to accept the boy's negative feeling as openly and as simply as she accepted his positive feeling, the ending of the case might have been very different. Limits were allowed to remain vague and uncertain, first allowing Charles to feel that he was the sole object of the therapist's affection, finally leaving the boy with the feeling that he had been betrayed. He felt that the therapist did not like him, because she had other ties, other contacts, which excluded him.

The Value of Limits to the Therapist

In the discussion up to this point, it has been stressed that limitations have a definite value to the client. Brief mention might also be made of the help they give to the therapist. In the first place, they allow the counselor to be more comfortable and to function more effectively. They provide a framework within which the counselor can be free and natural in dealing with the client. When the relationship is poorly defined, there is always the possibility that the counselee may make too heavy demands on the counselor. The result is that the counselor remains subtly defensive, on guard lest his desire to help should ensnare him. But if he clearly understands the limitations of his function, he can drop this defensiveness, can be more alert to the client's needs and feelings, and can play a stable rôle in relation to which the client can reorganize himself.

Is a Therapeutic Relationship Compatible with Authority?

A very practical question arises in connection with this discussion of the creation of a counseling atmosphere. As its various elements have been outlined, a number of readers will have raised the question as to how this type of relationship fits in with various present positions. Can the teacher carry on a counseling relationship with her pupils? Is it possible for the probation officer or court worker to build up a therapeutic relationship with the delinquents in his charge? What about the school counselor or dean, who is responsible for discipline as well as counseling? In the field of social work, what of the relief worker and the case worker in a protective agency? What of the personnel or industrial counselor in the business field? Is it possible for these professional workers, who have an interest in problems of individual maladjustment, to create and carry on a counseling relationship of the sort described?

The answer to these questions is not a simple one. As we analyze each of these situations, the problem proves to be primarily the compatibility of counseling and authority. Is it possible for the industrial personnel worker to be a satisfactory counselor if he is also responsible for hiring, firing, and job transfers? Is it possible for the college counselor to set up a satisfactory treatment relationship if he has the authority to say that a student shall be retained or sent home? Is it possible for the probation officer to be a counselor in the sense in which we have been using the word, if he is responsible for deciding whether the individual has broken probation and hence is to be sent to an institution?

Much thought and much research needs to be done in this field. It seems to the writer that the counselor cannot maintain a counseling relationship with the client and at the same time have authority over him. Therapy and authority cannot be coexistent in the same relationship. If this statement is amplified in terms of the description of the counseling situation which has been given in this chapter, the reasons for the incompatibility are plain. There cannot be an atmosphere of complete permissiveness when the relationship is authoritative. Is the student free to tell the college counselor that he cribbed on his last examination, if that same counselor is also responsible for discipline? If the student does talk over this behavior, the worker will have to make the difficult decision as to whether he is primarily a responsible authority or a counselor. Attempts to mix the two functions nearly always turn out badly for the student. If the relief worker builds up a permissive relationship, and the client tells how she hates the agency and how she has been systematically cheating the organization, what is the worker's rôle? If the delinquent accepts a counseling relationship with the probation officer and tells him of further delinquencies, the worker must at once decide whether he is therapist or officer. These questions are by no means academic, as countless bungled cases will testify. Nor are they solved by dropping the authoritative rôle. How many examinations may be cribbed before the counselor ceases to be and the college authority comes to the fore? How many delinquencies are necessary before the limit is reached, and the probation officer again becomes an officer? Mere leniency is not the answer.

There are three partial solutions to this problem, no one of them completely satisfactory, which merit consideration. The first might be termed the acceptance of authority as part of the framework of counseling. This viewpoint has perhaps been most completely worked out in the field of relief work. The case worker in this field may accept both the authoritative regulations, which she is required to apply, and also the client, with his need for protesting and resisting those rules. In effect she says to the client: "I accept you. I understand your needs. I understand your rebellion against the budget set by the law. But I also understand the need for a legal limit, and I accept and believe in the agency rules. Can we find a solution?" In taking this attitude, the case worker refrains from the authoritative attitude of "You must accept this budget." The client is free to express any resentment and hostility which he feels and to choose for himself how he will adjust to the reality of the situation.

In regard to the probation field, this viewpoint has also been expressed by Affleck.[8] She describes the relationship between the worker and the child in an agency which has certain pro. bationary authority delegated to it. "The worker does not use authority against him as must a court. She sees him really and yet accepts him as an individual. But she also accepts the

[8] Affleck, Doris Mode. "Therapeutic Utilization of Probationary Authority Vested in a Private Agency," *Journal of Social Work Process*, vol. 1, no. 1 (November, 1937), pp. 104–126.

society that has been harsh and possibly rejecting. She brings
these two sides together and gives an opportunity for the child
to get them into some kind of balance."[9] Where the worker
maintains this viewpoint, he does not deny the authority, does
not become merely lenient, but remains a helpful and non-
authoritative person himself. A further quotation from the
same source will show how this attitude is translated into action
in such matters as the keeping of appointments for probation
visits. The worker says in effect: "The court has asked us to
help you and expects you to come in every week. You may or
may not be able to do this; we cannot say about that. If you
break this arrangement, you do it on your own responsibility,
since we cannot release you from it. This is an opportunity for
you to use if you can. Since you are having trouble, there must
be some reason for it. Maybe you can do something about it
if you want to."[10] The child is thus left with both the freedom
to make his choice and the responsibility for abiding by the consequences of the choice which he does make. It allows the probation officer to exercise his probationary function and to make
plain to the child that both of them are under certain legal and
authoritative obligations. At the same time, it permits him
to remain a counselor, with all that is implied by that term.
Free expression of attitudes is possible, within a situation so
defined, and there is freedom from personal coercion.

A second partial solution to this problem of authority versus
counseling, which has been attempted by some counselors, is
for the worker to function in two different capacities at different
times. Perhaps this is best illustrated by the teacher who in
the classroom has certain authority, imposes certain duties, and
has obligations to the group welfare which often conflict with
attitudes she might wish to take toward an individual. She
may, however, be able to build up outside of the classroom a
genuine counseling situation in which her relationship to the
pupil is distinctly different from their classroom relationship.
If this is done, it becomes doubly necessary to define clearly the
limits of the relationship, lest the pupil expect that the char-

---

[9] *Ibid.*, p. 109.　　[10] *Ibid.*, pp. 108–09.

acteristics of the counseling hour — the complete interest of the
teacher, the freedom to express all attitudes, the absence of
pressure and authoritative control — will carry over into the
classroom.

There are no doubt a number of instances where such a dual
rôle can be played satisfactorily. This is particularly true
where the issues in the counseling situation are not the same
as the issues in the authoritative situation. Thus, the teacher
may carry on sound counseling of a pupil in regard to the
child's difficulties with his parents, and at the same time have a
normally authoritative relationship with him in the classroom
situation. If the pupil's primary problem, however, is his dislike for the curriculum, the teacher is likely to become defensive
and a poor counselor. Likewise, a college dean might carry on
effective counseling when the primary issue is one of vocational
choice. When the student's problems are those of infraction of
college rules, which the dean is partially responsible for formulating, the difficulty of satisfactorily playing two rôles becomes
very much increased.

A third type of solution, which in the long run may hold the
most promise, is to separate the counseling function from authoritative functions in our schools, colleges, social agencies,
courts, and industries. This solution has its disadvantages
and needs to be carefully planned if the insights gained in counseling are to be integrated and made effective, "plowed back,"
as it were, into our organized institutions. Yet perhaps this
solution is not as impossible as it seems. There is an increasing
tendency on the part of schools and colleges to recognize that
counseling should not be made a part of the disciplinary or
administrative set-up, but should be established as a separate
function. Guidance clinics have almost ceased to play a
double rôle in any case, though records of a dozen years ago
indicate that frequently at that time they saw no conflict between authority and treatment. Most surprising of all, industry has begun to realize that counseling is most effective if completely divorced from authority. One outstanding example
may be cited.

In the careful research done in personnel problems by the Western Electric Company, it became evident that one of the most important elements in industrial production and harmony was the easily disturbed web of personal and interpersonal relationships which underlies the more official and better-recognized web of administrative relationships. A personnel counseling program was established in order to facilitate the harmonious functioning of these basic interpersonal relationships. As thousands of these personnel interviews were conducted, a philosophy and technique of counseling were developed which are in accord with the counseling approach as defined in this book. As the work continued, the divorce of counseling from authority was made complete.

> The plan itself is fairly simple. It consists of assigning a trained interviewer to a particular group of employees, both supervisory and nonsupervisory. Experience has shown that the size of such a group can be somewhere in the neighborhood of three hundred. This interviewer is given the right to interview employees and supervisors on a confidential basis, but he is not given any authority whatsoever, and in line with the interviewing method, he is trained not to make recommendations for action nor to give advice. To avoid any semblance of authority, he is called a personnel counselor and is formally attached to our Industrial Relations Organization. Thus he is not officially responsible to the line of authority in the group to which he is assigned. Obviously such a relationship is something entirely new in modern industrial organization.[11]

If this sort of separation of function is sound and feasible in industry, there is good reason to suppose that it may be worked out in similar fashion in other institutional settings.

Summary

The counseling relationship is one in which warmth of acceptance and absence of any coercion or personal pressure on the

[11] From a talk given by H. A. Wright, Chief of Personnel Research and Training Division, Hawthorne Works, Western Electric Company, before the American Council of Guidance and Personnel Association, St. Louis, February 22, 1940. For a more extended discussion, see chapter 26 of *Management and the Worker*, by F. J. Roethlisberger and W. J. Dickson, Cambridge, Massachusetts: Harvard University Press, 1940.

part of the counselor permits the maximum expression of feelings, attitudes, and problems by the counselee. The relationship is a well-structured one, with limits of time, of dependence, and of aggressive action which apply particularly to the client, and limits of responsibility and of affection which the counselor imposes on himself. In this unique experience of complete emotional freedom within a well-defined framework, the client is free to recognize and understand his impulses and patterns, positive and negative, as in no other relationship.

This therapeutic relationship is distinct from, and incompatible with, most of the authoritative relationships of everyday life.

The Directive Versus the Non-Directive Approach

BEFORE proceeding to further discussion of the process of therapy, it may be well to consider a basic objection which many will raise to the preceding chapters and which will apply equally to the chapters that follow. This objection is essentially that in counseling and psychotherapy as it has been described, and in the counseling relationship as pictured in the last chapter, the counselor takes no responsibility for directing the outcome of the process. Many a reader will have felt that this is not counseling as he has known it. Others will raise the question of whether the counselor can solve the client's problem by the process outlined. These questions are indeed important and deserve investigation. Without attempting to give a final answer, some of the basic considerations need to be clarified.

THE DIRECTIVE APPROACH

Let it be said plainly that the concept of counseling set forth in this book is by no means the only possible concept. There are other definitions of the counseling process, and other ways of defining the counseling relationship. Probably the commonest definition of the process is that the counselor discovers, diagnoses, and treats the client's problems, provided that the counselee gives his active cooperation in the procedure. The counselor, according to this viewpoint, accepts a major responsibility in solving the problem, and this responsibility becomes the focus of his efforts. Perhaps an illustration of this directive approach will serve to make a comparison more realistic.

A student who is taking a college study-habits course comes to a college counselor for a first interview. The counselor greets her, and the following conversation takes place (phonographic recording):

    C. I was looking over your data sheet and information and all.

    S. Mm-hm.

    C. And I see you are from Y——.

    S. Mm-hm.

    C. Did you attend Roosevelt High?

    S. Yes I did, mm-hm.

    C. I noticed that you stated that you enrolled in Psychology 411 [study-habits course] because you didn't know how to study well enough — uh — and then I checked over the problem list, and I saw that you went rather heavy on — you worried about low grades and poor memory and so on. How well did you do in high school?

    S. Well, I was just an average student.

    C. And what major did you have there?

    S. Ah, you mean ——

    C. In high school, you took college preparatory or commercial?

    S. It was an academic course. I took languages and English and history.

    C. What course did you like the best?

This interview excerpt is cited because it is so typical of a viewpoint in counseling which is very familiar. From the outset the counselor tactfully takes the full direction of the contact. He lets the student know that he already has some information to guide him. He selects from the problems the student has listed those with which the counseling will be concerned. Most important of all, he assumes direct leadership of the interviewing process. The student's function is to answer the questions he raises, so that he can get the necessary information to make an accurate diagnosis. Toward the end of the first interview the counseling relationship is more definitely defined.

    C. It seems to me that your problem is that you want to learn more about yourself. We'll be getting all these tests back, and there are these projects, and the way we do, I see you each week at this time and you'll begin to get a little better picture — and then I'll help you check it and I'll tell you if it's right —— (*Laugh.*)

S. Mm-hm.

C. So that we can work it out. I would suggest — I would more or less work this project out because you say you are having difficulties concentrating. All right. Well, now, let's check and see what they are.

S. Mm-hm.

C. If this doesn't cause it, some other thing may cause it. All right, we'll get that picture. Now it looks as if on the reading test, there's a problem.

S. Mm-hm.

C. Now, when we get the picture of the problem, then it would be your decision to say, "Well, now, here's what I need to work on." It doesn't look half bad, but then you have to decide the question, "How hard am I going to work?" because you do the work. And so my suggestion would be, if history's what you're having trouble with, if you bring in your history book and your note book next time, then I can check that and we will go on with the diagnosis.

S. Mm-hm.

C. I'd work out these projects. Then I think you'll find that we'll be getting a more and more complete picture of where your problem is.

Several characteristics of this interview may be pointed out. The counselor defines the problem and this fact even creeps into his phrase, "It seems to me that your problem is ——" The counselor also indicates that he will be responsible for discovering the causes of the problem and for the definitive outline of the diagnostic picture — "I'll tell you if it's right." He suggests what is to be done now to further the process of diagnosis, and will of course later make suggestions toward correcting the difficulty. The focus of the counseling process is on the problem — its causes, its treatment. The only responsibility of the counselee is the decision as to how far she will cooperate. Otherwise the direction of the process is entirely in the hands of the counselor.

From the viewpoint expressed in this book, certain comments might be made in regard to this excerpt. In the first place, we do not know that the problems selected by the counselor are the situations on which the student actually wishes help. Unfortunately, once the counselor has defined the problems, the student is likely to accept his statement as the area with which counseling is concerned. More important, the whole process of having someone else diagnose, suggest, and treat may serve only to make the counselee more dependent, less able to solve new problems of adjustment.

It will be evident that this type of counseling differs in all but one characteristic from the definition of the counseling situation that has been given. There would be agreement on the need of rapport and responsiveness in the counseling situation. There is not, however, complete freedom to express all types of feelings and attitudes, because the direction which the counselor gives tends to inhibit expression in any but the prescribed areas. There is no defined limit to the counselor's responsibility nor to the degree of dependence which the client may show. Far from minimizing personal influence, this type of counseling is built largely on the persuasive powers of the counselor.

CHARACTERISTICS OF DIRECTIVE AND NON-DIRECTIVE VIEWPOINTS

The difference between this viewpoint in counseling and the one described in the previous chapter is by no means a theoretical one. In the study previously cited, Porter [1] has some suggestive data regarding counselors that hold directive and non-directive views. The number of interviews concerned in his various comparisons are small, but the consistency of the results is impressive. Porter asked a group of expert judges to classify all the counselor responses and conversations in nineteen phonographically recorded interviews into various categories which will be described later. In addition, he asked the judges to rate each interview according to its directiveness. The instructions to the judges ran: "The value of 11 on the scale represents an interview in which the direction has been furnished entirely by the counselor. The value of 1 represents an interview in which the counselor has refused directly or in-

[1] Porter, E. H. *The Development and Evaluation of a Measure of Counseling Interview Procedures* (unpublished thesis).

directly to take the responsibility for directing and consequently has forced the client to accept the responsibility for directing the interview. You are not to judge whether the counselor did a good job of directing or of not directing. Rate the interview only on the relative degree of directiveness or non-directiveness."

When this rating had been completed and the more directive interviews were compared with the less directive, certain differences in pattern were strikingly suggested. By taking Porter's data and regrouping certain of his facts, these differences may be shown in modified tabular form. Of Porter's nineteen interviews, nine were rated rather low in directiveness, with ratings of from 1.5 to 5.6 on an 11-point scale, with an average directiveness score of 3.3. The remaining ten were quite definitely directive, with ratings of 9.3 to 10.8, an average of 10.2.[2] Five counselors were represented in the group which was low in directiveness, and six counselors were represented in the high-directiveness group, so that the results were not particularly influenced by the specific practices of any one counselor. In each group there were interviews conducted by both experienced and inexperienced counselors, and interviews from the first, middle, and closing phases of a series, the two groups being roughly equivalent in these respects. If we now examine the data to see whether certain types of counselor response or conversation are characteristic of either group, we find sharp differences. There are eleven categories of response which are much more heavily used by the directive group. There are three categories much more heavily used by the non-directive group, and four categories which are used about equally by both groups.

This material is shown below (Tables 2–4). It should be kept in mind that the whole study was confined to the counselor's part in the interview. There is no classification of client responses. In the tables there appear the descriptive categories as defined by Porter and used by the judges. One of the

[2] It is probable that this clear dichotomy is atypical of counseling as a whole, though further studies would be necessary to discover how directiveness would distribute itself on a continuum.

brief illustrative examples which was used by the judges is given with each item in order to put more concrete meaning into the definition. The number of each type of counselor remarks per interview for the directive and the non-directive groups is shown in the right-hand columns.

TABLE 2. COUNSELOR TECHNIQUES CHARACTERISTIC OF
THE DIRECTIVE GROUP

| | Average No. per Interview | |
Item	Directive Group	Non-directive Group
1a.* Counselor defines the interview situation in terms of diagnostic or remedial procedures.	1.7	.5
Example. "I don't know what your trouble is, but we can get at it in part through the tests you take and in part through what we do here in the interview."		
2b. Counselor indicates topic but leaves development to client.	13.3	6.3
Ex. "Would you care to tell me a little more about that?"		
2c. Counselor indicates topic and delimits development to confirmation, negation, or the supplying of specific items of information.	34.1	4.6
Ex. "How long ago was it that you took it?" "Here or at home?" "What course was that in?"		
3d. Counselor identifies a problem, source of difficulty, condition needing correction, etc., through test interpretations, evaluative remarks, etc.	3.7	.3
Ex. "One of your difficulties is that you haven't had a chance to compare yourself with others."		
3e. Interprets test results, but not as indicating a problem, source of difficulty, etc.	1.2	.1
Ex. "This indicates that 32 per cent of college freshmen read the test material more rapidly than you did."		
3f. Expresses approval, disapproval, shock, or other personal reaction in regard to the client.	2.6	.6
Ex. "Good! Grand! That's a nice start."		
4. Counselor explains, discusses, or gives information related to the problem or treatment.	20.3	3.9
Ex. "Well, I don't think that's the only reason. Some people who know a great deal about it get just as nervous as the ones who don't."		

* The number preceding each item is that used by Porter and shows the order in which they occurred in his sheet for rating interviews. In general, category 1 refers to those techniques related to defining the interview situation; category 2 to those techniques which bring out and develop the problem situation; category 3 to techniques for developing the client's insight and understanding; 4 to techniques of giving information or explanation; 5 to those techniques which sponsor client activity or foster the making of decisions.

| | Average No. per Interview | |
Item	Directive Group	Non-directive Group
5a, b. Counselor proposes client activity, directly, or through questioning technique, or in response to question of what to do. Ex. "I think that you ought to quit that job and put as much time in on your schoolwork as possible."	10.0	1.3
5c. Counselor influences the making of a decision by marshaling and evaluating evidence, expressing personal opinion, persuading pro or con. Ex. "Well it's up to you, but I'd at least give it a try."	5.2	.3
5f. Counselor reassures the client. Ex. "Now you may run across a lot of difficulty, but don't let it discourage you. You'll come out all right."	.9	.2

TABLE 3. COUNSELOR TECHNIQUES CHARACTERISTIC OF THE
NON-DIRECTIVE GROUP

| | Average No. per Interview | |
Item	Directive Group	Non-directive Group
1b. Defines the interview situation in terms of client responsibility for directing the interview, reaching decisions, etc. Ex. "And sometimes people find that by talking over their problems with someone else they get a much better picture."	.5	1.9
3b. Counselor responds in such a way as to indicate recognition of expression of feeling or attitude in immediately preceding verbal response. Ex. "And that makes you feel pretty low."	1.2	10.3
3c. Counselor responds in such a way as to interpret or recognize feeling or attitude expressed in some way other than in the immediately preceding response. Ex. "Maybe you didn't want to come this morning."	.7	9.3

TABLE 4. TECHNIQUES COMMON TO BOTH GROUPS

| | Average No. per Interview | |
Item	Directive Group	Non-directive Group
2a. Counselor uses lead which forces the choosing and developing of topic upon client. Ex. "What's on your mind this morning?"	.6	.6

3a. Counselor responds in such a way as to indicate recognition of subject content.
    Ex. "And that test comes up Tuesday."
    "Humph! So neither method worked."
	6.1	6.0

5d. Counselor indicates decision is up to client. Ex. "That's up to you."	.4	.6
5e. Counselor indicates acceptance or approval of decision. Ex. "I think you're on the right track there."	.8	.6

Some Significant Contrasts

Examination of these three tables will bring to light several significant differences between the two therapeutic approaches. In the first place, the more directive counselors are more active in the counseling situation — they do much more of the talking. There are on the average one hundred and seven classifiable items of counselor response per interview in the directive interviews, and only forty-nine in the non-directive interviews. Conversely, of course, the client does much less talking. In an analysis of word count in these interviews, Porter found that the ratio of counselor words to counselee words ranged from .15 to 4.02. In other words, at one extreme the client talked nearly seven times as much as the counselor. At the other extreme the counselor talked four times as much as the client — a statistical example of what it means to try to "get a word in edgeways." If we compare these two extreme counselors, the second talked more than twenty-five times as much as the first.

There was a striking relationship between the ratio of words spoken by counselor and counselee and the degree of directiveness. In the ten directive interviews, the average ratio was 2.77, the counselor talking nearly three times as much as the client. In the nine non-directive interviews the average ratio was .47, the counselor talking less than half as much as the client. It will be noted from these two ratios that the directive counselors used on the average almost six times as many words as the non-directive — one of the sharpest differences found in the whole study. This makes graphic the fact that in non-directive counseling the client comes "to talk out his problems." In a directive contact the counselor talks to the client.

We find in these tables that differences in method center around such techniques as persuading the client, pointing out problems needing correction, interpreting test results, and asking specific questions, all of which are much more characteristic of the directive approach than the non-directive; or around such a technique as recognizing and interpreting the client's verbally expressed feelings or his feelings as expressed in actions, a technique characteristic of the non-directive group. Here again we note the fundamental contrast in emphasis, the directive group stressing those techniques which control the interview and move the client toward a counselor-chosen goal, the non-directive group stressing those means which cause the client to be more conscious of his own attitudes and feelings, with a consequent increase in insight and self-understanding.

Since the comparison in Tables 2, 3, and 4 is somewhat clouded by the fact that the directive counselors are so much more active in the interview, another comparison of the same material will be made by listing in parallel columns in Table 5 the counseling techniques most frequently employed by each group, listed in order of frequency. Only the seven techniques most frequently used are listed for each group, as the others are used very little. In this table the techniques are rephrased from the more formal definitions used in the previous tables. The number in parentheses following each item indicates its average frequency per interview.

TABLE 5. TECHNIQUES MOST FREQUENTLY EMPLOYED

(in order of frequency)

Directive Counselor Group	Non-directive Counselor Group
1. Asks highly specific questions, delimiting answers to yes, no, or specific information. (34.1)	1. Recognizes in some way the feeling or attitude which the client has just expressed. (10.3)
2. Explains, discusses, or gives information related to the problem or treatment. (20.3)	2. Interprets or recognizes feelings or attitudes expressed by general demeanor, specific behavior, or earlier statements. (9.3)
3. Indicates topic of conversation but leaves development to client. (13.3)	3. Indicates topic of conversation but leaves development to client. (6.3)
4. Proposes client activity. (9.4)	4. Recognizes the subject content of what the client has just said. (6.0)
5. Recognizes the subject content of what the client has just said. (6.1)	5. Asks highly specific questions, delimiting answer to yes, no, or specific information. (4.6)
6. Marshals the evidence and persuades the client to undertake the proposed action. (5.3)	6. Explains, discusses, or gives information related to the problem or treatment. (3.9)
7. Points out a problem or condition needing correction. (3.7)	7. Defines the interview situation in terms of the client's responsibility for using it. (1.9)

From Table 5 we might draw certain tentative conclusions based, it must be remembered, on study of a very small number of interviews, whose value, however, is enhanced by the fact that they are completely recorded through electrical recording devices. It might be said that counseling of the directive sort is characterized by many highly specific questions to which specific answers are expected, and by information and explanation given by the counselor. These two techniques account for more than half of the counselor's part in this type of treatment interviewing. The counselor further gives the client opportunity to express his attitudes on specified topics, and points out to the client problems and conditions which he, the counselor, has observed to be in need of correction. He clarifies or restates or recognizes the subject content of what the client has told him. He endeavors to bring about change by proposing the action the client should take, and by bringing to bear both evidence and personal influence to insure that such action will be taken.

On the other hand, counseling of the non-directive sort is characterized by a preponderance of client activity, the client doing most of the talking about his problems. The counselor's primary techniques are those which help the client more clearly to recognize and understand his feelings, attitudes, and reaction patterns, and which encourage the client to talk about them. One half of the counselor items fall into these categories. The counselor may further achieve this aim by restating or clarifying the subject content of the client's conversation. Not infrequently he gives the client opportunity to express his feelings on specified topics. Less frequently he asks specific questions of an information-getting sort. Occasionally he gives information or explanations related to the client's situation. Although not the type of technique which could be used frequently, there is considerable redefinition of the interviewing situation as being primarily the client's situation, to use for his own growth.

A Program of Non-Directive Counseling. It is of interest to compare the formulations just given with the rules which have been set up to guide the counselors in the Western Electric Company in the conduct of their interviews. These rules are as follows: [3]

1. The interviewer should listen to the speaker in a patient and friendly, but intelligently critical manner.
2. The interviewer should not display any kind of authority.
3. The interviewer should not give advice or moral admonition.
4. The interviewer should not argue with the speaker.
5. The interviewer should talk or ask questions only under certain conditions.
    a. To help the person talk.
    b. To relieve any fears or anxieties on the part of the speaker which may be affecting his relation to the interviewer.
    c. To praise the interviewee for reporting his thoughts and feelings accurately.
    d. To veer the discussion to some topic which has been omitted or neglected.
    e. To discuss implicit assumptions, if this is advisable.

It will be very evident that these rules, with their stress on the absence of advice, persuasion, and argument and with their clear emphasis on the fact that the interview is the client's, providing him with an opportunity to talk freely, are in harmony with the non-directive approach, as factually delineated, and quite opposed to most of the characteristic techniques of the directive approach.

Some Practical Implications. It may seem to some that the writer has gone to unnecessary lengths to indicate that there is a real and fundamental difference in the directiveness of different counselors and therapists. The reason for endeavoring to make these differences as plain as possible is that there is a definite tendency for all counselors to consider themselves as being non-coercive and non-directive. Most of the counselors who received high directiveness ratings did not believe that they took the lead in the interviewing, selected the goal, suggested what the client should do, and persuaded him to do it. Consequently, there is a tendency to assume that all counseling is basically alike and that differences in techniques are minor.

Porter's study is significant in illustrating that this is certainly not the case, and that progress in our understanding of psychotherapy will be advanced by recognizing the sharp contrasts which exist in therapeutic viewpoints, rather than by assuming a harmony of ideas for which there is no basis in fact.

If the reader wishes to test out some of the facts which have been given above, he may apply a crude device to any interview which is recorded verbatim. If he reads alternate items only, one of the following will be found to be true: (1) He may find that reading the counselor conversations alone is enough to give the gist, the general trend, of the interview. If this is the case, the interview is definitely directive. (2) He may find that reading the client items only will give a reasonably adequate picture of the interview as a whole. If so, the counseling is definitely non-directive. (3) He may find that reading alternate items gives nothing but confusion, and that either counselor or counselee items by themselves give little picture of the gist of the interview. If this is true, the interview would represent some midpoint between directiveness and non-directiveness.

Underlying Purposes

Back of these differences between the directive and non-directive approaches lie deeper differences in the philosophy of counseling and the values which are assumed to be important. In the field of applied science value judgments have a part, and often an important part, in determining the choice of techniques. Hence we shall do well to understand the implicit purposes of both directive and non-directive counseling.

The first basic difference in purpose centers around the question of who is to choose the client's goals. The directive group assumes that the counselor selects the desirable and the socially approved goal which the client is to attain, and then directs his efforts toward helping the subject to attain it. An unstated implication is that the counselor is superior to the client, since the latter is assumed to be incapable of accepting full responsibility for choosing his own goal. Non-directive counseling is based on the assumption that the client has the right to select his own life goals, even though these may be at variance with the goals that the counselor might choose for him. There is also the belief that if the individual has a modicum of insight into himself and his problems, he will be likely to make this choice wisely. This viewpoint is unusually well phrased by Robert Waelder, who, because of his background, clothes his ideas in Freudian terminology. "The basic idea of Freud's psychoanalysis . . . is impartiality toward the patient's inner conflicts. . . . Without taking any part in these never-ceasing struggles, psychoanalysis aims exclusively at letting light and air into the battlefield by making conscious the unconscious elements of the conflicts. The idea is that if the mature ego of an adult has full access to all the forces involved, it should be capable of finding an adequate and tolerable, at least nonpathological, solution to these conflicts, and capable of finding a workable proportion between satisfying desires and keeping them under effective control." [4]

The non-directive viewpoint places a high value on the right of every individual to be psychologically independent and to maintain his psychological integrity. The directive viewpoint places a high value upon social conformity and the right of the more able to direct the less able. These viewpoints have a significant relationship to social and political philosophy as well as to techniques of therapy.

As a consequence of this difference in value judgments, we find that the directive group tends to focus its efforts upon the problem which the client presents. If the problem is solved in a manner which can be approved by the counselor, if the symp-

[4] Waelder, Robert, in "Areas of Agreement in Psychotherapy," *American Journal of Orthopsychiatry*, vol. 10, no. 4 (October, 1940), p. 705. It is of interest that this statement of Dr. Waelder's was made in order to emphasize a viewpoint which he felt was distinctive of Freudian psychoanalysis. The representatives of other viewpoints in the symposium made it plain, however, that this was one of the basic principles of all effective psychotherapies, and Dr. Goodwin Watson, the chairman, in summing up the discussion observed that "we seem to have reached the conclusion that psychoanalysis did give much of the initial impetus toward a relationship in which the therapist tries not to let his own values influence the patient, and that the past twenty years have seen all other psychotherapies move toward much the same ideal." *Ibid.*, p. 708.

toms are removed, the counseling is considered successful. The non-directive group places its emphasis upon the client himself, not upon the problem. If the client achieves through the counseling experience sufficient insight to understand his relation to the reality situation, he can choose the method of adapting to reality which has the highest value for him. He will also be much more capable of coping with future problems that arise, because of his increased insight and his increased experience in independent solution of his problems.

It will be evident that the approach of the non-directive group applies to the overwhelming majority of clients who have the capacity to achieve reasonably adequate solutions for their problems. Counseling, from this viewpoint, cannot be the only method for dealing with that small group — the psychotic, the defective, and perhaps some others — who have not the capacity to solve their own difficulties, even with help. Neither does it apply to children or adults who are faced with impossible demands from their environments. For the great bulk of maladjusted individuals, however — children, young people, or adults — some reasonable adjustment between the individual and his social environment is possible. For this group a therapeutic approach which encourages growth and responsible maturity has much to offer.

PART III

The Process of Counseling

Releasing Expression

IMPORTANT as are the aspects of counseling which have been discussed, they are nevertheless in the nature of preliminaries to the counseling process itself. We come now to a consideration of what many would regard as one of the central features of any type of therapy — the release of feeling. Certainly one of the significant goals of any counseling experience is to bring into the open those thoughts and attitudes, those feelings and emotionally charged impulses, which center around the problems and conflicts of the individual. This aim is complicated by the fact that the superficial attitudes, and those easily expressed, are not always the significant and motivating attitudes. Consequently the counselor must be skilled indeed in providing release for the client in order to bring about an adequate expression of the basic issues in his situation. The counseling relationship itself, as has been pointed out, aids in this process. In this chapter we shall concern ourselves with the ways in which the counselor may handle the interview situation in order to assist the client to express those attitudes which he can helpfully reveal.

ENCOURAGING RELEASE

The Client the Best Guide. The surest route to the issues which have importance, to the conflicts which are painful, to the areas with which counseling may constructively deal, is to follow the pattern of the client's feeling as it is freely expressed. As a person talks about himself and his problems, particularly in the counseling relationship, where there is no necessity of defending himself, the real issues become more and more evi-

dent to the observant listener.   It is to some extent true that
the same issues may be uncovered by patient questioning in
all of the areas in which the client may be experiencing concern.
As we shall see, however, this is likely to be a costly process in
terms of time, and the difficulties which are uncovered may
turn out to be difficulties of the counselor rather than of the
client.   Consequently, the best techniques for interviewing are
those which encourage the client to express himself as freely as
possible, with the counselor consciously endeavoring to refrain
from any activity or any response which would guide the direction of the interview or the content brought forth.

The reasons for this approach are not far to seek.   Few problems are solely intellectual in nature, and when they are intellectual only, counseling is not called for.   If the student's only
problem is that he cannot comprehend a binomial equation or
does not understand how to score a psychological test or is puzzled as to the difference between a cretin and a mongoloid, additional information of an intellectual sort is obviously called for.
Such problems are solved in the realm of the intellect.   But
problems of adjustment are rarely of this type.   The intellectual factors in adjustment difficulties are often childishly
simple.   It is the unrecognized emotional factors which are
usually basic.   These emotional factors are most quickly understood by the client and the counselor if the counseling recognizes and follows the pattern of the client's feeling.   Thus, a
perplexed student tells of his difficulty in choosing between two
vocations.   He describes them in terms which give to each occupation scrupulously equal advantages, so far as his own future
is concerned.   They seem to be mathematically equivalent in
value to him, and hence his dilemma appears insoluble.   It is
only as he talks further, revealing that his choice of college was
nicely balanced between two institutions and solved only by
the intervention of a friend, and that he frequently cannot
choose which movie to attend, but follows the lead of a companion, that the true configuration of his problem begins to
appear in terms of its emotional elements.   The fact that indecision has a value to him comes gradually to light.   The client

is the only one who can guide us to such facts, and we may rest assured that the patterns which are sufficiently important to cause difficulties in life adjustment will crop up again and again in conversation about himself, provided that conversation is free from restriction and inhibition.   One of the most widely accepted tenets of psychoanalytic therapy is that "all roads lead to Rome," that any path of expression, freely followed, leads to revelation of a basic conflict.   The interviewing approach suggested here is merely a more direct and less mystical use of this fact.

Response to Feeling versus Response to Content.   Probably the most difficult skill to acquire in counseling is the art of being alert to and responding to the feeling which is being expressed, rather than giving sole attention to the intellectual content. In our culture, most adults are schooled to pay close attention to ideas and none to feeling.   Only children or poets show a deeper understanding, or playwrights, who recognize in such works as *Strange Interlude* that emotional attitudes are concomitants of all our utterances.   To recognize and help in bringing to expression these concomitant attitudes is an effective aid to counseling.   Some examples will assist in clarifying this point.

In the following excerpt the counselor responds to the content rather than the feeling.   A student, in his first contact with the counselor, states his problem as follows (phonographic recording):

> *S.* I've always realized that my methods of study, my study habits, are wrong.   I don't feel as though I am a very brilliant person, but I don't think I am as stupid as my grades indicate.

The reader will do well to ask himself what this student is feeling when he makes this statement.   It is plain that he is feeling disappointed at the discrepancy between his ability and his grades and concerned lest his grades be taken to represent the true measure of his ability.   To make some response to this feeling would have been a move toward deeper revelation of the problem, but the counselor responds:

> *C.* Well, how bad are your grades?   I thought they were pretty good.

S. My cumulative average is about 2.3 or 2.4. I had a 3.1 last quarter.

C. Um-hm.

S. Now, I realize I have to work very hard to support myself most of the time I go to school, but other people are doing it and other people are getting grades. I want to know why I can't.

C. Um-hm.

S. I'm not through with school yet. This is my fourth year in school.

The counselor, by responding to one of the intellectual elements in the conversation, diverts progress temporarily, but the student returns to his problem, his feeling of puzzlement and disappointment becomes more plain, and a hint of his determination ("I'm not through with school yet") becomes evident. Response to these elements would bring further light, but the counselor again pays attention to one of the content elements, the question of whether his outside work is affecting his grades.

C. Well, of course, you have to take a restricted schedule because of your work?

S. No, I have never taken one; I've never had any restricted schedule.

C. Oh, you haven't.

S. You see, I hope to get into medical school, and it doesn't look like I will now, because of my grades. I am majoring in music at the present time and still fulfilling my medical requirements, and hope to get into medical school.

C. Um-hm. Well, supposing you don't. What does that mean?

S. It means that I'll probably have to teach music.

C. Is it as bad as that?

S. Oh, it isn't as bad as that, but I've had my mind set on medicine for a long time, and I don't think there is anything I'd like to do as much as that. Not that I'm going to save the world or anything like that, or cure the world. I just want to do it.

C. Um-hm. Well, certainly nothing wrong with that ambition; I don't mean to defy that. I just wondered what it means to you, if, as you suggest, you aren't going to be able to go on, what the alternative is, and how that looks to you.

With the exception of the question, "Is it as bad as that?" the counselor's comments in each case lead away from the feeling aspect of the client's situation into one or another of its intellectual aspects. For a time the client resists this and continues to bring up his real feelings, but following the conclusion of this excerpt, he succumbs to the counselor's lead, and some time is spent discussing, on an intellectual plane, the relative merits of music and medicine. A genuine opportunity for expression of the client's motivating attitudes and of the deeper issues in his problem has been lost.

Here is a comparable instance in which another student is concerned about a problem, but in which there is more adequate response to the feeling expressed. In a second interview, Paul is speaking of the fact that his college work is going more badly than at the time of the first interview (phonographic recording, with items numbered for the sake of easy reference):

1. *S.* I haven't written to my parents about this at all. In the past they haven't been of any help to me in this respect, and if I can keep it away from them as much as possible, I'll do so. But there's a slight matter of grades to explain, and they're not good, and I don't know how I'm going to explain without telling them about this. [Meaning his upset emotional condition which, he has said, accounts for his problems.] Would you advise me to tell them about it?

2. *C.* Suppose you tell me a little more what you had thought about it.

3. *S.* Well I think I'm compelled to, because ——

4. *C.* It's a situation you've really got to face.

5. *S.* Yes, there's no use getting around it, even if they can't take it the way they should, because I've already flunked my gym course. I just haven't come. I've just been negligent about it. Now, they'll know that you can't flunk in gym without being negligent about it. They'll ask why.

6. *C.* It will be fairly hard for you to tell them.

7. *S.* Yes. Oh, I don't know if they're going to sort of condemn me. I think so, because that's what they've done in the past. They've said, "It's your fault. You don't have enough will power, you're not interested." That's the experience I've had in the past. I've been sort of telling them that I improved in this respect. I was — I was all right the first quarter. Well, I wasn't entirely all right, but I just got worse. (*Pause.*)

8. *C.* You feel that they'll be unsympathetic and they'll condemn you for your failures.

9. *S.* Well, my — I'm pretty sure my father will. My mother might not. He hasn't been — he doesn't experience these things; he just doesn't know what it's like. "Lack of ambition" is what he'd say. (*Pause.*)

10. *C.* You feel that he could never understand you?

11. *S.* No, I don't think he is — is capable of that, because I don't get along with him, don't at all!

12. *C.* You dislike him a good deal?

13. *S.* Yes, I — I did feel bitter toward him for a while and I've gone out of that stage, and now I don't feel bitter against him but I — I'm sort of ashamed. I think that that's it more than anything else, an experience of shame that he is my father. (*Pause.*)

14. *C.* You feel he isn't much good.

15. *S.* Well, he's putting me through school but [few words unintelligible] I'm sorry to say that, but that's my opinion about it. I think he had a lot to do in forming it, too.

16. *C.* This has been something on which you have felt pretty deeply, for a long while.

17. *S.* I have. (*Long pause.*)

18. *C.* Have you worried a lot about this matter of writing home?

19. *S.* About this? Well, yes, because it's going to be a pretty difficult proposition to put it across. I haven't got any idea of what action they're going to take.

20. *C.* You sound as though you feel a little bit like a prisoner before the bar.

21. *S.* (*Laugh.*) That's just about it. I — I don't know, I feel sort of strangled; that's how I feel.

22. *C.* Strangled?

23. *S.* By the world. I feel licked.

24. *C.* It's kind of tough to feel that you can't fight back. (*Long pause.*) You feel more licked now than you did awhile ago?

25. *S.* I do. I didn't feel this way last quarter, I just was hopeful, but, uh, when I went home Christmas time, my father and mother had a very serious quarrel, in my presence, and I really — I wasn't shocked, because I knew they were capable of having such a quarrel, but — it might have had an effect. My sister just left the day before, and she was spared it, and I saw it all.

A careful comparison of the counselor techniques in this inter-view with those in the preceding excerpt will show some sharp contrasts. Note that the counselor in responding to Paul either gives a neutral response which does not direct the interview (see item number 2) or responds directly to what Paul is obviously feeling (see numbers 4, 6, 8, 10, 12, 14, 16, 20, 22, 24). In most of these instances the counselor simply restates the attitude which Paul has been expressing, thus clarifying the feeling and helping the boy to realize that he is understood. Only once is there any evidence that the counselor changes the train of Paul's thought and feeling. (See number 18, to which Paul replies, "About this?" showing that he has been thinking about something else.) It is also obvious that by responding to the feeling which is being expressed, the counselor helps Paul to talk through the superficial problem of mustering courage to break the news to his parents and gradually reveal the much more basic antagonism and conflict in regard to his whole relationship to his parents. He goes on in the interview to give the details of the upsetting quarrel between his parents and to discuss his feeling that all his bad qualities are inherited. This lays the groundwork for a much more fundamental facing of his problems in subsequent interviews.

Another way of studying this fragment is to think of the multitude of ways in which the counselor might have responded to the content of Paul's words. It is then easy to see why counselors who respond to the intellectual aspects of the client's conversation find it very difficult to see any elements of orderly progress in an interview. After Paul's first statement, the counselor might have raised such questions as "How low are your grades?" or, "Why have you kept things from your parents?" In response to his second major statement (number 5) the counselor might have asked, "Why did you cut your gym classes?" or, "In what way were you negligent?" or even, "When did you learn that you flunked?" Following Paul's next statement (number 7) the counselor might have responded to any of several intellectual aspects, depending on his own emotional patterns. He might have asked about past experiences in which the parents had condemned the boy, or what Paul thinks of his will power, or he might have raised questions about what Paul meant by getting worse. This by no means exhausts the possibilities of counselor response to these three statements. It indicates clearly that when we respond to the intellectual content, the process is unpredictable and more dependent upon the counselor patterns than upon the client patterns.

The result is quite different when the same material is examined in terms of responding to the client's feeling. If this is the purpose, we find that the counselor's responses, though they might be differently worded by different counselors, would lead to approximately the same results in self-revelation on the part of the client. For example, in response to Paul's first statement, the counselor might more accurately have responded to his feeling by saying, "You feel that you need some help in facing your parents on this problem." Certainly this would have led to the same type of expression that actually took place. In response to Paul's later statement (number 7), the counselor might have recognized his feeling in several ways, such as, "You've kept this from them because they have been so critical in the past," or, "You've been through all this before and know what to expect," or, "You don't know whether they will blame you, but you think so." Any of these responses would be in line with the boy's feeling as he has expressed it. Any one of these counselor responses would have encouraged Paul to bring forth the feelings and attitudes which he did express.

In other words, when the counselor is alertly responsive to the client's expressed attitudes and recognizes and clarifies these feelings, the interview is client-centered, and the material which comes forth is the material which is emotionally relevant to the client's problem. On the other hand, when the counselor responds to the intellectual content, the direction of the interview follows the pattern of the counselor's interest, and only very slowly and with much winnowing and sifting do the essential problems of the client become evident. At its worst, this process leads to a blocking of the client's expression of his own problems and follows only the pattern set by the counselor.

It may well be that this skill in recognizing the client's feelings is partly intuitive, but it is also clear from examination of recorded interviews before and after counseling instruction that it is a skill which can be developed and trained.   Since it is so important an aspect in effective counseling, an additional example will be discussed.

In a second interview, Ted, a sophomore student, after responding to many direct questions on the part of the counselor, begins to express himself quite freely as to the dissatisfaction he feels in his fraternity relationship.   He knows he is regarded as too "cocky," and feels that he is not generally liked by the other fellows.   He continues (phonographic recording):

1. *S.* There's nothing I feel I can do about it, except I'm disliked by a couple of the fellows who are more active than I am and who are liked by the majority of the other fellows — they are maybe not liked, but they are not disliked.   And, therefore, I'm kind of disgusted with the whole fraternity and I just don't give a damn what happens to them, and if I can get my meal down there, my evening meal, just as cheap as anywhere else and get a better meal, I'll go down there!   And I'll go to their dances and — not for the love of the dear old fraternity (*very scornfully*), but merely for my own enjoyment!   However, it is damned depressing sometimes (*laugh*) if you don't have the right attitude.   Some days you wished you lived there and were — really had that intimate association with the fellows that are there, but ——— You see, my brother was in college last year — he graduated — and he belonged to the fraternity.   He wasn't exceptionally active.   He studied hard, he didn't run around any, he studied week-ends — he'd bring his beer in (*laugh*) and keep right on studying, and they just ——— He was never very active, and I more or less followed in his footsteps, all except studying ———

2. *C.* Did he get you in?   Did he get you pledged?

3. *S.* Well, I suppose, yes.

4. *C.* Are you an active?

5. *S.* I'm a pledge, not initiated.

6. *C.* Do you feel you want to join it?

7. *S.* Oh, I'll join it if I get the grades.

8. *C.* What do you have to have?

9. *S.* A two-point average — cumulative, I guess.   (*Pause.*)

10. *C.* Ah — what do you think are the main reasons you are not liked there?

11. *S.* Well — ah — to some fellows you make remarks. All right, that never goes, and I've had that art blessed on me, I guess, because I do it unintentionally; and with another fellow you use the opposite, and he will say you are cocky. There is one fellow down there that is a prune as far as I'm concerned, and he is the one that doesn't like me, and yet he is very active in our chapter. And he is more or less the serious type or the not-joking type, and somehow I have insulted him or acted cocky in front of him. Anyhow, I have picked up, on the sly, that in the discussion of myself at the meetings — I went to hell week — it was brought against me that I was too cocky.

12. *C.* Is he an active?

13. *S.* Yeah.

14. *C.* Well, what do they do? If they think the pledges are cocky, don't they take it out of them?

15. *S.* Well, they never did anything to me.

16. *C.* Is he the only one that thinks you are cocky?

17. *S.* Well, I couldn't say.

18. *C.* But you don't feel very much at ease when you go around there.

19. *S.* No.

20. *C.* How often do you go around?

21. *S.* Every night. I eat supper there. I usually get in around five-thirty, eat supper at six, and I leave around seven-thirty or eight. (*Pause.*)

22. *C.* Well, it may be that you should make some changes there. Of course, it is up to you. I think you should consider —· if you aren't happy with them, if you really don't want to join perhaps you shouldn't.

23. *S.* Well, now (*in a rising tone*), I can't get into any *other* fraternity — any fraternity that I want to get into — so, hell, if I can't get along with that group, I'll just pledge the darn thing and get my advantages from the fraternity elsewhere.

This portion of an interview is of special interest, because it illustrates how crucial in importance is this matter of response to feeling. Rapport in this contact is obviously excellent, and Ted talks freely and without inhibition. There is also no doubt that he is talking about problems of real concern to him. Yet in spite of these favorable factors, he is twice diverted from the significant aspects of his problem, and at the conclusion the counselor feels under the necessity of making a suggestion which Ted definitely resists. The recorded inflection of his "Well, now, I can't get into any *other* fraternity" is convincing evidence of his resistance. In the subsequent portion of the interview he refrains from expressing his feelings so freely.

Without doubt the crucial points of this excerpt are counselor responses number 2 and number 12. In each case the counselor merely picks up some point of intellectual interest in Ted's statement and responds to it, thus sidetracking the emotional attitudes which are being expressed. He continues to follow these unproductive intellectual leads in items 4, 6, 8, 14, 16, 20. Responses 10 and 18 are the only ones that have some relevance to the client attitudes which have been expressed. It is probable that had the counselor said nothing at points 2 and 12, the interview would have gone forward more profitably than it did. Or he might have responded to the feeling so clearly expressed in the student's first statement by saying, "You think they dislike you, and you're disgusted with them, and yet sometimes you wish you were one of them." Had this ambivalence been recognized, Ted could have gone more deeply into both sides of his conflicted feeling. It would then have been plain that a suggestion that he drop the fraternity could not be accepted by the boy. It is precisely because he feels critical and antagonistic to the group, and at the same time desires to be accepted by them, that he has an adjustment problem.

To summarize this discussion: when the counselor responds on an intellectual basis to the ideas which the client expresses, he diverts expression into intellectual channels of his own choosing, he blocks the expression of emotionalized attitudes, and he tends wastefully to define and solve the problems in his own terms, which are often not the true terms for the client. On the other hand, when the counselor continually keeps himself alert not only to the content which is being stated, but to the feelings which are being expressed, and responds primarily in terms of the latter element, it gives the client the satisfaction of feeling deeply understood, it enables him to express further feeling, and it leads most efficiently and most directly to the emotional roots of his adjustment problem.

A Pertinent Research. It could hardly be expected that any experimental proof of these statements would be forthcoming as yet. That they may be susceptible of proof is suggested by some of the data from Porter's study, previously mentioned. If the directive and non-directive interviews in this study are considered in relation to their position in the series, and divided into those that took place early in the contact with the client, those interviews from the midpart of the series, and those which constituted the closing phases of the counseling, certain suggestive trends are noticed. These are shown in Table 6. It will be observed that the counselor responses which define the counselor-client relationship tend, as would be expected, to decline to an approximate zero in the closing interviews. This is true of both the directive and the non-directive counselor groups.

When we consider all those items which may be regarded as eliciting and drawing out the problem situation, the non-directive counselors show a definite trend, but the directive counselors do not. In the non-directive counseling there are many items of this sort in the early interviews, but these diminish as the interviews continue and the client envisages his problems more clearly and turns to their solution. In the directive approach the counselor is still endeavoring, in the closing contacts as much as in the initial interviews, to discover the essential elements of the problem and is still asking as many questions as at the outset. This interpretation, which is admittedly tentative, is to some extent corroborated by the findings in regard to word ratios. The non-directive counselor takes nearly as much part in the initial interviews as the client, but as the process continues, and the client finds freedom to express himself and work out his own solutions, the counselor takes a smaller and smaller quantitative part in the process. The directive counselor, however, having taken the lead in defining the problem and guiding the expression, is compelled to continue this, and takes as much, or more, part in the later interviews as in the earlier. There is the implication that the non-directive counselor has been more successful in helping the client to find

TABLE 6. CERTAIN TYPES OF COUNSELOR RESPONSE AS RELATED TO EARLY, MIDDLE AND LATE INTERVIEWS *

	Average per Interview		
	Early	Middle	Late
Counselor items which define the interview situation:			
Non-directive counselors	5.6	1.0	.5
Directive counselors..........................	6.0	.7	.3
Counselor items which bring out and develop the problem situation:			
Non-directive counselors	14.0	10.6	5.5
Directive counselors..........................	49.7	46.7	45.0
Ratio of counselor words to client words:			
Non-directive counselors	0.69	0.45	0.28
Directive counselors..........................	2.24	3.74	2.44

* These data are reworked from facts given in the unpublished doctoral thesis by E. H. Porter, *The Development and Evaluation of a Measure of Counseling Interview Procedures.*

the problems on which he can work. The directive counselor continues to work on the problems he sees, which may or may not be those of the client. Because of the small number of interviews, these facts are suggestive rather than conclusive, but they hint at research studies which may throw much light on the therapeutic process.

Responding to Negative Feelings. As has already been mentioned, although the pattern of the client's feeling constitutes the most efficient road to a mutual understanding on the part of client and counselor of the basic problems to be dealt with, it is by no means an easy road to perceive. The counselor needs to develop a fresh mind-set, different from his mind-set in reading a book, carrying on a social conversation, or hearing a lecture. He needs to learn to pay attention to the feeling tone of what is being said, as well as to its superficial content. In following this aim there are several problems which occur with sufficient frequency to deserve special comment.

It is generally not too difficult for the counselor to recognize and help to bring to conscious expression hostile attitudes which are directed toward others — toward employers, parents, and teachers, or toward rivals and enemies. When the negative attitudes being expressed are directed toward the client himself,

or toward the counselor, then too often we find ourselves spring-
ing to the defense of the client out of our sympathy for him, or
rising to our own defense as counselors. It should be recognized that in these areas, also, the counselor is most effective
when he aids in bringing the feeling consciously into the picture
without taking sides. Here it is especially important that he
should recognize his function as that of a mirror which shows
the client his real self and enables him, aided by this new perception, to reorganize himself.

When the client is thoroughly discouraged, when he feels
that he is 'no good,' when his fears are overwhelming, when he
hints that he has thought of suicide, when he pictures himself as
completely unstable, completely dependent, entirely inadequate, unworthy of love — in short, when he is expressing any
type of negative feeling toward himself, the natural tendency
on the part of the inexperienced counselor is to try to convince
him that he is exaggerating the situation. This is probably true,
and the counselor's argument is intellectually logical, but it is
not therapeutic. The client feels worthless, no matter how
many good qualities may be objectively pointed out to him.
He knows that he has contemplated suicide, no matter how
many reasons may be pointed out for not doing so. He knows
that he has worried about going insane, no matter how unlikely
that possibility may be made to appear. The counselor is giving
more genuine help if he assists the client to face these feelings
openly, recognize them for what they are, and admit that he has
them. Then, if he no longer has to prove that he is worthless
or abnormal, he can, and does, consider himself more comfortably and find in himself more positive qualities.

The case of Paul, previously mentioned, gives an instance of
such a situation. In the first interview with Paul, who is highly
intelligent, but physically somewhat unprepossessing and below
average in stature and strength, this conversation takes place
(phonographic recording). Paul has been talking about the fact
that he regards himself as abnormal, and goes on to express
other negative attitudes toward himself.

    S. I — uh — have the opinion that I'm inferior. That's the
— that's the opinion I have.

C. You just know darn well that you don't measure up, is that it?

S. That's right. (*Pause.*)

C. Want to tell me some more about that?

S. Well, I'll tell you. I've been interested in anthropology to some extent, and especially criminal anthropology. (*Pause.*) Well, I'm continually — uh — I continually compare physiques of people, and I feel that mine is inferior, and I don't stop — I don't — I also believe that the behavior of an individual is an approximation of his physique, you might say. That's what my belief is. I've read too much of Hooton (*laugh*). Did you ever hear of him? (*C. nods.*) I expected you did.[1]

C. And — uh — as you look about on other physical types, you just feel that yours is inferior, the lowest of the low.

S. No, not exactly, I wouldn't say that.

C. But you're far down in the scale?

S. Yes, (*laugh*) that's the way I feel. And I'd have to have some real basis to change my mind about it.

C. And you feel that in your present experience nobody could convince you otherwise.

S. Yes. (*Pause.*)

C. I expect when you have as much of a conviction as that, it's probably backed up by other experiences?

S. Well, I — let's see — how did — how did I get interested? (*Pause*) I — can't recall exactly how I did get interested in that thing. I guess it was just a natural process, no certain thing that caused me to be interested in physique. I guess it was part of my development — to think along those lines. I can remember very distinctly in my life I've had — it was all associated with physique. At first I wanted to be — I wanted to weigh a lot, to tip the scales very high, and another time I wanted to be very tall. I thought that happiness was proportional to height. (*Laugh.*) I — when I look at it right now, I think it's very silly.

C. At the time, you believed those things very much.

S. Yes, very much. (*Pause.*)

C. Any notion as to why you thought of yourself that way?

S. Well, for instance, I was small, and I envied people who

---

[1] This is the sort of situation in which the counselor is very likely to respond to content rather than feeling. The counselor might have gone into a discussion of the truth or falsity of Hooton's theories. This would be thoroughly unprofitable. This boy feels inferior, and consequently he has drawn from his reading those elements which reinforce his attitude. If he were intellectually convinced that Hooton's book did not prove him inferior, he would merely find some other source which did. The counselor would not be touching the basic problem.

were large. I was — well, I took beatings by boys and I couldn't strike back. I guess that had something to do with it. And I resented being always licked. I guess that has something to do with it.

C. You've had plenty of experiences in being the underdog.

S. Oh, yes. I've repeatedly taken setbacks. (*Pause.*)

C. Tell me about some of those.

The interview continues with Paul telling a number of specific experiences which have caused him to feel personally and socially inadequate, and stating how strongly he has wished he were "master of the situation."

C. Yet you feel that actually you can't be anywhere near the top.

S. No. It isn't my ability. Of course, there's no reason why I should think that I should be at the top, but I think there is some reason for not being where I am. I think I shouldn't be where I am right now.

C. Shouldn't be?

S. No. (*Pause.*)

C. You think you should be further along than the progress you have made, is that it?

S. M-hm. I do have abilities and I realize some — among them I have a certain knack for mathematics. I think I do. And I've always been more advanced than my fellow students in that, I think I can safely say.

C. Then there's one thing at least in which you really excel most of the students that you work with.

Several elements in this excerpt are worthy of comment. As Paul's negative feelings about himself are accepted, he can begin to recognize in himself some of his assets. When he has faced his worst feelings about himself, then there comes the constructive realization that even if all these self-accusations are true, they still do not constitute the whole picture. It is interesting and typical that when the counselor overstates Paul's attitude, suggesting that he feels he is "the lowest of the low," Paul objects, already giving a hint of the fact that his evaluation of himself is not all negative. It is also of interest to note that by implication he asks for evidence which would prove himself to be worth while — "That's the way I feel. And I'd have to have some real basis to change my mind about it." It would have been quite futile for the counselor to try to give him this basis. It is only as he looks into the darkest recess of his fears and inadequacies and finds that they can be accepted that he develops the courage to see for himself the basis for changing his mind.

This interview also indicates the way in which the experience of catharsis can lead to insight. As Paul's feeling is recognized, it leads him into a revelation of those experiences which created it, a process which can gradually lead to self-understanding.

Another significant point is the fact that so long as Paul is tortured by his feelings of inadequacy, his whole desire is to be quite completely the "master of the situation." When his feelings have been calmly accepted as being simply elements of the total picture, then he can reduce his goal. "There's no reason why I should think that I should be at the top, but I think there is some reason for not being where I am." This is a much more reasonable goal, aiming at progress rather than perfection, and productive of much less conflict.

Responding to Ambivalent Feelings. In endeavoring to be alert to the emotionalized attitudes of the client, many less experienced counselors tend to handle poorly those attitudes which are ambivalent rather than clear-cut. An excellent example of such an attitude has already been given in the case of Ted (page 139). Where the client is conflicted in his feelings, where both love and hostility, attraction and repulsion, or both sides of a difficult choice, are being expressed, it is particularly important to recognize this clearly as an ambivalent attitude. Some of the sorts of recognition which may be given are exemplified in such statements as, "You feel you should go into commerce, but music is the thing you really like"; "In spite of your bitterness toward your father, you do like him"; "You want to come for help, yet still at times you feel it is too difficult"; or, as in Ted's case, "You dislike the fraternity, yet at the same time you wish you really belonged." A forward step in therapy is made when such ambivalences are definitely clarified. The conflict is well along toward solution when the client feels it to be a conflict with clear-cut choices.   On the other hand, to recognize only one aspect of such muddled feelings may retard therapy.   As we saw in Ted's case, the counselor's assumption that Ted had only critical feelings toward the fraternity led to rejection of his suggestion that Ted might drop out of the group.   To recognize only an attitude of hostility toward a parent, when elements of affection are also being expressed, may make it difficult for the client to bring out more fully these positive feelings.   Consequently, ambivalent attitudes need to be brought into the discussion as openly as positive or negative feelings, since it is through their clarification that the client is enabled to find a solution for them.

It need not disturb the counselor that feelings which are expressed may be in direct contradiction to one another.   Often it is these contradictory feelings that constitute the most significant ambivalences which are serving as sources of conflict. Thus, a student talks in the bitterest of terms in regard to his father.   He dislikes his father.   He has always been ashamed of his father.   It was his father's unreasonably harsh and contemptuous criticisms which were responsible for the attitudes of inadequacy which have crippled his life.   Yet after several interviews of this type, he slowly recognizes that he admired his father's scientific interests, admired his father's disregard for convention, looked up to his father for his independence of the maternal control which the boy was experiencing.   These attitudes are contradictory, but not in the sense that one is true and one false.   They are both true feelings, the hostile attitude conscious, the attitude of admiration never before having been recognized openly by the student.   As they are both brought openly into the counseling situation, the client is able to reach a much more realistic emotional evaluation of his relationship to his father, and finds himself free of conflicts which previously he has been unable to understand.

If, as feelings are expressed, the counselor refrains from a too-sympathetic identification with and approval of the attitude, and likewise from a critical and disapproving response, the client will be free to bring out other and contradictory feelings which may be hampering him in any clear-cut approach to his problems of adjustment.

Attitudes Toward the Counselor. In any counseling which is more than superficial, the client is likely to indicate, by one mode of expression or another, either positive or negative feelings toward the counselor and the counseling situation. The counselor will be likely to handle these more effectively if he can genuinely recognize and accept the fact that these expressions are directed not toward him as a person, but toward the counseling experience, in terms of the pain or satisfaction which it is at that moment giving to the client.

With most of the positive attitudes expressed, there is probably little that the counselor needs to do beyond accepting them as a casual part of the situation. Thus, in the treatment of one adolescent girl such statements cropped up rather frequently. As will be seen, some of these statements are directed toward the counseling experience as a whole, some toward the psychologist, who was a man.

> At the beginning of the third interview, she remarked that a number of her problems were troubling her, but they were not so hard to face "because I have this to look forward to."
>
> At the beginning of the fourth interview she said, "I'm beginning to look forward to this."
>
> At the end of this interview, "Oh dear, I hate to stop, just when we're getting started."
>
> In the fifth interview she gives quite the other side of her feeling. "To tell the truth, I haven't felt so well since I started all this."
>
> A little later in this interview she says, "I just wait for Wednesday to come so that I can talk things over." She again feels that the hour is too short.
>
> At the end of the sixth interview the counselor said, "Time's up." She replied, "Oh, those two words! I don't like them."
>
> During the seventh interview she tells of a letter to her father and reads part of it. She seems emotionally blocked for a few seconds and says, "I added this too. 'Maybe it will make a psychologist of me.' Well, I wasn't going to say that. I didn't think I'd bring that up. But it seemed to me over the week-end that that is the summing up of all my desires. After all, I've

always wanted a Ph.D. and I've always wanted to do things for people. Maybe some day I'll surprise you by letting you know that I'm a Ph.D. in psychology." The counselor replies that surely her experience here will give her a better understanding of herself and of other people, and that is the important thing, whether or not she goes into psychological work.

These reactions are rather typical of the positive expressions which are made during the early and middle phases of counseling. We will discuss at a later point some of the positive feelings which are brought out in the concluding phases of the process.

In responding to these feelings of warmth and affection on the part of the client, the important element is that the counselor should leave the client free to alter this feeling without any sense of guilt. Essentially the counselor's attitude must be, "You feel very warmly toward me now, but the time may come when you also will feel resentful, and the time will certainly come when you no longer will feel the need of this relationship." While it is probably infrequent that this interpretation would be fully given, this is the attitude which should lie behind whatever response the counselor makes.

Negative or hostile attitudes toward the whole counseling experience may be shown by tardiness in keeping appointments, (though one must not interpret an unreliable streetcar system as being evidence of client resistance), or by a desire to leave the appointment before the time is up. Sometimes the client shows such attitudes by his inability to discuss his problems, even though good rapport has been previously established. Usually these resistances occur because the counseling process has been painful. Material has been brought into consciousness which the client has been reluctant to face. Decisions have to be made which are painful to make. Naturally the counselor and the counseling situation become something to avoid. When these attitudes become quite evident, it is best to recognize them in the same manner in which any other negative attitude would be brought into the open. An example is given in the following section, and will be discussed there.

Although much has been written on the subject of resistance in therapy, the present writer is inclined to disagree with most of the opinions which have been expressed, and offers another hypothesis, which may be tested, it is hoped, as our knowledge of therapy increases. This hypothesis is that resistance to counseling and to the counselor is not an inevitable part of psychotherapy, nor a desirable part, but that it grows primarily out of poor techniques of handling the client's expression of his problems and feelings. More specifically, it grows out of unwise attempts on the part of the counselor to short-cut the therapeutic process by bringing into the discussion emotionalized attitudes which the client is not yet ready to face. Whether this hypothesis is correct or not, these "short cuts" constitute a sufficiently frequent error in treatment to deserve separate discussion in the following section.

SOME RISKS IN THE PROCESS

In the various types of haphazard counseling which are carried on in many schools, colleges, and other organizations which employ counselors with little psychological training in counseling, errors in treatment interviewing are difficult to recognize with assurance, and their effect is even more difficult to evaluate. Hence we find among these counselors little specific discussion of mistakes and their consequences. The type of counseling which we are discussing in this book carries no such light responsibility. It is a more orderly process, and elements which interfere with that process are more readily recognized. It is more effective in reorganizing personality, and to that extent errors are more serious, more damaging. Consequently, it is important to point out, in each stage of counseling, those mistakes in handling which may prove serious.

For the most part the process of "talking out" is a helpful one which is not likely to go astray. When the counselor is in doubt as to his correct course, he is usually safe to let the client talk. But there is one risk which we should rather thoroughly explore.

The Recognition of Unexpressed Feeling. The point of view has been stressed that the counselor must be alert indeed to be responsive to the client's feeling. It should also be emphasized that only those feelings should be verbally recognized which have been expressed. Often the client has attitudes which are implied in what he says, or which the counselor through shrewd observation judges him to have. Recognition of such attitudes which have not yet appeared in the client's conversation may, if the attitudes are not too deeply repressed, hasten the progress of therapy. If, however, they are repressed attitudes, their recognition by the counselor may seem to be very much of a threat to the client, may create resentment and resistance, and in some instances may break off the counseling contacts. Two instances of this type of handling, one constructive and one harmful, will make the discussion more concrete.

In the fourth interview with Sally, the resistant twelve-year-old who has been mentioned before, the following conversation takes place. She has been talking much more freely than in the initial interviews.

> Suddenly she opened her mouth, put her hand over it, and said, "Oh-h, I forgot!" I asked, "What is it?" "I forgot about detention. Because I didn't have my story in this morning, I was supposed to have forty-five minutes detention, and I forgot. Oh, that's terrible! How will I explain it? If you don't stay when you are supposed to you have to stay two or three nights the same week. But detention is really not so bad. There's a whole bunch of kids there, and we have fun. There's a bunch of bad boys, and it's fun to see them act up and sass the teacher. But I wouldn't do anything like that." "But you maybe feel like doing it sometimes." She looked up to see if I might perhaps be intending to be critical and then she admitted, "I sure do." "Maybe you often feel like doing it a lot more than you dare and more than your manners will let you." She nodded and replied, "Yeah."

The last two remarks of the counselor are shrewd guesses. Sally has not admitted any desire to "sass" the teacher, and only from her knowledge of the total situation can the counselor assume that this attitude exists. Yet there is no evidence that any damage has been done, and this feeling has been brought into full consciousness more rapidly because of this type of recognition. It is of some interest that the topic changes immediately after this paragraph, but since the recording is not phonographic, we cannot be sure exactly how or why this took place. In any event, here is an instance in which the counselor openly recognizes an hostile feeling which the client has not expressed, without affecting the therapeutic process adversely, so far as can be determined. Tentatively we might say that this was not damaging because rapport was well established, and the attitude was not deeply repressed by the child. Another example indicates that this type of handling may have a much less fortunate outcome.

Sam is a brilliant high-school student who is completing his senior year. He came to the counselor ostensibly because he wished to discuss prospects of going to college, but when given an opportunity to talk freely, made it plain that his main interest in college was that it provided an opportunity to get away from home. He then talked with a great deal of feeling about the friction between his parents and the fact that his home might be breaking up.[2] He felt that in this situation he was being left "out in the cold."

Rather extended excerpts from the second and third interviews are presented here, because they seem rich in counseling in which, although the counselor's alertness to emotionalized attitudes is obvious, the results are poor. The reason appears definitely to be that the counselor moves too rapidly in recognizing feeling which has not been expressed. This, it will be seen, tends to frighten Sam and make him fearful and resistant,

---

[2] Counselors need more recognition of the fact that the ostensible problem frequently is not the real problem. If the counselor had quickly classified Sam as a problem of "educational guidance" and given him information about college entrance and the like, the contact would have closed without ever having touched the real problem. The same comment applies to "vocational guidance." Human beings do not fall into our neat categories, and a "vocational" problem may turn out to be a conflict over sex matters, an ostensible problem of choice of college courses may turn out to be a fear of committing suicide. There is a need for counselors who can help people to make adjustments, not counselors who grind out solutions to one category of problem and are blind to all else.

his resistance growing stronger in the third interview and cul-
minating in the breaking of the contact.

The second interview opens with a bit of casual conversation,
and then the counselor refers to the previous discussion of the
home situation (phonographic recording).

1. *C.* What thinking have you done about what we talked
about last time, the general problems there? (*Pause.*)

2. *S.* Oh — ah — not too much. (*Rather long pause.*) My
mother thinks she's going to get her job in ——. And if it's
not there, she has another possibility, and she will attempt to
follow them up if possible.

3. *C.* She rather definitely wants to get away?

4. *S.* Oh, very definitely; there's no doubt about it. I think
she would go today if she got the opportunity, and the opportunity is sure to present itself. She is a social worker, by the way.
She drives everybody nuts talking about her clients all the time.
(*Pause.*)

5. *C.* You feel that perhaps she pays more attention to them
than to you?

6. *S.* Well, I — ah — more or less. Oh, I don't know — it
doesn't bother me or anything like that. I know she likes me,
but she does carry it to an awful extreme. But it can easily be
accounted for. I mean, she's just buried herself in that, you
know.

7. *C.* You feel that it is sort of an escape from the family
situation? (*Pause.*) What is your father's general attitude
about her going away?

Sam replies by telling of some specific quarrels which his
parents have had, the counselor making comments. Sam summarizes his attitude:

8. *S.* I don't think I am biased or anything of that sort either
way. I know from experience that he just doesn't get along
with people, while my mother does. That's strange, too, because
his work is dealing with people. But I think he tends to look
down on people. (*Pause.*)

9. *C.* That makes you resent him because he looks down on
you.

10. *S.* I don't think he looks down — well, he looks down on
me some, but not like he does on the majority of people. Why,
he speaks as if the majority of people were just imbeciles or some-

thing. I don't know — that kind of gets me. Because, well, I don't dislike anybody, except one or two people. Everybody has something, you know.

11. *C.* But you rather thoroughly dislike him, don't you?

12. *S.* No, I don't think I dislike him exactly, I don't want to dislike him exactly, but he just doesn't give me much else to do.

13. C. You want to do — you want to do what one would naturally expect a son to do in relation to his father, but you just can't quite do it.

14. *S.* Yeah, but I don't know how. It's sorta like — I know I've heard about kids' fathers playing with kids and stuff like that, and the most common thing he did was to hand me my coat and tell me to get out. I didn't know it at the time, I mean I never thought about it at the time, I just thought it was the natural thing, but —— (*Pause.*)

15. *C.* Just in — just in the last few years you have begun to ——

16. *S.* Yeah, after I got out and started looking around me a bit, I noticed there were other possible situations. (*Pause.*) He blames it all on my mother. (*Pause.*)

17. *C.* Which, again, you rather resent, don't you?

18. *S.* Oh, yes. (*Pause.*) Oh, I think I have a pretty fair picture of everything, but I don't think anything can be done.

19. *C.* Perhaps there is not much that can be done for — for the relationship there between your father and mother, but you may be able to do something — you can do something about straightening out how you feel about it. You can recognize these feelings and openly admit them, and if you do that they are not quite so hard to put up with and live with.

20. *S.* Oh, I think I know how I feel. (*Pause.*) I expect after I don't have to live with him, I'll start liking him. You know there's that kind, the less you are around them the better you —— (*Pause.*) I wish he would join a club or something. Gosh, it seems funny not to have him associate with anyone. Oh, once in a while somebody will call him up and want him to do something with them, and, "Naw, I've got a headache," or something like that. And they don't call him any more. He doesn't bowl or anything like that. I wouldn't like to bowl myself, so I don't suppose I could expect him to do that, but he could at least — oh, I don't know — he doesn't even go to church, and yet he insists on my going.

21. *C.* You not only feel badly toward him for his attitude toward you, but you're not able to make yourself very proud of him, are you, in relation to other people?

22. *S.* No. He always embarrasses me when I bring in my friends.

23. *C.* You feel that perhaps sometimes he does that on purpose?

24. *S.* Oh, yeah, I know he does. A lot of times he embarrasses me in front of company by calling attention to some little mistake I make or something.

25. *C.* And you rather resent that.

26. *S.* I suppose he's trying to improve me by doing that, but that isn't the right way to go about it. (*Pause.*) He rather resents my liking for art, too. (*Feeble laugh.*) He thinks I'm a sissy because I'm not as he was when he was in ——. He was raised on a farm. (*Pause.*)

27. *C.* And does that worry you, this particular feeling he has?

28. *S.* No, it doesn't worry me as long as he isn't around. I can't — I think I just don't think about it much any more when he isn't around, but when he's around he does sorta seem to act in such a way that I can't help but notice it.

29. *C.* And it makes you feel pretty uncomfortable.

30. *S.* Yeah. It doesn't when he isn't around. Oh, I don't think I am in danger of going insane or anything like that. It could be lots worse, I know there are a lot of people who are worse off ——

The client's resistance to the counselor's remarks is obvious. The interview continues in much the same vein, with the counselor endeavoring toward the close of the contact to give Sam an intellectualized interpretation of his behavior which is not accepted.[3] In the third interview, when the counselor suggests that Sam talk about whatever he wishes, Sam launches into an abstract discussion of the creative impulse in art and shows no desire to talk about his own problems. When there is a pause, the counselor interjects a direct question.

31. *C.* What decision has your mother made about this job?

32. *S.* She's still trying to get one. And she'll get it. I don't know. (*Long pause.*) She just enjoys argument. One of the most common arguments around there, whenever we buy crackers, why, my father likes round crackers, and my mother likes square ones. Can you think of anything sillier? (*Weak laugh.*)

---

[3] The reader may wish to refer to Chapter II (page 26) for this portion of the interview.

33. *C.* That does seem pretty bad.   What's the significance of that, though?

34. *S.* Oh, that each wants to have their own way and——. (*Pause.*)   That's just simple.   (*Pause.*)   That's nothing compared to some of the nice ones they get into.   Well, I don't like to talk about it so much.

35. *C.* It worries you pretty greatly though, doesn't it?

36. *S.* Yeah, but I don't like to talk about it; nothing can be done anyway and ——

37. *C.* I think there's something that can be done about it ——

38. *S.* Well, I think that the best thing for me to do is to take it for granted that, like it's apt to rain sometimes, but — (*mumbling*) before trying to invent a way to stop it.

39. *C.* Well, there is one thing you can change, though, and that is what this situation means to you.   Apparently you are worrying pretty much about it, and ——

40. *S.* Oh, I don't worry about that especially.   I got over worrying about that, but I still have some of the effects or something — and I sorta feel the need for companionship with the opposite gender, and they won't have anything to do with me.

The counselor who desires to understand the subtle but definite line between effective and damaging techniques of recognizing feeling will do well to give careful study to these contacts with Sam.   A definite pattern of counselor error and client response will be seen.   First, the counselor shrewdly suspects an attitude which Sam has not expressed.   Thus he intuitively realizes that Sam resents his father's attitude (item 9), and brings this feeling clearly into the open — "That makes you resent him because he looks down on you."   There is no doubt of the accuracy of this statement.   Sam himself gives ample evidence of this when he tells of the lack of companionship (items 14 and 16).   But his immediate reaction to this premature disclosure of his deeper feeling is to deny it — "I don't think he looks down — " though he then feels compelled to admit that this is partially true.   This resistance is increased as more and more of his underlying attitudes are brought out before he himself is ready to acknowledge them.

If the reader will examine counselor items 5, 9, 11, 17, 27, 29, 35, 39, and the client statements which immediately precede and follow these items, he will find that they all follow this identical pattern. First the counselor gives verbal recognition to an emotionalized attitude which the boy has not expressed. It is shown to be an accurate recognition by later conversation. It is met by partial denial ("Yes — but," item 18; "No, it doesn't," item 28, and so on). The client then goes ahead to express this feeling, but in a fearful and guarded fashion quite different from the uninhibited expression of feeling we have seen earlier in this chapter. The net result of this process, repeated a number of times, is for the boy to react against expressing his feelings, to become fearful of free conversation, and eventually to leave the situation. In the third interview he avoids his problems by discussing an abstract problem. Then he avoids his problems by frankly stating that he does not wish to talk about them. Then he endeavors to escape by changing the subject (item 40). Finally he avoids his problems by leaving the situation entirely, failing to keep his next appointment.

With almost mathematical precision, we find a different result when we change the counselor aspect of the equation. In those rare instances when this counselor accurately recognizes a feeling which has been expressed (items 21, 23, 25), we find that Sam goes forward to reveal his feelings more deeply. Thus, items 21 and 23 accurately reflect the feelings the boy has been expressing — his disappointment in his father, his lack of pride in him, his feeling that his father intentionally causes him distress and pain. In each case this recognition is followed by further revelation. Item 25 is also a reflection of the feeling expressed in words and even more as shown in the inflection. Here again, Sam goes deeper into his self-revelation.

If this case makes plain the dangers of premature attempts to have the client face his deeper feelings, it also provides proof of the fact that to "stay with" the client's attitudes is almost certain to lead to more helpful catharsis. If the counselor can be alert to the emotional aspects of the client's expression, if he can respond to those attitudes as they are expressed, without going too rapidly, more complete and constructive revelation of basic problems is almost sure to ensue.

Less Important Errors. There are many other ways in which the release of feelings may be poorly handled. They are less likely to produce serious results than the error discussed in the previous section, though they may slow up the progress of therapy. For example, the counselor may be entirely inaccurate in his recognition of the client's feelings. The client is most likely to deny such intended clarifications, and no damage is done if the counselor merely accepts his mistake and does not argue the point. Repeated errors of this sort give the client the feeling that he is not understood and undoubtedly delay the counseling process.

A frequent source of puzzlement, especially to the less experienced counselor, is the client who talks about his problems in such a confused way that his own attitudes in regard to them are far from clear. In such instances, it is well to realize that entirely neutral responses such as, "I don't believe I quite understand," "Can you tell me more about that?" are often adequate to lead to further expression which will make the feelings more plain.

It has probably been clear from much that has gone before that one error in this phase of counseling is for the counselor to talk too much. For the most effective counseling, it is the client's attitudes, not the counselor's, which need to be expressed.

Some Special Problems

Thus far we have considered those elements of the initial phases of counseling which are common to most cases. There are, however, a number of special problems which deserve our attention. The first of these is the problem of how to encourage expression and release of feeling in the case of the client who did not feel a need for help and who was forced into the counseling situation.

The Resistant Client. An excellent example has already been given of the initial handling of a highly resistant adolescent (see the interview with Sally, Chapter III, page 69). A re-examination of that excerpt will help to indicate those techniques which are most important. In the first place, the one outstanding feeling of the client, betrayed by every action and gesture, by silence as well as by word, was her antagonism to the counselor and everything she stood for. Ample recognition was given to this feeling. To recognize that the client is opposed to the contact, and to make it plain that this feeling is acceptable to the counselor, largely removes it as a barrier to counseling. In the second place, where the counselee is so completely resistant as Sally, a certain amount of neutrally toned conversation (in discussion with students in training the writer has termed it "sawdust") is necessary to keep silences from being too prolonged, embarrassing, and filled with antagonism. In essence the counselor is saying: "I realize that you dislike me and you dislike coming here. I accept that attitude on your part and regard it as natural. We can, if you prefer, talk about topics which are not painful, and you may decide whether you wish to talk about anything of importance." If this attitude can be maintained, if the client's antagonism can at appropriate times be recognized and accepted, then the counselor is making it as easy as possible for the client to express himself. Whether or not this approach will be successful will, of course, depend on some of the factors discussed in Chapter III. Often such neutral contacts may run through two or three interviews before there is any real beginning of expression. Time after time, the counselor fails to learn whether he might have been successful, because his patience gives out and he begins to probe and question in regard to the problem. This may lead to valuable diagnostic information, but it is unlikely to lead to any sort of psychological reorganization on the part of the client.

The Client Who Demands an Answer. The Waterloo of many a beginning counselor is the client who presents his problem and then demands, in effect, "Now tell me what to do." It has been proved time and again, from our phonographically recorded interviews as well as from experience, that such clients do not wish an answer. This is a fact which the less practiced counselor finds it very difficult to accept. Until he has experienced the situation several times, he does not realize that such a question is asked either in hope of getting the counselor to take the client's side and give the answer he already wishes to accept, or in order to use the counselor as a symbol for his hostilities, in case an answer is given which is emotionally unacceptable.

An amusing and convincing example may be taken from the counselor's third treatment interview with Sally. Sally has been voicing her feeling about the school very freely. It is, she thinks, stupid and useless to study grammar. It is equally absurd to learn about angles and how to tell how tall a tree is by measuring its shadow and the angle. She continues:

> "Why learn all that? I don't see any use in it. What is it really good for, to tell how tall things are?" At this time she was sort of standing on one knee in her chair and leaning toward me and talking quite earnestly. I said, "You really want an example of its use?" "Yes, I do." I decided to answer her question for fear that she might get the feeling that I was sidetracking her question and the rapport which was beginning to be built up would not carry over until a more stable basis for our contacts had been established. So I said, "Well, on a camping trip you might want to know the distance across a stream, and maybe could work it out in some such way." She looked very doubtful that that would be of any value and said, "Phooey — you could just estimate."

If clients were able to be more frank, many besides Sally would respond with "Phooey" when the counselor endeavors to turn the counseling experience into a schoolroom. To understand the reason for Sally's question, we have only to follow the interview a little farther, when we learn that in asking about mathematics her real purpose was to find out whether the counselor sided with her or with her mother.

> As it was time to close, I said, "Well, today we've been sort of talking about things at school, and you've been 'griping' about things you don't like. You can't do that around school,

where the teachers will hear you, and get away with it." With considerable feeling she said, "No, you can't!"

I went on, "But it does help to do that sometimes. Now here, in talking with me, you can talk all you want to." Sally replied, "Oh, I talk to the other kids sometimes, and to Mother. But *she* (with resentment) thinks all the school stuff is *reasonable!*"

Here it is plain that if the counselor had responded to Sally's original question by saying that school demands often were absurd, Sally would have gone home and used her remark as a weapon against her mother. By holding the view that school tasks have their use, the counselor unwittingly sided with the mother, and to a minor degree increased Sally's antagonism to the counseling situation. In either case, the counselor is not making progress toward the goal of counseling, which is to help Sally herself to achieve a more constructive attitude toward her relationship with school and with her mother.

If another example is needed, it may be found in the contact with Paul, cited earlier in this chapter (page 135). Paul tells of his problem of facing his parents and says, "Would you advise me to tell them about it?" The counselor's neutral response that Paul might tell more about his own thinking reveals the fact that he already knows what the answer must be, and that he plans to face his parents. Yet if the counselor had advised such a course, Paul could have placed the responsibility for the decision on the counselor and could have felt that he was being forced into such action. If the counselor had advised against telling the parents, the boy would have been thrown into real confusion.

The student who must have an answer, the mother who brings a notebook and demands to know how she shall handle her child so that she can write it down — these very human situations are not always easy to handle comfortably. Yet the principle of dealing with them, the principle which is consistent with the whole hypothesis of this book, is simple and clear-cut. It is to recognize understandingly that the client would feel great satisfaction in finding an answer to his problem, but that the only realistic answer that can possibly be found is in terms of his own abilities and desires to deal with the situation.

An example of this type of handling is found in the fifth interview with Mrs. L., whose problems with her ten-year-old son Jim were pictured in Chapter II.   By the time of the fifth contact, Mrs. L. had made considerable progress in understanding, but she opens the conversation by telling of a very upsetting quarrel which she had with her son over a bottle of ink.   He wished to take it to school, and she felt there was no reason to do so.   He became insolent and hid the ink, and she whipped him.   She continues (phonographic recording):

> *S.* Then I told him to get the ink, and he said he wouldn't do it.   So I said, "Well, are you going to get the ink, or will I give you another whipping?"   And he wouldn't get it, so (*laugh*) I gave him another whipping.   And he just got so upset — he was almost hysterical.   But I couldn't — I don't know.   It didn't seem to me that I should let him get away with that.   On the other hand, a bottle of ink seems a very trivial thing to cause such an upheaval in the house.   Now I wonder what you — what is the answer?
>
> *C.* Well, I doubt that there is any one set, particular answer to — that would fit all cases like that.   You — you were probably pretty much upset by the time it was over, too.
>
> *S.* I was extremely upset and ——
>
> *C.* Both felt all up in the air and, as you say, probably felt it was a trivial beginning, at least.
>
> *S.* Well, I said to my husband afterwards — I — he — he was — the boy was very upset and — oh, he got to the point where he was sobbing, you know — he couldn't get his breath or anything, so I took him upstairs and put him in the tub and let him play in the tub — that almost always calms him down.   Then I gave him a boat or something and washed him and let him play while I did the dishes.   And I said to my husband when it was over, it was probably all my fault and I was sorry I had refused him the ink in the first place, but having refused it once, I felt I had to (*laugh*) carry it through.
>
> *C.* M-hm.   That's often the case, isn't it — the feeling that you must go on with what you've done?

Here is the kind of situation which frequently occurs.   A problem has arisen, and the mother wants to know, "What is the answer?"   When the counselor avoids her question and

responds instead to the feeling that she has been indicating —
"You were probably pretty much upset" — the mother is able
to go on and to admit that she herself was as much if not more
at fault than the boy.   To realize the amazing significance of
this, one must recall the hostility which this mother showed
toward her boy in the initial contacts, and her complete assurance that he was the problem (see Chapter II, page 36, for a
sample of her attitudes).   The basic answer to her question
does not lie in any suggestions the counselor might have made
in regard to discipline.   The mother herself gives the basic answer in her changed attitude of genuine recognition that she
may be at fault as well as the boy.   It is this underlying emotional shift which will assure a better, more sensitive, more constructive handling of their relationship in the future, no matter
what type of problem appears.   The counselor has helped the
mother to arrive at this fundamental answer by refusing to be
cast in the rôle of an all-knowing authority.

Reassurance — Does It Reassure?   In various expositions of
the principles of psychotherapy, much is made of the need of
reassuring the client in order to keep his anxiety from getting
out of bounds.   A comment on this point may be in order.   If
the counselor has been successful in "staying with" the client's
feelings, recognizing and clarifying those which have been expressed, but avoiding the error of bringing to light those attitudes which the client is not yet ready to reveal, it is unlikely
that verbal reassurance is needed or will be helpful.   There is
one underlying form of reassurance which the client is receiving
at all times as he tells of his socially unacceptable impulses and
attitudes.   This is the reassurance which comes from finding
his most "shocking" revelations accepted without shock by the
counselor.   It is doubtful that in most instances any further
reassurance is necessary.   It is only when counseling has blun-
dered, as in the case of Sam (pages 153–157), and the client has
been led to reveal unconventional or repressed attitudes before
being ready to do so, that reassurance may be a needed prop to
counseling.

It should be pointed out that, in any case, the only type of reassurance which has any promise of being helpful is that which relieves the client's feeling of peculiarity or isolation. To know that he is not the only one who has suffered with such problems, nor the only one who has been torn by strongly conflicting desires, may lighten a sense of guilt or make the individual less anxious.

On the other hand, cheery reassurance that the client's problems are not serious, or that he is much more normal than he feels, or that the solution to his problems is easy, has a thoroughly bad effect on therapy. It denies the client's own feelings and makes it well-nigh impossible for him to bring his anxieties and conflict and sense of guilt fully into the conversation when he has been assured that they should not exist. No amount of assurance will eliminate the fact that they do exist.

Some Devices

Our knowledge in the field of personality study has been much advanced by various devices — inkblots, series of pictures, the use of toys to construct dramatic situations, as well as the more familiar devices of paper and pencil tests. Are there any devices which can be used to accelerate therapy or to insure more adequate facing of real problems? It would seem to the writer that there are relatively few such devices as yet, but attention should be called to those that are available in order to stimulate further thinking along this line. Specific techniques can never be a substitute for a consistent viewpoint, but they may, if properly selected, implement such an approach.

The use of silence may, curiously enough, be one such technique. In an initial interview, long pauses or silences are likely to be embarrassing rather than helpful. In subsequent contacts, however, if fundamental rapport is good, silence on the part of the counselor may be a most useful device. Often in an interview the client reaches the limit of his expression on a particular topic. He has either verbalized his attitudes fully, or more likely, has said all that he is ready to reveal at the time.

There comes a pause. If the counselor now changes the subject, raising some new question, he runs the risk, as we have already mentioned, of directing the flow of expression into some relatively profitless area. If, on the other hand, he simply waits, freeing the situation from embarrassing tension by continuing to make notes on the interview, by lighting a cigarette, or by some other inconsequential activity, the burden of reopening the conversation is placed upon the client. Frequently this leads to conversation of a most significant sort. Feeling that he must say something to break the silence, the client is likely to find that the topic which comes first to mind has an important relation to his problem.

While this device, if we may dignify it by such a name, has real value, of course it may be misused. It is not likely to be helpful to a client who is resisting counseling. It may, however, be of help when the client is having difficulty in bringing his real problems into the situation. Sometimes fruitful silences may last for as long as sixty seconds, as we have determined from phonographic recordings, provided the counselor can so conduct himself as to keep the situation free of mutual embarrassment.

Some counselors have encouraged clients to express themselves in writing between contacts. Autobiographical sketches, or descriptions of feelings in certain situations, are devices of this sort. To the writer it seems that such compositions are likely to lend themselves to an intellectual type of discussion, rather than to concentration upon present feelings, but there may be fruitful ways of using them. Some counselors give their clients "homework" of some variety between contacts, topics they are to think about, aspects of their situation which they are to observe. Such assignments may be highly directive, and hence unsuitable from the viewpoint of this book, or based on the client's own feelings and hence more helpful. Chassell [4] makes use of a rather directive assignment of this sort, giving the client a copy of his "Experience Variables Record" to study

[4] Chassell, Joseph O. "A Clinical Revision of the Experience Variables Record," *Psychiatry*, vol. 1, no. 1 (February, 1938), pp. 67–77.

during intervals between contacts.   This instrument contains many questions about the client's emotional relationships to many aspects of his past and present situation — family, social group, sexual situation, and vocational adjustment.   In the subsequent contact the client is allowed to talk about any aspect of the total situation which the questions have brought to mind.

One area which needs to be explored is the adaptation of play-therapy techniques to adolescents and adults.   Such techniques offer an easy and symbolic way of expressing feeling and conflict, and if they can be adapted to the older individual, should be helpful devices.   The writer has known of instances in which finger puppets have been very helpfully used by adolescent girls to act out dramas in which their own conflicts were only faintly disguised.   Murray and Homburger[5] have shown that adults under the guise of constructing dramatic situations with toy materials, will reveal their own emotionalized attitudes to a considerable degree.   Such devices may be developed further. To the extent to which these techniques leave the client entirely free to express his attitudes and provide easy and comfortable ways of doing so, they are helpful.

THE PARALLEL TO PLAY THERAPY

It was pointed out early in this book that no attempt would be made to discuss fully such approaches as play therapy except as they illustrated and clarified the general therapeutic process. It is in relation to this matter of releasing expression that the most striking parallels appear.   If we consider typical instances of treatment through play therapy, we shall find that in the structuring of the relationship, in the recognition of negative and positive feelings, in the matter of giving full expression to forbidden and repressed attitudes, in the gradual acquisition of a certain measure of insight, play therapy is very similar to counseling of a verbal nature.   In some ways the process

5 Murray, H. A., *et al.   Explorations in Personality.*   New York: Oxford University Press, 1938, pp. 552-582.

stands out more clearly because it makes use of nonverbal media.

The treatment of a four-year-old and his parents is interestingly described by Baruch and is quoted below. It will be noted that almost all the major principles which have been enunciated in regard to counseling appear in this case. The treatment of the parents is clearly indicated, and is carried on. The play situation with the teacher in this very modern preschool gives evidence of the permissiveness and warmth which has been commented upon in relation to counseling, and also indicates the limitations which help to structure the situation. The gradual increase in depth of feeling, as attitudes are accepted and recognized, is very noticeable. The degree of aggression and hostility is extreme, no doubt because the repressions have been extreme. The eventual appearance of positive feelings is dramatic and striking. The effect of all this release upon behavior is of interest. The case can best be given in Baruch's own words:

> Raymond was four years and two months when he came into the preschool. He remained for three semesters. On entrance he was extremely withdrawn. He did not talk. He did not play. He seemed impervious to what went on about him. There was no gross abnormality in physical health according to the pediatrician. His mother reported that at home he would sit and sit for hours without moving and that he seemed to be within a shell that no one could penetrate. She was worried about his lack of speech.
>
> Chief among the items that might have caused such maladjustment, was the fact that the parents were in extreme tension in their relationship to each other. To the worker they avowed hatred of each other. They claimed, however, that they did not fight openly, that instead they "held things in." The mother drank for relief and thrashed the child, letting out onto him the antagonism she held against her husband.
>
> To the worker the parents in their own separate conferences expressed their hostilities. They talked, they got mad, they ranted against each other. To her they let out many of their ranklings. And as they let out, they apparently gained enough relief so that within approximately six months' time they were able to accept each other on a different basis — without such a weight of piled-up resentment.

They were able, too, to accept the child on a different basis. The mother no longer felt "red anger" against him. She could be more acceptant and have greater patience. But the child had introjected so much of her old emotion that he could not accept the new.

From the beginning he was given extra chances for contact within the group situation. But for the first months he was fearful of any but casual approaches. Releasing experiences were obviously impossible for him when he was not utilizing materials. However, the fact that demands were few and restrictions fewer, may have given him some sense of ease. Slowly observable trust in one of the teachers came, but this was deep enough to permit release in her presence only after he was in his third semester. Only then would he leave the group without near panic at being alone with an adult.

He was the child who began tapping a key of his teacher's typewriter, saying "pee-pee, pee-pee," with sly looks and great silliness, and a shade of defiance.

He ran the gamut of several distinct types of activity during his subsequent period with her. He expressed aggression through bowel movements of clay. He even defecated actually on the linoleum floor several times in the room where these periods took place. He became exhibitionistic, showing his penis repeatedly to the teacher and masturbating in front of her. Finally he attempted to make a very crude clay figure and demanded her help.

The figure became his mother to him. He would pound her, trample on her, urinate on her, poke his penis at her, pull her arms and legs and head off.

The teacher remained acceptant. She reiterated that children often do feel mean and mad to their mothers, that she understood how he felt, and that he could keep on telling her and showing her about it. A couple of times, he attempted to hit her and smear clay on her, but here she erected limitations, feeling that the relationship would be jeopardized if she permitted him to do to her what to him would symbolize harm. Hurting the one person whom he could thoroughly trust might lead into too great fear of desertion and into too great anxiety and guilt.

Finally one day, after an extreme orgy of biting and cutting and mashing of the mother figure, he became suddenly relaxed. For the first time his voice carries in it a sympathetic note. "Oh, she died, poor old nasty."

He then picks up the mutilated clay mother and very softly whispers. "Poor thing. She got runned over. Call the am-

bulance. Poor old nasty thing. She's dead all right." He
pats the figure gently — "Let's see what she has inside her."
He scratches the clay figure open. "Oh, there's blood. Blood
is coming out. Put her in the ambulance." He picks her up
again. "I don't want to hit you, Mother." Then turning to
the teacher he asks her to "fix the mother all right again."

She repairs the clay figure and meanwhile interprets that it
looks as if his old mean mother were dead and that perhaps this
is a new mother whom he wants.

He picks up the figure. Calls it his new good mother. One
of the legs that the teacher had put hastily on, falls off. He
picks it up and himself makes another leg and carefully molds it
back on. These are the first tender, caring-for, positive expressions toward his mother ever evidenced in his play. A short
while later, when his time finishes, instead of demolishing the
mother as on previous days, he places her carefully in the clay
can, covers her gently with the oilcloth, saying gently, "The.e
you are."

Apparently, through having let out hostility against the old
mother, he has at last become able to accept a new mother.

Great changes are apparent in his behavior. He no longer
stutters. He begins to defend his own rights. He becomes
overly aggressive to other children as a swing from earlier with-
drawal and submission. He is less frequently silly or shrill, and
more capable of demanding response through affectionate approaches. All in all, he is a much less tense and a much more
open, natural person.[6]

Experiences with play therapy, such as are described in this
case, add to the conviction that therapy is very definitely a
process, a process which follows certain fundamental trends.
It is as we see these trends operating in the most diverse situations — with employees in an industrial plant, with adolescents in high school, with parents in a clinic, with small children
in a play experience, with young people in a vocational counseling setting — that this conviction grows.

[6] Baruch, Dorothy W., "Therapeutic Procedures as Part of the Educative Process,"
Journal of Consulting Psychology, vol. 4 (September – October, 1940), pp. 170–172.

The Use the Client Makes of Catharsis

The values which uninhibited expression has for the client have been implied if not always stated in each of the interview excerpts which have been given. These values have long been recognized and need only to be mentioned here.

As a first step, the client gains emotional release from those feelings and attitudes which he has been repressing. Often it is possible to observe the physical relaxation, the release of physical tension, which accompanies such catharsis. Once free of such tension-creating feelings, it is possible for him to be more comfortable and objective about himself and his situation.

An opportunity for free expression also enables the client to explore his situation much more adequately than, in most instances, he has ever done before. Even where emotional factors are at a minimum, talking about one's own problems, in an atmosphere calculated to make defensiveness unnecessary, tends to clarify the adjustments which one must make, to give a more clear-cut picture of problems and difficulties, to give possible choices their true values in terms of one's own feelings.

Not only is the situation thus clarified, but also the client's understanding of self. As he talks freely about himself, he becomes able to face the various aspects of himself without rationalization or denial — his likes and dislikes, his hostile attitudes as well as his positive affections, his desires for dependence as well as independence, his unrecognized conflicts and motivations, his wishful as well as his realistic goals. Amid the pressures of real life situations, it is almost never possible to do this. Some sort of defensive "front" must be maintained in every situation. But in the counseling relationship, freed from any necessity of being defensive, the client for the first time has an opportunity to take a frank look at himself, to go behind the "front" and make a true evaluation.

As he finds that this unconventional self, this hidden self, is comfortably accepted by the counselor, the client is also able to accept this hitherto unrevealed self as his own.   In place of anxiety and worry and feelings of inadequacy, the client develops an acceptance of his strengths and weaknesses as being a realistic and comfortable point of departure for progress in maturity.   Instead of striving desperately to be what he is not, the client finds that there are many advantages in being what he is and in developing the growth possibilities which are genuinely indigenous.

It is these values in catharsis which make it truly therapeutic in counseling.   The counselor endeavors to create a releasing atmosphere in which the individual may express himself.   The client finds that expression leads also to the releasing of new forces within himself, forces which heretofore had been utilized in maintaining defensive reactions.

Even if counseling goes no farther than this phase of free expression, it is helpful and constructive.   It is this fact which makes the type of counseling described here most satisfactory for short-contact counseling.   The counselor is often faced with situations in which he knows that he will be limited to but one interview, or in which he is sure that he cannot carry on any extended treatment.   In such instances, the common practice is to be completely directive.   Since time is short, the counselor quickly grasps the problem as he sees it, giving advice, persuading, directing.   The results are almost inevitably and thoroughly bad.   If, however, the counselor makes use of this limited time to free the client to "talk out" his attitudes, positive results ensue.   The client leaves without, to be sure, any artificial "solution" to his problem, but with his situation much more clearly defined in his own mind, with possible choices clarified, and with the comforting reassurance that someone has understood him and, in spite of his problems and attitudes, has been able to accept him.   He is now more competent to meet his situation than the client who leaves the interview with much half-digested advice, resentful toward some of it, feeling that he has been wrong in many of his own actions, and less sure of himself than before.

Summary

This chapter has endeavored to explore rather thoroughly the process of catharsis, and to consider various issues and problems which arise in the conduct of this phase of interview treatment. A brief summary of the viewpoint which has been presented may be of assistance in structuring the material.

In effective counseling and psychotherapy one of the major purposes of the counselor is to help the client to express freely the emotionalized attitudes which are basic to his adjustment problems and conflicts.   In carrying out this purpose, the counselor adopts various methods which enable the client to release his feelings without inhibition.   Primarily the counselor endeavors to respond to, and verbally recognize, the feeling content, rather than the intellectual content, of the client's expression.   This principle holds, no matter what the type of emotionalized attitude — negative attitudes of hostility, discouragement, and fear, positive attitudes of affection and courage and self-confidence, or ambivalent and contradictory attitudes. This approach is sound whether the client's feelings are directed toward himself, toward others, or toward the counselor and the counseling situation.   In each case, the counselor aims to recognize and respond to the feeling expressed, openly accepting it as an element in the problem and in the counseling relationship. He avoids the verbal recognition of repressed attitudes which the client has not yet been able to express.

In this process the client finds emotional release from feelings heretofore repressed, increasing awareness of the basic elements in his own situation, and increased ability to recognize his own feelings openly and without fear.   He also finds his situation clarified by this process of exploration and begins to see relationships between his various reactions.   This is the beginning of and the basis for insight, which we shall now consider.

The Achievement of Insight

THE free expression of emotionalized attitudes, valuable though it is to the client, is by no means a complete description of the processes included in successful counseling or therapy. This will have been evident in the preceding chapter. The experience of relating feelings hitherto inhibited involves more than bringing about a sense of release. It inevitably gives the individual a somewhat changed perception of himself. This has been clear in some of the case material cited. It is true even in the case of the child who is releasing his feelings through play therapy. Gradually he comes to orient himself in a new way and to show by his actions that he is playing a new rôle. It is the purpose of this chapter to turn to a consideration of these new perceptions, which we call insight, recognizing, however, that they are inseparably linked to the experience of catharsis and that they are based upon it.

In the concluding portion of the chapter we shall take up in greater detail the description and the meaning of the experiences which we class as insight. For the present it may be adequate to say that the term implies the perception of new meaning in the individual's own experience. To see new relationships of cause and effect, to gain new understanding of the meaning which behavior symptoms have had, to understand the patterning of one's behavior — such learnings constitute insight.

This is a difficult process to discuss effectively, largely because it is a piecemeal affair, rarely if ever occurring all at once. Such learnings are likely to be only partially expressed, or to be shown as much in actions as in words. They are learnings with deep emotional concomitants, not learnings of intellectual content, and hence may or may not find clear verbal expression. Nevertheless, insight is a highly important aspect of counseling treatment, and as such deserves the closest scrutiny. It is also an aspect of treatment which is little understood and often is seriously misunderstood. Consequently, careful study of considerable of the raw data of interviewing experience seems wise, if our thinking is to be realistic.

What Insight Means to the Client

Seeing Old Facts in New Relationships. In order to examine some of the various facets of this phenomenon of insight, let us look first at a simple example — almost a microscopic sample — of one type of insight. Mrs. R. is a talkative, garrulous mother of rather overpowering bearing, whose thirteen-year-old son, Isaac, is mentally defective. The whole pattern of the situation is one which is all too familiar to clinicians. The boy is obviously defective, and the psychological examination reveals that he is functioning at about an eight-year level. The greatest barrier to constructive handling of the problem is that the mother has never accepted the fact of her son's mental defect. This is not for lack of intellectual interpretation. A number of professional workers have carefully explained the facts, without observable result. But when the mother is allowed to talk out her feelings in an accepting situation, insight begins to develop. An excerpt from the latter portion of the first interview makes this evident (phonographic recording). The mother is talking about her struggles to keep the boy in health and to make him learn.

> C. You feel that the whole thing rests on you, don't you? You've got to make him eat, you've got to make him learn, you've got to make him wear his brace [for a cracked collarbone], and all.
>
> S. I don't know. Today, tomorrow, then what? You know, time runs away before you know it. He's grown up, and what can he do? Nothing, absolutely. He tells me he'll be able to —— when I say to him, "What's going to happen? You won't

be able to read and write," he says, "I'll be able to drive a truck; I can fly an airplane; I can lay linoleum; I can hang window shades." He has an argument for everything to tell me what he can do. I said, "You can't fly an airplane if you can't read and write. There's numbers on the dial," and then I don't know a thing about an airplane to tell him about it.

C. You think that perhaps he can't learn some of those things that you'd like to have him learn.

S. I don't believe that he *can't*. Now, I may be blind from a mother's point of view; understand, I may be blind, but I don't think so. I think that Isaac has a little stubborn streak in him. If I could get to the bottom of that I think that he *could*, but I don't know.

C. But you've tried for quite a few years to make him learn, haven't you?

S. Maybe I haven't tried hard enough.

C. Maybe you've tried too hard.

S. I don't know, I don't know. I went to this baby specialist, and he asked me two questions, and then he said to me, "Well, take him home and let him be," and I said, "If there is something wrong with him, why don't you tell me the truth?" (*Voice rising to crescendo.*) I'd like to know the truth, then I would know exactly how to go about it and know that I've got to make up my mind, and I'll hire him out for a carpenter or cement mixer or something! Tell me the *truth* —!

C. (*Sympathetically.*) Don't you know the truth already?

S. (*Very quietly — voice very much changed.*) I don't want to know it. I don't want to believe it. I don't want to know it. (*Tears come to her eyes.*)

What has occurred in this fragment? It would seem that the essential fact is that the mother, in ways and for reasons which we shall consider later, now sees familiar facts in a definitely new relationship. She has learned no new facts about the problem. The problem itself is an objective reality that has not been altered. But the problem as she sees it has been decidedly changed. At the outset the problem is, as it has always been, something external to herself, though necessarily affecting her. The problem is her boy and his stubbornness. The problem is the doctors who give her no help and who refuse to tell her the truth. Quite suddenly the situation changes. It is her own attitude which she begins to see as a part of the problem, and her own adjustment which she recognizes as difficult to make. Having once become conscious of this as an integral part of the total problem, her own behavior in regard to the situation is bound to undergo change.

There can be no doubt that in many instances insight has this sort of meaning to the client — a process of becoming sufficiently free to look at old facts in a new way, an experience of discovering new relationships among familiar attitudes, a willingness to accept the implications of well-known material. As we see in the previous history of Mrs. R., such insight cannot be gained from being talked to; it is an experience which the client achieves.

The Gradual Increase in Self-Understanding. It cannot be sufficiently stressed that such instances of insight are but steps in the total process of better self-understanding. Insight comes gradually, bit by bit, as the individual develops sufficient psychological strength to endure new perceptions. In our phonographic recording we have captured one minute example of this gradual growth which illuminates the topic as a whole. In one of the interviews with Mrs. L., whose problems with Jim, her ten-year-old son, have provided several illustrations for the previous discussion, the conversation indicates that she comes almost to the point of recognizing her rôle in the situation, and then avoids completing her statement. It is one week later, in her next interview, that her courage is adequate to accept this new perception and to complete the sentence begun seven days before. In the earlier interview of the two, Mrs. L. tells of praising Jim — a rare event — for some helpful behavior which he has shown. This leads to a discussion of his highly annoying behavior, which she feels demands punishment, and his occasional "good" behavior. The interview continues (phonographic recording):

> *C.* I wonder which he feels more strongly — that you disapprove of things he does, or that underneath you really love him?
> *S.* I don't know. I don't know how he really feels. I know how I talk to him, but —— Of course he hasn't said it recently, but he used to say that we didn't love him, because we corrected

him. And then when he'd say that, I'd say, 'Now, listen, Jim, if I
didn't love you, I wouldn't care what you did at all. You could
do just exactly what you pleased, and if I didn't love you it
wouldn't make any difference to me. I wouldn't care how you
turned out, but I want you to turn out to be a good man."

C. Sometimes people get a good bit of pleasure and good
feeling out of just a little show of affection and love entirely
separate and apart from any behavior situation. (*Pause.*)

S. (*Slowly.*)   I suppose I've worked so hard at trying to correct him that I haven't taken time off to —— I'm not a very
affectionate person by nature, not with anybody. (*Pause.*)
My mother often remarked about that in regard to her. I never
did go around kissing, even my mother. My brother did, and
my mother used to remark that I must not love her as much as
my brother did. I just didn't care anything about it.

C. Do you feel sometimes that you would like to show more
affection than you do show?

S. (*Laughing, almost giggling.*) Oh, no. (*Long pause.*)

One can see, as in a slow-motion camera study, the coming of
new insight to this mother as she thinks out loud, "I suppose
I've worked so hard at trying to correct him that I haven't
taken time off to ——" Obviously the concluding portion of
the idea is "to be affectionate," but Mrs. L. cannot face or
accept the self-accusation which this implies. She shifts the
conversation to defend herself, even though she has not been
attacked. She must prove that she cannot be affectionate,
that her attitude to Jim is not different from the one she showed
to her own mother. When the counselor tries to help her complete her unfinished sentence, she laughs in a very self-conscious
fashion and denies the whole idea. Throughout the remainder
of the interview she refrains from taking up this line of thought
again.

During the following week, however, this dawning perception
begins to grow, because she has not been made defensive in
regard to it. As in all cases of genuine insight, it becomes a
potent factor in bringing about a new orientation. In the succeeding interview, she not only tells of the fact that Jim's behavior is better and that she protected him from too violent
criticism from his father and that she has felt less nervous, but

she also comes around, in the closing minutes of the interview, to finish the sentence she commenced the week before. "Perhaps," she says, "what would do him the most good would be for him to have some affection and love and consideration entirely apart from any correcting. Now, I guess that we've been so busy correcting him that we haven't had time to do anything else." [1] She has reached the point where she can bear to look at the fact that her own lack of affection, her own desire to punish, has had a part in making Jim a problem.

One might search a long time for an instance which would tell more about the development of insight. In the first place, the contacts with the counselor have gradually given her assurance that she does not need to defend herself against any attack, direct or implied. In this new freedom she begins to sense her own rôle in the situation. But she does not dare to put it fully into words and denies her perception when the counselor tries to make it easier for her to state it. It is the satisfaction which comes during the ensuing week from putting the new perception into action that gives her the courage to state it fully in words.

It is scarcely necessary to point out that this genuine acceptance by Mrs. L. of her rôle in creating a problem is a far cry from the easy verbal statement of some such attitude, adopted as a defense. Many mothers come to a clinic with the statement that "My child is bad, and I'm sure I'm all to blame." This is merely the intelligent individual's best method of defense. It is a very different experience when these individuals *feel* that they have actually had a part in creating the child's difficulties.

Recognition and Acceptance of the Self. The development of insight often involves not only the recognition of the rôle which the individual is playing, but also the recognition of repressed impulses within the self. So long as the individual denies certain attitudes which he finds within himself, so long will he keep up compensatory attitudes of a defensive character. When he

---

[1] This statement was previously quoted in Chapter II (page 41).

can face clearly, and can accept as a part of himself, these less praiseworthy feelings, the need for defensive reactions tends to disappear.

An excellent example of the development of this type of insight may be taken from the case of Cora, an adolescent girl of seventeen who was brought to the guidance clinic and to the children's court by her stepfather because of ungovernable behavior at home. The mother was an invalid, having spent periods in the hospital and a sanitarium. The stepfather had assumed much responsibility for Cora, and had also shown a peculiar attitude toward her, being jealous of her boy friends and behaving in ways which indicated a direct sex interest in the girl. As the friction in the home was extreme, Cora was placed in a foster home by the court, and after a short time the girl asked if she might again talk with the psychologist with whom she had had several contacts at the time she went to court. When she came in, she expressed a desire to talk about her family, and much of her conversation revolved about her stepfather. She told indignantly of the way in which he checked on her behavior, even while she was in the foster home, and how disturbed he seemed to be when she had any contact with her boy friend. The interview continues:

> Finally counselor said, "Why do you think these things happen?" Cora said, "I think he does it for meanness. I can't understand why my mother doesn't stop him. Why does she always believe him?" Counselor said, "I have talked with your mother since you were here. Your mother has talked about this. She understands. Perhaps some day she'll explain it to you. Would you like to have me tell you what your mother and I talked about?" Cora expressed no interest in this, but went right on with the problem of her stepfather's behavior. "I think he just wants me home. I think he wants me to help with the work. I think he's jealous. Several people have said it. The adviser at school said so, you remember I told you. I don't see why he should be jealous; what could he be jealous of? He hates to see me go out with a boy. I don't know how to explain it. I think he's not all there. Sometimes he is, and sometimes he isn't. He doesn't like it if I go with Italians. He doesn't like any boys to take me out. He's jealous. I don't understand it.

If he were a boy my age it would mean he wanted me just to go with him. But he's married to my mother. I don't understand it. A boy would come out and say it. He doesn't. He just acts that way. He acts as if he wanted to go with me. Why, that couldn't be true. He's married to my mother. That's hard to think of." She was very disturbed and silent for a long time; became very fussed and fidgeted.

Counselor: "Talk about it some more."

Cora: "I don't know what to say. It seems awfully unfair to my mother if that's it. After all, he married my mother. It wouldn't be fair to my mother. I haven't any feeling for him. I don't see why he should feel that way. I go crazy if he even touches me. He seems so devoted to my mother. I think he is. I realize it's been hard for him, my mother being in the hospital. If he must be like that, why pick on me? He might better go out with someone we didn't know, some woman we didn't know."

Counselor: "Why should he especially like you?"

Cora: "I don't think it's because I'm especially like my mother. People say I am. He says I am. I don't think I am. Maybe I am. There's nothing else to say. It makes me sort of horrified — my own mother. The only reason would be that I remind him of my mother."

She talked about how wonderful her mother was. "He's married to my mother. He shouldn't feel that way. Why doesn't he say something? Why take it out on me? My mother's right there. Why doesn't he give her all his affection? Maybe it's because I'm younger, in better health, or something. I don't think it could be sex, because — unless" — (there was a long pause) — "I know he couldn't have any sex life with my mother. She's sick. I don't even like to talk about such things. What else is there to say?"

There was further conversation along this same line, devoted largely to discussion of the stepfather and his behavior. Two days later Cora came in for her next interview.

Cora looked very sober when she came in. "I'm still in a fog. I've thought and thought. It seems impossible. It's hard to believe. I can see the sense in it. It all adds up, and still I can't believe it. How could that be, when I see that it makes sense?"

Counselor explained to her something of how one could understand how a thing could be and still not emotionally accept it. Cora then said, "It's hard to believe that it's real. Nothing like that ever entered my head. I don't think about things like that anyway."

Counselor: "What is it that is hard to believe?"

Cora: "It's hard to believe, and yet I believe it. It's hard to believe that people would have feelings like that. He doesn't seem clean. When I think about it, I shudder. That was not included in my education. It ought to be for every girl, that there are such things. The idea that my stepfather would have such feelings. I'm not like my mother. I don't see why he should feel that way. I don't know how to say it."

During the remainder of the interview she talked about family frictions, and about the fact that she did not think she would ever wish to go home.

Cora missed the next two appointments which were given to her. It seems entirely reasonable to suppose that the painfulness of this increasing insight was the major factor in her failing to keep these appointments. Consequently, it was two weeks later that she came in for her next appointment.

Cora explained that she had made a mistake about the time of her appointment. "I didn't try to forget it. It was an accident. I've been thinking about what we talked about last time. It all makes sense, but I can't believe it."

Counselor said, "When you were here last time, you were trying to answer the question of what had been your part in creating this situation." (No such statement is included in the counselor's account of the previous interview. If such a question was raised by the counselor, it no doubt accounts for Cora's failure to keep the appointments.)

Cora: "I don't know what it is. I can't think it out."

Counselor: "When your mother was in the hospital, your stepfather did things for you and gave you things and took you places. You were pleased, weren't you? How did you show it?"

Cora: "Oh, I'd jump up and down and be very gleeful. I might have hugged and kissed him. Sometimes I show my pleasure in that way. Sometimes I kissed him and made a great fuss."

Counselor: "Did you ever do something for someone else and have them show pleasure? How did you feel?" Cora thought for a few moments and then gave several examples of having done things for the foster mother. "I felt pretty good that she was pleased." She thought a long time. "I liked her maybe a little harder for a few minutes after that."

Counselor: "Go back again to when you and your stepfather were together and your mother was in the hospital."

Cora talked about the things her stepfather had done for her, particularly taking her places. "He did those things then to please my mother, not for me. I was pleased and showed it. He was pleased because my mother was pleased. When she was pleased, he was more willing to do more for me. Then I got a feeling toward him, hero worship. No, I guess that isn't right. Something different. Sometimes I thought he was very nice, and sometimes I didn't like him. I was also jealous that he had married my mother. I would be grateful to him, but then I would think it was my right that he should do things for me. No, it wasn't hero worship. I can't quite say what it was. He did things for me that pleased me. I guess he was a sort of Santa Claus. You get to expect and expect when people do things for you. Then the person gets kind of sick of it. Then you learn how to get things. I guess that's what I did. I learned how to get things from him."

Counselor: "What did you do?"

Cora showed embarrassment, paused a long time. "Oh, I don't know. I have a lot of tricks. It wasn't hard to get him to go out. He didn't like to sit at home. I'd do a lot of things. When I wanted girls to go with me, I'd pick the girls he liked to get him to take them along." She paused a long time and counselor waited, then said, "Anything else?"

Cora: "I suppose my voice was soft and persuasive and my face had a happy expression, the way I knew it would get him to do things." She talked about this for a little while, showing more and more embarrassment.

Counselor: "When you want a boy to take you some place, how do you get it?"

Cora: "I probably look sweet and defenseless." Then very quickly: "I'm not conscious of all this, but I guess I do. I know how to look that way, but it never works on my mother. I guess I learned how to do it particularly in thinking up ways to get things from my stepfather. I didn't consciously bring about this situation." She went back to discuss the idea that her stepfather liked her very much and identified her with her mother, again saying, "It makes sense, but I don't believe it."

Counselor: "Do you like this situation?"

There was a long pause. Cora flushed, fidgeted, and then hesitated. "No, but I do like my stepfather to pay attention to me." She was silent for a long time.

Though the counselor's approach in this situation seems too forceful and directive, the insights gained in this case are of considerable interest. First Cora faces more clearly the fact of her stepfather's sexual interest in her, and the consequent reasons for his jealous behavior. Gradually, however, she comes to recognize that she has herself been encouraging his special interest in her, and that she has adopted various wiles to cause him to continue this rôle of an older "boy friend." It is of interest that as long as her insight is limited only to the step-father's behavior, she speaks of him with disgust — "He doesn't seem clean." When she is able openly to recognize her own feelings in the situation, she no longer talks in this way, but faces her very ambivalent attitude toward him. In this last interview, a few moments following the excerpt quoted, the counselor asks, "How have you felt toward him?" and Cora replies, "I guess as a Santa Claus, and yet I hate him, but I do like him, too."

In a case of this sort, where counseling treatment has revealed the conflicts which are present, the symptomatic behavior of rebellion, sex delinquency, truancy, and the like becomes more understandable. Also the importance of genuine insight is emphasized. Until Cora was able to achieve a considerable degree of insight, all attempts at treatment were futile. With this insight, she was capable of assuming a more adult rôle, and aggressive behavior was less necessary as a substitute for her conflicts.

It is evident that the insight which was gained was first of all a clearer understanding of her relationship with her stepfather, but the more dynamic insight was her recognition of the tabooed feelings within herself, and the fact that she and the stepfather had each played a part in creating the situation.

The Sequence of Developing Insights. The instances which have been given are examples of partial insight, but scarcely give an adequate reflection of the process of insight as it develops throughout a complete series of psychotherapeutic contacts. To show the variety and richness of insights which may develop, and also to point out the deeper and more significant quality of insights as the contacts continue, we may turn to the case of Barbara.

Barbara is a sixteen-year-old high-school junior, brought up in a family of very strict religious traditions. Her father is in religious work, and Barbara greatly admires him, particularly for his academic and scholarly achievements. The father is a stern individual who has never shown much affection, but who has taken some pride in Barbara's excellent school marks. Barbara's social life has been extremely limited, not because of parental restrictions, but because she herself has strongly disapproved, on religious grounds, of most adolescent social activities. During her junior year she had a "nervous breakdown" which came on her very suddenly, bringing with it fears and sensations of an overwhelming sort which were very troubling to Barbara. She was unable to attend school, and was placed in the home of relatives for a time on her doctor's advice. Some months after her "break," she came to the clinic for help. During a period of about twelve weeks the psychologist had sixteen counseling contacts with Barbara in which the girl worked out many of her problems. Following this she was able to return home and again enter school successfully. The unusually complete record of these interviews has been carefully considered, and the excerpts which follow represent most of the instances in which there seemed to be clear-cut evidence of increased insight, or in which the counselor endeavored to interpret the situation in order to bring about more insight. The progress from partial and dubious insights to more complete and assured insight is very clear. The content of the interviews cannot, of course, be given in a limited space, but the more significant issues are clearly implied in these conversations in which insight is evident.

First and Second Interviews. No instances of insight noted.

Third Interview. Talking about the heavy feeling of responsibility which she has always had, Barbara says:

"All the opportunities are at my feet if I can take advantage of them. I wish to get everything out of every opportunity."

Counselor remarked, "You have to be perfect, don't you?" She replied, "Yes. People would say, 'Everyone has to have his faults.' I didn't think so. I couldn't see any reason for that. It seemed to me I could do everything just right. Maybe, (*pausing thoughtfully*) maybe some of those ideas are too high-powered for me. Is that the reason for my break?" Counselor asked what she thought, and she felt that maybe it did have something to do with it.

Fourth Interview. Barbara has been talking of the fact that she has never had anything but a brotherly interest in boys, while a girl whom she detests had come between her and one of these boys with "sweetheart stuff." The record continues:

There was a hesitation, and then she said, "Should I tell my likes and dislikes?" Counselor said, "You get further when you talk about how you feel." She said, "There is only one person I like, a boy here in L——. I missed him when we moved to D——. Maybe he likes me. I don't know. Of course, I'm not interested in getting married and I've never thought of him like that. His name is Frank. He came in last night with Jack, the other boy who is going to teach me to dance. Frank was even more like a brother to us. He used to come to our house, and my sister and I knew him very well. I liked him and I've thought a good deal about him since leaving L——."

Counselor remarked, "Maybe those feelings have something to do with your questions about dancing and about doing your hair." "Maybe they do. Yesterday in thinking about whether to have my hair cut, I thought of it as something for Frank, but then I tried to snap that out of my mind." She laughed and giggled somewhat self-consciously. "I guess I have a tinge of love. I hate to admit it. I fight it, I guess."

Later in the same interview, after some confused remarks and a long pause, she says:

"Before all this, I believed in controlling oneself, in complete mastery of my mind and feeling." Counselor discussed this, saying that what she was gradually learning was that there was no such thing as complete control of mind and feeling; that it was rather hard for her to recognize that the part she was shutting out was a part of herself. She said, "You know that motto, 'Be yourself.' I used to hear that, and I couldn't understand it. I didn't think that I wanted to be myself, or that I knew what it meant to be yourself. I guess I have acted that way so long that I don't quite know how to be myself."

Fifth Interview. Talking about some highly ambitious intellectual plans she had discussed with one of her teachers, Barbara says:

"He calls them our heavy ideas. I call it high-powered thinking. Maybe you'll tell me that I ought to stay away from that sort of thing for a year or so." Counselor said, "Do you want me to tell you that?" "Well, I will anyway, whether you say to or not." Counselor remarked, "Good for you." Barbara went on, "I've changed so much. Why, I almost used to accuse the young people of being too 'flippy.' When I go back I'm going to go to a show once in a while, go to a movie."

Sixth Interview. Barbara, after much blocking, tells how, after one recent evening

"that brotherly relationship with Frank changed a little. He kissed me several times, and that changed things." She goes on to talk about this incident and adds, "Most of the girls run around after boys — I don't know — I have just such an unselfish feeling toward Frank. I'd do anything for him. Of course, I don't think of him for marriage, why, he isn't even eligible. I guess I think I'm in love. Still, love and marriage usually go together. I don't know. I try to figure it out mentally, but there is no mental pattern. So far as Frank being my ideal — why, of course he has good qualities, but he doesn't anywhere near measure up to my ideal. (*Pause.*) I didn't say anything about all this at first, though it is one of my most prominent feelings." Counselor said, "It isn't easy to talk about our deepest feelings, is it?"

At another point in this interview, after counselor had commended her for the progress she had been making, she said:

"I used to try to think it all out, but I couldn't do anything about it. Lately I've been doing more as I feel. I don't mean that I lose control of my emotions, but I just do more what I feel like doing. That's why I knew last time that I was going to tell you about Frank."

Later in this interview, she says that she is taking up sewing, an occupation which she had formerly scorned. Counselor remarks that she has definitely changed, adding:

"When you left home you were a little girl." Barbara replied, "Do you think so? I feel younger now." Counselor said, "I think that when you left home you were a little girl who was trying to act very, very old. Now I think that you have grown up and that what you are going to do is to try to be yourself and act your age." She smiled and said, "Maybe so. You know Wednesday after the appointment here I went all over town to find a jacket just like I wanted. Back home I liked those jackets with writing on them. All the girls wore them. They had lists of their boy friends on them and all sorts of crazy things. That was the real me, I guess, that liked those jackets. Of course, I didn't get one then. I felt it wasn't dignified. I guess I had a streak of fun in me, but I didn't want to let it out. So Wednesday I decided I would get one. I had to walk all over town and nearly blistered my feet getting it. But I finally got one." She shows the counselor a plain linen jacket which she had laid over a chair when she came in. "You see, it hasn't any writing on it yet, but the next time I come in it will have. It will have lots of writing on it." She points to the collar. "Along here it will say, 'No arms allowed.'"

Seventh Interview. Barbara has been expressing her attachment to the counselor by saying that she has now decided to be a psychologist.

"Of course, there's the fact that I'm a woman. I suppose — are there any women that get anywhere in psychology?" Counselor told her there were a number of women who held leading positions, and went on to say, "You hate to think that you're a woman, don't you?" She said, "Yes, it seems I admire masculine qualities so much that I wish I could be a young man. Maybe somebody ought to set me straight and show me that I could be a fine young woman."

Later in the interview she remarked:

"About the time of my 'break,' when the doctor told me that my thoughts and all were like a man of thirty, I felt it was sort of a pat on the back. Maybe, though, I was just trying to be masculine, when all I could do was to be feminine."

Eighth Interview. At one point Barbara says that some people used to tell her that these high ambitions of hers would die out and she would "sort of settle down."

"Is that necessary? Will I have to lose my ambitions? I think I'm doing more like I feel, but if I just do the things I feel,

where will that get me? It's all so puzzling." Counselor interpreted to her that after all the progress she has been making is
not just in doing what she feels, but in being willing to accept her
feelings. Pointed out that formerly she had always denied to
herself that she had any desire to have a good time or to be social.
She had denied that she had any sex feelings or any desire for
boy friends. She had denied that she wanted to look attractive
or to have her hair bobbed like other girls. Now she is reaching
a point where she can accept the fact that she does have all these
feelings. Of course, this does not mean that she will follow all
her impulses, but that she will not be afraid of herself or of the
feelings which she finds herself having. Ended by saying, "A
year ago you wouldn't have talked with the boy at the meeting
[an incident she had described]. You wouldn't have admitted
to yourself that you were interested in him or that you were attracted to him. Now you can realize it. Of course, what you
will do about it will not be simply to follow your impulses, but
to decide how far you want to go in following up that interest."
She laughed at this and said that she had hardly dared to admit
to herself the extent to which this boy had interested her. "But
it is true lately that I feel I want more masculine friends." The
counselor added, "And you will be willing to admit that you have
both an intellectual interest in them and also an interest in them
as boy friends."

Ninth Interview.

Barbara says, "You know I talked to you about children the
first time I came in and said I didn't like them. I want to analyze that a little." She talks about her dislike for small children,
but the fact that children seem to like her. "Maybe my dislike
has been more or less forced. Maybe I just thought I'd be that
way."

Tenth Interview. She talks with concern about her educational plans and the fact that she does not always get the very
highest marks.

Counselor remarks, "You still have to be perfect if you start
something, don't you?" She replies, "Well, I am feeling that
way some. I've always tried to be the ideal girl that you read
about. Older people always like me. I always do nice things for
them, and young children, they're always fond of me. I guess
young people are my problem." Counselor interpreted the fact
that perhaps her willingness to do things for older adults and

children was partly due to her realization that she could not get along with her own group. She said, "I guess so. I guess boys don't like that missionary-minded sort of person that I was. I was just a girl full of sweet ideas. Well, you know what I mean."

Eleventh Interview. Barbara discusses her educational plans again, laying great stress on Latin, scholarly pursuits, and the like.

Counselor mentioned that this would be one type of goal. Reminded her, however, that throughout her interviews here her greatest satisfactions have come when she has chosen to do something which would make her more like other young people — her jacket, her haircut, her plans about dancing, and the like.

She sits for a moment, and then speaks more to herself than to the counselor: "Maybe I am foolish to think of those things. Other people don't appreciate them. I don't do them just to show off. Maybe that all seems so worthy, but maybe it's all cowfodder." She stops and bursts into laughter. "Where did I ever get that word! Cowfodder!"

Twelfth Interview. In the middle of the interview she laughs and says:

"You know, about the fourth time I came in I sniffled over Frank. That must have seemed awfully silly to you. Now it just seems like nothing much at all. I feel as though I'm ready to drop him when I get back to D——. I'd like to see him once more before I go, but when I go back I'm going to forget him. You know, before I was sort of a martyr to love. I guess that's what you'd call it. Now I laugh at myself. First I thought I'd never get over it. Now I think I'll find somebody else to take his place when I get back. Still I'll always have a kind of soft spot in my heart for him." Counselor encouraged her as to the way in which she had worked through this whole problem.

Thirteenth Interview.

Barbara says, "Is there any problem I'm not quite facing squarely?" Counselor says that she would know best whether there were problems she had not fully faced. "Well, it's that marriage question. I'm still kind of mixed up on it. I don't know what I want myself. I kind of want to dodge it." She goes on to discuss in quite confused fashion her mixed attitude toward children, her fear of childbirth, her fear that marriage would interfere with a career. She hesitates for a bit and then remarks on how much she has changed. She has come across a couple of *True Story Magazines* and has really rather enjoyed them. "And then when I see someone high wide and handsome going down the street, that interests me too. I don't know myself what I want."

A moment later she remarks:

"You know, I have always liked masculine companionship, not sex so much, just the companionship of mind to mind." She hesitates and says, "Well, here's something. If I had to make a choice like I did about my hair as to whether I'd be a boy or a girl, I don't know now which I'd choose."

She talks a little about some of her experiences during her "break" and says, "Maybe because I wanted to be a boy I tried to emphasize mind. I've sort of tried to mingle ——" She stops, puzzled. "I didn't like girls. I liked boys, because a boy was what I would like to be." Counselor said, "I think that you felt that boys were above girls." She replied, "Yes, mentally superior. It seemed as though they could stand much more than girls could. I wanted to dodge being a woman. I wanted to develop that intellectual side of me. I thought I was getting there — and then I broke." Counselor said, "Perhaps you're learning now that you can be feminine and mentally superior." "Well, before I was all mind and no body. I was evading that situation just as far as I possibly could. I think that had something to do with it."

Toward the end of the interview she remarks:

"In the *American Magazine* a few months ago there was some sort of a test on masculine and feminine traits. I took it and I found that on all but one of the items I gave the feminine response. It made me so mad at the time!"

Fourteenth Interview.

"That last time I came in — you know we didn't settle too much last time — yet on the bus going back I was just thinking that it meant so much to me. I think lots of little things are coming to a head now, and some time soon I'm going to spill them all to you."

Fifteenth Interview. During this interview Barbara is talking about the problems she will face when she goes back home.

"My friends are going to ask, 'How are you?' I don't like that

I can't tell them how I feel, and if I say I'm all right, then they'll wonder why I'm not at the Young People's Society. You know, I just feel like it's a new world I'm living in, and I'm different from what I used to be. They used to ask me to pray in the Young People's Society. I don't want that saintly, pious attitude now. You know, I read the Bible for the first time in months this morning. It really seemed as though things have changed. The things I read seemed to have a new meaning for me. You know, I still aim for perfection, but it's a different sort. Before, I would read the Bible and I would find in it reasons for not dancing and not doing other things, but now it looks different to me."

About the middle of the interview Barbara says:

"You know, I've thought about that femininity thing again and I'm going to see if I can put it into words. I'm a girl. I'm going to accept it, not as fate, not in a spirit of submission, but as meant for the best. If there is a God, I think he must have meant it for the best. I can be a better woman than I can be if I try to acquire masculine desires. I can probably do a lot more good by being myself and developing my own talent rather than trying to do something different. I'm going to accept it as a challenge. I feel that I've almost lost that feeling that I wanted to be masculine. I just want to be myself. Maybe before I get through I'll really be glad I'm feminine. I'm going to learn to cook and I'm going to be a good cook and make an art out of it."

An Attempt at Analysis. It will be obvious even to the casual reader that Barbara's ways of perceiving herself have undergone a profound change during this counseling experience. If an effort is made to analyze or group these new perceptions, they seem to fall into four categories. Barbara has come to accept a more realistic view of her abilities and her ultimate achievements. She has been able to achieve an acceptance of her own inhibited social desires. She can admit her heterosexual desires. She has shifted from a complete repudiation of her feminine rôle to a rather complete acceptance of it. It helps to clarify the process through which she has gone, if the succession of self-percepts in each of these areas are listed, approximately in the girl's own terms. The reader may check the accuracy of these self-percepts by reference to the interview material quoted.

I. Barbara's views of her goals of achievement.

Third Interview. Perhaps my previous ideals were too high-powered.

Fourth Interview. I used to want complete self-control. Now I think I want to be myself.

Fifth Interview. I'm going to relinquish my too high-powered ideals.

Eighth Interview. But it is a real loss to give up my fantastic ambitions. If I am simply myself, where will that get me?

Tenth Interview. I used to want to be a "sweet," ideal girl. Now I want to be a natural young person.

Eleventh Interview. My previous goals, too lofty and too high-powered, are "cowfodder."

II. Barbara's views of her social self.

Fifth Interview. I disliked "flippy" young people. Now I admit I have some "flippy" desires.

Sixth Interview. I used to disapprove of the girls who wore undignified and silly linen jackets. Now I admit that the real me has always wanted to do the same thing.

Tenth Interview. I want to get along with other young people.

Fifteenth Interview. I'm no longer an ultra-saintly person, afraid of my social instincts. I'm very much changed.

III. Barbara's views of her heterosexual interests.

Fourth Interview. I hate sweetheart stuff. Yet truthfully, I have a tinge of love myself.

Sixth Interview. Love and marriage go together. I want love, but not marriage. Or do I?

Eighth Interview. I am interested in boys and in having boy friends. I can admit that now.

Twelfth Interview. I realize that what I've had was puppy love. Now I look forward to other contacts which will bring love.

IV. Barbara's views regarding being a woman.

Early Interviews. I dislike children. I don't want marriage. I wish I were a man, or could act like a man.

Seventh Interview. I have hated to be a woman. Maybe someone will convince me that I should be a woman.

Eighth Interview. Perhaps I like children rather than dislike them.

Thirteenth Interview. I don't want to be a woman. Still
I do. If I had my choice, I'm no longer sure. Perhaps
trying to be a man caused my breakdown. I guess I am
really quite feminine.

Fifteenth Interview. I am a woman. I am going to be a
woman. I like the idea.

Such statements are, to be sure, a crude, but possibly an
effective, way of showing the reorientation which gradually
developing insight has brought about. Or the alteration may
be described in more formal terms. During the period of her
counseling contacts Barbara has changed from a person who
feels she must be perfect, must be a man, must refrain from
many social activities, a person who dislikes any "sweetheart
stuff," to a person who can have comfortable goals of achievement, who desires social activities, looks forward to heterosexual contacts, and accepts her feminine rôle. Whether we
describe this change in terms of changed goals, changed motivation, release of repressions, or change in self-percepts, it is obvious that the change is a highly significant fact. It is a process
of sufficient dynamic potency to command our full attention.

The examples of insight which have been given thus far
indicate that its meaning to the client may be described in
different ways in different instances. It may mean the perception of new relationships between old facts, illustrated again in
Barbara's perception of the connection between her nervous
breakdown on the one hand and her ultra-lofty ideals and her
desire to be a man on the other. Or it may mean the facing
and acceptance of hitherto repressed attitudes and impulses. It
may mean a willingness to face and recognize the rôle one has
been playing. As we consider the process from the counselor's
viewpoint, other aspects of this significant chain of psychological experiences will suggest themselves.

How the Counselor Promotes the Development
of Insight

The Primary Technique. This reorientation and reorganization of the self, which has been illustrated in the case of Barbara,

is certainly the major aim and goal of counseling. It is natural that the question should be raised as to how the counselor can promote this increased self-understanding, this reorientation around new goals. The answer is bound to be a disappointing one to the overeager. The primary technique which leads to insight on the part of the client is one which demands the utmost in self-restraint on the counselor's part, rather than the utmost in action. The primary technique is to encourage the expression of attitudes and feelings, as discussed in the preceding chapter, until insightful understanding appears spontaneously. Insight is often delayed, and sometimes made impossible, by efforts of the counselor to create it or to bring it about. It is probably not delayed, and certainly never made impossible, by those interviewing approaches which encourage full expression of attitudes.

It will be noted that although other techniques are evident in the case of Barbara, techniques which we shall discuss, the most profound and helpful insights, the understandings which are most effective for reorganization, are those which she expresses spontaneously. Thus the main aim of the counselor is to assist the client to drop any defensiveness, any feeling that attitudes should not be brought into the open, any concern that the counselor may criticize or suggest or order. If this aim can be accomplished, then the client is freed to look at the total situation in its reality, without having to justify or protect himself. It is then that he can see relationships clearly, and can recognize the hitherto hidden impulses within himself.

This course of action imposes much self-restraint upon the counselor. The reason is simple. As the client reveals himself more and more fully in the counseling interviews, the counselor begins to develop insight into the client's problems. Not infrequently the major patterns of reaction are relatively clear to the counselor at the end of the first or second interview. There is the greatest temptation to most counselors, whether they are psychiatrists, psychologists, guidance counselors, or social workers, to inform the client as to his patterns, to interpret his actions and his personality to him. We have already seen

(Chapter II, page 26) the type of reception this is likely to receive. The more accurate the interpretation, the more likely it is to encounter defensive resistance. The counselor and his interpretations become something to be feared. To resist this temptation to interpret too quickly, to recognize that insight is an experience which is achieved, not an experience which can be imposed, is an important step in progress for the counselor.

Indeed, it might be said that for the less experienced counselor it is safer and more satisfactory to make use of no interpretive or special techniques for the promotion of insight. If the counselor adequately recognizes the client's attitudes, helps in the process of clarification of feelings, and promotes free expression, new insight will come of itself and can be recognized by the counselor as it occurs. There are, however, certain other types of counselor effort which seem to promote the development and increase the scope of the client's self-understanding, and these deserve our attention.

Examples of Techniques Which Clarify Relationships. Under certain conditions, it is possible to interpret to the client some of the material which he has been revealing. When the interpretation is based entirely upon statements which the client has made, and when the interpretation is merely a clarification of what the client has already perceived for himself, this type of approach can be successful. An example of this type of interpretation has already been given in the case of Barbara, in the eighth interview (pages 188-189). The counselor summarizes much of what Barbara has brought out in the interviews by pointing out that where formerly she denied that she had any social or sexual feelings, now she can accept such attitudes as part of herself. This interpretation Barbara not only accepts but expands. This acceptance is important. Unless an interpretation is fully accepted, it creates resistance and is of very doubtful value in therapy.

In order to gain a more concrete view of such counselor techniques in action we may turn to a fragment of a fourth interview with Herbert Bryan, a young man in his late twenties.[2] Mr. Bryan came to the clinic because he was suffering from a variety of neurotic complaints — physical pain which had no organic origin, lethargic and discouraged moods which made him ineffective, and a general lack of success which he blamed on his neurosis. He was a man with a brilliant philosophical mind who had read widely in psychology and used psychological terms freely and accurately. During his early interviews he discussed in highly abstract and intellectual terms the difficulties which troubled him. During the fourth interview he brought out spontaneously that whenever he felt blocked from playing "a manly, vigorous rôle," he tended to retreat into his neurotic symptoms, which were definitely satisfying in certain ways. He then reviewed all the efforts he had made in the past to rid himself of his symptoms. He goes on in the portion of the interview which is quoted below to recognize quite clearly the choice that is ahead of him — the continuance of the neurotic rôle, or the struggle toward normal adjustment. The reader will note how the counselor aids in the development of insight by recognizing clearly the feelings which Mr. Bryan has been expressing, by clarifying the choice with which he is faced, and also by interpreting some of the relationships which exist in his situation. The recording is phonographic.

    C. That brings you up to the present, where you ——
    S. Yes, where I made the decision to come to you. As I mentioned to you before, I felt that the efforts on my part were not wholehearted, otherwise — otherwise they would have worked, and that what I was doing was just a sop to the minority,[3] as it were. So I believed that a trained man such as yourself could point the way to a key whereby I could make my change.
    C. At least a part of that key, in what you're saying today, seems to lie in a pretty clear recognition of the choice that you are making. I mean, you certainly have brought out much more plainly the contrast between going ahead, which involves responsibility and involves both satisfactions and dissatisfac-

---

  [2] This case is reproduced in full in Part IV of this book. The segment given here may be read in context on page 351.

  [3] He has previously spoken of the "minority" in himself, the healthy impulses, and the "majority," the neurotic impulses.

tions, or slipping back into the easier possibility of simply living with your symptoms.

S. In the last analysis, it comes down to this, that I enjoy the neurotic symptoms more but respect them less.

C. Yes, that's a good way of ——

S. Or to use other words, I suppose I'm beginning to value self-respect more now, otherwise I wouldn't give a damn.

C. That's right. That's, uh — you talked when you came in the first time about the fact that here was this picture; now, where could the motivation come from to change it? Well, a large measure of the motivation to change it comes from that much clearer recognition on your own part of what aspect of this whole situation you wish to preserve on a permanent basis.

S. I have a subtle philosophic way of cheating myself on that, though, that I ought to mention. Of course, as a philosopher, I know that there is no way of evaluating values. I know that any attempt to say that one set of values is superior to another set of values always resolves itself into one of two things. It either is a logical tautology, where you repeat the same idea in different words and say, "Well, these values are better because so-and-so," and what you're really saying is that they are better because they're better; or you come back to some sort of a fiat — either a divine fiat — "These values are better because God says they are," or some sort of a naturalistic fiat, which of course are philosophically not provable. So that when I find myself, uh — I find myself valuing the intellectually more desirable values, that is, when I find myself valuing the good rôle, another part of me says, "Well, you can't prove that that set of values is better." I have such a philosophical fetish that if I could prove — if there were some cosmic yardstick, some sort of a cosmic absolute, uh — comparable to the religious person's absolute trust in God, you see, uh — then I could have a philosophic proof that one set of values was definitely better than the other, but this way I know that I cannot have such a philosophic proof, or at least I haven't run across it. We can never prove values — we always have to assume them. I think as a philosopher you'll have to agree with me.

C. I don't know whether it's as a philosopher, but I certainly would agree with you that, in situations of this kind, I don't think there is any proof that could be advanced that would prove one set of values rather than the other.

S. Nothing out in the universe. It all must lie within ourselves.

C. It comes right back to the naked self pretty much, doesn't it? Here are two general roads; which do you prefer? It comes right down to a personal and probably quite unphilosophical choice.

S. Yes. In other words, I can't — I can't look to the cosmos and say, "Now, which of the two roads do you approve of?" I can't ——

C. You can, and some people do, but it's doubtful if that is what really settles it.

S. Yes, I imagine that when a person does make a change they oftentimes think that they're doing it for God, but they're really doing it for themselves. Well (*thoughtfully*), perhaps I don't need anything out in the cosmos, then.

C. Well, there's just the chance that you've got enough within yourself.

S. Yes, that's a good point there. The — uh, my philosophic searching for something in the cosmos to justify my taking one of the two roads was really searching for something that I knew I would never find.

C. M-hm.

S. Because I had the intellect to know that I would never find a cosmic command to take a certain path. And then I allowed myself to utilize the absence of such a cosmic command as a rationalization for my own lack of motivation.

C. Nothing wrong with your understanding of yourself when you let it loose.

S. Well, I guess that's about the first thing — know thyself.

C. Right.

S. That's what I'm going to work on now — is, to not seek a proof for my values, but go ahead and assume the ones that I can have the most self-respect and satisfaction for.

C. The ones that you most deeply want. I think that it is a real choice, and different individuals take different roads. There are, as you know, certain satisfactions connected with — well, with evading life, with building up things that make it unnecessary to go out and fight some of these battles and assume some of these responsibilities and so on. Some people choose that road. On the other hand, there certainly are satisfactions connected with the tougher road too.

S. I think that my religious conditioning has made me sort of dependent on some kind of a cosmic sign. Originally, I had to depend upon God's approval. As I lost a belief in a personalized sort of deity, then I sought signs from nature and other things like that. But I must learn to assume my values without the justification of the outside. That boils down to what I really want. (*Pause.*) I think it's a pretty close battle.

    C. I think so too.   To be quite frank with you, I think so too.
    S. It isn't just a case of Rotarian optimism and saying, "Well,
now my better judgment is going to have its way."
    C. No.
    S. I don't think it's that.
    C. No.   I think — uh, I think your whole experience shows
that it's a very close choice indeed.

    This is a good example of the cooperation between counselor
and counselee which produces the deepest insight.   The first
counselor response from this excerpt involves the recognition
of feeling which has been expressed earlier in the interview, but
it also involves a clearer interpretation of the fact that the
client is facing a choice, with satisfactions resulting from either
decision.   Being accepted, this leads to the highly significant
realization on Mr. Bryan's part that he enjoys the neurotic
symptoms more, but respects them less, a beautiful statement
of the basic conflict between infantile and adult desires.   As the
counselor reiterates the notion that he is faced with a choice,
the client retreats somewhat, pointing out that nothing can
prove that the road which makes for growth is better than the
road which escapes into neurotic symptoms.   When this somewhat discouraged feeling is accepted and recognized, the client
gradually comes to the deepest insight of all, that perhaps the
forces which will make the choice lie within himself — that he
has himself the capacity for growth and independence.
    Here is the type of counselor response which increases insight.
No interpretation is made which is not accepted by the client.
Most of the counselor responses merely recognize and reinforce
the insights which the client has already achieved.   Note that
when this process is followed, the insight gained is immediately
reapplied in a new situation, as when Mr. Bryan faces the fact
that looking for "cosmic proof" was merely a rationalization
which aided in putting off the real choice.   Note also that the
counselor makes no attempt to weight the choice for the client,
but points out that there are satisfactions either in being
neurotic and evading difficulties, or in being more adult.   As
was pointed out earlier, real therapy relies for its motivation

upon the impulses toward growth and normality which exist in every individual. Unless those are strong enough to make the positive choices possible when those choices are clearly seen, it is doubtful that therapeutic success can be hoped for.

Since the techniques which the counselor uses to promote insight are subtle ones, and the line between successful and unsuccessful interpretation is difficult to draw, another example of counselor procedures will be given. In this instance, the counselor is more hasty, does not wait for the spontaneous expression of insight, and tends toward more direct interpretation. Consequently, the total outcome is less satisfactory, and while insight is almost certainly increased to some extent, there is more question as to whether the insight is genuine and lasting.

Paul, the student from whose record we have quoted before, spent a portion of his second interview discussing the fact that he had inherited the abilities he does not want — musical and literary abilities — and few of the abilities he wants. He hates his musical and literary interests because they are concerned with the emotions. In his boyhood he was ridiculed and humiliated for having these "sissy" interests. The interview continues (phonographic recording, with items numbered for easy reference):

1. *C*. You feel that you'd be a lot happier if you were just like the other fellows and not emotional.

2. *S*. That's right. Of course, I'd like to be — not, not experience these fears. (*Pause.*) I'd like to be calm and be clear-thinking in all situations.

3. *C*. Instead of those things you find yourself to be somewhat emotional.

4. *S*. I go haywire! (*Laugh, followed by pause.*)

5. *C*. You've thought a lot about that. What is your ideal person?

6. *S*. Uh, well, some scientist. That is what I consider an ideal person, preferably a physical scientist, in chemistry or physics or an engineer, one who — one who serves society by constructing, or by making things more convenient. I like everything modern.

7. *C*. Someone who deals only in things, and not in emotions.

8. *S*. That's right, something tangible.

9. *C.* So you'd really like to solve this difficulty by being someone very different from yourself.

10. *S.* Yes. That's why I'm in engineering college. I have an opportunity to — well, just to experiment with myself and see actually what talents I do have in that direction. They're not so bad, but I lack some — some of the very fundamental things that a good engineer should have; that is, being calm, sticking right to it, and forgetting about things that have come up. A good engineer is not emotional, that's about one of the worst things he could —— No person who is emotional is a good engineer.

11. *C.* So that in some respects you've gone into engineering because you felt it would be awfully good discipline for you, is that right? Make you stop being emotional?

12. *S.* That's right.

13. *C.* It was that, perhaps, rather than being interested in engineering.

14. *S.* Well, it was mingled with a certain genuine interest. There was some, that's true. But it was largely due to that, exactly what I said, to a considerable extent.

15. *C.* You don't suppose that part of your trouble is that now you're wondering whether you want to be your real self. Could that be part of it?

16. *S.* Uh, what's that?

17. *C.* Well, I just wondered. You're trying so hard to be some other fellow, aren't you?

18. *S.* Yeah, because I'm not satisfied with myself.

19. *C.* You feel that the self that you are isn't worth being.

20. *S.* Yeah, that's right, and unless you can change my mind about that, then I'll continue thinking along the same line.

21. *C.* (*Laughing.*) Why, that almost sounds as though you were wishing that somebody would change your mind about it.

22. *S.* (*Very soberly.*) Yeah. Because I don't know how I can solve it the other way.

23. *C.* In other words, you're finding it a pretty tough proposition to try to be a calm, unemotional engineer when really you're something quite different.

24. *S.* Right! Yeah, that is a very tough proposition. I find it impossible, and I hate the idea that it's impossible.

25. *C.* And you hate it partly because you feel there's nothing worth while about this real self of yours.

26. *S.* Yes.

27. *C.* What are some of the things your real self would like to do?

28. *S*. Oh, let's see. Well — uh, I told you I was interested in mathematics. That's one thing. Also, I was interested in anthropology. At the same time, I was interested in music and in — well, now, I used to like novels, but I don't care for them any more, but — I would like — I think I have a gift for writing, too, and I'm ashamed of those gifts.

29. *C*. You're ashamed of those two, and your interest in anthropology you used to prove to yourself that you're no good.

30. *S*. (*Laughing*.) I've been tremendously influenced by a certain anthropologist, Hooton. (*Pause*.)

31. *C*. Well, I think you're up against a very hard problem and one that people often have to face, at one point or another: whether they're going to be themselves, trying to discover what that self really is, or whether they're going to try to be three other fellows. (*Very long pause*.)

32. *S*. Well, I haven't decided to be myself.

33. *C*. No, I realize that. As I say, that's the thing you are still very much up in the air about. As a matter of fact, you don't want to be yourself.

34. *S*. That's right. (*Pause*.)

35. *C*. Still, you're not quite sure that you want to be an engineer, either.

36. *S*. Well, it's —— No, I don't think I can be one, not the way I am right now. I'm not getting anywhere.

In considering the counseling techniques in the above interview, it will be noted first that there is no instance of spontaneous insight — no point at which Paul himself recognizes, without aid, some new aspect or pattern of his situation. Any statement on his part which seems to involve insight is merely an acceptance of a relationship which the counselor has pointed out. (See, for example, Paul's responses numbered 22, 24, 26.) We might make a rough classification of the counselor's techniques into three types. In the first place, insight has been aided by some responses which endeavor, not always with entire success, to recognize and reflect feelings which Paul has expressed. (See items numbered 1, 3, 7, 19, 33, 35.) In other instances, the counselor has suggested relationships which may or do exist between feelings Paul has expressed at different times. For example, Paul has condemned himself for being emotional and has painted as his ideal the physical scientist who deals in tangible things.   The counselor points out the possible relationship by saying, "So you'd really like to solve this problem by being someone very different from yourself."   (This is item 9.   For other examples of this technique see items 11, 23, 25, 29, 31.)   A third method which the counselor has used is to suggest interpretations of Paul's behavior which are not based upon attitudes already brought into the interview situation. For example, "You don't suppose that part of your trouble is that now you're wondering whether you want to be your real self.   Could that be part of it?"   While it is likely that this statement is to some extent an accurate interpretation, it is not based upon material which Paul has been ready to express.   It gains a certain type of acceptance, but it is doubtful that this acceptance goes very deep, and doubtful that it will prove a dynamic for change.   (See also items 13 and 17 for similar techniques.)[4]

The Use of Techniques Which Clarify Relationships.   We may summarize certain of the principles which govern the techniques we have been discussing in the following way.   Insight and self-understanding are most effective when they arise spontaneously. If the counselor has been successful in freeing the client to look clearly at himself and his problems, the most valuable type of insight will develop on the client's own initiative.   The counselor may aid this process by reformulating insight already achieved, by clarifying the new understandings at which the client has arrived.   He may be of assistance in helping the client to explore and recognize the choices, the possible courses of action, which lie before him.   The counselor may, in addition, suggest relationships or patterns of reaction which seem to be evident in material which the client has freely stated.   To the

[4] Four examples which have been cited constitute something of a continuum in techniques of interpretation   In the case of Sam (Chapter II, page 26), interpretation is very direct, formulated entirely by the counselor, definitely resisted by the client. In the case of Mr. Bryan (pages 197–200), insight is largely spontaneous, interpretation is at a minimum, and the insight is genuine.   The cases of Paul and Barbara (pages 185–192) would fall in between, the techniques in Paul's case bearing some resemblance to those in Sam's, while the counselor's approach in Barbara's case comes closer to that in Mr. Bryan's.

extent that these patterns or relationships are accepted and re-applied by the client, they no doubt represent added elements of insight. The counselor will do well to refrain, however, from giving interpretations of the client's behavior, the elements of which are based, not on the client's expressed feelings, but on the counselor's judgment of the situation. Such interpretations tend to be resisted and may delay the achievement of genuine insight.

Some such formulation as the above would seem to represent the present state of our knowledge in regard to counseling techniques for promoting insight. These statements need careful evaluation by many workers, evaluation based on study of the development of improved insight in actual counseling situations.

Some Cautions. Before leaving this topic, some cautions may well be given, particularly for the benefit of the less experienced counselor. For clarity, these may be listed.

1. When the counselor feels unsure of himself, interpretation of any sort is best avoided.

2. In any interpretation, it is best to use the client's terms and symbols. If Barbara sees her conflict in terms of bobbing or not bobbing her hair, or if Paul sees his difficulty as between his emotional self and his scientific desires, those are the terms for the counselor to use. Acceptance is more ready and more genuine if the symbols are those which the client has already been using in his own thinking.

3. It is always best to deal with attitudes already expressed. To interpret unexpressed attitudes is definitely dangerous.

4. Nothing is gained by arguing an interpretation. If an interpretation is not accepted, the nonacceptance is the important fact. The interpretation should be dropped.

5. If genuine insight has been gained, the client will spontaneously see its application in new areas. If this evidence is not forthcoming, the counselor can be quite sure that he, and not the client, is the one who has achieved insight. This is not the desired goal.

6. After the client has achieved some particularly vital new

insight, the counselor should be prepared to observe a temporary relapse.   To recognize one's shortcomings or the infantile
nature of one's reactions is a painful procedure, even though it
has been gradual.   Having taken such a step, the client tends to
recoil from it and is likely to drop back into conversation which
is reminiscent of early interviews, relating over again the
difficulties with which he is faced, the seeming impossibility of
making progress, and a certain amount of dissatisfaction with
the counseling aid which he has had.   It is highly important
that the counselor should simply recognize his discouraged feelings and accept them, rather than attempt to argue him back
into the insightful attitudes which he had achieved.   If the
counselor will be patient and understanding, the client will soon
give ample evidence that this is but a temporary retreat from
the struggle involved in growth toward maturity.   Barbara,
after having achieved some highly significant insights into herself and having made some important decisions in the direction
of progress, relapses in the fifth interview into complaints.   "To
tell the truth, I haven't felt so well since I started all this.   I felt
best the first week I came to see you.   Since last Saturday I've
been feeling quite miserable."   This whole interview is relatively unproductive and shows evidence that Barbara is feeling
sorry for herself.   But in the following interviews she again
goes ahead.   This type of irregular advance is very common in
therapy.

WHAT IS INSIGHT?

Having examined various interview situations in which the
development of insight is evident, we may now return to the
question of what, specifically, is meant by the term.   Various
phrases have been used by different writers in discussing insight.   It involves the reorganization of the perceptual field.
It consists in seeing new relationships.   It is the integration of
accumulated experience.   It signifies a reorientation of the self.
All these statements would seem to be true.   All lay sound
emphasis upon the fact that insight is essentially a new way of

perceiving.   There appear to be several types of perception which we group together as insight.

The Perception of Relationships.   In the first place, there is the perception of the related nature of previously known facts. Mrs. L., for example, is well aware of the struggle she has had in disciplining Jim.   She tells of her own hostile feelings toward him.   She becomes aware, through talking of the situation, of the fact that he does many things to gain attention.   Then comes the perception of these elements in a new relationship — she has helped to create his problem by concentrating upon correction to the exclusion of bestowing any affection.   She has come to see these facts in a new relationship, a new configuration, a new gestalt.

We are familiar with this type of phenomenon in the intellectual and perceptual realm.   It often occurs in the solution of a puzzle.   Various elements have been observed.   Suddenly they are perceived in a new relationship which provides the solution. Sometimes this experience is called an "Aha!" experience, because of the sudden flash of understanding which accompanies it.   Evidently this type of perception is possible in counseling and therapy only when the individual is freed from defensiveness through the process of catharsis.   It is only in such a state of emotional release that a reorganization of the perceptual field can take place.

Why is it that we cannot save time by telling the client these relationships, instead of waiting for him to arrive at this new perception himself?   Experience indicates, as has been pointed out, that this intellectual approach is futile; but why is it futile? The usual answer is that emotional as well as intellectual acceptance is needed.   Precisely what this means from a psychological point of view is not as yet entirely clear.   We perhaps see a parallel in the intellectual sphere.   To be told that a certain cloud looks "like a discouraged old man with a long nose" is practically meaningless until we can perceive the cloud in that way ourselves.   Thus we cannot transfer perceptions even in such a simple and concrete situation, where such a

transfer is desired by both parties.   It becomes easier to understand why, in the realm of emotionalized attitudes, where the
new perceptions are likely to be unflattering, where defense
reactions are very easily aroused, any transfer of perception
from counselor to client is a process filled with difficulty.   It is
then evident that the spontaneous development of these new
perceptions is likely to be the most rapid road to insight.   Nevertheless, there are many unanswered questions here, and experimental investigations of changes in self-perception, in the
field of emotionalized attitudes, are urgently needed.

The Acceptance of Self.   A second element in this process of
insight is the acceptance of the self, or, to put it in perceptual
terms, the perception of the related nature of all impulses.   The
accepting atmosphere of the counseling situation makes it much
easier for the individual to recognize all attitudes and impulses.
There is not the usual need to deny those feelings which are
socially unacceptable, or which are not in conformity with the
ideal self.   Consequently, Cora can come to recognize that she
has had some sexually tinged courtship attitudes toward her
stepfather.   Barbara can admit that she has wanted to be
social, undignified, and silly, although these impulses conflict
with her ideal.   Mr. Bryan can face the fact that he has had
satisfactions out of his neurotic suffering.   The client can see
the relationship between his own self, as he has usually thought
of it, and these less worthy, less acceptable impulses.   He is thus
able to bring about an integration of his accumulated experience.   He becomes a much less divided person, much more of a
functioning unit, in which every feeling and action has its admitted relation to every other feeling and action.

The Element of Choice.   There is a further element involved
in insight which seems to have been little recognized.   Genuine
insight includes the positive choice of more satisfying goals.
When the neurotic sees clearly the choice between his present
satisfactions and the satisfactions of adult behavior, he tends to
prefer the latter.   When Mrs. L. sees clearly the satisfactions

she has been obtaining through punishing her son, and the satisfactions she might gain through a more comfortable and affectionate relationship, she prefers the latter. When Barbara
perceives clearly both the satisfactions she has obtained from
striving to become a man, and the satisfactions she might
achieve by becoming a woman, she prefers the latter. Therapy
can only help an individual to find increased satisfactions, to
adopt a course of action which is in the long run more rewarding. All too often the counselor acts as though he were endeavoring to force the client to give up satisfactions. This is quite
impossible, unless more meaningful rewards are substituted.

It is this act of choice which has been termed "the creative
will." If one implies that this term signifies some mysterious
new force which enters into the situation, then there is nothing
in our knowledge of therapy to justify such a supposition. If
one limits the term to the kind of choice which always occurs
when the individual is faced with two or more ways of satisfying
his needs, then the phrase may have some meaning.

Let us restate this matter in a somewhat different fashion.
The maladjusted person has adopted some type of behavior
reaction which brings satisfaction — not complete satisfaction
and contentment, but some type of gratification of his basic
needs. Because he is unhappy and threatened by others or by
circumstance, he cannot consider clearly or objectively the
alternative courses of action which may offer less in the way of
immediate gratification, but more in long-time satisfactions.
Like Hamlet he finds that the situation

> ... puzzles the will,
> And makes us rather bear those ills we have
> Than fly to others that we know not of.

It is the fact that the counseling relationship is a releasing, non-
threatening relationship which makes it possible for him to consider his choices with greater objectivity and select those which
offer the deepest satisfaction. It is here that the therapist finds
himself in league with powerful forces — biological and social —
which tend to make growth and adulthood a rewarding type of
satisfaction. That they are generally more rewarding than in-

fantilism or escape from growth is the one fact which gives therapy its hope of success.

Still another aspect of this choice might be recognized. In counseling, insight generally involves a choice between goals which give immediate and temporary satisfaction, and those which offer delayed, but more permanent, satisfactions. In this respect, the type of "creative will" which acts upon the situation is no different from the choice exercised by the child who decides to forego the immediate ice-cream cone in order to save his nickels for the prized roller skates. He chooses the course which gives him the greater satisfaction, even though that satisfaction is delayed. Thus, Barbara gains immediate satisfaction out of self-approbation as she condemns other young people for being frivolous, undignified, and social. She has the satisfaction of considering herself much more nearly perfect than they. When able to face the choice freely, however, without defensiveness, she definitely prefers the satisfactions which will come from being one of the group and engaging in social activities. She makes this choice in spite of her recognition that the first steps in this process of socialization will be difficult and painful and that the rewards will be delayed. Or, in the case of Mr. Bryan, the client sees clearly enough the satisfactions of escaping life and responsibility through his neurotic symptoms. Yet, after considerable uncertainty, he chooses the course of adult development, not for its immediate, but for its long-time satisfactions.

An understanding of this third element of self-understanding will add finality to the conclusion that insight must be earned and achieved by the client, and cannot be given to him by educative means or by a directive type of approach. It involves choices of a sort which no one can possibly make for the client. If the counselor fully recognizes this limitation and can stand by with an understanding attitude, clarifying the issues, but making no effort to influence the choice, he thereby greatly increases the probability that the choice will be constructive, and that positive actions will be taken to put this constructive choice into effect.

POSITIVE ACTIONS RESULTING FROM INSIGHT

As insight is developing, as the decisions are made which orient the client about new goals, these decisions tend to be implemented by actions which move the client in the direction of the new goals.   Such actions are, indeed, a test of the genuineness of the insights which have been attained.   If the new orientation is not spontaneously reinforced by action, it is obvious that it has not deeply involved the personality.

In actual counseling practice, such positive steps are almost invariable concomitants of insight.   The counselor should not be deceived by the fact that, from an objective point of view, they may be insignificant.   It is their direction which is important.   A striking example of the kind of action which is meant may be gleaned from the case of Barbara.   It is especially revealing, because the record gives a clear picture of this action from the time when it was a step which Barbara could not take, through the period when it was a fearful struggle, to the actual carrying out of the action, and the satisfactions obtained in having moved toward her newly chosen goal.   All this deeply significant emotional process revolved about the matter of bobbing her hair — an issue which to those unfamiliar with counseling might seem to have no possible meaning of any lasting sort. It will be best to let the record speak for itself, with all the material which bears on this minute, but deeply important, decision gathered together from the various interviews with Barbara.

> *Second Interview.* Barbara says, "About this narrow-minded stuff.   Before my break I went to the movies a few times with my sister.   Recently, though, I've gone more.   I think it's all right.   Now I wear some make-up.   I've had my hair done up too.   It gives me something to do and think about.   I've wondered about having it cut off.   My church believes that women should have long hair.   My mother wants me to keep it long, but still I wonder if it would make me feel sixteen rather than sixty.   If it would make me feel better, I would be willing to have it cut off.
>
> "I used to think I would improve suddenly.   I would lay on

the bed and think, 'Perhaps in five minutes something will click in my mind and I'll be all well.' Now I realize it will come slowly."

Counselor agreed with this and said that it would all be made up of decisions, such as decisions about cutting her hair.

"If I had to decide, I would leave it long. But if it would help me, I'm sure my mother would be willing to have it cut." She repeats this idea in different ways. Counselor says, "You wish that I would decide it for you, don't you?" She replied, "Well, if it would help me, I would be willing to have it cut."

Third Interview. "About my hair. I haven't decided yet whether to have it cut off or not. Do I have to decide that soon?" Counselor laughed and pointed out that she was still trying to get him to decide the matter one way or another. "Well, I'm going to a beauty parlor and I'm going to get advice as to how I would look best. I think it would look better with my hair cut. It would make me look different, but I don't know whether I want that different feeling. It would make me look younger, but still I feel quite old." Counselor pointed out that she had a hard time deciding whether she wanted to be young or not.

Fourth Interview. At the beginning of the interview she said, "Yesterday I had one of those terrible times again. I was out on the field playing ball, and I just felt that awful feeling that I have described before. It's terrible. (*Pause.*)

"I guess I'm going to have my hair cut." She went on to tell of her visit to the beauty parlor and the way she thought she would have her hair cut. "Maybe that's one of the reasons I had those feelings. It was terrible. Nobody knew that I was having any trouble. I went on as though nothing had happened."

Fifth Interview. Again her first remarks were about her hair. "I've heard from my father and mother. It's all right with them to have my hair cut, but I was going to have it cut anyway. It's funny, I've thought and thought about it, and it seemed awfully hard to decide when I first came to see you, but now I'm just going to have it cut. I am going to see how it makes me feel."

Sixth Interview. "Ever since I've had my hair cut I've wanted to come for this appointment." She apologized for the way her hair looked and the fact that it was not as well trained as it would be in time. "I've wanted to dress like a little girl for this time. See, I have ankle socks on and the widest skirt I could get." She got up to demonstrate her swing skirt. "And I just wanted to be more youthful. I feel so different. I felt so good yesterday." She runs her hand through her hair, curling up the ends with a very feminine gesture.

In this instance, as in other similar therapeutic actions, the client is fully aware of the fact that the contemplated steps have symbolic value far beyond their objective importance.   Barbara first hopes that the counselor will take the responsibility for deciding that she should be younger, gayer, more social. Then in the third interview she decides tentatively to explore this possibility herself, but basically she still is not sure whether she wants the different adjustment to life that she knows it would symbolize.   Between the third and fourth interviews she makes her decision, but it is so difficult for her that her old neurotic symptoms return in full force.   It has been a real struggle, and she feels discouraged.   By the time of the fifth interview she has assimilated this decision and feels comfortable about it.   In the following interview she has taken the positive step, and fully exploits the meaning that it has for her.   It means she will be youthful, feminine, less repressed, a different person, oriented toward a different goal.   It cannot be doubted that the satisfactions accompanying this action, the increased confidence in her ability to direct herself toward healthy goals, will be a significant force in carrying her forward in other areas demanding decision.

Since we have also followed the treatment of Mrs. L. in some detail, it may be well to give one further example of such self-initiated action from the counseling contacts with this mother. During one interview she is complaining about Jim's behavior, though not so violently as had been her custom during the first interviews.   She then goes ahead in the following excerpt to tell of his disorderliness, and to relate how impossible it would be for her to overlook this attention-getting device on his part.   Gradually she admits to herself that she might be able to overlook such behavior, but that it would be very difficult.   In the following interview, she tells of having tried this policy, and of having found it very successful.   Interestingly enough, she still hesitates to adopt full responsibility for the step, and refers to it as the counselor's suggestion.   The two portions of the record involving these gradations in positive action are as follows.

She went on to say some more things about the children doing things which annoy her and made the remark that it is "pretty hard on Mama." Then she asked, "Should I just let it go?" I replied, "What might happen if you did?" She said, "Well, he got dressed all right this morning, but usually he comes down-stairs for breakfast, on Saturdays, in his bathrobe. Then he goes back upstairs and gets something to read and goes back to bed. And he usually gets all the quilts and covers off all the beds and drags them around and gets them in one pile and tears up the upstairs in general. And I just get after him and try to get him to get dressed and straighten up the place." And I said, "He evidently gets some satisfaction at your reaction to the situation."

She asked, "Well, what would you do? I hate to have my house all littered up all morning." I asked something about it being his own room that he played in. And she said, "No, it's the whole upstairs. It isn't just his own room that gets messed up." I said, "What are some of the things you might do in the situation?" She replied, "Well, I might just let him do it and not say anything to him. Just let him have the house all messed up." (Her tone implied that that solution wouldn't suit her at all, and that if she tried it she would feel considerably abused.) I replied, "But you would still feel pretty strongly about it." She replied that she wouldn't like it very well. "He's too big to do things like that. He's just too old to do some of the things that he does." I said, "Well, sometimes people don't seem to act according to their age." And she said, "Yes, I guess that's right."

She paused, and I asked, "How might he *feel* about situations in which he does things that you don't like? You know how *you* feel — pretty upset, perhaps angry about it, perhaps somewhat hostile toward him because he does do so many things that you think that he shouldn't." She looked very thoughtful for a moment and said, "Well, I don't know quite how to say it — I don't know what word would be right. But I believe he feels sort of devilish or triumphant; has sort of a 'ha-ha' feeling when he is doing things that he knows I don't like. Now, I may be wrong about that." I said, "But it does seem to you that he might get that sort of feeling from it." And she replied, "Yes, I do think that must be the way he feels about it." From the way she looked I judged that she hadn't before thought of an-alyzing or thinking of what his feelings might be in such situa-tions.

As she sat thinking about it I said, "The whole thing on the part of both of you seems to be pretty much mixed up with your feelings about it." Then she said, "Well, now, maybe if I would just let it go and let him act that way and not get after him —— But you can't imagine what it is like to have him go around like that, just getting the whole house messed up, keeping it in a mess all the time." I said, "Yes, of course it would be hard to let him do that." I felt that her saying "maybe if I would let it go" was much more of an acceptance of the idea than the time before when she said, in tones with much more feeling, that she might try that. She hadn't then seemed to have accepted the thought that she really could. This time she seemed to be really considering it and felt more willing to take the consequences.

In the following contact she indicates that she has initiated the type of handling which she has so doubtfully discussed above.

During the interview she said, "I tried what you suggested last time, when you asked what would happen if I just didn't say anything about Jim not getting dressed and downstairs on time in the morning. This morning Marjorie came downstairs and had her breakfast. I didn't say anything to him about coming down, and when I walked through his room I didn't pay any attention to his having the covers all piled up. Then when Marjorie was about through with her breakfast, here he came, all dressed and ready for his breakfast." It seemed that she was quite pleased with this, and I merely recognized that feeling.

The counselor who has made directive suggestions to clients (and what counselor has not?) will perceive the sharp differences between the type of positive action here described and the grudging, incomplete type of action which follows a direct suggestion, in those cases where the suggestion is not disregarded entirely. In response to direct suggestion and advice the client delays taking action. He carries out part of the suggestion, but not the crucial portion. He carries it out in such a way as to defeat the counselor's purpose. He carries it out halfheartedly, and then reports its failure. All this contrasts very sharply with the type of action taken by the client who has been freed by the counseling situation to a point where he can attain insight and formulate actions in line with his newly chosen goals. Here is no halfheartedness, nor action taken only after prodding.

The step is taken in clear-cut fashion. The client is pleased with the results. Frequently the counselor is given no inkling beforehand. The client simply takes the positive action and reports it. It is as though the client were saying, "I am able to handle this by myself. I am working toward my new goal. I am enjoying becoming independent of your help." This attitude is one of the real achievements of therapy.

It is because these positive actions have this meaning of a growing independence that their full significance should be recognized by the counselor. It is as the client sees these new actions clearly as his first move toward new goals, that he can begin to contemplate the end of the therapeutic relationship without fear, and can find increasing satisfactions in his own independence. It is a consideration of this question which leads us into the whole problem of constructively closing the counseling relationship, and this we shall discuss in the following chapter.

SUMMARY

The free release of the client's feelings and emotionalized attitudes in an accepting type of counseling relationship leads inevitably to insight. This development of insight comes for the most part spontaneously, though cautious and intelligent use of interpretive techniques can increase the scope and the clarity of such self-understanding.

The client's insight tends to develop gradually, and proceeds in general from less to more significant understandings. It involves the new perception of relationships previously unrecognized, a willingness to accept all aspects of the self, and a choice of goals, now clearly perceived for the first time.

Following these new perceptions of self, and this new choice of goals, come self-initiated actions which move toward achieving the new goals. These steps are of the most significant sort for growth, though they may relate only to minor issues. They create new confidence and independence in the client, and thus reinforce the new orientation which has come about through increased insight.

CHAPTER VIII

The Closing Phases

As THE client gains in the insight and self-understanding which have been discussed in the last chapter, there comes a definite change in the quality of the counseling relationship. The client is under less strain. He has a more confident approach to the problems he is facing. He less frequently endeavors to become dependent upon the counselor, and gives more evidence of working with him. The relationship becomes a more genuinely cooperative one, in which both counselor and counselee are discussing the next steps which will achieve greater independence for the latter. Because the client has developed an ability to accept himself as he is, he is less defensive and can more constructively evaluate suggestions and advice, though it is doubtful if much is gained by giving him suggestions, even at this stage of treatment. He is, not infrequently, in need of information to aid him in reaching his new goals, and the counselor may be able to supply this knowledge, or may be able to indicate other sources to which he may turn.

THE EXTENT OF RE-EDUCATION

It is during these closing phases of counseling that a certain amount of re-education takes place. This term has been widely used in discussions of counseling, and perhaps overemphasized. It should be pointed out that in the client-centered type of therapy which this book describes there is no attempt to solve the client's problems through re-education. It is not expected that his problems will all be solved through counseling, nor is this assumed to be a desirable goal. Satisfying living consists, not in a life without problems, but in life with a unified purpose and a basic self-confidence which gives satisfaction in the continual attack upon problems. It is this unified purpose, this courage to meet life and the obstacles which it presents, that is gained through therapy. Consequently, the client takes from his counseling contacts, not necessarily a neat solution for each of his problems, but the ability to meet his problems in a constructive way. It follows that re-education is not, as has been sometimes supposed, the retraining of the individual in all aspects of life. It is rather a sufficient practice in the application of the new insights to build up the client's confidence and enable him to carry on in healthy fashion without the support of the counseling relationship.

These re-educative experiences are, for the most part, the achievement of an expanding insight and the multiplication of the positive steps already initiated. Thus a graduate student whose life has always been dominated by an eccentric father, and who has come to understand this fact and to choose a more independent course of action, finds to her delight that she can actually discuss with her father, without scenes, tears, or explosions, her plan to purchase a car for herself out of her own earnings. She obtains a tremendous increase in confidence in her own adulthood out of her handling of this situation. A married man, whose many difficulties have revolved in part around his relationship with his oversolicitous and demanding mother, finds that he can tolerate a visit from his mother without being upset and that he can oppose his mother's wishes in a healthy and constructive manner without arousing antagonism. He derives much pleasure from this fact. A student, who has been completely blocked by indecision, finds rather suddenly that he may have to take a special examination in order to get into the field of training which he has at last selected. "But I didn't do what I used to do — run around and ask people what to do. I just went around and got the facts." He feels great satisfaction in his more self-reliant, more mature handling of his situation. A man who has tried to avoid some of his basic conflicts by accepting very inferior jobs gains much insight into his own behavior. He comes in during one of the closing interviews and says: "I took the bull by the horns. I walked into the office of the general manager and talked to him. We talked for two hours. I told him, like I've told you, how I'd gotten into the manual labor end of it, how I'd had a hard time making up my mind what I wanted to do, and all that. I explained that I didn't want to keep on working with my hands, but with my head. He seemed to understand, and suggested that he might be able to get me an accounting job. I have a call today to go back in and see him about it." It is this type of re-education in actual experience which is most vital, and which forms a significant portion of the closing interviews in a counseling relationship.

One more example might be given. A student who has struggled with the problem of vocational choice has come to understand his earlier confusion and has made a clear-cut choice, deciding to go into the Commerce course for business training. In one of the later interviews he implements this new insight, and amazes the counselor by giving himself a special assignment in his new field. In view of his status as an academic failure at the time counseling was initiated, such a step has very real significance. A brief excerpt (phonographic) illustrates this bit of positive action.

> *S.* After — I've been thinking a whole lot about this lately — after I finish with this job [paid work for his self-support] I think I'll study a little more economics outside — put my time in on economics in my extra reading that I want to do. I think I'll try and write a term paper on some phase of economics just for my own benefit. It'll give me some initiative to read the material. I think maybe if I start something like that I'll probably read more than if I just decided to go to the "libe" and read something.
>
> *C.* You're beginning — you're beginning to feel somewhat responsible for your own study activities now, aren't you? That is, you feel that you get something out of doing an additional assignment like that, one you give to yourself?
>
> *S.* Yeah.
>
> *C.* If you quit this job — when you quit this job, too, then you feel that will give you more time for this additional work that you plan to do.

S. Yeah. I thought if I would get started on something like that and found it interesting, I'd probably do more on it and work a little more on it, if I had to take notes on it to write a fairly decent term paper. And possibly I'd get more out of it.

C. You feel then that you are beginning to get your academic problems pretty well ironed out, don't you?

S. Yeah. I feel a lot more confident of myself than I have heretofore down here at school.

If the reader inquires wherein this self-initiated action differs from that described in the previous chapter as growing out of insight, the answer is that there is no fundamental difference. The client continues to take such positive actions and will continue to do so after counseling has ceased. In these later contacts it is important only that the client should implement his insight sufficiently to acquire the confidence that he can continue without help. This is the extent to which re-education is a part of such client-centered therapy.

Ending the Counseling Interviews

What It Means to the Client. When the counseling process has been successful, and the client has come to understand himself with sufficient clarity to make new choices and to reinforce them with appropriate actions, the possibility of concluding the counseling interviews inevitably comes to mind. Toward this possibility the client has the familiar ambivalent attitude which accompanies every growth experience. He feels fearful that if he leaves the counselor, all his problems may recur and he may be unable to cope with them. Often he shows rather plainly that he fears the counselor may be disappointed and regard him as ungrateful if he leaves. At the same time, his increased insight and increased self-confidence cause him to desire to meet his further problems without assistance, to be independent of any counseling help. The various ways of showing this deep ambivalence constitute the characteristics of the end of counseling.

Not infrequently, if the counselor is the first to recognize that independence is nearly achieved and the first to mention that little more help is needed, the client will respond by presenting all his old symptomatic behavior anew. The fears and doubts and confusions and conflicts which he discussed in the earliest contacts are brought into the picture again, as though they were matters of much concern. The experienced counselor will understand that this is a temporary phenomenon, brought on by the fear of losing the support of the counseling relationship.

A very similar reaction is shown by the client who in the closing phases of therapy brings up a number of new problems, all of them requiring the counselor's assistance in their solution. If the counselor in these instances merely recognizes plainly the client's feeling of a need for help, his feeling that these problems are too much for him, this recurrence of a dependent attitude will be found to be very short. The satisfactions of independence and growth far outweigh the comfort of remaining dependent, and the client is soon ready to face the problem of leaving. This vacillation and uncertainty is not different from the fear and uncertainty of the small child who leaves the shelter of home for his first experience at school, or the fluctuating feelings of the man who has just been promoted to a position of heavy responsibility. Whether a similar psychological vacillation takes place even at birth, as Otto Rank supposes, must for the moment remain a matter of speculation, but we do know that such anxieties accompany most experiences of psychological growth toward maturity.

This basic ambivalence, which the client exhibits even after he has developed the insights which would allow him to become independent, is, if properly handled, a genuinely therapeutic issue and can make for further growth. If the counselor helps the client to recognize clearly, as they are expressed, his feelings of loss about leaving, and also his positive and independent desire to manage his own affairs, this recognition becomes a source of fresh insight for the client. Facing a clear choice of remaining dependent or of taking complete responsibility for himself, he assimilates this choice and prefers the latter. He can then contemplate the prospect of leaving with much less conflict, and can bring the contacts to an end without losing confidence.

There is, in closing any successful therapeutic contact, a healthy feeling of loss and regret, which is natural, and which is to some extent mutual. A close and understanding relationship has grown up, a relationship which has had vital meaning for the client, and in which the counselor too has found satisfactions, particularly the satisfaction of watching an individual grow and develop. It is entirely natural that there should be some regret at the dissolution of such a relationship, and the counselor will do well to recognize this fact, and to admit his own as well as the client's feeling about the matter.

An interesting phenomenon which occurs in many instances is the changing type of interest in the counselor which the client shows as the counseling comes to a close. As he feels himself to be more adult, more on a psychological par with the counselor, and as he faces the thought of dissolving the relationship, the client takes, for the first time, a personal interest in the counselor. He inquires about personal matters, the counselor's health, where he lives, his views on current news issues, and the like. He may pursue the notion of keeping up the relationship on a social basis. The counselor should recognize these positive feelings toward himself, but in most instances will be wiser to close the contacts on a therapeutic, rather than a social, basis. A good example of handling this type of situation may be taken from the worker's contacts with Mrs. J., who with her daughter Patty had been coming to the clinic for treatment help.   Mrs. J. and the worker had previously discussed the matter of closing, and toward the end of the final interview the following exchange takes place. Mrs. J. has been discussing some of the practical future problems regarding school for Patty and expressing her assurance that she can handle the situation.

> Her eyes filled with tears and she said, "I hate to think that this is the last regular time we will come." Counselor responded, "I hate to think of it too. I shall miss you." Mrs. J. nodded and said, "I wonder if you wouldn't come and visit us. I'd like you to see our whole family, to know our whole family. I'd like

it so much." Counselor responded, "I'd like it very much too. Not just because I know you here, but because I like you." Mrs. J. nodded and said, "I was getting around to that too." Counselor continued, "However, I know that much as I appreciate the invitation, I must not accept it because, as you have said to me before, you cannot go to your friends with your problems. I know that if I am to be of use later on, I had better stay here in the clinic to be used when need be." Mrs. J. protested that she thought this wouldn't be necessary, since I knew so much about the family already. Counselor responded that that's the way it might seem to her, but that it probably would not work out that way. By this time our time was up. We shook hands and agreed again that our work together had been very pleasant.

When the counseling contacts are well handled by the counselor, they are not likely to dwindle off or break off gradually. The conclusion is just as significant, just as clear-cut, just as helpful to the client as any other portion of the therapeutic contacts. Where the interviews tend to "fade out," growing less significant, ending with broken appointments, the counselor may be sure that he has in some way failed adequately to recognize and respond to the feelings of the client.

Meeting the Problem of Closing — An Example. In order to make more plain the type of problems which occur in concluding the therapeutic contacts, and the counselor's approach to them, illustrations may be drawn again from the case of Barbara, the high-school girl whose progress in insight was discussed in the last chapter. In her case, the matter of closing the interviewing contacts had an unusual degree of finality. Barbara was not living at home during her contacts with the psychologist, but she knew that eventually she must return to her home in another city. The gradual alteration of her feeling about leaving is well pictured in the following excerpts. All those portions of the interviewing which revolved directly around the problem of closing are included. The first mention of the possibility of leaving comes in the eighth contact.

Eighth Interview. In talking about her present place of residence and certain changes which will occur in the next few weeks, Barbara wonders how long it will take to finish here. She doesn't want her father to run up too much of a bill. In this conversation she seemed to be fearful that it might be too long a process. The counselor said that the interviews would be finished when she felt ready to go home and take up her work and go on with her life. Mentioned that with the progress she was making perhaps a few weeks might be sufficient. She seemed satisfied with this idea. Counselor added, "Would you like to see whether we can accomplish enough in the next two or three interviews?" Her expression immediately changed. "You mean that that would be all? Oh, no, I don't want to rush this. I'm willing to stay here just as long as necessary. Six months, if need be. I might not want to get over it if I thought I had to be all through here in three visits." Counselor said that he had merely raised the question because he did not want her to think that she had to keep on coming for a long time. Reassured her and asked if she would prefer to come in next Wednesday or to put it off until Saturday. She decided she would prefer to come in on Wednesday.

The usual ambivalence about leaving the counseling situation is well illustrated in this instance. Barbara has made enough progress in insight and independence to feel that some day she will want to leave. When it appears that this might be soon, the other aspect of her feeling comes to the fore. She is sure that she does not yet have sufficient independence, and recognizes correctly that a hasty conclusion might undermine her present determination to "get over it," to solve her problems. It is probably significant that she wishes to come in soon for the next appointment. It is not until the last of the eleventh interview that she again brings up the question of leaving.

> *Eleventh Interview.* At the close of the interview the counselor compliments her on the progress she has been making. She says, "You know, maybe I'm nearer through than I thought I was." The counselor agrees that this may be true. She continues, "But, of course, if I thought this was the last interview I just couldn't bear to think of it." Counselor agrees that she should come back, and refers to the appointment which has just been made.

Barbara has now made sufficient advance in her own independence so that she can look at the prospect of leaving without nearly so much fear. Her only concern is that the present interview should not be the last. There is no further mention of separation from the counseling contacts until the end of the fourteenth contact, when the problem is brought up, this time by the counselor.

Fourteenth Interview. Counselor mentioned that the hour was nearly up, and that perhaps we could discuss the future a bit. Added, "I wonder when you think you will be ready to go back home?" With no hesitation Barbara replied, "I think I will be ready very soon. There are just a few more problems to solve. Maybe one or two visits more will do it." Counselor pointed out that of course the problems would not all be solved at any time, but that perhaps she had learned a new method of attacking them. She agreed that this was so and that she would not be disturbed at taking some of her problems home with her. Plans were made for two more interviews.

The constructive attitude which she has been able to adopt, and the growing confidence in her own abilities, are very evident. When the next interview arrives, however, with its implication that it is the next to the last, her courage temporarily wanes.

Fifteenth Interview. After some rather casual conversation, she sat for a moment and then said, "I thought I'd spill out everything this time. I haven't had time to collect my thoughts, I guess. I guess I just haven't been so well lately, and these feelings that I've had bother me." Counselor reminded her that the last time she had such feelings she was able to tell why. She said, "I don't know why I should have them now. I can't guess. Can you tell me?" Counselor said, "How do you feel about going home?" She said that she was looking forward to it, and had been looking forward to it increasingly. Counselor suggested that while this was true, going home also meant facing a number of problems. She discussed this for a moment and then sat silent for a little while. "You know, I've thought so much of this appointment I've almost dreamed of it. I thought I'd come bouncing into the office and laughing, and here I am crying. I just can't keep a lump out of my throat. I don't know what's the matter. It's my nerves, I guess." Counselor said, "When an experience has meant a good deal to you, it's hard to think of its ending."

This excerpt has several interesting facets. Faced with the reality of breaking off the counseling relationship, Barbara finds herself clinging to it, in spite of her basic willingness to leave. The counselor at first interprets her attitude as a fear of the future, but Barbara rejects this interpretation. When the counselor recognizes the real feeling of personal loss and regret, Barbara is able to go on and, following the quoted fragment, discusses her plans for going home, states very clearly the new insight she has gained, and toward the end of the interview tries to put into words the new integration she feels. To quote the record at this point:

> She recognized that it was time to leave and got up to go. She raised a theoretical question: "Are the mind and the personality different things, or are they the same thing? I used to feel they were sort of in conflict. Now I'm all in one piece." Counselor replied that the question she was raising would all depend on definitions, and that the important thing was that she felt that she was all in one piece and could carry forward in that way. She continued, "Well, sometimes I'm sort of asunder, but most of the time I think I'm in one piece." She left in a cheerful mood.

In the final interview Barbara shows much less emotion than in the one just described. She tells how people see a change in her and how she is looking forward to going home. She tells of a recent gathering in which there were a number of young people whom she had known several years previously.

> *Sixteenth Interview.* "You know, the people all said, 'You've changed so.' The boy who came to see me the second night afterward said, 'I'd hardly know you, you've changed so much. You're more one of us.' He seemed to think I'd changed a great deal. Once he said, 'You're more like a human being.' I guess before I acted too superior to people. Now the girls wish I was staying longer and would come to their parties. They'd be kissing parties, I guess. I don't suppose we'll have any of those back home." She talks on about the fact that she feels so much better adjusted socially and so much better liked by young people.

Only at the close of the interview does she again show a slight tendency to cling to the counseling experience, but she definitely relinquishes it.

> She still tries to prolong the interview, although the time is now up. She looks down her list again, tries to remember things she has forgotten. Counselor says, "We could go on talking for a long time, couldn't we?" She says, "Yes, but I think I've raised all the questions I want to." She then begins to bring the interview to a close, talking about the improvement she feels in herself. "You know, before I was just interested in accomplishment and achievement. Now I think that accomplishment and fun with young people will be managed all together. I'll do some original things, and they may not even know about it, but I'll have a good time with them too, and I won't feel different from them or better than they are." She thanks the counselor sincerely for the help she has received, and says good-bye.

These excerpts picture a satisfactory conclusion of a series of counseling contacts. The client has been made to feel free to leave as soon as she has sufficient independence and self-confidence. She has been frightened by the thought of becoming entirely independent, but finds this problem no more difficult to face and assimilate than the other issues she has been facing from week to week in the interviews. Gradually she comes to the point where she wishes the contacts to end and carries this resolve through, feeling, as she says, "a lump in my throat," but recognizing that this is temporary. The counseling process has achieved its desired goal of helping her to become a better-organized person, oriented around healthy goals which she has clearly seen and definitely chosen. She has not been freed from problems, nor has there ever been any attempt to achieve an artificial goal. She has been able to free herself of hampering conflicts which have made it very difficult for her to meet her problems, and is thus enabled to be a more effective and more mature individual in the future. She has not achieved complete insight into her behavior, nor has this ever been the goal of counseling. She has achieved what might be called a "working insight," sufficient to enable her to meet her present problems, and to make continued growth inevitable. She may, at some future time, need additional help, but the likelihood of this has been greatly diminished by the increased emotional maturity which she has attained.

The Counselor's Part.   The example just cited makes plain much of the part which the counselor plays in drawing therapy to a healthy conclusion.   We may, however, state in a more generalized form certain elements of the counselor's function in these concluding phases.

It is important that the therapist should be alert to the client's progress and that as soon as increased independence is evident, he should bring up for consideration the eventual ending of the contacts.   If this is not done, the client may feel that the counselor does not want him to leave.   In the contacts with Mrs. J., in the next to the last interview, she tells how successfully she has been handling her daughter, stressing that "things are different now."

> There was a long pause.   Counselor said, "Since things are coming so smoothly and seem to have worked out, I wonder how much longer you and Patty will want to come down to us." Mrs. J. laughed and said, "I have been wondering the same thing."   After some discussion, we agreed that we would meet once more.

It is evident that Mrs. J. feels a certain sense of relief that the counselor has brought this matter out into the open.

It is perhaps unnecessary to add that the counselor should make no attempt to hold the client because he does not feel that the problems are all solved, nor the insight complete. If the client has selected appropriate goals, and has the courage and confidence to work toward them, the effectiveness of his understanding of himself, and the effectiveness of his actions in reaching the goal, will increase rather than decrease after the conclusion of counseling.   The counselor must learn to get his personal satisfaction in this progress of the client toward growth, not in keeping him dependent.

Some therapists, notably Rank, have maintained that at

times an arbitrary time limit should be set for the conclusion of treatment. This would seem to be unwise. The ending of the counseling interviews should be set primarily by the client, with the counselor serving again to clarify the issues that arise in connection with leaving. Once these issues are clarified, we may be assured that the client will adopt the more mature choice.

On the whole, the end of counseling is likely to come sooner, rather than later, than the counselor expects it. We are so prone to think in terms of unsolved problems that we may not be sufficiently aware of the client's readiness again to "paddle his own canoe." Not infrequently the pace of the concluding interviews is so much more rapid than those that have gone before that the counselor fails to recognize the full significance of all the material. So many steps have been taken, so much confidence is displayed, that the counselor looks forward to continued interviews of this sort which will record the solution of all the difficulties with which the client is faced, forgetting that these steps and this confidence are already an indication that the end is near and that further help is not needed.

COUNSELING AS THE CLIENT SEES IT

Occasionally in the last interviews, the client endeavors to put into words something of what the experience has meant to him. These spontaneous expressions are of interest, because they tend to confirm the viewpoint toward counseling which has been expressed in this book. Living through an experience of a new sort, the client tries to describe it in his own words, and from his own feeling to make plain the value it has had for him. Sometimes these statements are very brief. One young man, whose previous life has been literally crippled by feelings of inadequacy, says: "I know now what I want to do, and I feel some confidence in what I think. My wife sees a great change in me." A woman who has been struggling with marital problems and with the question of handling her maladjusted boy comments on all that she has gained: "It is quite different from going to my physician. I tried to talk to him about these things, but it didn't work. Here I feel that no one is pushing me; there is no advice and no prejudice." This statement is especially significant since this same woman earlier in the counseling contacts had insisted that the counselor must tell her what to do, must give her the answers to her problems.

An adolescent girl gives her views of what her counselor has meant to her, and incidentally her concept of the counseling process, in this statement:

> "I've been thinking about what you are to me. It's as though you were myself — a part of me. You're a balance wheel; you're not a person. It's almost as if I were talking to myself, but with someone listening and trying to think on it. I'm not getting rid of anything but a lot of stored up feeling. I don't come for advice. No, sometimes I do. But then I'm conscious that I want advice. It really bothers me when you become a person. What you do is let a person talk and put in comments that keep it going instead of stewing in a circle. That's why I say that you're a balance wheel. It's different now. When I first met you, you were a person. I disliked you because you were touching sore spots. Now I know you'll be a person when I need you to be. Other times you're someone to blow off steam to and to talk to so I can make up my mind." [1]

Her concise picture of counseling as a process in which you "let a person talk and put in comments that keep it going instead of stewing in a circle" is a priceless statement of the releasing aspect of expression, and the counselor's function in it. And when she concludes that the counselor is someone "to talk to so that I can make up my mind," she has added another essential function of counseling, the creation of a situation in which choices can be clearly made.

Perhaps the most eloquent statement of the way in which counseling comes to be understood by the client is captured in one of our phonographic recordings, from one of the last in a successful series of interviews with a student. In his faltering,

[1] Quoted from "Intensive Treatment with Adolescent Girls," by Virginia W. Lewis, *Journal of Consulting Psychology*, vol. IV (September–October, 1940), p. 184.

stumbling way, obviously groping for words to describe what has been a totally new type of experience for him, this student manages to summarize most of the essential elements of a satisfactory counseling experience.

> S. Well, that's about all, I guess, that's on my mind right at the present time.
> C. O.K. Well, you remember our arrangement — whenever we run out of anything to say we postpone ——
> S. Till the next time.
> C. — the meeting till the next time, and if you would ever feel that you didn't have anything particular to say at that time, why, just come in and we'll dismiss right at the beginning.
> S. All right. Well, I — uh —— Right here's something I'd like to talk about. I don't know just how to put it, but I enjoy these things. I mean — uh — if you talk to somebody like this, it brings the thing open in your own mind, something you've kept — that you've tried to avoid, and that you can avoid, easily, in your own mind; but you walk in that door and you get gumption enough to — when he's here — to tell him, so you tell him, and it not only — it may not impress you, but when you say it out loud and hear it, it makes you think about it, and it makes you sometimes do — do something about it.
> C. Well, you feel then that maybe it has been helpful.
> S. Yeah, I'm certain it has.

Note how beautifully this grammatically confused utterance explains what therapy means to the client: the release of hitherto inhibited attitudes which the client has "tried to avoid"; the clear facing of the self and the situation — "when you say it out loud and hear it, it makes you think about it"; and finally the courage to take positive action — "it makes you do something about it." Such statements indicate that the structuring of the situation by the counselor, and the efforts that the counselor makes to restrain himself from directive activity in the counseling, are slowly recognized by the client as being extremely helpful in finding a new orientation. They seem to indicate very definitely that the process we have been following is a genuine sequence of progress, felt and experienced by the client as well as recognized by the counselor.

SPECIAL PROBLEMS

What is the Length of the Counseling Process?   Many a practical-minded reader will before this have been raising the question, "How long does this take?"   There is, of course, no hard and fast answer to such a question.   The length of the counseling process depends on the degree of maladjustment existing, upon the skill of the counselor, upon the readiness of the client to receive help, and perhaps to a slight extent upon the client's intelligence.   Nevertheless, we do not need to leave the subject with this indefinite comment.

There seems good reason to believe that the length of the counseling process bears a direct relationship to the subtlety and accuracy of handling by the counselor.   If free expression is unhindered by counselor bungling, if emotionalized attitudes are accurately recognized, if insight is increased by well-selected interpretations, the client is likely to be able to handle his own affairs after six to fifteen contacts, rather than fifty. These figures are only the crudest approximations, but there does seem to be a rhythm of therapeutic progress which is likely to be complete within three months of weekly contacts, rather than a year.   Where maladjustment is not extreme, where the individual is not deeply neurotic, two, four, or six contacts are often sufficient for the client to find the needed help, though in such instances some of the steps of the therapeutic process may appear only in very abbreviated form.

The writer is convinced that in most cases where counseling contacts have greatly exceeded the number mentioned, it is generally true that the therapeutic process has won out in spite of, rather than because of, the counselor's approach.   So strong is the individual's drive toward maturity and growth that counseling is often successful in such cases in spite of much mishandling along the way.   This conviction is borne out through careful examination of recorded interviews, where one may see, not infrequently, instances of delay caused by counselor errors of the sorts previously discussed in this book.   Such errors may postpone, throughout an interview, significant attitudes which the client was ready to express, and which do not appear until the following interview because they were inadvertently blocked by the counselor. A succession of such blunders may decidedly prolong the counseling contacts. Somehow the unfortunate attitude has grown up that the number of therapeutic contacts bears a direct relationship to the depth of those contacts. This is not necessarily true. On the other hand, the desire to find short cuts, to hasten the client, nearly always increases the number of interviews necessary for improvement. The shortest successful series of therapeutic-counseling interviews is the one which is handled with the greatest skill, the one which is the most completely client-centered.

Some of these comments automatically raise questions about psychoanalysis, particularly Freudian analysis, which often prides itself upon the years of daily contacts necessary for any real psychological reorientation. The writer has refrained, throughout this book, from any attempt to argue the merits of one school of thought as against another and does not wish to begin such an argument at this point. Perhaps certain questions could be raised, however, to which fruitful answers might be found. What is the goal of Freudian analysis? Is it to enable the individual to move forward independently, or to acquire a complete topographical map of his personality? Is the goal that of healthy, self-directed action, or a complete insight into the causes of all of one's behavior? Is it not true, in Freudian analysis as in the client-centered therapy which is described, that the attempt to impose preconceived interpretations always delays, rather than hastens, therapy? Might it not be true that Freudian analysis could to some extent be shortened by a more careful analysis of technique? Such questions are not meant as criticisms, but merely to cast doubt upon the fetish of length as a significant indicator of value in the counseling process.

The Conclusion of Unsuccessful Counseling. Although it is the whole thesis of this book that failures in counseling may be avoided through adequate consideration of basic principles governing the appropriateness of counseling as a treatment approach and through the adequate handling of the therapeutic process, we must nevertheless recognize that counselors are human and failures do occur. Such failures in counseling may be allowed to do real damage, or they may be handled in a manner which at least holds promise for the future. More attention needs to be paid to this problem.

There are several reasons which may account for a particular client's failure to find help in the counseling interviews. Undoubtedly the most frequent cause of such a failure is the bungling of the contacts by the counselor. In the rush of daily work, it is very easy to suppose that good intentions will take the place of painstaking skill. Time and again the counselor must learn the hard lesson that this is not so. There are, however, other reasons for failure, most of which may be summed up by saying that the client was not a suitable candidate for counseling in the first place. Perhaps the environmental obstacles to growth were too overwhelming, or the individual has too little control over his life situation to make change effective. Perhaps an error in judgment was made, and an adolescent was accepted for counseling in the belief that he was relatively independent of his parents, time proving that only by counseling both parent and child could success have been achieved. Certainly most, if not all, of our counseling failures belong in one of these two major categories, being failures either because the clients were never suitable for counseling help, or because the counselor has failed adequately to help them to see themselves and take positive action.

Every experienced counselor can trace some of the typical developments in these unsuccessful cases. In some instances the client becomes annoyed, increasingly resistant, more hostile to the counselor and the counseling situation as the continued contacts bring no improvement or help. The counselor, feeling that the process has miscarried, exerts an increased effort, a more persistent pressure, a more direct attack upon the problem. The client fails to return. The case is closed "for failure to cooperate." In other instances the client makes a certain amount of encouraging progress, but gradually becomes more and more dependent upon the counselor. This unhappy individual, alarmed at the extent to which he has taken over the direction of the client's life, endeavors to push him away. He finds it difficult to see the client, the contacts become more brusque, the counselor at last insists that the client should manage his own life, and the relationship is broken, with the counselor's puzzled sense of guilt the only remaining evidence of the work done.

In most cases of unsuccessful counseling, both counselor and client sense the fact that progress is not what it should be. Unable to analyze the reason, they both become defensive and punitive, and the contacts cease with the possibility of real damage on both sides. Such a deteriorating type of contact is not necessary, even in those instances where the cause of the failure is beyond the power of the counselor to analyze.

When counseling seems to be going astray — when the counselor finds himself wondering why he has encountered such resistance, why the client is making no progress, why the situation seems worse than it did at the outset of the contacts — the first step is naturally to investigate the possible causes. This is the time for the counselor to consider carefully whether an error was made in relying upon counseling to help this particular client. This is the time for him to make a careful study of his record of the contacts, endeavoring to discover his mistakes. Has he been too directive? Has he endeavored to push the process too rapidly? Has he been using interpretation unwisely? Has he been trying to solve the problem in his own way rather than in the client's? Has he in some way made it difficult for the client to reveal his feelings? These and other questions, which have been considered earlier in this book, should be carefully evaluated. Often the cause can be found and remedied. It is a vastly encouraging fact that so anxious are individuals to grow, to discover the way out of their difficulties, that even though many mistakes may have been made and much poor counseling carried on, constructive results may be obtained by correcting those mistakes. It is never too late to make an exhaustive study of the causes of failure.

If we are realistic, however, we shall recognize that in some instances the counselor is too close to his work, too defensive in regard to it, to recognize his errors. He does not always have the help of a supervisor or colleague in uncovering these blind spots. In short there are some cases which will be counseling failures in spite of the counselor's well-intentioned efforts to discover the cause. What may be done in such instances?

A frank recognition of the failure by both counselor and client has very real value in preventing defensive actions on both sides. The counselor says in effect: "We seem to be making no progress. Perhaps it is owing to my lack of skill. Perhaps it is owing to some unwillingness on your part. At any rate, without trying to blame anyone, it is plain that we are not getting results. Shall we call a halt to our contacts, or do you wish to continue them for a while in the hope that we may find them more satisfactory?" Such a clear-cut statement of the situation is most helpful. It relieves the client of any need of attacking the counselor. It also opens up several possibilities.

It may lead to a closing of the counseling contacts, mutually agreed upon by both parties. If so, the break is clean cut, without antagonistic or guilty feelings. The client will feel free to return at some later time, or to go to some other counselor if he feels that someone else can offer more help. On the other hand, it may lead to a clarification of the barrier to counseling progress, and thus to new therapeutic developments. The writer recalls one series of contacts with a mother in which the counseling had been badly bungled, as seen in present perspective. Since no progress was being made in her handling of her son, the counselor simply stated that it appeared that the contacts were not fruitful and that perhaps they should be discontinued. The mother seemed to accept this, and the situation apparently was closed, when she remarked, as she got up to go, "Do you ever accept adults for treatment?" When the answer was in the affirmative, she sat down again and began to reveal all her marital unhappiness, which was basic to her mishandling of her son, but which she had been reluctant to reveal as long as her boy constituted the ostensible reason for the clinic contacts.   In other words, if the impasse which has been reached is clearly stated and recognized, both client and counselor may be able to accept it without too much emotion and to find the way in which it may be overcome.   If not, at least the contacts will be closed without hostility and guilt being uppermost.

One caution may be given.   Counseling should not be allowed to drag on at great length unless progress is being made. If in several contacts a careful study of the interviews reveals no significant development, no movement in the direction of therapy, the counselor should consider whether it might be well to close the interviews.   Contrary to the opinion of the inexperienced, the unsuccessful interview is more likely to run over the time limit than the successful one.   Likewise, the contacts which run on and on with relatively little change point in general to a counseling failure.   It is best in such instances to try to discover the causes of the impasse, and failing in that, to draw the counseling to a close.   While such an ending admits the lack of success, it will not generate future conflict nor make it harder for the client to seek help on another occasion.

SUMMARY

As the client develops in his insight and self-understanding and selects new goals around which he reorients his life, counseling enters its closing phase, which has certain distinctive characteristics.   The client gains in self-confidence as he gains fresh insight and as he takes an increased number of positive actions directed toward his goal.   In his confidence he desires to be finished with counseling, yet at the same time he fears to leave its support.   Recognition by the counselor of this ambivalence enables the client to see clearly the choice ahead of him and to develop the assurance that he is capable of handling his problems independently.   The counselor aids by helping the client to feel entirely free to end the relationship as soon as he is ready.   Ordinarily the counseling ends with a sense of loss on both sides, but with a mutual recognition that independence is another healthy step toward growth.   Even when counseling has not been successful, it may often be closed in a constructive fashion.

The length of the therapeutic process is as much dependent on the skill of the counselor in keeping the contacts client-centered as it is upon the severity of the maladjustment or upon any other factor.

Not infrequently it is plain in these closing contacts that the client has clearly perceived the unusual structure of the coun-seling situation and realizes how he has used it for his own growth.   The spontaneous statements of clients lend weight to the thesis of this book, that a client-centered counseling rela-tionship releases dynamic forces in a manner achieved by no other relationship.

Some Practical Questions

In the preceding chapters an attempt has been made to convey to the reader some sense of the definite and understandable process by which counseling achieves its goal. The aim has been to develop an appreciation of the fact that this process has unity and sequence, that its unfolding is predictable and orderly, and that its aspects may be subjected to objective scrutiny. In thus focusing attention on the essential principles of counseling, many questions which might legitimately be raised have been ignored. Questions which might cause us to fasten our attention upon the nonessential rather than the essential aspects of counseling, questions based upon entirely different concepts of counseling, questions which lead only to speculation, have been avoided. Having completed our survey of the process of therapy, however, we may now take up some of the more persistent practical questions which are frequently raised about counseling in general, or about a client-centered type of therapy in particular. No attempt will be made to answer all such questions, but certain comments may prove helpful in stimulating more adequate thinking. The questions which follow are arranged in no special order, except that some of the weightiest and most basic queries have been placed at the end. In order that the reader may select most easily those portions of interest to him, each topic is stated as a specific question.

How Long Should Counseling Interviews Be?

We do not have the necessary experimental knowledge to answer this question. It seems certain that a known limit, whether that limit is fifteen, thirty, forty-five, or sixty minutes, is a more important factor than the actual length of the inter-view. The writer feels that more than one hour for a single in-terview is unwise, though the counselors in the Western Electric Company, whose purpose is largely to encourage full expression of attitudes, find that their interviews average eighty minutes.

Some interviews of an hour in length, particularly at the out-set of counseling, are completely filled with significant mate-rial. As feelings are expressed and the interviews center more around the achievement of insight and the decisions regarding new steps, the client may utilize part of the hour in conversa-tion which avoids the real issues with which he is struggling. In such instances it is only the approaching end of the counsel-ing hour which enables him to express the thoughts or make the decisions about which he is ambivalent. In some such cases, it seems likely that as much progress would be made in a short interview as in a longer one. Experimental counseling, with recorded interviews, would be needed to settle this question.

How Long an Interval Should Come Between Interviews?

This, too, needs experimental study. It would seem clear that appointments should not be too close together. There probably is no sound justification for the daily contacts which classical psychoanalysis has made famous. Such daily con-tacts are necessary only when the process is centered to a con-siderable degree in the therapist rather than in the client. In-terviews several days or a week apart seem to be most effective, giving the client an opportunity to assimilate his gains, to achieve a certain amount of new insight, and to take the actions which implement his new impulses toward growth.

What Should the Counselor Do About Broken Appointments?

In many organizations where a directive type of counseling is practiced, broken appointments may constitute a large fraction of the total. The writer does not expect to be believed when he says that in the client-centered therapy which we have been discussing, broken appointments are almost nonexistent. Nevertheless, this statement is true. Illness may occur, trans portation systems may break down, but when these obstacles crop up, the client notifies the counselor. The appointment is not broken without notice unless there has been some bungling of the counseling itself.

In the case of broken appointments, there are two important steps for the counselor to take. The first is to study his notes, particularly regarding the last interview. Have his techniques been of a pushing sort, likely to create resistance? Has there been too much premature interpretation? Has the client faced a very difficult choice before he was ready for it? Has he shown by his progress that he is ready to cease contacts, and was this new independence not recognized and accepted? It is likely that some such factor will be discovered which accounts for the failure either to keep the appointment or to notify the counselor.

The second step is to make it as easy as possible for the client to return, at the same time helping him to feel that if he chooses not to return, this outcome is also acceptable to the counselor. Often a letter is a good means of carrying out this step. Such a note might be phrased in some such style as the following: "When you did not come in for your appointment on Wednesday, I thought that it might mean that you no longer wished to continue our discussions. I know that sometimes people reach a point where they do not wish to carry such discussions further. If, however, you would like another appointment, I should be glad to arrange it. Please feel free to telephone me at any time when you might wish to see me, and I will arrange a mutually convenient hour." This is not presented as a model note, but to indicate certain points that may well be kept in mind. The counselor gives no indication of disappointment, since this would only create the false impression that the client has failed in some way to help the counselor, or that he is coming only because the counselor wishes it. The

letter does not give another appointment, but leaves the initiative with the client. It is still his responsibility as to whether
he wishes help. The note is such that even if the client never
replies in any way, he will have a minimum of guilt in regard to
breaking the contacts. This is important, since it means that
the client will then feel free to return at some later date if he
needs help.

Should the Counselor Take Notes During the Interview?

For some reason, this question seems to cause great distress
to most counselors. It may be said with assurance that the
success of therapy bears a direct and positive relation to the
adequacy of the record. In engaging in a counseling relationship, we are dealing with delicate and subtle factors. The more
faithfully we can record the process, the more accurately we
can determine what is actually occurring and the mistakes that
are being made. The truth of this is completely borne out by
the striking educational efficacy of the phonographically recorded interviews upon which this book has drawn so heavily.
Counselors invariably testify that listening to their own interviews, even without critical comment, but especially with the
benefit of constructive criticisms, has been one of the most
educational experiences in their counseling training.

It goes without saying, therefore, that very complete notes
should, if possible, be taken during the interview, notes which
record the counselor's statements as well as those of the client.
A dialogue form, with statements condensed and abbreviated,
has proved helpful.

The basic reason for hesitating to take notes has not yet been
touched. The counselor is fearful that the client will think he
is trying to "put something over." These fears arise out of the
counselor's own feelings of guilt. If he is not trying to "put
something over," if the contacts are genuinely designed as a
place in which the client may learn to help himself, then the
client will not be disturbed by the note-taking process, pro-

vided its purpose is explained. The counselor may say something of this sort: "I hope you won't mind if I jot down the things we say. I like to study them afterward to see what we've accomplished." One counselor of the writer's acquaintance tells the client that he may look at the notes himself any time he wishes. Occasionally such a request is made toward the end of the counseling process, with the result that the client develops a very clear insight into the progress he has made.

To what extent such notes should be dictated or written out or made part of a permanent record is a more difficult question. Every counselor should write out fully, and study very carefully, some of the cases with which he works. For permanent-record purposes, however, in many agencies, interview notes would serve as the working record, and at the conclusion of counseling a brief summary of the problems presented, the issues faced, the insights gained, the positive steps initiated, might be sufficient for the permanent record. When, however, two counselors are working with the same situation, one with the parent and one with the child, it is essential that each should have full knowledge of the work of the other. Often a complete record is the best means of obtaining this knowledge. In general, such questions must necessarily be determined by the purpose and function of the organization, whether that purpose is primarily training and research or purely service. More complete records are necessary in the former than in the latter type.

What if the Client Makes Statements Known to be Untrue?

In discussions of counseling practice, this question never fails to lift its hoary head. In making diagnostic studies of maladjusted individuals, it may at times be important to know whether a statement is objectively true or false. In studying a delinquent it may make some difference in the diagnostic formulation of the problem to know whether he committed a particular delinquency and is now denying it, or whether he is truthfully denying his participation. In counseling treatment, however, such objective facts are quite unimportant. The only facts which have significance for therapy are the feelings which the client is able to bring into the situation.

Consequently, we need not be concerned about whether the client's statements are "true" or "false." His emotionalized attitude is the element that has importance. Thus, whether a student is "truthful" in saying that he received a low grade in a course because the professor was prejudiced against him, is of much less importance for counseling than the fact that he feels that he was persecuted. As he is allowed to talk out his feelings, he will also come to evaluate the facts more truly, and eventually the counselor is likely to know the objective truth, but this is not absolutely necessary for counseling.

Interviewing may be used, of course, to endeavor to determine objective fact. This is a legitimate purpose in legal work, for example. It is not, however, counseling or therapy. In most instances of good counseling, a complete recording reveals a number of flatly contradictory statements on the part of the client as to attitudes, or facts, or both. These are, for the most part, examples of contradictory attitudes within the individual which have not yet been integrated. They represent both of the dynamic sides of an ambivalent desire. If the counselor challenges this contradiction on an intellectual basis, he is not likely to help the individual to achieve an integration which will unify the attitudes themselves.

Does Charging a Fee Affect Counseling?

There are many counseling situations in which fees are entirely inappropriate. In dealing with high-school students, for example, the student is unable to pay a fee himself, and the payment of a fee by his parents may emphasize the dependence from which he is struggling to free himself. On the other hand, when the client is an adult, or in child-guidance work where both parent and child are coming for help, a fee may have a real place in therapy. The payment of a fee, adjusted to the income level, may be a channel by which the client can indicate his seriousness in coming for help, and a means of maintaining his self-respect while accepting help from another.

There are several issues of therapeutic value which are raised when a fee is charged. In the first place, the setting of a fee, which should be frankly talked over in the first interview if there is to be a fee at all, provides a definite measure of responsibility which the client can decide to accept or reject. It is his first step in a new direction, an initial assumption of the effort necessary to face his situation. In the second place, a fee provides motivation toward rapid progress. To be paying for each contact encourages the individual to talk as freely as possible, to work for his own improvement in the shortest possible time. Payment of a fee also does away with any necessity of feeling dependent or grateful when the therapeutic goal is reached. The services are paid for. Both sides have contributed to the process.

It should be stressed that these advantages accrue if the fee is genuinely adjusted to the economic resources of the individual. A charge which the client cannot pay without cutting deeply into the necessities of his budget may, of course, hamper treatment, becoming a real block to continued contacts. In the guidance center of which the writer was the director, it became the practice to discuss fees with every parent who referred a child for help. In the hands of a skilled case worker, this gave an opportunity for making the client feel that he was doing all that it was reasonable to expect, even though the fee was ten cents per visit, or there was no fee at all.

In some student-counseling services, the arrangement is made that a flat fee is charged to every student for guidance and counseling service, and that the student may consequently use these resources to the extent that he needs. This is no doubt a good method of supporting the services, and it has the advantage of making the student feel that he is a self-respecting person who is paying for help received. It does not, however, have the other advantages that have been mentioned.

In concluding this brief discussion of fees, the point should very definitely be made that non-directive counseling can be carried on with great success whether or not fees are charged. In this respect it differs from orthodox psychoanalysis, in which a fee is almost a necessary part of treatment. In the type of counseling under discussion here, the client is putting much effort into the process himself. The whole therapeutic procedure throughout is such as to emphasize his fundamental autonomy, which is the basis of self-respect. Hence, he can use this helping atmosphere in a constructive way, without feeling that he must pay financially. The writer can see no great difference in process or outcome between those clients who have paid for the service and those who have not.

Does Client-Centered Counseling Demand Less of the Counselor in the Way of Concentration, Study, Records, and the Like?

This question is raised in good faith by individuals who are accustomed to a directive style of counseling. It could best be answered by talking to counselors in training who are endeavoring to learn the non-directive approach. They testify to the much greater effort necessary in client-centered treatment. The fact that the counselor talks much less carries with it the obligation of thinking much more. To remain constantly alert to the client's feeling, to use words not as bludgeons but as surgical tools to release growth, puts a heavy strain upon the counselor.

Essentially client-centered counseling is endeavoring to raise treatment interviewing out of the prescientific stage where "anything goes," provided it is backed by good intentions, to a point where every expression, whether by counselor or counselee, is recognized as having its importance and its effect, either retarding or stimulating, upon the psychological growth of the client. Consequently, records need to be much more complete, and they are records for use, not merely busy-work. Between interviews, such notes and records need to be studied carefully. What feelings has the client been expressing? What mistakes in recognition have been made? What is the full meaning of statements which in the rapid flow of the interview were only dimly felt to be significant? What are the attitudes which the client is likely to bring to the next contact? The counselor will be far more alert to the real feelings if he has thus minutely studied the previous contact, and has recognized the probable direction which the next interview will take.

The careful scrutiny of phonographic recordings will be convincing evidence of the fact that most counseling and so-called psychotherapy is comparable to dissecting a gnat with a butcher knife, or cultivating tiny seedlings with a huge tractor cultivator. What is vitally needed is the recognition that the process which goes on in interviewing is so subtle that its potentialities for growth may be utterly destroyed by the "forceful" handling which is characteristic of most of our relationships. To understand the subtle forces operating, to recognize and cooperate with them, needs the utmost in careful concentration and study, and in the completeness of records which picture the process.

Can Counseling Be Carried on if Only a Brief Contact Is Possible?

This question has already been touched upon in Chapter VI (page 172). We need only repeat here the fact that a counseling relation of the sort described in this book is particularly essential if the contact is to be a short one. The seeming advantages of the directive approach in a short contact are completely spurious. If we have any reasonable regard for the complexity of human life, we should be able to recognize that in one hour, or less, it is highly unlikely that we can reorganize the life structure of the individual. If we can recognize this limit and refrain from playing a self-satisfying Jehovah rôle, we can offer a very definite type of clarifying help, even in a short space of time. We can enable the client to express his problems and feelings freely and to leave with a clearer recognition of the issues with which he is faced.   If we utilize the time in trying to direct him, we gain satisfaction only because we do not see the confusion, the dependence, and the resentment which follow our unwarranted interference with his life.

CAN COUNSELING BE CARRIED ON WITH FRIENDS AND RELATIVES?

Not infrequently the question is raised, particularly by less experienced counselors, as to how they may effectively counsel some friend who is in difficulty, or a roommate, or even a wife or husband.   In such instances the desire to be of help to another individual is natural and commendable.   Clear thinking is needed, however, as to the ways in which we can be of help to other individuals.

As has been evident in previous chapters, counseling is effective primarily because the counselor, not being deeply involved in the situation from an emotional point of view, is able to recognize the feelings of the client, able to bring them into conscious consideration, and able to allow the client to formulate, out of this increased insight, his own course of action.   It should be clear that the more deeply we are involved emotionally the less we are able to carry on these functions of the counselor.   The husband will not be able to be a satisfactory counselor for his wife.   Nor will the close friend find it possible to be both a good friend and a counselor.   It is more important that the husband should be an understanding husband, facing with frankness and sympathy the mutual problems of himself and his wife.   The friend may best serve by being a good friend, sharing viewpoints, acting as an understanding listener and a source of emotional support.   In so doing, many of the insights gained through counseling may be of help, provided they are used with full recognition that this is a situation in which both individuals are emotionally involved.

Where the relationship is not so close, as in the instance of the casual friend who seeks counseling assistance, counseling may satisfactorily be carried on if the therapeutic contacts are kept strictly separate from the occasional friendly contacts.

This discussion merely re-emphasizes the point of view which was explained in Chapter IV. The counseling relationship is a different relationship from that of friendship or any other close emotional tie. We gain nothing by confusing various relationships. As parents we may build up a good parent-child relationship, but this does not mean that we are the best counselors for our children. We may develop strong bonds of attachment to our friends, but if we endeavor to be both counselor and friend, we are likely to become unsatisfactory both as counselor and as friend. Even the doctor does not operate upon his wife or his child. He knows that he cannot be fully objective, cannot have the confidence in his own judgment which he would have in other situations. Much the same reasoning applies to the counselor.

As a matter of fact, in those instances in which an individual feels that he should act as a counselor for a friend or relative, it is very often because he desires to "make over" the other individual. This fact is in itself sufficient to make real therapy impossible.

WHAT IS THE RELATIONSHIP OF PSYCHOMETRICS TO COUNSELING?

Psychometric tests have been thought by some to be an integral part of any counseling program, and readers with this point of view may have been puzzled by the fact that tests have scarcely been mentioned. Our use of psychometric devices, like our use of the case history (mentioned in Chapter III, pages 80–83), needs to be reconsidered carefully in the light of our advancing knowledge regarding treatment processes. No attempt will be made to give a complete or final answer to this question here, but a very tentative answer, which may stimulate more adequate consideration, will be given.

There can be no doubt that psychometric tests of abilities, achievements, aptitudes, interests, and personality traits or adjustments are genuinely useful in making diagnostic studies of maladjusted individuals. The diagnostic evaluation of the maladjusted school child, the study of the juvenile or adult delinquent who is to appear before a court, the study of job applicants or army recruits in order to classify them on the basis of aptitudes and skills — all work of this sort relies heavily and rightly upon the information which psychometric tests can give. In the statements which follow there is no intention of questioning the great value of testing in work of this sort.

It is the place of tests in counseling treatment which is not nearly so clear-cut. The disadvantages of using tests at the outset of a series of therapeutic contacts are the same as the disadvantages of taking a complete case history. If the psychologist begins his work with a complete battery of tests, this fact carries with it the implication that he will provide the solutions to the client's problems. The point of view consistently maintained throughout this book is that such "solutions" are not genuine and do not deeply help the individual, but tend to make him either resentful or overdependent.

This is not to say that tests have no place in a counseling process. It is likely that they can be very effective in a number of cases, if they are used toward the conclusion of counseling, essentially upon the client's request. A student may, for example, have come to understand his problem of vocational choice and be ready to move forward. He may, however, sincerely maintain that he does not have a sufficiently objective picture of his interests and aptitudes to make an intelligent choice. Here the counselor can tell him of available tests which might throw light on his vocational possibilities. Would he like to take them? If he does, the results can be very constructive, as the results of the tests are discussed and evaluated in relation to his understanding of himself.

Barbara, the adolescent girl from whose record excerpts were given in the two preceding chapters, finally decided to take an intelligence test. Rather early in the contacts, when she was talking about her "high-powered" intellectual ambitions, she raised a question as to her real ability. The possibility of taking a test was mentioned, but she was very fearful of such a procedure. It was plain that she felt that a test might destroy the basis for her ambitions, might prove that she did not have the ability. Later, as she became more able to accept herself, she spoke of a test with less fear, and in one of her last contacts definitely requested that she be given a test. When the test showed her to be of superior but not exceptional ability, she was able to accept this result. If a test had been given earlier, the counselor would have obtained an earlier evaluation of her mental level, but Barbara would have been either crushed by the result, or forced to rationalize regarding her performance on the test. If she had not been given the results, she would have been extremely anxious.

It is when tests are used to meet a felt need of the client, rather than merely as information for the counselor, that they function therapeutically. A student has decided that his interests lie in commerce rather than in his present field, but is he actually fitted to take commerce? Tests can helpfully give him the answer. A high-school student has worked through his maladjustments and now wishes to know whether he is college material. Tests can help to provide the facts on which he may make his decision.

It is this last statement which provides the clue for the proper use of tests. From the point of view of effective therapy, tests are of value when they can be used constructively by the client in making decisions or in taking positive actions. Their use as instruments to provide information for the counselor seems not to be indicated, with the single exception of determining at the outset whether an individual is a suitable subject for counseling. Here, as in the use of the case history, tests may be necessary in a preliminary study to determine whether the individual meets the criteria set up in Chapter III. Such a preliminary study probably makes treatment somewhat more difficult, but it is a necessary precaution in those instances in which it is doubtful whether a counseling approach or an environmental approach should have the primary emphasis.

We may summarize this tentative answer as to the relation of testing and counseling by saying that, apart from their legitimate diagnostic use, tests may wisely be used, usually in the latter stages of counseling, when they meet a real need of the client for further information which will implement his insight and give clearer direction to the positive steps he is taking. That this position is a radical departure from present practice in many organizations is obvious.

DOES A CLIENT-CENTERED TYPE OF COUNSELING HAVE ANY APPLICATION IN SUCH FIELDS AS VOCATIONAL GUIDANCE AND EDUCATIONAL GUIDANCE?

To many workers in this field, guidance means the giving of information to the individual. He is informed as to various job openings, or given information in regard to courses, grades, the requirements for degrees, and the like. He may be given information about himself — test results on vocational, educational, or aptitude tests. There is no question of the wisdom of such education for the appropriate groups. Where the individual is making a normal adjustment and merely needs further information, supplying such information is a helpful type of education.

Counseling is especially adapted, as has been pointed out before, to the individual who is conflicted, maladjusted, struggling with himself or with his environment. For the individual who is vocationally confused or educationally maladjusted, or whose personal conflicts are resulting in vocational and educational failure, a client-centered type of counseling has a great deal to offer. It would seem logical that every organization or agency which gives general educational help of the sort that has come to be labeled "guidance," should also provide an opportunity for counseling help for those who need it and can use it.

In addition to this specific type of application, the principles outlined in this book, as to the paths by which the individual comes to more independent and mature choices, have deep implications for any work which calls itself "guidance," thereby implying the guiding of the less able by the more able. It is entirely possible that much of our guidance work is based upon principles and policies which do not encourage independent psychological growth. Certainly more thought is needed to adapt the findings in the field of therapy to the various other fields which are closely allied, yet which have specific possibilities and limitations of their own.

Who Is Qualified to Carry on Counseling?

It is obvious that both personal and professional qualifications enter into our evaluation of an individual as a counselor. The discussion here will deal with the personal qualifications, since the matter of professional training is considered in the next section.

In some discussions of counseling the ideal counselor is pictured as some sort of psychological superman — all-knowing, all-wise, above the petty reactions of ordinary men. This is an unrealistic point of view. There are certain personal qualities which should be present if the individual is to develop into a good counselor, but there is no reason to believe that these are any more rare than the qualities which would be necessary for a good artist or a first-class aviation pilot. This is definitely true if we are talking of the client-centered type of counseling and therapy which we have been describing in this volume. The directive counselor, to be sure, has need of more omnipotent qualities. Even in our phonographic recordings we find these counselors deciding with assurance such diverse issues as how to study history, how to get along with one's parents, how to solve the issue of racial discrimination, and what is the proper philosophy of life. From other records we know that such counselors decide issues of marital adjustment, questions of vocational choice, problems of discipline, and, in fact, all the puzzling personal questions which a perplexed individual can face. Obviously a generous portion of supernatural wisdom is required of the individual who takes such an attitude toward counseling. When the goal is more modest and the aim is to help the individual to free himself so that he can decide these

issues in his own way, then the necessary attributes of the counselor are reduced to a human dimension.

Perhaps the first qualification for a counselor is that he should
be a person who is sensitive to human relationships. This is a
quality which is difficult to define satisfactorily, but which is
evident in almost any social situation. The person who is quite
obtuse to the reactions of others, who does not realize that his
remarks have caused another pleasure or distress, who does
not sense the hostility or friendliness which exists between himself and others or between two of his acquaintances, is not
likely to become a satisfactory counselor. There is no doubt
that this quality can be developed, but unless an individual has
a considerable degree of this social sensitivity, it is doubtful
that counseling is his most promising field of effort. On the
other hand, the individual who is naturally observant of the
reactions of others, who can pick out of a schoolroom group the
unhappy children, who can sense the personal antagonism which
underlies an outwardly casual argument, who is alert to the
subtle differences in actions which show that one parent has a
comfortable relationship with his child, another a relationship
full of tensions — such a person has a good natural foundation
upon which to build counseling skills.

If we regard this social sensitivity as a basic qualification,
there are certain other attitudes which are also essential for the
good counselor. The following paragraphs briefly describe
these attributes. Although these statements were written to
apply to the counselor who works with children, they apply
with equal force to those who counsel adults.

Objectivity. It is generally conceded that to be helpful as a
therapist the clinical worker needs to have an objective attitude.
This has been variously described as "controlled identification,"
as "constructive composure," and as "an emotionally detached
attitude." The term as used in clinical practice is defined somewhat differently than in the strictly scientific field. There is
included in the concept a capacity for sympathy which will not
be overdone, a genuinely receptive and interested attitude, a
deep understanding which will find it impossible to pass moral
judgments or be shocked and horrified. A person with this at-

titude differs on the one hand from the cold and impersonal detachment of the individual with Jovian tendencies, and differs quite as sharply from the deeply sympathetic and sentimental individual who becomes so wrapped up in the child's problems as to be quite incapable of helping. It is, to come back to the first description of it, a degree of sympathetic "identification" with the child sufficient to bring about an understanding of the feelings and problems which are disturbing the youngster, but an identification which is "controlled," because understood, by the therapist. . . .[1]

Respect for the Individual. A second qualification of the effective therapist is a deep-seated respect for the child's integrity. If the child is to gain real help to grow in his own way toward goals of his own choice, the therapist must create a relationship where such growth can take place. The worker who is filled with a reforming zeal, or who is unconsciously eager to make the child over into his own image, cannot do this. There must be a willingness to accept the child as he is, on his own level of adjustment, and to give him some freedom to work out his own solutions to his problems. . . .[2]

An Understanding of the Self. Another essential element in the personality make-up of the therapist is a sound understanding of himself, of his outstanding emotional patterns, and of his own limitations and shortcomings. Unless there is this considerable degree of insight, he will not be able to recognize the situations in which he is likely to be warped and biased by his own prejudices and emotions. He will not be able to understand why there are certain types of children or types of problems which he is unable to treat satisfactorily. Thoroughly to understand and be objective in regard to the child's problems, the therapist must have some insight into his own personality.[3]

It is probable that this degree of self-understanding is most satisfactorily gained through adequate supervision while in training. As the counselor-in-training deals with cases himself, he becomes much more aware of his own blind spots, his own emotional needs, and the ways in which he has satisfied these. The supervisor has a rare opportunity to assist the individual to gain insight into himself in this training process. Not infrequently this may involve a counseling relationship

[1] Rogers, Carl R. *The Clinical Treatment of the Problem Child*, p. 281.
[2] *Ibid.*, p. 282.   [3] *Ibid.*, p. 283.

between student and supervisor, if the counselor-in-training comes to feel the need of such assistance.

Psychological Knowledge   Finally, the therapist can scarcely expect to do satisfactory work without a thorough basis of knowledge of human behavior and of its physical, social, and psychological determinants.   It might seem more logical to put this qualification first, but the experience of every clinic would bear out the viewpoint that a full knowledge of psychiatric and psychological information, with a brilliant intellect capable of applying this knowledge, is of itself no guarantee of therapeutic skill.   The essential qualifications of the psychotherapist lie primarily, as we have pointed out, in the realm of attitudes, emotions, and insight, rather than in the realm of intellectual equipment. [4]

WHAT SHOULD BE THE TRAINING OF THE COUNSELOR?

This is a question upon which a number of professional groups are focusing attention.   It would be presumptuous to attempt any final answer.   Certain broad trends, however, are fairly well agreed upon and may be pointed out here.   The characteristics of a satisfactory course of training should, it would seem, include the following:

1. An adequate program of selection which will choose for training as counselors those individuals who are interested in service in the field of human relationships, and who have the personal qualifications already outlined.

2. Basic work which leads to a fundamental understanding of human relationships.   Courses in sociology, social psychology, and anthropology would help to meet this need.   Experience in group work or teaching or in the field of industrial relationships is also valuable in this connection.

3. Basic courses leading to an understanding of the psychological development and adjustment of the individual.   A considerable portion of the training period should be devoted to such work.   Courses in the biological development of the individual are of some importance here, but special emphasis

[4] *Ibid.,* 284.

should be given to work in genetic and developmental psychology, child, adolescent, and adult psychology. Courses in the dynamics of human adjustment help to lay a basis for study of various types of adjustment problems — family and marital adjustments, vocational adjustments, the adjustments of deviates such as the abnormal, the subnormal, the delinquent, and other groups.

4. Training in research methods, in order that the counselor may have adequate techniques for evaluating his own work and that of others, and thus a sound basis for progress.

5. Courses in the techniques of counseling, in which the individual can become acquainted with various viewpoints toward counseling and psychotherapy.

6. Supervised experience, in which counseling is carried on with ample opportunity for detailed criticism and evaluation by a qualified supervisory individual.

If one asks where such training is available, the answer is that it is only partially available in most institutions which provide professional training. Several professional groups, notably those concerned with social case work, clinical psychology, clinical psychiatry, and educational guidance, endeavor to give training for work which involves counseling. Each of these professional groups exhibits certain characteristic strengths and weaknesses in its professional training for counseling. Social workers have been especially successful in developing supervised practical experience. They have tended to be weak in the acquisition of basic knowledge and in the field of research. Psychologists, on the other hand, have developed perhaps the best training in the basic knowledges required, and have adequate training in research, but until recently have had few satisfactory courses in counseling and have been weak in supplying the necessary supervised field experience. From the point of view of future development, it may be significant that the psychologist is more free to concentrate his training solely upon the psychological problems of the individual than are the members of the other professions mentioned. The social worker must devote a large part of her training to problems of relief administration, legal aspects of social welfare, and the like.   The psychiatrist devotes the great bulk of his preparatory years to the organic problems of the individual.   The worker in the field of educational guidance must devote much time to gaining an understanding of educational administration.   The clinical psychologist alone is free to devote the bulk of his training to gaining understanding of the psychological development and adjustments of the individual.   The psychiatrist's training has been notoriously weak in any basic training in the psychological development of the normal individual, and he has been handicapped by the fact that his training concentrates to such an extent upon the organic problems of the individual that insufficient time is given to the psychological aspects.   Psychiatric training has, however, been rightly noted for the extent of practical experience which is given in interneships, at its best giving the young psychiatrist well-supervised training, and at its worst permitting him to develop a rule-of-thumb approach to psychotherapy which has little to commend it.   In the field of educational guidance there has been much attention given to environmental methods of bringing about adjustment, but relatively little to the counseling approach, in spite of the large numbers of counselors employed in educational institutions.

The above generalizations do not, of course, apply in all cases.   They are intended merely to show what every thoughtful worker in the field recognizes, that no one avenue of professional training can be said to offer the ideal preparation for counseling maladjusted individuals.   What is needed, and what may one day be achieved, is a new type of professional training in the adjustment problems of human beings and the professional skills which are helpful in meeting those problems.

PART IV

The Case of Herbert Bryan

The Case of Herbert Bryan

INTRODUCTION

THE REMAINDER of this book is unique. It is the complete account, phonographically recorded, of the counseling process as it was carried on with on~ individual. So far as the writer is aware, this is the first time that such a presentation has been made. Of case histories, many are available, in all degrees of detail. In the last decade there have been a number of case accounts of treatment, particularly in th field of social work, which describe rather fully the various measures which were adopted and which contain at least summaries, and in some instances dialogue accounts, of portions of the interviews. But to have all the material of a series of counseling interviews — to have the counselor's statements as well as the client's — to have an account in which every spoken word is included — to have an account in which neither bias nor wishful thinking has had any influence — this is a new opportunity. It is this opportunity that the writer and a number of co-workers have had in their use of phonographically recorded treatment interviews, and it is this opportunity which it is desired to make more widely available, through the publication of one complete case.

Scientific progress in counseling can only take place as we have an adequate research analysis of adequate data. Up to the present time we have never had adequate data. All accounts of interviews have been very incomplete and influenced to an unknown degree by the bias of the interviewer. Brief illustrations are always unsatisfactory from a scientific point of view, not only because of their brevity, but because they have definitely been selected to prove a point.   What is needed is the complete material of interviewing, permitting the student to study the course of therapy in leisurely and exhaustive fashion.   It is such material that is presented in the case of Herbert Bryan.

The Selection of a Case.   No one individual can be said to be typical of all.   Mr. Bryan is an adult.   He is not a child, nor a parent.   His problems are those of a neurotic, not the problems of the delinquent, nor of the student with educational problems.   He is one individual, with special difficulties of his own, which are not those of any other individual.   Yet from the viewpoint of this book, this is not a serious disadvantage.   If counseling is looked upon as the solving of problems, then a multitude of cases will be necessary to show how each problem or each type of problem may be handled.   But if counseling consists of creating an atmosphere in which the client can develop insight and begin to redirect his life in new directions, then an illustration of the ways in which a counselor has created such an atmosphere in one case is, in a very real sense, typical of what the counselor can do in all cases.   Consequently, the fact that the case which follows is that of but one individual, who can by no means be described as "typical," is not a matter for apology.

The Preparation of the Case Material.   The interviews which follow were all phonographically recorded and have been transcribed from the records.   They have not been edited in any way, except where it was necessary to delete or change identifying information.   Fortunately Mr. Bryan (and this, of course, is not his real name) tended to put his problems in general terms, and hence a minimum of such editing has been necessary.

The Use of the Material.   There are several ways in which this material may be used constructively by the reader.   In the first place, it may be read as an example of treatment interviewing simply in order to get the "feel" of the movement and progress which take place as the interviews continue. It is printed in such a form that the reader may follow only the recorded material, without any reference to the notes and comments which have been made. A second use of this material is to regard it as a basis for research. The changing types of counselor and client response as counseling progresses, the changing self-concepts of the client, the type of counselor statement which is usually associated with a certain type of client statement — these are some of the more obvious research possibilities. A third use is to read each interview carefully, considering also the comments which have been added. The counselor who desires to assimilate the principles advanced in this book will find this a profitable method of procedure, since the various aspects of the counseling process which we have discussed are pointed out as they occur in the case. A fourth use is perhaps the most significant for the counselor who wishes to consider and improve his own techniques. If he will read each statement of the client, covering the next response of the counselor with a sheet of paper, he may ask himself, "What would be my response?" He is thus faced with a real interviewing situation, but without any of the feeling of pressure or haste which is likely to be a part of an actual interview. He may formulate his response thoughtfully, compare it with the response made by the counselor in this case, consider which is better, and evaluate both in the light of his own principles of counseling. This is perhaps the most profitable way of using such interview material for the person who has a serious professional interest in counseling.

The Case. Without further preliminaries, let us introduce Mr. Herbert Bryan, a young man in his late twenties, who came to a psychological counselor for assistance. He stated that he wished help with his problems and that he regarded them as deep-seated. He started to tell of his difficulties, but the counselor informed him that he would prefer to postpone such discussion until a regular appointment, when there would be more time.   There were several difficulties in the way of making a series of appointments, and these were discussed, but an arrangement was reached.

These remarks are sufficient to introduce the first interview, since it is all the information which was available to the counselor at that time.   However, it might be added that Mr. Bryan turned out to be a highly intelligent, definitely neurotic young man, verbalistic and intellectual in his interests.   This last trait makes his interviews particularly valuable, in that he verbalizes attitudes which most clients probably hold, but which few of them state with such clarity.

From a traditional point of view, Mr. Bryan would be regarded as a difficult individual to treat.   It develops that he has read widely in psychology, and he knows and uses psychological terms intelligently.   He has sought help before; he attended an institute for those with speech difficulties, and he went to a college counselor for help.   In addition, he has tried self-hypnosis and a number of other techniques in order to rid himself of his problems.   Hence he enters the counseling situation not as a naïve individual, but as one who has tried such help and found it wanting.

❧ FIRST INTERVIEW ❧

*C*1.* Well, now, we were so concerned yesterday about these various aspects of whether or not we were to go ahead with it, that I don't know that I have as clear a picture as I'd like to have of what's on your mind, so go ahead and tell me.

*S*1. Well, as accurately as I can convey the idea, I would term it a blocking which has manifestations in several fields.

*C*2. M-hm.

*S*2. The — in my earlier childhood the symptom of blocking which was emphasized on my consciousness most was in speech. I developed a speech impediment along about the sixth grade. Then, as I matured, I noticed a blocking in sexual situations. However, not — not in the voyeuristic situation, only in an intercourse situation; oftentimes I had difficulty there. Also an unpleasant tight feeling in the lower abdomen, as if, to use an analogy, there were some sort of a cold, hard axe or some other such thing pressing against the libido in such a way as to block it.

*C*3. M-hm.

*S*3. Now, another interesting angle there, this negative feeling was at first referred to my chest. There was sort of a dull, cold ache there. I'd get cold hands and have an increase

---

*C*1. The counselor by this very broad kind of opening question makes it easy for the client to discuss his problem in any way he wishes. Note that *S*1, 2, and 3 are all in response to this one question.

*S*1, 2, 3, 4, 5, 6. This sequence of client statements is a classical example of a neurotic's description of his problems. The bizarre physical symptoms, the feelings of tension, are typical. As the case progresses, the reader will wish to compare the problems as at first presented with the real problems which cause the basic difficulty. Note that this sophisticated individual gives a very sophisticated

---

* Throughout these interviews the responses of the counselor (*c*) and the subject (*s*) are numbered for easy reference. The footnotes which accompany the interview material are numbered correspondingly.

in heartbeat at certain times, in certain situations where I was blocked.   And then that feeling began to go down, as it were. That's the best way I can describe it.   I mean, I guess actually — I mean, that's the way that I referred the feeling, as traveling downward.

*C*4. M-hm.   And does it cause you more distress than it used to, or is that no different?

*S*4. I hardly know what to say there.   I used to be very distressed about my speech, although that's not as bad as it was.   I used to, uh — I used to be a very bad — a very bad stutterer, uh — then I sort of — sort of — sort of got my mind off of it and more or less forced myself to ignore it and to go ahead anyway, even though it was a terrific tension for me to go into certain situations.

*C*5. M-hm.

*S*5. But — uh, in later years, the actual feeling itself seems to have — that is, the feeling seems to have been — seems to have been, shall we say, compressed, as well as moved.   That is, I feel that it has been intensified and in moving downward has become more compressed.   I mean, that's the sensation I get.

*C*6. M-hm.   M-hm.

*S*6. It's only a vague sort of cold and dull feeling in the chest, then it became more and more intensified as it moved down lower.   And sometimes it gets very excruciating.   I just seem to be held down, as it were, blocked in all realms of life.

---

picture of his problems.   The naïve individual will give a naïve picture of his problems.   In either case, it is unlikely that the problem as initially stated is the fundamental formulation.

*C*4. Here is a moderately directive question, limiting the client to a specified area for discussion.   However, the question is distinctly a response to the feeling of distress Mr. Bryan has been expressing, rather than to the intellectual content.   It might have been better for the counselor simply to recognize the material expressed, in some such statement as, "You've noticed a real change in these symptoms?"

*S*4. As soon as he mentions his previous problem of stuttering, Mr. Bryan begins to stutter, and this continues in *S*5.

*C*7. A feeling of real pain, is that what you mean?

*S*7. Oh, yes.

*C*8. M-hm.

*S*8. And then sometimes for short periods it mysteriously goes. I mean, there's no particular ideology with its going. I get release, and then I'm very active and very happy during these short periods — I'd say they occur — oh, I have one or two good days a month when I'm practically free of it, but I never know when they're going to come on, or when my bad periods —

*C*9. And you say that you feel this does block you in a good many areas of life?

*S*9. In practically all areas of life — anything which you could mention. I hesitate to meet people — I hesitate to canvass for my photographic business. I feel a terrific aversion to any kind of activity, even dancing. I normally enjoy dancing very well. But when my inhibition, or whatever you wish to call it, is on me powerfully, it is an ordeal for me to dance. I notice a difference in my musical ability. On my good days I can harmonize with other people singing.

---

*C*7. This counselor response is definitely helpful in bringing progress. It must already be evident to the counselor that these are psychological, not organic, sufferings. The usual reaction is to question, in some way, their validity. Any such implication would have thrown the client on the defensive and made him intent on proving that his pain was real. The counselor's recognition that he is describing real pain helps Mr. Bryan to feel that he is genuinely understood, and makes it possible for him to go ahead and tell of times when he is not suffering (*S*8).

*C*9. Here it seems evident that the counselor has just assimilated the second half of the client's statement *S*6, and is now responding to it. Our phonographic records indicate that this occurs quite frequently and that responses are often made, not to the preceding speech, but to an earlier one. This is not necessarily a criticism. The feeling that is thus verbally recognized is a real one, and the recognition of it leads Mr. Bryan to expand it more fully, bringing it more completely into the open. This is the usual result of recognition of feeling.

*S*9. Here we gain the first diagnostic inkling as to what purposes Mr. Bryan's symptoms may serve. They may help to keep him from work activities and from social contacts.

*C*10. M-hm.

*S*10. I have a good ear for harmony then. But when I'm blocked, I seem to lose that, as well as my dancing ability. I feel very awkward and stiff.

*C*11. M-hm. So that both in your work and in your recreation you feel blocked.

*S*11. I don't want to do anything. I just lie around. I get no gusto for any activity at all.

*C*12. You just feel rather unable to do things, is that it?

*S*12. Well, I actually feel pressure on me just like that (*pointing to abdomen*), as near as I can refer it, uh — pressing down right on my dynamo, as you might say.

*C*13. M-hm. And you — In spite of the difficulty that it causes you, you feel pretty sure that it isn't physical?

*S*13. Oh, I know that it isn't physical. Well, for several reasons — I've had thorough physical check-ups for one thing. For another, the fact that it leaves me, and leaves me very, very suddenly. Within a half a minute, I can have a complete change.

*C*14. Is that so? (*Pause.*) Can you tell me about any of those times?

---

*C*11, *C*12. Good instances of entirely non-directive responses which simply recognize the feeling being expressed, make conversation easy, and enable the client to continue to explore his attitudes.

*C*13. This question and its answer seem to be the one unit of a strictly diagnostic nature in the whole series of contacts. Here is a client who seems obviously suitable for counseling help. He is adult and sufficiently in control of his environment to be carrying on a business. He is under psychological stress, as indicated by his conversation. His intelligence is clearly above average, as indicated by his vocabulary. He seems to meet all of the criteria set up in Chapter III, provided these tensions are primarily psychological and not organic. This one question is settled at this point. Whether consciously planned for this purpose or not, the counselor has shrewdly put his finger on the one point on which diagnostic knowledge was necessary.

*C*14. The one directive diagnostic question, *C*13, puts the client in the question-answering frame of mind, and hence there comes a pause which the counselor has to break, this time with a less directive question.

*S*14. Well, it's just the painful weighty feeling leaves me. And it never leaves me with the same ideological counterpart. I mean, I might be thinking about something else or I might be working on a self-psychoanalytic technique which I thought would be helpful. And sometimes certain thoughts help my release. Other times those exact same thoughts — the exact same self-technique doesn't work at all.

*C*15. M-hm. So that you feel that it goes and comes absolutely beyond your control.

*S*15. Yes. My impression is that the whole thing is — has nothing to do with my conscious thought or it is not under my conscious control. So that except under the voyeuristic situation I mentioned — If I were to be feeling bad, and then would look out and see a woman undressed, then I'd feel happy.

*C*16. At those times you wouldn't have any of this feeling of pressure or distress.

*S*16. No. Oddly enough, that's the one touchstone that always seems to ——

*C*17. You feel that's some kind of a clue to it.

*S*17. Well, yes, I think so. Now, sometimes I can have an enjoyable intercourse — other times, it isn't enjoyable — it's almost a mechanical process — I don't get very much sensation.

*C*18. So that in that situation, you're not at all sure that you'll be free of this feeling, or free of difficulty.

*S*18. Well, I know beforehand that if I have a bad day, why it isn't going to do me much good. Although I have had the difficulty leave me, and leave me rather suddenly, so that I was able to carry on O.K.

*C*19. But, I mean, that may or may not happen, where as I understand it, in what you described as a voyeuristic situation, you're pretty sure there that ——

---

*C*15. This is the type of response which shows that the counselor has been thinking deeply about the emotionalized attitude which the client is expressing. He responds very definitely to that feeling and not at all to the content.

*C*18, *C*19. Evidently a clumsy attempt on the counselor's part to respond to Mr. Bryan's statement that it is only in "the voyeuristic situation" that he feels satisfied.

*S*19. I always have the euphoria there, yes.

*C*20. Well, you've thought of that yourself as a clue. Do you have any notion as to what that ties up with, or what the origin ——

*S*20. Well, I can trace the origin. When I was very young, back in the first grade, we had a couple of girl student roomers with us, and they used to exhibit to me; that is, I think they actually did it deliberately, and I got quite a sex kick.

*C*21. When was this, you say? What grade? You said something about the grade you were in.

*S*21. First grade.

*C*22. I see.

*S*22. I was about five then. That's my earliest form of sexual pleasure, and it was associated with that sort of a phantasy. And I think I've analyzed it further — the actual feeling is one of vicarious exhibitionism; that is, it's more intense when I know that the girl is actually exhibiting to me, rather than just being accidental.

———

*C*1 to *S*19, inclusive. Note how necessary it is to follow the pattern of the client's feeling if the counselor is to discover with any accuracy what the real issues are. Up to this point, the counselor might, with the best of intentions, have seized upon any of these problems as being the one upon which to focus attention — the abdominal physical symptoms, the voyeuristic satisfactions, which sound vaguely compulsive, the sexual maladjustment, the difficulties in adjusting to social situations. To investigate each of these areas by questioning might indicate which of these problems is most significant, but might never discover some deeper problem underlying all. This would be a most time-consuming process, with no guarantee of success. Obviously the swifter and more realistic method is to encourage expression, in full confidence that the client will gradually take the counselor to the heart of his problems.

*C*20. Evidently the counselor again feels the need of using a moderately directive question in order to keep the conversation going. While the question follows the lead given by the client in *S*16, a simple recognition of feeling, "That's the one situation in which you're sure of satisfaction," would probably have been more helpful.

*C*23. M-hm. You've analyzed this thing quite a bit as to various aspects of it. Can you tell me any more of your thinking about it? You say that you feel this is perhaps the origin of it ——

*S*23. Well, of course that would account for the positive feelings. Now to account for the negative feelings. I was raised in a very Victorian and puritan manner. My mother even whipped me one time for talking with a friend of mine. She thought it was terrible. We had noticed, well, different animals and so forth, and she was very horrified. I remember she worked up to quite a dramatic climax. She said, "Well, did you talk about locusts?" and "Did you mention animals?" and then "Did you mention human beings?" Worked up to a climax, and then she whipped me for, well, for even mentioning the facts. I suppose I assumed that if it were horrible to talk about, it would even be more horrible to do. Then my father had very definite ascetic notions — it's a medieval concept — "mortification of the flesh" — that sort of thing. When he was a young man he went on a fast and all that sort of thing to make himself more spiritual. He's outgrown that sort of thing, but he was very intense that way as a young man. I think that comes from his mother. She was very much of a Calvinist — very much opposed to card playing, dancing, things like that. He had quite an attachment to his mother. I'm sure she dominated his life.

*C*24. So that you feel your folks are somewhat the basis of some of your difficulty?

*S*24. Well, psychologically and of course philosophically you can carry it back there, I'm sure. But, yes, I'd say this is

---

*C*23. A very broad, non-directive type of lead, which, as usual, is productive.

*S*20, *S*22, *S*23. Note how Mr. Bryan, in these items, places all the responsibility for his problems upon others. The counselor catches this underlying feeling and responds to it at least partially in *C*24.

*S*24. Intellectually, this client "knows all the answers." Unless counseling has more to offer him than intellectual content, it is obviously doomed to failure.

entirely a matter of conditioning.   But I don't know whether realizing one's conditioning should effect a therapy or whether there must be something more.   I used to have the idea that if I would recall all the childhood events consciously and bring them up to my consciousness from the subconscious, there would be release there, but either I haven't thought of something, either there is something there that hasn't been thought of, or realizing it hasn't done any good.

*C*25. Whatever you've done hasn't worked enough to free you from the problem, is that it?

*S*25. No, when I do think of unpleasant childhood episodes, it seems to intensify rather than do it any good.   So I ——

*C*26. Then you've simply lived with this for quite a number of years.   Why is it any worse now, or why are you trying definitely to do something about it?

*S*26. Well, it's just reached the point where it becomes unbearable.   I'd rather be dead than live as I am now.

*C*27. You'd rather be dead than live as you are now?   Can you tell me a little bit more about that?

*S*27. Well, I hope.   Of course we always live on hope.

*C*28. Yes.

*S*28. But — No, I don't have any conscious suicidal urge or anything like that.   It's just that — looking at it rationally, I feel that I'm — that I'm in the red now and I wouldn't want to keep on living in the red.   (*Pause.*)

*C*29. Well, can you tell me in any more detailed way what

---

*c*25. This is a point where it would have been very easy for the counselor to become involved in an intellectual discussion of therapy. It is to his credit that he responds only to the feeling.

*c*26. Why did the counselor interrupt here?   This seems to be a quite unnecessary directive question breaking into the flow of feeling. It leads to brief client responses ending in a pause (*S*28), which the counselor has to break with another rather directive question.   This in turn leads to a repetition of the symptoms originally described (*S*29), and it is only following this that a fresh start in recognition of feeling is made.   This is a minor example of the way in which clumsy handling by the counselor can delay progress.

— in what way it blocks you so much that you really feel sometimes that you'd be better off dead?

*S*29. Well, I don't know if I can any more accurately describe the sensation. It's just a — a very impressive and painful weight as if an axe were pressing on the whole abdomen, pressing down, I can almost — I can almost sense the position and I feel that it's oppressing me very radically, that is, that it goes right down to the roots of my dynamic energy, so that no matter in what field I essay any sort of effort, I find the blocking.

*C*30. It really just cripples you as far as anything else is concerned.

*S*30. Yes. M-hm. And that even has a physical counterpart. When I walk, that is, when I'm feeling badly, I walk hunched over and sort of like I had a bellyache, which I actually do have, psychologically.

*C*31. M-hm. It just makes you more or less half a man, is that it? And only half able to do your work ——

*S*31. Yes. It's just as if I had an axe in me literally, you might say. I feel it in my very core of energy — it's blocked and oppressed in that painful way. It's a deep-seated thing, because conversely when I get the release I feel a deep-seated flowing of energy.

*C*32. When you feel all right — you feel very much all right.

*S*32. Oh, yes, yes. Very dynamic — my mind works much more rapidly and everything's all right. Anything I try I do successfully.

*C*33. And what you want is to find ways of increasing the amount of time that you have that dynamic self, is that it?

*S*33. Oh, yes. Be that way all the time. I don't see any reason why I couldn't be. The whole thing is psychological, and I want to get at it.

*C*34. Well, I think possibly one way of doing that might be

---

*C*30, *C*31, *C*32, *C*33. These responses constitute a productive following of the client's pattern of emotionalized attitudes.

*C*34. This is the first attempt on the part of the counselor to define verbally the counseling relationship, and it is only a minor gesture to talk somewhat more about the ways in which it does block you, I mean, what — in your work, for instance, and some other things.

*S*34. Well, the blocking is so universal, almost anything I could mention, it would hold true. Now, do you want me to go ahead and mention the ways?

*C*35. Well, possibly not. But you feel that it really prevents you from doing anything that you might wish to do?

*S*35. On my bad days I just can't do anything, and it isn't what you would call lethargy, although that is what it would seem to the observer. It's actually a tying up; that is, I feel the conflict going on within me. I have an intense inward feeling that the impulses and the inhibitions are so accurately blocked and counterbalanced that it leads to inertia.

*C*36. Plenty of energy there, but it's just lost in the balance.

*S*36. Yes. I'm quite aware of that.

*C*37. You say those feelings mean a good deal of conflict. Can you tell any more about those?

*S*37. Well, I referred there to the tone, which is one of energy, with the inhibition cracking down on the energy, no matter in what realm I wish to be energetic. That is, if — well, if I'm feeling that way and somebody wants to give a party or there's work to be done or there's something I want to read or some intellectual problem I want to think about, why, I'm not able to do it. But when I have my good days, I do achieve so much, you see, that it's very disheartening to me to have bad days, because I know what I can achieve when I have my release.

---

in that direction. However, every counselor response tends in one way or another to structure the relationship, and the client must have, even at this point, some recognition of the unusual freedom of the relationship and its lack of any strongly directive aspects. Following this brief explanation, there is the usual slight amount of difficulty in getting the client to take the lead again in the conversation and to talk freely and without restriction (*S*34 and *C*35). From this point, however, the client goes on, picturing his difficulty for the first time as a conflict.

*C*38. You feel that if you were at your best, your abilities and achievements and all would really be topnotch.

*S*38. I've done some writing which the professors at M—— University have liked. Now I find that that's blocked — that was one of the last things to be blocked, by the way. I could write up until I was a junior and that became blocked.

*C*39. M-hm. And then there was a time when you couldn't even do that?

*S*39. Yes. I haven't been able to write since, except in a very sporadic manner. But I like to write, and that is perhaps my main ambition — to write novels. I had a course at M—— in novel writing and liked it very much — did A work in that.

*C*40. And tell me, what sort of thing stopped you from writing — I mean, if you could do it up to a point.

*S*40. It was a feeling that stopped me. That is, my impression of my ailment is that it is a feeling — there is never any constant ideological pattern. It's simply blind feeling.

*C*41. And gradually this feeling grew to a point where you couldn't write?

*S*41. I don't know whether it grew up to that point, or whether writing came under its influence independent of its quantitative growth.

*C*42. I see. Well, then, perhaps it became focused more on writing.

*S*42. Well, writing came into the fold and it blocked that too.

*C*43. So that gradually that circle has grown until everything you might want to do is within that circle of blocked activities.

*S*43. Except voyeurism.

---

*C*40. This direct question is in line with the client's feeling, and in the rapid give and take of the interview we cannot expect perfection. Nevertheless, it is plain that a better response on the part of the counselor would have been, "You like to write, but this blocking keeps you from it." It often seems difficult to catch and bring into the open the ambivalent impulses.

*C*43, *S*43, *C*44. Adequate recognition of attitudes brings the flow of feeling around again to the same point which was poorly recognized

*C*44. So that the satisfaction you get from voyeurism is almost the only thing from which you're sure at the present time that you can gain satisfaction?

*S*44. Well, yes, that and food.

*C*45. Appetite is still good.   M-hm.

*S*45. M-hm, although when I'm in awfully bad condition, I lose my appetite to a very considerable extent.   That doesn't happen very often.

*C*46. Well, I think that the sort of thing that perhaps we can do in our discussions together is to explore this thing pretty fully — uh, find out what it means to you and why it has blocked you in different situations and gradually see if we can find ways of dealing with it.   I think that's the ——

*S*46. As I analyze myself, I'm sure that there is some impulse for me to cling to it — that it's ——

*C*47. That there is some what?

*S*47. An impulse for me to retain my inhibition — it's paradoxical.   I get some sort of inner satisfaction out of it evidently.

_____

at *C*18, *C*19.   The phonographic recordings indicate that this frequently occurs.   If the client expresses some attitude which has significance for him, and this is misunderstood or inadequately recognized by the counselor, the same attitude is likely to be expressed again later.   Adequate recognition, on the other hand, tends to lead to further and deeper expression.

*C*46. Here the counselor makes a more complete and satisfactory attempt to define the type of help which the client can expect from counseling.

*S*46, *S*47. Is it because the counselor's remarks sound almost as though he were bringing the interview to a close that Mr. Bryan is able to reveal this highly significant feeling?   Or is it merely that having revealed his superficial symptoms, he is now ready to recognize that they are to some extent symptoms that he wants?   At any rate, in this one interview, he has gone through three levels of expression of his problems.   At first they are described as pain, suffering, maladjustment.   Then (*S*35) they are described as conflicting forces within himself.   Now they are recognized as symptoms to which he clings, in spite of his desire to change.   This is actually the beginning of insight, a clearer degree of self-understanding.

*C*48. There is a feeling you have a certain tendency to cling to this, even though you don't like it.

*S*48. And, of course, that's invariably borne out — I feel this way about psychological changes — if a person wholeheartedly wants to change, the change automatically occurs. Of course, perhaps that's a little bit tautological. I don't know. My own impression of these things, or my intuition about them, I should say much more accurately, is that if the person really wants to change, why the change occurs, so there must be some reason, or must be some — and I do sense that I have an emotional something that's clinging to my neurosis — not willing to give it up.

*C*49. You feel that conceivably if you wanted wholeheartedly to get rid of it, possibly you could get rid of it.

*S*49. Why, I know that I could get rid of it then. But, of course, that's defining wholeheartedness in terms of getting rid of it, so it becomes tautological.

*C*50. Yes. M-hm. But you say that at times you do sense a certain amount of tendency to cling to it. Can you say any more about that, or times when you felt that?

*S*50. I wrestle with it, but I know that I'm not wrestling powerfully enough. I know that the other aspect of my personality wants to preserve the *status quo*. Well, after all, the whole thing is occurring within me, and it's what might be termed a war within my own house.

*C*51. Part of your problem is to discover who and what are the enemy in your own home.

*S*51. Yes. I feel that there's some sort of a hidden touchstone that provides the driving force for the oppression, and

---

*C*48. Fortunately the counselor recognizes and states clearly the ambivalent feeling which is being expressed. This enables the client further to express his feeling in what are the most significant items of this first interview. They show clear progress in exploration at more than a superficial level.

*C*51. Here the counselor takes the opportunity to define again what counseling can mean, putting it in terms of the client's symbols, which is always a sound device.

that there is — I feel that it is a blind impulse, rather immune to logic, but of course not necessarily immune to change, that is, I mean, there are other ways besides logic, of course ——

*C*52. In other words, you haven't been able to reason yourself out of it — nor has anyone else, is that it?

*S*52. Yes. In other words, I even get the impression that I have a full cognitive appreciation of the difficulty and that even if I were — even if there were no more new ideas to come out, that that would have nothing to do with the change. That is, of course, I have a theory of persuasion anyway. Of course, that's in the philosophic realm. I don't believe that anybody is ever persuaded by logic or reasoning — it's emotional undercurrents which undergo the change, and logic, that's just a rationalization — sort of a rack to hang your coat on.

*C*53. In other words, you feel that nobody could persuade you out of this situation.

*S*53. No. I feel that I already know the logic of it, but that doesn't effect a cure. Now, I feel that in the last analysis — I think that psychoanalysis is probably a matter of prestige — prestige persuasion. I feel that if I get a confidence in you, that you know more about it than I do — that regardless of the logic — that is, I feel I am your equal in logic, but that you are my superior in certain emotion-changing techniques.

---

*S*52. This intelligent and sophisticated client can put into words what most clients feel — that they cannot be talked out of, or argued out of, or persuaded out of, their problems.

*C*53. Here, again, the counselor must have been tempted to agree or disagree. He wisely does neither, but merely clarifies the attitude that is being expressed.

*S*53. Here the client refers to the process as psychoanalysis. In *S*48 he refers to his neurosis. It is the client, not the counselor, who is using the technical terminology. Whether the counselor should endeavor to correct him, to explain the difference between this counseling process and a classical analysis, is doubtful. It would almost certainly become an intellectual detour, delaying real progress.

*C*54. In other words, if you felt that gradually you had enough confidence, and so on, in me, I might be able to bring about some change in you, but you couldn't very well do that by yourself.

*S*54. Well, let's put it this way. Right now, the part of my personality that wants to change is outvoted. We're going to have to change the balance of power. Now, how to change that — how to get a majority in the house — I don't know. I've tried several techniques on myself and had some talks with a man at M—— University; and I feel this way — now it sort of comes down to a sort of philosophic — what shall we say? — sort of a get-nowhere thing, that is, when you're in such a position where the negatives outweigh, how are you going to get the motivation to change the situation?

*C*55. You feel that you've got this thing fairly well analyzed; you realize it is a balance of power within yourself ——

*S*55. But I can't lift myself up by the bootstraps, as it were.

*C*56. Yes. I think you do have a remarkably good intellectual analysis of the situation, and you feel quite rightly that you can't lift yourself by your bootstraps. It's possible, though, that as we explore this thing you can at least decide clearly whether you want to vote the same way you're voting now, or whether there may be other ways of ——

---

*C*54. This is an interesting point. The counselor might have used this opportunity to define his rôle in this type of therapy. Instead, he merely recognizes the client's dependent feeling. Probably this was the better choice. If he had failed to recognize it, undoubtedly it would have cropped out again.

*S*54, *C*55, *S*55, *C*56. In this interchange the client is clearly asking the counselor to supply the motivation which he needs. The counselor neither agrees nor refuses. He further defines the relationship as a situation in which a clear choice can be made. At the conclusion of *C*56, in the statement "whether you want to vote the same way," he implies a unity in the client which has by no means been expressed. This is really a very subtle beginning of interpretation, which could easily be overdone.

S56. Well, to draw another analogy, I feel that I have so much energy, so much reservoir of energy — now, what I want to do is to get the negatives to desert to the positive side. Which will be a double-barreled gain, you see, and will probably occur very rapidly once the ball gets rolling. But when the negatives are in power, why, of course how can the ball begin to roll?

C57. Can you, uh — not today, but one question that you may want to be thinking over is, what are these negative votes?

S57. Well, as I have it analyzed now, it seems to be just a blanket feeling operative in all these realms. You mean, can I refer the feeling — you mean would there be any ideological aspects to it?

C58. I think we might get further if we talked about it in specific terms. You say you like to dance, for example. And still this thing crops up there, too, and blocks you from enjoying dancing. Well, can you tell me more about that — I mean what your feelings are while you're dancing, or what it is that seems to ——

C57. Here is the second blunder of the hour. The counselor departs from sound recognition of feeling. Instead of some such response as "You feel that someone else must start the ball rolling," he asks a direct question which goes deep into the client's situation. If Mr. Bryan were fully aware of why his "negative" side was in power, he would have little need of help. The counselor draws nothing but a confused and somewhat defensive answer (*S57*), and follows it with another direct question which endeavors to tie the client down to a specific situation, that of dancing (*C58*). The client makes a partial response, and then definitely retreats into a long philosophical statement (*S59*) which has no direct relation to his problems and is as far as possible from being specific. The counselor only brings him out of this by a recognition of the pleasure he is getting in being philosophical (*C60*). However, this whole section of the interview, from *C57* to *C67*, is much less profitable because of two directive questions. This indicates how easily the course of constructive therapy can be diverted by errors which may not be recognized as errors at the time.

*S*58. M-hm. Well, I enjoy music very much and especially creative music, that is, improvised music — that is, where the musicians are not reading — where they close their eyes and play as they feel. I like the creativeness of that sort of thing, and I like powerful rhythm, and I feel that when I'm dancing, that's a form of expression which gives me satisfaction when I'm not blocked. I don't ——

*C*59. M-hm. You like the rhythmic expression, you like the musical aspect of it.

*S*59. I don't marshal the universe to favor dancing — it's not necessarily a superior form of activity — that is, I don't — well I don't have any notion that it is superior. Our values are our private absolutes. There are no cosmic yardsticks whereby to measure our values — that is, we either like a thing or we don't. There's no use moralizing about our likes and dislikes. One form of enjoyment is not superior or inferior to any other form of enjoyment. In other words, I don't evaluate values philosophically. Of course, we all do it psychologically. I think that's what the Latins meant years ago when they said, "De gustibus non disputandum." Concerning feelings — one should not rationalize — one should not evaluate. One can evaluate means, but I don't see how they can evaluate ——

*C*60. You like to consider the philosophical implications of most of your ideas, don't you?

*S*60. Yes. I get an intense enjoyment out of philosophizing. I have several friends — we sit for hours and philosophize.

*C*61. You really do like that?

*S*61. Yes. Especially (*he names a certain school of thought*). I'm very much interested in that.

*C*62. M-hm. And when you're discussing philosophical issues, what about this problem of blocking — free from it, or not?

*S*62. No. That's the thing that saddens me quite a bit. When I wax enthusiastic philosophically, I oftentimes have quite a blocking in my speech — maybe you notice how I hesitate. Now, my hesitation is not a groping for words, although that's a sort of a — well, I want to make it seem so, for sort of what you might call protective coloration.

C63. Defend yourself a little bit that way?

S63. Yeah. I like to make people think that I'm groping for just the exact word — that I'm a careful thinker, but actually I know right off what I want to say, and when I am fluent, I get very exact and nice diction without having to grope for a word.

C64. So that in that particular situation your blocking keeps you from being your best and fluent self. And in that situation, it's speech blocking that is primarily ——

S64. Well, yes. I mean it seems like — well, there wouldn't be any other blocking. No other form of activity than speech is going on, and that's the thing, of course, which I notice — that is, of course the thought — my thought is also to a certain extent blocked — that is, they sort of go hand in hand. When I'm able to speak more fluently, I'm able to think more fluently.

C65. M-hm.

S65. But even when I can think clearly, my speech is sometimes blocked. It is the blocking that would be the last to go. When I'm in a philosophic discussion, I feel very angry that I'm not as fluent as the others, because I know that I'm just as intelligent as they are. Be able to hold up my end just as well only I'm not able to have the actual oral expression.

C66. If you could express yourself as well as the others, you would be as good or better than they are in the discussion. (*Pause.*) Well, what other aspect of this whole thing comes to your mind?

S66. Let's see, we've mentioned — music, work, and sex. I feel, to reiterate, that it's just sort of a pan-operative thing.

C67. And, I gather, feel very much discouraged about it.

S67. I feel this — that it is keeping me so far under my ceiling that I think that's an essential part of it. If — well, of course, if I were unimaginative and unintelligent, perhaps — well, I don't know, it's hard to say; maybe everyone thinks they have a ceiling that's a lot higher than they are, but regardless of comparisons, I don't — I'm not interested primarily in comparing myself with other people. I just want to fulfill my own personality as much as I can.

*C*68. And you feel quite confident within yourself that ——

*S*68. Not a bit of doubt of it. I know that I have far greater potentialities than I have achieved yet. In the artistic realm and in the intellectual realm ——

*C*69. So that up to date your whole life situation is simply that you would be really outstanding except that this blocking keeps you from it. And then, too, as you say, you feel that to some extent you keep that blocking there in some way.

*S*69. There's some impulse — there's some reason why the negatives are in power and why, even when I wrestle with the negative feeling, I know that the wrestler is in the minority and the negative feeling outweighs.

*C*70. You know you're licked before you start to fight?

*S*70. Yet I always have a hope that I will come upon some sort of touchstone that will set the inhibition free. No, I'm a hopeful person — sometimes I wonder — I think I've been very unhappy, comparatively speaking, and yet I sometimes wonder why I am so cheerful, in a way — that is, I have a hopeful, cheerful disposition and all of my friends regard me as a very happy person, yet I know that I have undergone years and years — and sometimes the awful monotony of my miseries is appalling — day after day to have the same feeling and then also at night. I have nightmares lots of times, and my sleep doesn't at all rest me, such times.

*C*71. M-hm. M-hm.

*S*71. So I feel that I have an incubus, as it were, year in and year out. Sometimes it gets rather appalling.

---

*C*69. The counselor summarizes two of the important attitudes which have been expressed. This statement might also serve as a description of the typical neurotic pattern. "My life would be noteworthy," says the neurotic, "were it not for the fact that my neurosis prevents me and excuses me from attempting to live it."

*S*70. The client, having made real progress, now returns temporarily to a restatement of his original symptoms. Acceptance of this attitude (*C*72) leads to more positive views.

*C*72. M-hm.   A steady grind.   And yet in spite of that steady grind, you feel that you — you still feel you may find your way, or fight your way out.

*S*72. In my phantasies I always imagine myself as being cured and achieving certain goals.   I never have pessimistic phantasies.   The alter ego that I set up is one of me cured, so that my potentialities may fulfill themselves.

*C*73. Yes.   What sort of achievements do you phantasy about?

*S*73. Well, I want to write — I want to be musical and dance, and I want to be a connoisseur of beautiful women, and I want to have a reasonably luxurious standard of living — say about twenty-five, fifty thousand a year.

*C*74. So that you have a generally high ——

*S*74. I know that I can do it.   I know damn well I could do it, because I've had flashes of what I can be when I'm without this, and although they are short flashes, the achievements that I make within those short flashes could be very accurately reduced to an arithmetical projection which would show me what I would do if I were completely released all the time.

*C*75. So that you, minus this blocking, would really go places.

*S*75. That sounds a bit Rotarian.   Perhaps I should clarify my position.   I don't have a bourgeois ambition in that I want fame alone.   I'm the sort of fellow that, if I got what I wanted, I would not mind whether the world applauded or booed — I'm my own supreme court.

*C*76. M-hm.

*S*76. But — well, perhaps that's not significant — I don't know.

*C*77. Well, it is significant — you have your own — you say you have your own standards and it's by those standards you gauge what you do ——

*S*77. If I wrote a novel, I would like it to make money, but if it didn't make money, it would be all right if I were satisfied with it.   The money angle wouldn't be too important.

*C*78. Well, you've given me quite a good all-round picture of your situation. I think probably that's as much as we can do in one session.

*S*78. I think perhaps, to sum it up, that the origin is sexual, but that a sexual blocking, that is, is such a fundamental blocking that it blocks all. I don't know whether that's too Freudian for you, but I feel that sex is sort of a dynamo and is the source of energy for other activities too.

*C*79. Well, now, I'd put it this way, as to the way we can go at that. I think that the best way to work through some of this is for you, when you come in next time, to take up those aspects of it about which you feel the most concern or which are disturbing you most at the moment. Maybe it will be the sexual aspect; maybe it'll be something very different from that. Whatever the thing is that is of greatest concern at the moment, let's work that through and explore it. Perhaps we can find out what some of these negative votes are. I mean, if you can get a little clearer feeling as to what this balance of power consists of — why it is that in some ways you wish to keep this painful problem — then we'll be further along.

*S*79. Well, I think I know why I want to keep it. I want to keep it for the voyeuristic pleasure, because I know that when I don't have it I get no enjoyment from voyeurism at all.

---

*C*78. The counselor begins to bring the interview to a close. He lapses temporarily into a doctor-patient description of the relationship, but there is no evidence that this does any damage. He could just as easily have said, "You have explored many aspects of your problems, and that is probably all we can do for today."

*C*79. The first portion of this conversation is helpful in that it defines the client's responsibility for the direction of the counseling interviews. In the last portion the counselor returns to the same direct question which delayed therapy before (*C*57) and unwisely tries to give this problem as a "homework assignment." This would seem to be the third blunder in the interview.

*S*79, *S*80, *S*81, *S*82. The client is determined to answer the counselor's questions at once. To some extent this represents further insight. To some extent it is almost certainly an attempt to prolong the interview. The counselor has definitely to call a halt (*C*85).

On the other hand, I get pleasure from intercourse when I'm
without it, but when it returns, the remembered intercourse
wouldn't be pleasurable, you see.

*C*80. M-hm.

*S*80. In other words, we remember, not in the past, but in
the present, so that when I'm neurotic I can't pleasurably
remember an experience that was pleasurable to me **at the**
time when I happened to be released.

*C*81. M-hm. All right, that is helpful. That's one value
that it has to you — that it enables you to — while you have
your problem, bad as it is, it does give you one certain type of
satisfaction that you can't get ——

*S*81. M-hm. And I think another angle on that would be
that that would always be available, whereas intercourse
wouldn't be. Perhaps that's one reason why I cling to the
neurosis, because I can always get a voyeuristic phantasy.

*C*82. M-hm.

*S*82. I'm sure that this — that the inhibition is a fear.
And I admit that I do have these Victorian fears of sexual
activity, and probably in the Victorian concept, probably
voyeurism would be less terrible than actual intercourse.

*C*83. That's why you feel perhaps less guilty about that ——

*S*83. M-hm. Well, it's more powerful ——

*C*84. — and less fear of punishment ——

*S*84. — and a feeling of guilt. Here's the way I can perhaps
illustrate it diagrammatically. Here (*pointing to head*) and
here (*pointing to chest*) I am pretty balanced. I know exactly
what I want and how to get it. But down here (*pointing to
lower abdomen*) there's blocking. Now it used to be that the
disturbance here (*chest*) rather confused me up here (*head*),
but since the negative feeling has gone down to here (*abdomen*),
what it amounts to is — that I'm a pagan intellectually and
in my heart, but in my guts I'm a perfect puritan.

*C*85. Yes. That's an excellent statement. Well, let's
consider various angles of that next time you come in. Now,
we should — I was looking over my calendar just before you
came. I could see you next Tuesday at four o'clock; would

that be a convenient time for you? I thought perhaps we might try to work in a couple of contacts next week — I'm not sure that I can make them as frequent as that later on.

*S*85. Well, I imagine at the outset it's probably better to have more frequency, isn't it?

*C*86. If it can be arranged, m-hm.

*S*86. Well, now my time can be adjusted to suit yours. I mean, this thing's so important to me, that you just name the date and I'll adjust myself accordingly.

*C*87. Well, let's say Tuesday at four and Friday at four.

*S*87. Tuesday and Friday at four.

*C*88. Is that feasible, or not?

*S*88. I see my dentist at 1.45 Tuesday, and yes — he'll be through with me before four.

*C*89. Well, then I'll put those on my calendar.

*S*89. Tuesday and Friday, both at four?

*C*90. Both at four.

*S*90. All right, sir.

*C*91. O.K. We'll see what we can do on it.

*S*91. All right.

General Comments

This interview illustrates many of the issues raised in Chapters III, IV, V, and VI. The client has been judged to be a suitable candidate for counseling help, and he has begun the expression of his attitudes regarding his problem. The counselor has helped to clarify these attitudes and to make plain the structure of the counseling relationship and the ways in which the client can use it. In only three instances has there been any real departure from the hypothesis underlying this book, and in these instances progress would seem to be only slightly delayed, rather than seriously hampered.

It will be a valuable exercise for the counselor who is endeavoring to improve his techniques to make a list of the outstanding feelings which have been expressed in this interview. The gradual change in these attitudes as the interviews progress is striking. To the writer, the following would seem to be a fair summary of the outstanding attitudes which have been spontaneously expressed:

I suffer from a blocking which interferes with my sexual life, my business life, my social life.

I suffer excruciating pain from this blocking.

I feel well at times, but I don't know why and have no control over the change.

My only satisfaction is voyeurism.

Others — particularly my parents — are to blame for my problems.

I want help.   I would rather be dead than continue as at present.

I actually have outstanding ability, but this blocking keeps it from being evident.

My energies, positive and negative, balance themselves in a conflict-producing inertia.

I have a tendency to cling to my symptoms.   In some way they give me satisfaction.

I cannot bring about change.   Motivation must be given to me.

I'm at war with myself.   I'm a pagan intellectually, but a puritan in my guts.

This list could, of course, be made longer by making it more detailed.   It would seem to include, however, the most prominent attitudes expressed.   To make a list of this sort at the conclusion of an interview is an excellent way of fixing the essential elements, and a review of the list is perhaps the best preparation for the following interview.

❧ SECOND INTERVIEW ❧

*C*92. Well, how are things today?

*S*92. Well, I noticed something that I was rather looking for — a sort of a reactionary movement over the week end, since the interview. It would almost seem as if the neurosis were resisting the change and seeking to augment itself, because it had been monkeyed with ——

*C*93. (*Laugh.*) Things were really worse?

*S*93. Yes. I was very restless. Matter of fact, I kept roaming around from night club to night club all week end, and I'd come home late — say about four or five, and then my parents would want me to get up in the morning — say, "What are you lying around all the time for — is something wrong with you?" — all that sort of thing. So I'm sort of worn out.

*C*94. You feel that part of that is due to the fact that some part of yourself is probably resisting any change?

*S*94. Resisting any change. That's right.

*C*95. What makes you feel that?

*S*95. Oh, just a hunch. It's sort of a deduction. I mean, if a part of me — if a major part of my energies want to be that way — well, we see the analogy anywhere we look. When

---

*S*92. Notice how Mr. Bryan tends to externalize his problem, regarding the neurosis as something outside of himself, for which he does not take full responsibility.

*C*94. This is a type of response which occurs several times in this interview. The client has been saying, "My neurosis has been resisting change and has been making trouble for me." The counselor recognizes this feeling, but adds a slight edge of interpretation to his response, pointing out that the neurosis is "some part of yourself" rather than something external, as the client has been picturing it. Repetition of this technique brings difficulty.

*C*95. This question is a dubious type of directive response. A pause would probably have elicited further attitudes from the client.

a majority is threatened, it sort of intensifies and cracks down. We see it in sociology. Of course, after all, it probably might be *post hoc ergo propter hoc* reasoning, but at least ——

*C*96. At any rate, you feel that the conflict is, if anything, sharper than it was ——

*S*96. I'm not discouraged about that, because I have rationalized it this way — that if the neurosis did not feel threatened, why, it wouldn't have had that reaction, so at least we're threatening it. Making it feel uneasy.

*C*97. You feel we're threatening *it*, that is, it's something sort of outside of yourself, isn't it?

*S*97. That would have to be answered two ways. Of course, philosophically everything happens within one's own nervous system, but psychologically I regard it as an alien, I think. Some sort of an enemy alien.

*C*98. You don't really claim any ownership of the problem that you have?

*S*98. Well, I realize that it's my feeling, but I tend to regard it as being perverted and unhealthy, not from any moralistic criterion. As I mentioned before, values are private and absolute — no way of evaluating them philosophically, but psychologically we can say that such an emotion would be destructive to harmony of the organism as a whole. If we evaluate it that way, then we make it a means — that is, simply describe it as a means to total harmony which we can do scientifically. We can scientifically describe means, even though we are unable to do that to values.

---

*C*97. Here, as in *C*94, the counselor's response involves recognition and also interpretation. As we shall see in other instances, interpretation leads this client to retreat into abstract and philosophical discussions, and to some extent this begins in *S*97.

*C*98–*S*103. *C*98 is an interpretive type of response. It would have been definitely preferable simply to recognize the attitude expressed in such terms as "You feel it is something foreign to you." The client retreats from the interpretation offered by the counselor into an intellectual discussion. In *C*99 the counselor definitely pushes his interpretation. The client fails to understand — perhaps does not

*C*99. Then it's the neurosis that resents any attack on it — not you that resents any attack on the neurosis?

*S*99. What's this again?

*C*100. Well, I was just interested — you seem to be saying that it's — the neurosis perhaps resented the fact that we were trying to change it.

*S*100. M-hm.

*C*101. And you evidently feel pretty sure that that's the situation rather than that you might inwardly be resisting the possibility of losing it?

*S*101. Well, is there any difference between those two statements?

*C*102. No, not really.

*S*102. Oh, but of course there would be psychologically, wouldn't there? That is, the fact that I would say — use the third-person pronoun rather than the first person.

*C*103. I just wondered if there was any significance there.

*S*103. M-hm. Well, I imagine that for egotistical reasons I don't like to own it, as you say, because my better judgment is so opposed to it, and we always have a tendency to put our better judgment forward when we're in any kind of social situation. (*Pause.*) You said you wanted me to think in terms of present situations rather than delve into the past. I had done some thinking about that one time myself — I was wondering whether an original cause of a neurosis might with the passing of time tend to become insignificant, yet the

---

wish to understand — and indicates a desire to argue the point at *S*101. The counselor retreats from the interpretation in *C*102 and *C*103, and the client gives an intellectual type of partial acceptance in *S*103. It is plain that the client regards this segment as a detour, and after a pause he returns to his own line of thought, taking up the "homework" which the counselor had assigned to him at the close of the first interview.

*S*103–*S*107. These items are concerned with the "homework assignment" mentioned above. The client's thinking is good, and his consideration of the present usefulness of neurotic symptoms is intellectually sound. However, one has only to compare this portion

neurosis be retained for other purposes, to meet present situations, which would of course invalidate the older technique of digging into the past, since I'm no longer reacting to the past anyway.

*C*104. Have you had some reason to feel that that might be so?

*S*104. Well, I don't know — you're getting into epistemology there, and I don't know if I can tell you where I get these ideas — in the last analysis, they just sort of come. (*Pause.*) I can see where a neurosis — where the same neurosis might serve one function years ago and serve an entirely different one today ——

*C*105. M-hm.

*S*105. Yet it might be the same feeling. On the other hand, I can also imagine a sort of permanent condition, lasting for years without change. It's pretty hard to rationalize the feelings. I think that when we do rationalize a feeling, we don't describe the feeling — we merely show that we have a need for rationalization.

*C*106. And you like to see in rational and intellectual terms every possible angle of this, don't you?

*S*106. Yes, that's one of my emotional kicks — is to rationalize. I get an enjoyment out of that quite qualitatively different, yet just as quantitatively intense as many other things. Of course, everyone thinks, but I like to think about thinking.

*C*107. Everyone feels, but you like to think about feeling.

*S*107. M-hm. (*Pause.*)

*C*108. Well, I told you last time, you could figure on using this time in the way that seems most meaningful or most helpful at the moment. What are some of the things you'd like to ——

---

with the section of the interview which follows (*S*108 ff.) to realize that it is not as profitable as the material which the client spontaneously brings into the interview.

*C*108. This is a good general lead, non-directive in character, which also helps to structure the situation.

*S*108. Well, right now I have some photographic jobs lined up, but I'm sort of held from going out and doing them. I have a chance to make myself a nice little sum of money, but I feel inhibited about actually going out and doing it — that's very distressing for me. My partner's somewhat sick — he's at the hospital. I don't know when he'll be up on his feet. Working by myself is hard on me.

*C*109. And to go out and face whatever is involved in these jobs is — seems like a little too much at the present time?

*S*109. Well, you have to talk to people, you know, and outline the proposition to them, talk to the leader of the group you want to photograph, and that requires salesmanship, ease, and confidence — all that sort of thing which I don't have when I'm in my present condition.

*C*110. You couldn't at the present time face that kind of a situation.

*S*110. Well, a speech impediment, such as I have as one of my symptoms, tends to make people distrustful — they have that reaction. They think that perhaps you don't know your business, or you're perhaps not to be trusted — it gives them sort of a vague feeling of distrust that's harmful to business.

*C*111. And it's that that you would find awfully hard to face — I mean, that attitude on their part?

*S*111. Yes, when I'm not in a good mood, I realize that I'm not handling the situation well. That, of course, makes an overtone to the original negative.

---

*S*108–*S*117. This is spontaneous expression of feeling, skillfully handled by the counselor in ways that clarify the client's attitudes and lead him on in constructive fashion. *C*111 shows recognition of feeling which shades over into the type of interpretation which can be accepted by the client, because it merely puts into one thought what Mr. Bryan has been saying in *S*108, *S*109, *S*110. *C*112 and *C*113 illustrate good handling of a situation which often arises — an expression of attitude which is not understood by the counselor. *C*115 is perhaps the most doubtful of the counselor responses in this section, being definitely interpretive. The client, however, accepts it fully, as is proved by his amplification of the interpretation.

*C*112. I don't think I quite understand that.

*S*112. Well, you have an original negative, then you bungle the situation, so you get another negative from having bungled the situation.

*C*113. In other words, you feel somewhat fearful about meeting some of these situations, and quite sure that if you did go out and meet them, things would happen to make it that much worse, is that it?

*S*113. M-hm. Yes, my money motivation doesn't seem to be powerful enough to — once in a while I get such a powerful money motivation, that I go ahead anyway, but that of course creates a terrific tension and leaves me in a very exhausted condition.

*C*114. It's a pretty distressing situation if you do **try to** fight it openly.

*S*114. Yes, it creates quite a conflict. Uses up a lot of nervous energy.

*C*115. So that at present it seems the better — more comfortable way out to sort of drift along.

*S*115. Roam around night clubs at night. I find release in having some drinks and seeing floor shows, although I'm not really happy. It's just sort of the lesser of two evils. I feel very restless and caged up if I were to sit home, with everything quiet.

*C*116. M-hm. At least you do get some satisfaction **out** of ——

*S*116. Well, it's excitement. It's sort of a counteractive **to** the negative feeling, although not completely.

*C*117. More satisfying than staying at home, but not completely satisfying.

*S*117. Then, of course, it wears me out. I get in late, and my folks get up early, and they make no effort to keep quiet because they have a resentment at my being in bed after eight or nine.

*C*118. But they do resent your inactivity — what seems to them to be inactivity?

*S*118. Yes, the inactivity, and that's of course made even

worse by the night life. They would think that it's bad enough to be a loafer, but much worse to go to night clubs at night too.

*C*119. So that, from their viewpoint, you're both lazy and wicked, is that it?

*S*119. That's about it.

*C*120. Are other attitudes involved there, too, on their part?

*S*120. How do you mean?

*C*121. Well, I was wondering, do they resent the fact that you're not aggressively going out after jobs and so on, too?

*S*121. Well, they know that I have jobs lined up, and I have a convenient outlet there in that the camera has been being repaired, so that they realize that I couldn't actually be at work anyway, but they tend to suspicion — tend to have a suspicion that I'm not very ambitious anyway. But the camera is fixed now, so I'm going to have to do something about that. Have to have some results. Of course, I get my board and room, but I have a need for more than that. As I mentioned the other day, I need a certain amount of luxury.

*C*122. M-hm. That's one of the things that makes your problem more acute. You've got to have money, and still the things that bring money are among the things that you hate to face.

*S*122. It seems to me there's certainly a — some deep-seated

---

*C*118, *C*119. This is a minor type of error which can easily occur. The counselor ceases to recognize the client's attitude and endeavors to describe more clearly the attitude of the parents. This, of course, is a very different process. Mr. Bryan is talking about his own exhaustion and the fact that he feels that his parents are unsympathetic and critical. It is this attitude to which response might have been made. It is probably this deviation from the best techniques which brings the conversation to a halt at *S*119, and leads the counselor to put two directive questions which follow the same general topic. The client again picks up the thread of his own feelings in *S*121.

*C*122–*S*122. Here the counselor endeavors to show the relationships between the attitudes brought out thus far in the interview. While it seems to be a satisfactory interpretation from the point of view of fact, it should be noted that the client evades it completely, retreating instead into a description of symptoms similar to the views expressed

fear within me; that is, I would describe the neurosis as a compressed fear — fear that has been compressed down until it has an almost steel-like quality. That is, formerly I referred the sensation here (*chest*) and it was more vague, more generalized, not so compressed. And with the evolution of time, the sensation was one of being compressed and forced down deeper, both anatomically and psychologically compressed down deeper. I don't know why I have that conviction that it's a fear, but I should say it is.

*C*123. I understand that it's simply a conviction that it is a fear — it isn't that you feel fear?

*S*123. Well, it's so chronic that it can hardly be called the agitated sort of a fear — it's just sort of a permanent compression there till it becomes a pressure. Now, I notice from time to time, when I have a nightmare, why it seems to sort of bubble up in a way — I mean, sort of like an artesian well.

*C*124. Fear comes out in the open more?

*S*124. And becomes — then it agitates me more — they say it — that I yell out in my sleep and toss and turn — all my roommates have told me that, so I think that's one reason why I think that it is a fear. Of course, perhaps that's too general to be of any significance. It wouldn't — well, it could hardly be anything else but a fear, could it?

*C*125. Well, I think that the more significant elements are what you experience, not what you think intellectually it might be. I mean, if you experience fears in your nightmares — that's something. Any amount of thinking about whether or not it might be a fear is ——

*S*125. They don't seem to have any consistent imagery — that is, I can vision myself walking down the street in my dream and then all of a sudden being intensely afraid — no particular imagery there. I remember some very old night-

---

early in the first interview. Mr. Bryan appears to have forgotten completely his previous statement that his symptoms bring him a degree of satisfaction. When interpretations are made too rapidly or too directly, the client is liable to retreat even from the insights already attained.

mares that might be of interest. When I was very young, I could read at a very early age. I did a lot of reading. I read a book about Pike, the Western explorer after whom the Peak was named, and after I had finished the book I dreamed that I was ascending Pike's Peak, and when I reached the summit, there was my father, looking very, very stern. His aspect was very intensely forbidding. I had another dream where I had a popgun, and just as I was holding it, it mysteriously floated away from me with no apparent cause, and that terrified me too. I think the symbolism is clear there ——

C126. M-hm.

S126. The warning of my father about ascending the Peak. And then the phallic symbolism of the gun being taken away from me in a very mysterious and terrifying way. Those dreams have always lingered with me. I must not have been over — not over six years old, anyway.

C127. But more recent nightmares aren't nearly as specific as that?

S127. No — don't have any — seem to have any particular imagery. Just the feeling itself seems to dominate, rather than any particular concomitant imagery.

C128. You're afraid of something, but not entirely clear what, even in your dreams — is that it?

S128. It doesn't seem to be symbolized in dreams, or perhaps it would be more accurate to say that fear no longer requires any definite symbolism — it just goes ahead and hangs its hat on whatever I happen to be thinking of.

C129. That would be natural.

S129. I think too that I had some incest and homosexual fears in my early childhood, which would perhaps be more fearful than just a fear of normal sex. I mean, that's the usual way of our society — we react more intensely to homosexuality and incest than we do to normal sexuality. And I imagine — I don't know, I was going to ask you — would an

S123–S126. This sophisticated client is no stranger to the Oedipus complex or castration fears. The significant point is that rather clear intellectual insight of this sort is of no real therapeutic help.

incest fear tend to have a carry-over into the normal sex realm — or homosexual fear? I mean, could one be homosexually inhibited and then have that carry over into the normal sex?

C130. A good many things can happen in that realm. I think that it's your own experiences and feelings that really determine what direction it does take. What raised some of those questions in your mind?

S130. (*Pause.*) What did you ask me?

C131. Well, that is, I wondered what were some of the experiences or feelings that raised those questions in your mind?

S131. Well, my first sexual experience was with a playmate — he was about my own age, and he urged me to have an experience with him. Of course, I didn't have any inhibition against it at the time, so I let him go ahead. And the incest might be concerned with three possible persons. I've always had a feeling — I don't have any definite proof on it — that my mother was sexually frustrated because of my father's academic life — he was always reading everything. She's talented — as a matter of fact, a born genius, and has intense feelings — probably has a high libido, and I think that she tended to have subconscious sex feelings toward me, yet if I were ever to have an overt sex reaction, why, of course, she would slap it down right away — I mean it's sort of like offering a child a piece of candy and then slapping his wrist when he reaches for it. She told a girl one time that she didn't have enough sex life when she was first married, and the girl told

---

C130. The client's direct question is well handled, bringing his thinking back to the one aspect with which therapy can be effective — his own feelings and attitudes. It will be plain to the reader that any attempt to give an intellectual answer could have had but one outcome — a detour which would almost certainly have been unprofitable from the point of view of basic progress.

S130. At no point since the counselor's interpretation at C122 has Mr. Bryan been talking freely about things of present concern to him. He has been talking of intellectual abstractions, or of early experiences which have little present significance to him. His reverie at this point makes one wonder what unexpressed feelings have been going on during this period.

me — so I know that for a fact.   And I had an aunt — an old-maid aunt — that I used to live with quite a while.   And I never noticed anything overt about her, except she used to want me to sleep with her from time to time, but she didn't make any advances or anything like that.   And my sister — we took baths together when we were young, oh, up until maybe seven — maybe six years old — she's fifteen months younger than I — and I think that I probably got, uh — I probably got a sexual reaction from that.   Nothing terrific, but I imagine some sort of a sensuous experience there.

C132. I notice both in regard to your mother and your aunt, you describe simply their reactions.

S132. Yes — well, I take mine for granted — I've always had a high libido ever since I was very, very young, and I imagine I got a reaction from it.   I just — well, I don't remember it — I mean those things are awfully hard — I mean you might recall a situation where you did not have a reaction, yet have a reaction to it now and refer your present reaction to the past.   I mean, those things are pretty tricky, because you experience yourself in the present, so that such things can be temporally misreferred.

C133. And in any case, you prefer somewhat to think about the reactions of others or the intellectual aspects of the situation, rather than your own ——

S133. Well, I would say that the people that I have mentioned — after all, they were the ones that did the condition-

---

S131.   The evasion continues.   Here is no expression of real conflict, but rather an account of feelings which the client thinks "probably" he had.   The counselor notes this and in C132 attempts to elicit the client's genuine reactions.   Note how futile it is to probe for attitudes.   The only response on Mr. Bryan's part is to retreat into the splitting of philosophical hairs.

C133, C134. These statements of the counselor go somewhat beyond the feeling which is expressed, but they do recognize the underlying attitudes.   A better response at C134, for example, would have been simply, "You feel they are the ones who are responsible."   Because the counselor oversteps the feeling which has been expressed,

ing, and if they had not had an ambivalent reaction, why, then I wouldn't have been conditioned against them.

*C*134. But you had no real part in that, except as they made you a victim, in a sense?

*S*134. Well, yes, I do feel victimized. On the other hand, according to my philosophy that we're the product of our genes and our conditioning — I'm merely describing it from one point of view. Of course, from the other point of view you could say I had such and such a reaction, etc. You can't jump from one to the other — you have to take one of the positions. I think it would have been all right if there hadn't been any negative reaction to the incestuous sensation that I got in my early childhood. If it hadn't been moralized about or hadn't been preached against, why, I don't see how it could have hurt me. After all, our genes are so constructed that we're not responsible for these things.

*C*135. You feel that it's your mother's reaction to that, and so on, that ——

*S*135. Well, you know how children are — I mean they can intuit things and sort of read between the lines. I felt that Mother was having a sexy undercurrent and at the same time being overtly very much opposed to sex, so that I imagine that rather disturbed my sense of justice or sense of balance. And I mean — I don't see why a young child wouldn't have a sexual reaction toward his mother, I mean, due to fondling, caressing, and so forth; it seems to me to be quite natural. It just seems to me that I was unfortunate in that it could only be carried on behind the mask of mother love, that whenever I made any overt sex reactions, she immediately cracked down on me.

---

the client agrees, but immediately retreats into more philosophizing. (See the very similar example in Chapter VI, pp. 153–58.) This is followed by more intellectual discussion of attitudes which Mr. Bryan "imagines" he held as a child. It is not until the latter part of *S*136 and *S*137 that he is encouraged, by the counselor's adequate recognition of feeling, to return to genuine attitudes of significance in his present situation.

*C*136 And you feel that because she rebuffed any sex feelings that you had toward her that ——

*S*136. I don't remember ever having had any toward her, but that wouldn't matter — I mean she would rebuff them when they were turned toward her or anyone else — perhaps even more so out of her jealousy. Even if — she would probably crack down on me, perhaps a little harder for fooling around with one of the neighborhood little girls than she would if I were to react sexually while she was caressing me. She seems always to have been somewhat possessive — I imagine due to her frustrated life, I was probably centered upon more; and she finds fault with girl friends that I happen to bring around to the house.

*C*137. You feel that she's jealous of any normal reaction ——

*S*137. Anything that might lead me away from her. (*Pause.*) Of course, I dislike my parents for these things — but I can't blame them — if you get the distinction. Might as well blame God.

*C*138. And without particularly holding a feeling of blame, yet you do feel that ——

*S*138. I feel it would have been nicer had they gotten rid of their puritanism rather than leaving the job up to me.

*C*139. For you, you feel it's almost too much, is that it?

*S*139. Well, that's been my impulse so far. I have a rather irrational optimism about me anyway. I mean, I have no reason to feel cheerful, yet I do manage to be pretty cheerful. Even on very bad days, I still have my sense of humor.

*C*140. You can put up a pretty good front, and maintain pretty good spirits.

*S*140. Oh, yes. I feel now, though, that there will probably soon come a time when my dissipated life will begin to tell

---

*S*138–*C*139. Mr. Bryan puts in concise form the attitude which he has stated in various ways thus far, that others are to blame for his difficulties. In responding, the counselor goes somewhat too far. A more accurate recognition would have been, "It seems like quite a task to you."

on my health. I've an awfully strong constitution. I can do a lot of drinking and smoking and late hours without affecting my health too much. Of course, I can take more than the average fellow I know. There's no use in eating up my capital like that.

*C*141. I gather that you feel that now you're somewhat fighting yourself by those activities?

*S*141. Well, it's injurious to the health, yes. I imagine that if I were psychologically healthy, I'd still enjoy night life, but it wouldn't be such a compulsion. I'm sure that it would relegate itself to a less intense pattern.

*C*142. At the present time you have to carry it on to prove something.

*S*142. Prove? I hadn't thought about it in those terms. It just makes me feel less miserable. I hadn't thought about it in terms of proving anything.

*C*143. Well, I might be wrong on that.

*S*143. Well, as near as I can describe it — you go to a night club and you have the excitement of picking up girls and flirting with them and you see a floor show — maybe they have some nice-looking girls and you have your drinks and the jazz music — all that sort of thing tends to create an atmosphere which counteracts your negative feelings to a certain extent.

*C*144. Makes you feel pretty good for the time being.

*S*144. Well, no, I oftentimes tend to contrast my inner feelings with the outward atmosphere, but it must make me feel less miserable or I wouldn't do it. Once in a while I can sort of lose myself in that kind of atmosphere. If I pick up a pretty girl — why I get momentary pleasure.

*C*145. M-hm. But that quite definitely isn't enough — I

---

*C*142. The counselor again endeavors to interpret the client's actions, again finds interpretation resisted, and gives up the attempt in *C*143. A more satisfactory response would have been, "You feel it's injurious; still in a way you have to carry on such activities," or, "If you were healthy, you wouldn't feel it was so necessary."

*C*145, *C*147. These responses repeat the persistent error of this interview, going beyond the attitudes expressed by the client.

mean, that momentary kind of enjoyment isn't what you want?

S 145. Well, I don't object to momentariness *per se* — but I object to a return of the old negative feeling. That is, permanence *per se* is not of value to me. Satisfying affairs have ended just the right time. I feel that there's a certain artistry to be had there in making it last just the right time.

C 146. Not too long.

S 146. I've never had a mistress that I wanted to — that is, where I wanted to retain things longer than she did — sometimes it comes out even. Usually I find, though, that I get tired of them before they do of me. Of course, they're conditioned to permanence — I mean, they want marriage and family.

C 147. Yes, but you're very sure you don't want permanence?

S 147. Oh, no, no, it doesn't go to the other extreme. It's just that so far I haven't met a personality that makes me think in terms of permanence. Well, I met one girl that I thought it would be nice to get married to and have a family, but she wouldn't go out with me because of my reputation. But I don't know how long that feeling would have lasted. She didn't refuse to go out with me, but — I don't know, perhaps it was a sort of renunciation on my part. I didn't want her to suffer because of me — for her to lose her reputation by going with me. Or perhaps that's a noble rationalization from the fact that I didn't want to assume any serious responsibility. I mean, you can oftentimes have more than one rationalization and don't know which is the true one.

C 148. M-hm. At any rate you feel that you're as much responsible for that affair not going further as she was?

S 147–*C* 148. This very interesting statement goes through several levels of defensive expression, the client coming at last to the possibility that he did not want to assume mature responsibility. To this confused and complex statement the counselor gives a rather satisfactory reply.

S 148. Well, when I want a new affair, why, I just end it. Yes, I took active steps in making the ending.

C 149. And you're not quite sure, I take it, whether you really do want permanence?

S 149. I don't — I do not have a philosophic evaluation of permanence *per se*. In other words, an affair, that is permanence, should not be one of the factors one way or the other in evaluating such human relationships. I think we have to live automatically by the emotions, so that I would have no prejudice, no preconception either way. If I meet someone that I like and I think I want to settle up with permanently, all right. That'll automatically be taken care of by my emotions. But *per se*, I have no reaction to permanence or to temporariness. I think that my neurosis has a definite part in making my affairs temporary. That is, after all, there is such a thing as inertia when you have a beautiful mistress. I suppose the inert thing to do would be to go ahead and keep her, but I think weeks and months of it seems to exhaust me. I mean, since I'm doing it over the hump, as it were — over the inhibition. I imagine that's one reason why I choose to terminate them. And I notice, too, that when I become sexually attached to a girl, even though I have no emotion of love toward her, it intensifies my neurosis. If I imagine that she'd be going out with another fellow or something like that — I mean, there I get all of the inhibition against sex, but since I'm not in the situation, since another fellow would be in the

---

C 149. Again the counselor interprets, and again the client retreats into an intellectualistic consideration of the problem. A better response at this point would have been, "You feel you handle that sort of situation well." Throughout this section the client is expressing extremely self-centered attitudes, which show not the slightest regard for the rights or feelings of others. The counselor must surely feel tempted to set him right or to point out the selfish note which predominates. Such an approach would certainly fail. The only basic way of helping the client to understand these attitudes and desire to change them is to clarify them objectively, until the lient sees himself plainly.

situation, I don't get any of the counteracting pleasure — in other words, all of the inhibition comes down on the pleasure, to counteract it. And I find myself having phantasies — either with or without any evidence. Of course, sometimes twisting the evidence happens in those cases. I have painful thoughts that perhaps she would be unfaithful to me. I imagine that's probably due — that is, since I don't get satisfied completely from intercourse, I probably automatically assume that she doesn't and therefore she would seek her satisfaction elsewhere, and I build up the infidelity.

C150. M-hm. You feel quite sure that you couldn't really satisfy her because she doesn't fully satisfy you.

S150. Yes, I think that that is the emotional conclusion, although oddly enough my inhibition has oftentimes the opposite effect, and I prove to be very satisfying to my partner. So logically there's nothing to it, but I imagine that the emotional ——

C151. At any rate, that's the way you feel.

S151. M-hm. I feel it isn't satisfying and pleasurable to me. I automatically assume it isn't to her. She might go elsewhere. I don't have a feeling of inferiority about that — it goes deeper — it's just an intensification of the old feeling. And I sort of look at it this way — sometimes it's almost as if I were vicariously inhibiting the girl by inhibiting myself, if you get what I mean. Sort of like you see a friend in the street, perhaps approaching an accident — you sort of tense yourself up — say, "Put on your brakes."

C152. In this case, neither of you must have full pleasure out of it. Is that what you mean by vicarious inhibitions?

S152. Well, no. I want to inhibit her against other fellows.

C153. Oh, I see.

S153. That's one of my rationalizations for the feeling. Of course, you never know which one is right. Perhaps feelings — I'm inclined to think maybe feelings are absolutes anyway — that the imagery along with them has to do with another phenomenon rather than the feeling itself. I think that they are self-sufficient absolutes.

*C*154. Perhaps it's because they're absolutes that you're somewhat fearful of looking at them.

*S*154. Well, that's certainly true. I feel this — that the dice have been loaded against me. That is, my parents have said, now sex is painful and terrifying — now you keep away from it. All right — I go ahead and get into it — their prediction is verified. Yet intellectually I know that the dice have been loaded. Naturally, with that sort of preconditioning, why, the prediction is going to come true. In other words, that says nothing about sex. It merely describes my parents' nervous systems. But psychologically, thinking has made it so for me. Do you get what I'm talking about?

*C*155. I do. That is, that ——

*S*155. Well, they define sex in terms of pain and terror; when that's inculcated into my nervous system, then I also react to it that way. Yet I know philosophically that my parents have said nothing about sex, but have described themselves, yet that doesn't do me any good.

*C*156. Nevertheless, your feelings tend to prove your parents are right.

*S*156. Yeah.

*C*157. While you fight them somewhat in your actions, yet you feel, you say, that they were right and you were wrong.

*S*157. It isn't rationalized that much. It's just sort of a feeling — well, sort of an I-told-you-so feeling, like it's just what I had expected, and I'm sort of foolish to hope that sex could be pleasurable — that, after all, this is the way it is. Of course, I know that a prediction has to be universal to be valid — that is, everyone would have to react that way.

---

*C*154. After several satisfactory responses the counselor returns again to mild interpretation. This time it seems to be accepted.

*S*154–*S*163. This excerpt is marked by excellent counseling, and consequently by deeper and more significant attitudes, which lead to considerable insight. The counselor in *C*160 asks an unnecessary and directive question, but fortunately the client pays no attention. A cautious type of interpretation is given in *C*161, which summarizes attitudes expressed, and this interpretation is accepted. *C*156,

*C*158. But that doesn't alter your experience.

*S*158. M-hm. That's right. In other words, the only reality I have is the neurotic one, and I can't persuade myself by saying that an alternative reality would be better, because I haven't ever had the actual experience of any alternative reality. Well — or if I do get it temporarily, my neurosis comes back and I can only know that I had a good time — I can't *feel* that I had a good time.

*C*159. M-hm. *(Pause.)* So that adds to your feeling that you're sort of trapped in this state of development, or state of feeling.

*S*159. Well, I realize thoroughly now that a philosophic grasp cannot serve a therapeutic function — it can only serve a philosophic function. I get a slight enjoyment, somewhat ironically tinged, out of being able to analyze myself, but I don't think it's going to do any good therapeutically. What I think I need is some sort of a faith cure — that's what it would ultimately boil down to. Of course, faith ——

*C*160. Faith in what?

*S*160. In the last analysis, such a thing would have to be a jump of faith. I mean, we can have so much evidence, but whether we are going to accept that evidence and act on it is in the last analysis an act of faith rather than an act of reason.

*C*161. That's true, isn't it? And in a number of these things, that's where you feel blocked. For example, you know the jobs are there and they could be managed, and so on, but to have the confidence that would send you out on them, that's a different story. The same thing in the sex realm, as I get

---

*C*158, *C*162, *C*163 are splendid examples of sound recognition of feeling, which bring out the statement of *S*163, indicating that Mr. Bryan has gained some inkling of his part in the situation. In his statements from *S*159 to *S*163 there is a growing realization that intellectual analysis cannot bring about change, a feeling that some type of motivation, some dynamic force, must be discovered. He feels that at least a part of this force resides within himself. This is a much clearer picture of himself than he gave in his first interview, or than he expressed in *S*122 in this interview.

your feeling on it — other people enjoy sex, it is a normal thing and all that, but — there's always the *but* that keeps you from developing that confidence in yourself.

*S*161. Yes. To me, it's — I react just exactly as if it were painful and terrifying, so there isn't any difference at all psychologically. After all, truth is what we operate on, and truth, of course, is private to each individual nervous system. There you are — you can — two complete philosophic circles.

*C*162. The truth for you is that these things are painful and terrifying and that unless you can find some basis for faith or courage or something of that sort ——

*S*162. Some sort of an agent whereby the emotions can be changed; that is, where the negatives will change sides and go over to the positive side, as it were. If there were some way to proselytize the negatives, as it were. That's where the philosopher ends, and the psychoanalyst, you see, takes up. Some sort of a technique is needed to achieve it.

*C*163. Yes, that's where you feel you've come to a full stop, and that somebody else should to some extent take over.

*S*163. Well, I'll have to provide the energies and — I'll have to do it, but I feel that somebody else should flash the flashlight upon the key to the solution and I'll go ahead and grab the key.

*C*164. That's right. Now I think that's a pretty satisfactory way of looking at it, and the thing that still seems to elude our grasp somewhat, I mean, I noticed that although we've covered a lot of new territory today, we've come back to somewhat the same issue we were up against last time — what are some of the negatives? Well, you've defined that more — we're sneaking up on that — but I think that is our problem really. As you say, some of these things that have past origins are likely to be kept in the present primarily because they have some — some use to us.

---

*c*164. It would appear that the counselor is starting to bring the interview to a close. He becomes definitely directive in indicating that the counseling should concentrate upon the negative forces. This sort of attempt to summarize the interview is not likely to be satisfactory.

*S*164. That might be the same old use, and yet it might be a new use.

*C*165. Yes. M-hm. Quite right.

*S*165. Well, I've outlined the areas in which I feel inhibited. I don't know how I could particularize it any more.

*C*166. No, I think you've given quite a clear picture ——

*S*166. What I feel now would be somewhat comparable to this — that if — I need a key in the feeling realm, and some sort of a motivation to make me turn the key. That is, I feel that values are assumed and to change my feeling, I'm going to have to start some sort of a process there. I don't think it will be necessarily logical, although there might be some intellectual counterparts to it, and I feel that my intellect is not going to turn the flashlight on the key, due to the neurotic resistance itself. In other words, I feel that there is a key — I know that because I have had involuntary releases from my inhibition, and I know that I can have release, from actual empirical experience. But I can't put my finger on anything definite that I did to get that release — it all seems just to have happened automatically, and what I want to do is to have that release within full control of my conscious volition.

*C*167. M-hm.

*S*167. But I don't feel that the negative aspects of my personality are going to allow the intellect to turn the spotlight on the said key. Well, that is the conclusion to my self-sufficiency. I'm going to enlist your aid.

*C*168. The negative forces in your personality probably

---

*s*166. Mr. Bryan here shows better insight than the counselor. He states very clearly the point he has reached in his own insight, the recognition that the needed element is motivation and that (*S*167) he is relying on the counselor for help. Had the counselor simply clarified these attitudes, the interview could have been brought to a constructive close at this point.

*C*168–*C*170. Unfortunately the counselor endeavors to interpret the material of the interview, and meets definite resistance, which forces him to retire as gracefully as possible at *C*170. It may be said in the counselor's favor that in spite of unwise attempts at inter-

won't let you turn the spotlight on them, particularly as long as you regard them as something quite outside of yourself.

*S*168. I think they'll let me turn the spotlight on themselves, but not upon their therapy.

*C*169. Well, you'll make a good deal of progress as you can turn the spotlight on those negative forces.

*S*169. Oh, I think I've been doing that, haven't I?

*C*170. Some, yes. Yes, I think that's true.

*S*170. I can think about all of my experiences without recoiling from them. That is, I don't have the conventional values where I'd be embarrassed about it or anything like that — perhaps a slight embarrassment if they were to become common knowledge or anything like that.

*C*171. Well, you cast all of them on an intellectual plane. I don't think there's any aspect of your life that you indicate you would be fearful of looking at intellectually.

*S*171. Well, of course, here's the thing. Now perhaps — to use this example — I might intellectually recall and talk about my homosexual experience, for example, yet at the same time be unwilling to recapture the feelings that went along with it — is that what you referred to?

*C*172. Yes, or in another frame of reference — you might

---

pretation, he does cease to push the interpretation as soon as it is evident that it is not accepted. This whole difficulty could have been avoided very easily at *C*168 had the counselor simply recognized the attitudes expressed by saying, "You feel there are limits to what you can do, and you would like me to take over."

*S*170. Mr. Bryan's pride in his intellectual analysis explains very clearly his reason for putting his problem at first in such a sophisticated way. He is anxious to show that nothing is intellectually terrifying to him. Nevertheless, the prospect of giving up his neurotic symptoms can be a fearful situation for him, as we shall see in later interviews.

*C*172. A frankly interpretive response, but probably accepted because it is not as damaging to the ego as some of the other interpretations given. In reply, Mr. Bryan gives in concise form the philosophical basis for making an independent choice, and also makes one of his most positive statements as to his goal.

be quite willing to look at this job situation quite coolly from an intellectual point of view, but the feelings which — on both sides of the balance — toward going out after the job or staying home and recoiling from it — those are more difficult to face, I think.

S 172. Yes, one tends to abstract one's self so that one lives in the intellect alone. Yes, I often get this reaction — I say, "Well, your own feelings are blocking you, and after all it isn't any outside force or anything. Other people may have conditioned you, but you accepted the conditioning."

C 173. Yes, your own ——

S 173. In other words, I'm a determinist philosophically, but the fact that the will is not free does by no means say that the will cannot be unimpeded. I want the unimpeded will, and enjoyment and satisfaction from that unimpeded will, and it doesn't worry me emotionally that I have a deterministic philosophy. The fact that I'm reacting, rather than acting, doesn't make any difference to me psychologically. One can get just as much of a satisfaction from a reaction as one can if one was acting from free will, sort of in a vacuum — independent from preconditioning causes, I mean. That's of no emotional significance — purely academic.

C 174. Well, I suspect that our time is about up for today. I think that you're putting your finger on a number of things there that are highly important. And it is going to be a question of — you say your feelings are blocking yourself — can you look at them? Can you really consider your own reactions — not an intellectualized abstracted picture of them?

S 174. Yes, that might be an escape mechanism there, that overintellectualization.

C 174. The counselor gives another "homework assignment," and cannot resist an implied rebuke to Mr. Bryan for his tendency to retreat from real feelings into intellectualisms. The counselor seems quite unaware that his own overuse of interpretation is the most important single reason for these retreats. At any rate, his implied reproof is not missed, and *S* 174 to *S* 178 is something of a struggle of ideas, which is not therapeutically profitable. At last, in *C* 179, the counselor recognizes his mistake and again ceases to push the matter.

*C*175. Well, let's ——

*S*175. Of course, I am — I mean, in a sense a person faces his feelings sort of *ipso facto* when he has his feelings — I mean, they bring themselves pretty largely into the realm of consciousness, and ——

*C*176. Sometimes he doesn't own them.

*S*176. I'm conscious of my feelings practically all the time — of my negative feeling. Well, you feel that the — that one obstacle in the way of cure would be to regard the feelings as undesirable aliens rather than as worthy cripples?

*C*177. No, I guess that wasn't quite my notion. There's always a chance that they might not be aliens at all — they might be citizens right in your own country.

*S*177. Well, they're fifth columnists, then.

*C*178. (*Laugh.*) You're not going to own them, eh? (*Laugh.*)

*S*178. Well, I know that in the end one experiences only oneself, but I can't bring myself to put out the welcome mat for negative feelings.

*C*179. Well, I think probably I'm pushing you a little too hard on that, too. At any rate, let's explore into this situation further and see what some of the values are that it does seem to hold for you.

*S*179. Oh, I notice one other thing that would be of interest to you. Just before the interview, I seemed to feel better

---

*S*179. As in the first interview, the client saves up a significant attitude to bring out at the very close of the interview. This interesting statement of the conflicting desires within himself in regard to help is, on the whole, well handled by the counselor, although he cannot resist a slightly interpretive coloring to his remark in *C*183. In *C*184 he gives an excellent recognition of the feelings expressed, which enables the client to admit that at this time the feelings of not wanting help are strong indeed.

In this connection it is worth while to point out that this conflicted attitude toward obtaining assistance is very common and often very deep-seated. The client does want help, yet on the other hand he is fearful that he may be helped and will lose some of the satisfactions he gains at the present time from his maladjustments.

If the initial stages of counseling are badly handled, the contact is

— as if it were playing a trick on me by saying, "Well, you're going to be all right — perhaps you really don't need this." Then after the interview, why then I have a let-down. I've noticed that before.

*C*180. Yes, that's ——

*S*180. So I jot down things to report to you while I'm feeling badly so that when I feel well I won't have an absence of something to talk about.

*C*181. In other words, right within yourself there are the feelings that — "Oh, well, let's not do anything about this, there's nothing to it anyway."

*S*181. Just before the interview I feel pretty good and that, of course, tends to make me have not as much to say as if I were feeling very badly. If I were feeling very badly, I'd probably pour out a torrent of ideas.

*C*182. And, of course, one reason for that no doubt is that, as you pointed out yourself, you feel ——

*S*182. You think the neurosis can have such a diabolical cleverness, or am I overrationalizing that?

*C*183. I think *you* can have such a diabolical cleverness. (*Laugh.*)

*S*183. Yes, but on the other hand, the other aspect of me is even more clever, since I jot down things to say.

*C*184. That's right. And both of those parts of you are just as real as any individual or any person. I think that's the thing that strikes me — that you're just as much the person who writes down those things and who swears, by gosh, you'll get rid of this or else; and you're also the person who says, "Let's not — no use going into this thing too deeply."

*S*184. I realize that more and more. And oddly enough, I did go off without my notes.

---

likely to be broken and the client can then rationalize his conflict along these lines. He can say, "I wanted help, but all that the counselor did was to give me impossible advice. It proves that I have made every effort, but that I cannot be helped." A non-directive approach, in which the stress is upon the client's attitudes, not upon the counselor's judgment of these attitudes, avoids such a result.

*C*185. (*Laugh.*) That's a good one. (*Laugh.*)

*S*185. Let's see here — there's one more thing I had on my notes now that I haven't mentioned — oh, yes. Here's a very — sort of a subtle convolution. About the voyeuristic angle there — I think that I got the positive voyeuristic conditioning from my mother. She used to make comments about the girl roomers there — I mean she'd go to see their new underwear and everything, and I think she got a voyeuristic kick out of it herself; and I think that the girl roomers in turn got an exhibitionist kick out of it. Of course, that would make it homosexual — I don't know whether it was a matter of ego or whether it was an actual — what would you call that — vicarious exhibitionism?

*C*186. Well, perhaps so. Let's see if we can take up some of those things next time. Now let's see, we said Friday at four.

*S*186. At four. All right.

*C*187. Well, let's ——

*S*187. We couldn't have one before Friday, I suppose?

*C*188. No, I can't. I'm tied up tomorrow and ——

*S*188. Well, any extra periods that you might have ——

*C*189. All right.

*S*189. Oh, I told my folks I was being psychoanalyzed. (*Voices fade out as they leave the office.*)

General Comments

Mr. Bryan has expressed a great many significant attitudes in this interview, and has made progress toward the development of insight. The interview is marred and hampered, however, by the counselor's attempts to hasten the process. There are repeated instances in which the counselor goes beyond the feeling which has been expressed, or gives interpretations which are either resisted or only partially accepted. In connection with the counselor's errors it would be well to re-read the latter part of Chapter VII, particularly the portion beginning with p. 205, and Chapter II, pp. 25 ff., both of which

---

*S*185. This confused intellectualism, coming after such significant insight, seems to have but one goal — to prolong the interview. *S*187, 188 show the same desire. The counselor firmly brings the contact to a close.

discuss the misuse of interpretation.   The risks of recognizing unexpressed feeling are discussed in Chapter VI, pp. 152 ff.

In spite of these errors, there are sections of the interview in which
clarification of the client's feelings has been admirably carried out
and therapy moves rapidly forward.   Toward the end of the interview Mr. Bryan is able to achieve several significant insights, recognizing that he is conflicted in his desire for help and that he must
supply at least part of the motivation for change.

It is not so easy to list, for this second interview, the major feelings
which have been spontaneously expressed.   This is largely because
the counselor, having taken a more active part, tends to warp or
influence the course of the interview.   Nevertheless, the following
would seem to be the major attitudes:

> My neurosis is resisting treatment.
> We are threatening it.
> I cannot carry through the jobs I have lined up.
> In my present condition, I cannot face all the difficulties.
> If I do work it is a terrific struggle and it leaves me exhausted.
> I obtain partial release through night clubs.
> My parents disapprove of me.
> I think it is a fear that is holding me back.
> Perhaps my dreams indicate that it is a sexual fear.
> My mother, aunt, and others have conditioned me as I am.
> I am their victim.
> They leave a heavy burden on me.
> I pretend to be cheerful, but am not.
> Dissipation is eating up my strength.
> I keep my love affairs only as long as *I* want.
> I liked one girl, but was afraid of the responsibility of marriage.
> I feel jealousy about my girl friends, without reason.
> My parents are to blame for my lack of sexual satisfaction.
> I need some sort of faith.
> I need someone to help me.
> I could turn the key to my situation if someone could show
> it to me.
> I want the unimpeded will.
> I do want to improve, and I don't.
> I should like to prolong the interview.

Careful comparison of this list with the list from the first interview
will indicate that Mr. Bryan is talking much less about symptoms
and more in terms of causes.   He has become more outspoken about
his conflicted attitudes toward removal of his symptoms.   He recognizes that he must supply a part of the motivation for change.   These
differences show that he is beginning to move in the direction of
insight and positive choice.

❧ THIRD INTERVIEW ❧

*C*190. Well, how goes the battle today?

*S*190. I got your point right after I left the office the last time. The notion came to me that all aspects of the person-ality should be owned — that is, should be regarded as myself, and I was under the impression that if the neurosis were re-garded as an undesirable alien and I kept making a deportation struggle that there would be a resentment there and it would just entrench itself all the more deeply.

*C*191. M-hm.

*S*191. So I thought perhaps that this approach might be better — that is, we would say that we were all citizens as it were, and what are we going to do to make it a better country — working together?

*C*192. M-hm.

*S*192. So I've — in other words, I realized that to try to shove it out of me, as it were, would be resisted as — well, it would just be like — sort of like getting rid of a valuable por-

---

*C*190. A casual opening remark such as this is perhaps not so casual as it seems. The counselor has given the client an oppor-tunity to respond freely with either optimistic or pessimistic feelings or with any other topic which is uppermost in his mind. This type of opening is much more satisfactory than questions which are more directive — "Have you noticed any improvement since our last visit?" or, "Have you thought over what we talked about last time?"

*S*190–*S*193. This extended statement by Mr. Bryan is of consider-able theoretical interest, because it indicates the assimilation of an interpretation given by the counselor three days before. In spite of the fact that the interpretation was resisted and was not accepted at that time (see *S*92–*S*103, and also *S*176), it has gradually been ac-cepted during the interval. There is no doubt that some interpreta-tions, rejected at first, do gain acceptance. We know little as to the conditions under which this takes place.

tion of the personality. I mean, after all, it's my nervous energy there ——

C193. M-hm.

S193. — and any attempt to shove it out or get rid of it would be an amputation, as it were, of the personality, so that ——

C194. You feel that perhaps it is a part of you after all.

S194. Yes, and that I ought to change those — that is, to look upon the therapy as a change in personality rather than a getting rid of. It seems that with that in my conscious mind, there won't be so much resistance to the change as if I regarded the change as a throwing away of something.

C195. M-hm. And has that — you'd again like to look at all the intellectual aspect of that — has that made any difference in your — feeling about things, and so on?

S195. Well, I've adopted a nonintellectual concentration of it in my odd moments. I try to achieve a feeling of unity toward all aspects of my personality, and at the same time, not necessarily take them as they are without trying to change them, but at the same time not to regard myself as me and the enemy, but rather to make the me include all aspects. And it's a sort of a getting together with the negatives, and I don't know exactly how to make them change into positives, but at least I decided not to try to shove them away, because it'll be — I feel that there's some sort of resistance to loss there, that it makes the negative feelings entrench themselves just that much more deeply when you make an effort to shove them away, I think.

C196. M-hm.

S196. Now, on the other hand, I felt there might be a tendency perhaps on the other extreme to adopt too much of a Popeye attitude — "Well, I am what I am, and that's all I

C195. This is a quite unnecessary directive question. The reader can easily formulate a substitute response which would clarify the feeling just expressed. The counselor seems to be showing signs of the impatience which characterized the second interview.

am," and well, that's that. That's all right philosophically, but I don't think it would be all right psychologically.

C 197. Well, particularly not since you do feel quite strongly, I think, that there are pretty diverse forces, or forces working toward diverse goals, as far as you're concerned. You can't pretend more unity and more satisfactoriness than is there.

S 197. Well, what I meant was, I didn't want to get a placid self-satisfaction out of it by saying, "Well, I am what I am." I don't want to get self-satisfied, otherwise there won't be any motivation for a change. (*Pause.*) My work had a setback. The camera needs some more repair. It won't be ready till next week, but I think I can get ahold of another one. I notice I made an effort to locate another one, rather than wait till next week, till the first one gets fixed.

C 198. Do I understand that you really wanted to get to work on that?

S 198. Yes, I think that that would be the indication there. See, I could have waited till next Wednesday, until my own camera gets fixed, but I went out this afternoon and got one lined up from one of the downtown supply houses.

C 199. That really means something.

S 199. Yes, I thought that it did. I went over and talked to the manager quite a lot. It needed a good deal in the realm of persuasion there — it was a very unusual request. I felt that I talked him into completing negotiations so that I won't have to wait till next week.

C 200. And that makes you feel pretty good, I presume?

C 197. The counselor attempts some interpretation, based upon the last interview. S 197 shows that it is not accepted by the client.

S 190–S 197. It is interesting to see that up to this point the client is responding to the counselor's remarks in the preceding interview, made particularly in C 177 and C 178. He completes this topic in item S 197, and after a pause goes on to the more significant attitudes in which he is spontaneously interested.

C 198–S 203. It is important to be on the lookout for the minor actions which indicate that there has been a definite change of direction. The counselor is alert to this more mature move on the part

*S*200. Oh, yes. You see, I believe that some weeks ago I would have said, "Well, I believe I'll wait till Wednesday," and just seized the pretext to remain inert, but ——

*C*201. Something makes it different now?

*S*201. Yes, there is a barrier there, but not an insurmountable one. I walked in, anyway, and started talking to the manager. (*Pause.*)

*C*202. That sounds like quite a step.

*S*202. Well, I believe it is. Heretofore I've had to have circumstance more or less force me, or some outside force to sort of prod me into things, but I took the initiative. Of course, there is a pressure, but not a specific one.

*C*203. You could have gotten along without doing it.

*S*203. Yes. (*Pause.*)

*C*204. Sounds as though there must be more of a story behind that.

*S*204. Well, I don't know. I seem to be fluctuating now. I have periods where I have a lot of negative feeling, and then periods where I don't have so much. I seem to be fluctuating around the previous norm. And perhaps my parents' attitude was an incentive there. They have sort of a notion that I should do photography as a sideline and have some sort of a job — sort of regular job. They feel this way — that regularity in hours has a great value to them and that you should be subjected to the discipline of a certain routine. I've always had a spontaneous sort of life and no regularity at all. It's been very much of a sore point with them, and they're going to leave town on a trip and they want to make sure that — well, they want to lock up the house and they want to make sure that I've enough to get by on board and room — they don't

---

of Mr. Bryan and recognizes it in a helpful fashion, giving the client the support of knowing that his difficult actions that show more maturity are as well understood as his selfish and neurotic feelings.

*S*204. Mr. Bryan wishes to explain away some of his initiative and points out that it had a mixed origin, partly in his own desire, partly in the pressure of circumstances. He is looking at his situation very objectively.

— they want to use all of their money for the trip, rather than give me any. So making me get a job — that might have in turn put the pressure on myself to get the camera. But anyway, it happened, and I got a release there. I just finished with that camera deal just before I came here. Of course, I get a habitual euphoria before my interview, anyway. I wake up feeling well — now this is the day when I achieve another milestone with my psychology, and I feel in a good mood all day.

*C*205. M-hm.

*S*205. I don't feel any resistance to coming to the interviews — I thought perhaps I might. It doesn't seem to be working that way. But sometimes after the interview I have a worse fluctuation. But at least I am fluctuating — I think that I would rather fluctuate than have it a monotonous condition.

*C*206. Then, of course, that fluctuation is something very, very real, isn't it? I mean ——

*S*206. Oh, yes.

*C*207. — you have courage enough, and it must have taken quite a little to decide, "I'm really going to do something about this," so you came in to see me. Then — as you were saying last time — then on the other hand, you sort of trick yourself out of making use of it sometimes by feeling good in advance, and all that. I mean, you do fluctuate, but certainly there are very definitely the two parts of your motivation, very closely balanced.

*S*207. Yes, that's right. And I find on the upswing, things that would very definitely appall me to do, I do very nonchalantly — I mean, I actually enjoy doing them. It doesn't — things that I dread when I'm in the nadir I go at very

---

*C*206, *C*207. This interpretation is sound and is entirely based upon attitudes already expressed, so that it is accepted. Nevertheless, it is probably a second-best approach. A simple recognition of attitude, such as "At least some kind of change is taking place," would probably have been just as fruitful, and would not involve the risks which are inherent in every interpretation.

zestfully on the upswing. Perhaps actually get an enjoyment out of the social contacts of meeting people and in inducing people to cooperate with me in whatever enterprise I might have in mind.

*C*208. Any other things that have happened, or other elements that you want to talk about?

*S*208. Oh, I'm somewhat worried. Since the last interview, I didn't hear from one of my girls in ——, and I got the feeling that perhaps — the older feeling that I mentioned to you the other time, that perhaps during my absence, somebody else was getting in there, as it were. But I got a letter from her today. She's holding down three jobs — works from early in the morning till pretty near midnight, so that made it all right.

*C*209. That's an excuse. And that adds to your feeling that everything's going pretty well today, eh?

*S*209. Mm, yes, that's a factor in there. Although I have very illogical feelings of jealousy. My relationships with girls have been such that they have given what to a rational man would be every assurance of love and fidelity, and at the same time, I have an intensification of negative feeling, with imagery of infidelity when I don't have any evidence for such feelings or thoughts. And I imagine that that's a means I take of intensifying negative feelings, because that way I get all of the negatives of sex with none of the counteracting positives, so it seems to bite in deeper, as it were.

*C*210. Yes, you feel that you tend to punish yourself, perhaps, by some of those feelings?

*S*210. Well, I wouldn't know whether it would have a punishment motivation — there isn't any conscious thought

---

*C*208. It is difficult to see why the counselor did not respond to the genuinely positive feeling the client has just expressed. A significant opportunity is missed here.

*S*209-*S*221. Throughout this section of the interview, the client is spontaneously thinking through one aspect of his attitudes, and the counselor, through sympathetic listening and appropriate and simple recognition of feelings, helps him to go more and more deeply into the topic.

of punishment. Shall we say that I have a desire to make my condition worse, and that imagery ——

*C*211. — and you make yourself miserable, in a sense.

*S*211. — that imagery goes along with the worsification ——

*C*212. M-hm.

*S*212 — along with the worse negatives, I should say. So I feel that that's a means that I take to make myself react in that direction. I mean, that sort of imagery seems to be especially painful. That is, I think that's about one of the most painful thoughts I could have — would be a girl that I was interested in sexually being unfaithful to me.

*C*213. That greatly torments you.

*S*213. Yes, that makes the negative feeling very intense. (*Pause.*) Then, of course, I compensate there to a large extent. I get a joy out of going after other fellows' girls as a sort of a compensation there, which gets me in a lot of hot water. But my ideal would be that — I feel that the ideal reaction would be this — that it wouldn't particularly matter to me if the girls that I had a sexual relationship with — if they would have someone else, I would like to have no reaction to that. In other words — of course, I suppose that could be carried to extreme. I imagine if a fellow loved a girl with all of his personality rather than just sexually, why, he would have a certain amount of possessiveness. I suppose those attitudes can be overdone, although on the other hand, I have sometimes thought — perhaps it's a compensation thought — that monogamy was not necessarily a *sine qua non* of love, and the highest form of human relationship is to feel that — I can imagine a husband and wife having other affairs with perfect frankness, and yet not wanting to break up their marriage, yet always sort of being each other's preferred one, though not necessarily each other's only one. But at any rate, I do want to rid myself of the neurotic aspects of jealousy there, and of possessiveness.

*C*214. M-hm.

*S*214. But that's a bridge, of course, which can be crossed when it arrives. I'm convinced of this — that after my cure,

if I am possessive, it will be a much less painful form of possessiveness and will not be destructive. Do you recall the scene
in *Gone with the Wind* where Rhett thinks that his wife is
having an affair? Now, he doesn't like it, but at the same
time, it seems to make him more aggressive, rather than make
him lie down.

*C*215. M-hm.

*S*215. So perhaps that would be a healthy reaction.

*C*216. Do I understand that you feel that in your case it
torments you, but it doesn't tend to make you aggressive, is
that it?

*S*216. Well, the way I have been, if I had evidence of that,
it would be so painful to me that I wouldn't want to see her
again.

*C*217. M-hm.

*S*217. That is, that imagery would constantly be before
me — make me very pained. Of course, those things can be
rationalized to a certain extent — that is, you can say that a
girl's promiscuity says nothing about you, but only describes
her.

*C*218. But you feel in your case that that very definitely
isn't true — I mean that ——

*S*218. That I take it personally, you mean?

*C*219. Well, and you feel that way many times, even when
you have no real evidence of her promiscuity.

*S*219. Yes, I do. I get the feeling — and then of course I
tend to have an Othello-like reaction there — to seize on every
little bit of evidence and twist it. But — what was I going to
say? (*Pause.*) I've always had a feeling that women were
inclined to be promiscuous anyway — that it's only out of
social pressure that they idealize monogamy. I think to a
large extent that's lip service. And I've also had the feeling
that a woman's loving a man does not necessarily guarantee
her sexual fidelity to him. I've had experience with several
married women ——

*C*220. M-hm.

*S*220. — I can't relate the experiences — I mean they're

all regarded as very loving wives, and so on, so it has made me skeptical on that score.   I've never had any direct — any evidence of its happening to me when I was on the other end of the stick, but as I say, I don't need the evidence — so the feeling is just as real, whether I have any evidence or not. But that seems to be about the most intense — I mean, that is the imagery which is associated with my most intense neurotic feeling.   I can't imagine any worse neurotic pain, and oddly enough, the girl can be a tramp — the only prerequisite seems to be a sexual attraction — I don't have to admire her, don't have to respect her, don't have to love her, don't have to have any affection for her.   As long as my libido goes forth, it's a torture to me to think of her having relationship with anyone else.

C221. You feel that has a pretty direct and important relationship to your whole pattern, don't you?

S221. Well, it seems to me that the imagery that goes along with the utmost of negative feeling would have a bearing on it, some way or other.   Since that imagery is associated with the negative at its worst, I can imagine that it has some sort of significance.

C222. Yes, I think so, too.   You like so much to talk in rather general or intellectualized terms about some of these things — I mean, about fidelity of women in general, and so on, that it is perhaps a little hard to see what some of those connections might be.   Can you cast some of this more in

---

C222. The counselor endeavors to probe further, to get the client out of generalities and into specific problems, but the approach is quite futile, as it usually is.   S222 and S223 are no more specific than what goes before.   It is hard for the counselor to realize that each individual solves his problems in a frame of reference which is comfortable and natural to him.   Some clients would work through their problems entirely in terms of their relationship to specific friends or employers, or in terms of very concrete situations.   This client faces his problems in more generalized terms.   It is only when pressed by the counselor that he retreats into unprofitable philosophizing.   The client should be allowed to think through the issues in the ways which are real and natural to him.

your own frame of reference, in regard to your own experience, and so on?

S 222. Well, my own experience has been — I have a very easy time in attracting women. Always had a lot of success there, and a great many of them seem to love me pretty completely, that is, it isn't just a sexual thing with them — of course ——

C 223. It's different for them than your own feelings toward them?

S 223. Well, I think that they have a heart interest there — at least, they give the evidence of it, but I imagine that's sort of a sugarcoating. Most women, either to themselves or to others, would not acknowledge a pure sexuality — they would want it sugarcoated, as it were, with love. That is — I have found a few girls who say frankly that they can have sex without love, but most of them seem to feel that it's nobler to have love along with it — that love makes it beyond good and evil — that sort of thing. And I've never been dropped by a girl. I've always been the one to do the dropping. And I've never had any logical evidences at all of their infidelity — it just seems to be a phantasy of mine that I build up. Is that what you meant by getting out of the general?

C 224. Yes, that does help a little. In other words, you do get a good deal of — you get a more comfortable feeling that you have dropped the girl than you would if she had dropped you.

S 224. Yes, I would prefer it that way. I want to get over that. I don't want to have my ego tied up with such things. I want to make my ego tied up more with artistic achievement rather than with the vagaries of human emotion.

C 225. Keep yourself fairly clear from getting deeply involved in any emotional relationship?

---

c 224. Although a directive question did not help materially, sound recognition of feeling, as in this response, does lead to a deeper and more significant statement in *S* 224. It is not important that at this time Mr. Bryan sees none of the egocentrism portrayed in this statement.

S 225. No, I want to have deep experiences, but I want to be psychologically healthy enough that any outcome of those experiences — even the worst possible outcome, would not be a neurasthenic blow to me. That is, I would want to be able to take any outcome, as it were, and the way I have been, I feel that if I had a disastrous love affair it would be a higher price than I would want to pay for it. Of course, I realize that being neurotic heightens the chances of disaster anyway — that is, that a healthy fellow is both able to take a disastrous outcome and also at the same time has less likelihood of it happening; so that you get both edges of the sword when you're in an undesirable psychological condition. More likely to get dropped, and it will hurt you more.

C 226. Well, I wonder — can you tell any more about why you feel it would hurt you so if you really became involved in one of these affairs and then it didn't turn out too well?

S 226. Well, I don't know what we can say as to the why of a feeling. I just know that it would intensify my abdominal pain, as it were — what I've been describing to you, and I imagine I would feel inferior too. I mean, I'd probably react to my friends — I mean they would — they'd probably gloat about it, since it would mean a downfall to me, who have always had such success — I think they would seize the opportunity to gloat — I think they would needle me.

C 227. M-hm.

S 227. So one aspect would be partly ego, and mostly I think that — just pure pain.

C 228. At any rate, what you're saying suggests, or I get the feeling a little bit, that these affairs and so on have given you quite a sense of achievement, in one respect. I mean — that you can attract most women; you can get them in-

---

C 226. This kind of question does respond to the client's feeling and does not change the flow of the contact. It is not seriously directive. Its only disadvantage is that, if frequently repeated, it leaves the client with the feeling that he is being pushed or prodded, where simple clarification of feeling does not.

terested in you, but your own interest in them is pretty definitely limited to ——

*S*228. Yes, I don't know whether to call it a sense of achievement. Some fellows I know have a definite conquest angle there. One of my friends in —— has that to a very exaggerated degree; that is, he goes after girls more than his libido calls for — that is, he goes after them just for the sake of conquest. I don't believe I regard it as an egotistical achievement. I think I could perhaps better describe my reaction as an artistic kick — I like the process of using my amatory technique, and I get an artistic kick out of that sort of like a trumpet player would in a jam session, where he wasn't trying to set the world on fire — he was just playing his horn like he felt and enjoying the artistic technique of it.

*C*229. You feel that you're a skilled artisan or a skilled musician in that sphere ——

---

*S*228. A statement such as this (or *S*233) deserves careful consideration, because it is here that one's fundamental approach to treatment is most sharply tested. From a psychological point of view one may judge the client to be immature, because of the complete lack of any social feeling and the absence of any interest in, or regard for, the personality of his partner. From a moralistic point of view, one may evaluate the client as amoral in his attitudes and unconventional or even antisocial in his behavior. But from a therapeutic point of view, such evaluations and judgments are not made. It is the therapist's function not to pass judgment, but to clarify and objectify the client's basic attitudes, in order that the client himself may decide whether they are in line with his own life goals. To take such an approach involves a deep respect for the autonomy and integrity of the individual. It involves a belief in the right of each individual to self-determination. Not every professional worker has this degree of confidence in human beings, nor this degree of respect for the individual's right to make his own basic choices. Such workers will not find it possible to carry on therapy as it is outlined in this book and in this case. The approach will not be congenial to their beliefs.

*C*229–*S*241. Throughout this section the counseling techniques are very satisfactory. In *C*229, *C*230, the counselor attempts no moralization, no evaluation, but simply reflects the attitudes expressed. In *C*235, *C*236, and *C*237, his responses shade into interpretation, but these interpretations are mostly accepted.

S 229. Yes.

C 230. — but you mustn't become too deeply involved, either.

S 230. Well, not till I've achieved my cure. Then, of course, I feel that I can take anything. If it does have an undesirable outcome, why, it's not going to wreck me. (*Pause.*) Then too I have a sort of a fundamental — sort of realization of human behavior — that it is subject to variations anyway, and that I feel that the enlightened man should not find that a source of sadness. That should be one of the realities of life which should be accepted. Personalities do change, and even though people do stick together, they might not necessarily have the honeymoon feeling all throughout their lives. That can change to something else — something no less valuable, but at least I feel that the healthy mind is not saddened by changeability.

C 231. You feel that if you were healthier, you could take it as well as dish it out, is that it?

S 231. Yes.

C 232. — be more adaptable.

S 232. And then I wouldn't have these worries, and even if the actuality did occur, why, then I could take it all right. But this way I worry anyway. It's purely a case of phantasy.

C 233. It's pretty hard for you to assimilate even these imaginary infidelities.

S 233. Yes. They're just as real to me as if they were actual. And, well, my relationships have been with somewhat the exuberant sort of girl anyway — the uninhibited and exuberant type. And, of course, there's much more chance for infidelity with that sort of girl anyhow. But then, of course, they make better sexual partners. It's just a case of not being able to have your cake and eat it too. Then, of course, I have a great sadness there when my technique works so well up to a certain point, and then to have the inhibition blocking me is, of course, very hideous irony there to me. (*Pause.*) I worry constantly during the making process, — whether I'll be able to function properly, and all that sort of thing.

*C*234. M-hm. You don't feel quite sure of yourself in that kind of a situation.

*S*234. Yeah. I don't know but what I might have difficulties sexually that would make me look ridiculous.

*C*235. Again, a part of that, I take it, is the fact you just would find it awfully difficult to take anything that struck at your ego — that you would feel humiliated.

*S*235. I cast it in egotistical terms, but it goes a lot deeper than that. Well, I feel an acute sense of something very fundamental in life being wrong — so it would go deeper than a petty ego deflation. It's just——

*C*236. Deeper, but along the same line, is that it? I mean, that you feel that there really is something quite basically wrong with you — this is just one relatively lesser manifestation of it?

*S*236. Well, I feel that sex is very fundamental in life and that the least a man can do is to be a good copulater; that should be one of the fundamentals. Of course, he should be a lot more, of course, if he does have the potentialities, but at least any animal can do that.

*C*237. That's one of the reasons why it strikes you so hard if there is — if you have some doubt or some uncertainty as to your own abilities along those lines.

*S*237. Yes, I feel that there's something fundamentally wrong there — something wrong with the very foundation, as it were — that any other achievement I might have would not be adequate compensation for a blocking in that fundamental field. I used to think that perhaps I would become an ascetic — go in entirely for intellectual life, and so forth, but I couldn't bring myself to value that wholeheartedly. I had the definite conviction that no intellectual achievement could make up for that fundamental blocking there. (*Pause.*) I want to be a healthy animal first of all, then I feel that the super-elements there will grow out of that healthy foundation. I feel that any achievement that was the result of overcompensation would be pretty unsatisfying, no matter how great the achievement, no matter how great the world's applause.

My private knowledge of that fundamental blocking would bring me down so much that the world's applause wouldn't make up for it.

C238. In other words, you've got to have some respect for yourself on a pretty fundamental basis, in order to have any achievements in any line.

S238. M-hm. Of course, I overvalue sex now as a direct result of my inhibition. That is, I think more about it than I would if I didn't have the inhibition, but I want to put it somewhere between food and music. It has — well, you could make the analogy that it is somewhat like food; it's sort of a physical gusto, and on the other hand, it also has the artistry of music about it. And I feel that it can have an important place without being dwelt on, as it were.

C239. M-hm. You feel that somehow you've failed to give it the proper balance that it should have, somewhere between food and music, is that it?

S239. Well, I know that I haven't been able to get the gusto from it. So that, as an experience, it's very definitely dampened, you see, by the negative. But I know that that's the place it would assume if I were in a healthy condition. Of course, I'm talking now just about the more or less semi-permanent affairs — I feel that a great love with the right girl would be very important in my life, if I had a healthy psychological condition.

C240. But, as I gathered it from last time, when some opportunities come along for possible real love, you have tended to avoid them.

S240. Yes, that's entirely correct. I feel this way, as closely as I can analyze it — I don't want to enter into anything

---

C238 is a particularly good clarification of a complex conversation and brings the client to a very significant insight. In S238 he realizes quite frankly that he overvalues sex and places too much stress upon his thinking about sex. This is a result which would not have been obtained if the counselor had been in any way judgmental. C240 is a definite interpretation of the material from the preceding interview (S147), but it is accepted to some extent.

great as a psychological cripple. It would be very disheartening for me to compare myself with the ego image — that is, I would have an ideal self and my real self, and the contrast would be very distressing to me, most particularly in a situation of great love. So that I wouldn't want to enter into it unless I were my best self.

*C*241. M-hm. You feel you just wouldn't have a great deal to offer to a great love, perhaps.

*S*241. Yes, that's right. I'd feel that I'd be going along in low gear, as it were. But I definitely want to have a great love or loves, as the case may be.

*C*242. You want to, but nevertheless, you have a little concern over whether you could pay the price.

*S*242. That's a peculiar terminology, in a way. Whether or not I would want to pay the price, or whether or not I would have the money, now which do you mean?

*C*243. How would you put it?

*S*243. Whether or not I would have the money. Still you could put it another way. There's sort of a fluctuation there in my evaluation of it. Let's leave that analogy a minute. I would feel very disheartened were I to be in that situation, because I would constantly compare it with the ideal — that is, compare my real self with the ideal and be very aware of the blockings in my feelings and my actions. I'd feel that I couldn't be the great lover that such a situation would require.

*C*244. And that has some parallel in your feelings about other things, doesn't it? I mean that, here you are at your present status, and 'way up here is the ideal as you would like to see it, in regard to job or love or any one of several different things.

---

*C*242. Here is a direct interpretation which could not be accepted unless the client recognized some of his own self-centered tendencies. He has not arrived at any such recognition and does not accept the statement. The counselor wisely retreats in *C*243 and lets the client read his own meaning into the statement.

*C*244. The same comment might be made about this summarized interpretation that was made at *C*206. It is a second-best approach.

*S*244. M-hm.   That's right.   Sure, you could put it in any field.

*C*245. And that — any bridging of that gap seems pretty hopeless.

*S*245. I put it in the sexual field, because I think that's where it had its origin — if that isn't where it had its origin, at least the central dynamo of sex is the thing that is being inhibited, and of course that inhibits all, when you inhibit the dynamo.

*C*246. M-hm.   Well, I guess our time is nearly up for to-day.   Just before I came in, I looked over my calendar, and I'm not sure whether it conflicts with your plans or not.   The next hour I had down was Thursday at four.

*S*246. I was wondering now — I may be working from now on — you see, I haven't been doing any work.   Do you ever have any consultations in the early evening?

*C*247. No, I try to avoid that.   But it might be possible.

*S*247. Well, I might only have evening hours open, although I don't know for sure now, but I was just wondering — in that eventuality, if you would ever be able to take me in the evenings.

*C*248. I think that might be possible.   How about — just happened to think of another thing — would Monday at five be a possible time for you, or will you be tied up then?

*S*248. Monday at five?   Yes, that's all right.

*C*249. Monday at five would be all right.   All right, let's make it Monday at five, and I guess probably we'd better settle these as we go along, anyway.   We won't try to set another time.

*S*249. All right.

*C*250. I'll sort of tentatively save Thursday at four, but we'll see ——

*S*250. I'm going to — I'll probably be working on Monday — that's a good night, but that won't take place until about half past six anyhow, so ——

*C*251. All right — five o'clock'd be O.K.   (*Both stand up, preparatory to leaving.*)

*S*251. Well, how do I compare with others in my progress, or —

*C*252. I think you're definitely making progress, and the kind of thing that has more significance to me than some of the intellectual and philosophical aspects are the things that you do in the realm of feeling and action. I mean — I'm interested that you had guts enough to go talk to this fellow this afternoon and so on. And it's as we discuss —

*S*252. Well, it didn't take any guts. I mean, that's the nice part of it. I didn't have to force myself.

*C*253. M-hm.

*S*253. That's just my reaction there.

*C*254. And it's some of those things that —

*S*254. Do you want to leave any thoughts with me to dwell on between times, or don't you use that sort of technique?

*C*255. Oh, sometimes I do, but I often find it doesn't mean very much.

*S*255. M-hm. I see. You just want me to come in and talk about the things that I feel —

*C*256. Yes. I might make this kind of a suggestion — that when you find your symptoms rather bad or leaving you — I mean either way, when they're coming on or leaving you — the more honestly you can ask yourself, "What's this getting me?" the more progress you might be able to make.

*S*256. That's a good thought. Just to take the full responsibility for my feelings — say, "I'm the one that's making

---

*S*251. Mr. Bryan is plainly asking for encouragement and support. Perhaps the best response would involve more clarification and less outright encouragement. A helpful type of response would have been, "Of course you are concerned as to whether you are making progress. Certainly you are seeing yourself more clearly, and that is a first step." The counselor's attempt to focus attention on the forward step which has been taken may or may not have been helpful.

*S*254–*S*256. It is interesting that neither counselor nor client seem to be aware of the previous "homework assignments." It is also worth noting that the counselor rejects the idea intellectually and then gives such an assignment.

myself feel this way, and what is this feeling getting me — what good is it doing me?"

*C*257. M-hm.   Sometimes that ——

*S*257. Now I'm — I've done a little work with self-hypnosis, and I find that I can induce a quite interesting stage there. I raised a blister on myself one time by suggesting a cigarette burn.

*C*258. Well ——

*S*258. And I don't know what to do about that — we might go into that some time if you want to ——

*C*259. Well, I think that — well, we'll see — we can talk that over.   I think that has somewhat limited therapeutic value.

*S*259. Yes, it doesn't last long.

*C*260. It has a lot of influence on various elements ——

*S*260. I get quite a good trance state ——   (*Fades out. They leave.*)

General Comments

The third interview proceeds much more smoothly than the second. The counselor makes few errors of a serious sort, though there is still a slight tendency to interpret material rather than to recognize and clarify it.   With greater freedom from counselor pressure, the client freely explores various aspects of his situation, thinking deeply, and arriving at some new insights.   There is also one indication of a more mature and responsible attitude toward his work.   There is almost no mention of physical symptoms, except descriptions of such symptoms in the past.   Progress at this stage of therapy is not readily discernible from the content of the interview.   It is only as one

---

*S*257. This sudden attempt to bring in a totally new topic seems designed solely to prolong the interview.   In support of this view, it may be noted that neither this topic nor the one brought in at the conclusion of the second interview (*S*185) is ever referred to again by the client.   They seem to have had value only as a claim upon the interviewer's time.   The counselor might simply have responded, "I realize that an hour seems short, and that you would like to have more time, but it is the limit I've had to set, and we can take up other things at our next appointment."

compares the spontaneous attitudes with those expressed in previous interviews that change is evident. A tentative listing of the most prominent attitudes might be as follows:

I feel that my neurosis is a part of myself.

I'm trying to bring about more unity in myself.

I have put forth some special effort on my job and found it satisfying.

I feel that I am fluctuating in my goal and in my activities.

I find that I am enjoying some social actions which previously would have appalled me.

I feel irrational jealousy about my girl friends.

I can't endure the thought of a girl's being unfaithful to me.

I should like to be able to take such experiences in healthy fashion.

I do not want to be too deeply involved emotionally with any girl.

I pride myself on my amatory technique.

But I lack fundamental confidence in myself sexually.

I feel that I overvalue sex at the present time.

I shouldn't want to enter into real love until I am cured.

I should like reassurance as to the progress I am making.

A comparison of this list with those from the two previous interviews will bring out several facts. In the first place, there is relatively little repetition. When feelings are adequately recognized, it is rare for the individual to go over and over the same ground. Even where the same topic is discussed, as in his conversation about his irrational jealousy, he goes much further in his exploration in this interview than in the previous conversation. A second fact is the increase in positive attitudes. Where the first interview stresses his misery and suffering, there is comparatively little of this in the third interview, and a number of forward-looking and positive attitudes are expressed. A third fact to be noted is the acquisition of a degree of new insight in each interview. Mr. Bryan is somewhat unusual in that he shows some evidence of insight even in the first interview. At that time he recognizes his desire to cling to his symptoms. In the second contact he achieves some understanding of the fact that he must play a part in the dynamics of change — he expresses his willingness to turn the key, if it can be shown to him. In the present interview he realizes his compensatory overvaluation of sex. In short, these three interviews show a wider and wider exploration of his attitudes and a clearer recognition of them. They show a gradual accumulation of partial insights. They lay the groundwork for more complete insight, and for positive decisions and actions based upon such understanding.

❦ FOURTH INTERVIEW ❧

S261. I think this will be an important session.

C261. Is that so?

S262. I wonder if I could ask you to take rather complete notes. I don't know how complete you're in the habit of making them.

C262. M-hm. O.K.

S263. I find myself reacting quite strongly to the war situation. I have this very definite feeling — that if I were to be involved, that is, inducted into the army ——

C263. M-hm.

S264. I feel it would not only be catastrophic to me in my present condition, but even if I were to have a cure in the meanwhile — my healthy ideals have always been that of — well, an abhorrence of regimentation, and I feel a love of

---

S261. It is typical of this type of therapy that important advances take place between contacts, as well as during contacts. The counselor who is used to a more directive approach finds this difficult to understand. He is used to "selling" the client a suggestion or an idea during one contact, only to find that the conviction has faded by the time of the next interview. It is often a surprise to find a therapeutic approach which releases forces that continue to operate outside of the interview contacts.

S262. Such a request is quite unusual and is probably related to the neurotic's high degree of interest in himself. Yet it is also one indication of the fact that note-taking, if accepted (and in this case it has been accepted without explanation), helps to give a business-like and serious tone to the contacts.

S263–S270. This segment is a sound bit of counseling. The client talks through his fears and resentments at the war situation, and these attitudes are adequately recognized.

This is an appropriate point at which to consider the effect of new environmental forces upon the progress of therapy. Will fear of being drafted, for example, prevent progress or undo any progress

individual initiative and private enterprise — that sort of thing, which seems to make a war situation very much intolerable to me. I had thought I would not be called (gives his reasons), but now I think I might be called, so it's had a very disturbing effect on me.

*C*264. You feel that would be just more than you could take.

*S*265. Even if I were up to my psychological ideal, I would find that such a life would be absolutely against my grain — the way I've been raised — the ideals that I've been taught to hold to, and the individual way of life that I have always pursued myself. (*Pause.*) So I'm reacting very much to that situation.

*C*265. M-hm. You've found it quite upsetting to you?

*S*266. Yes. I feel that even aside from my neurosis I would have — that I have — that my healthy temperament would also find it very intolerable. I'm sure that I couldn't make an adjustment to it, even though I were in a sound condition. My life history has always been one of — I've always had those ideals of independence and private initiative — always had a distaste for regimentation. That's reflected in the occupation that I have chosen. It's my own business — that is, I'm not working for anyone else. I like to take the initiative and take the risk and take the profit.

*C*266. M-hm.

*S*267. That's why my condition has been — one of the reasons why it has been distressing to me — because my business is one that requires a good bit of initiative and a good bit of working for one's self. And that's why I want to change my condition to a healthier one — because I know — I have

---

which has been made up to this point? On the whole, it may be said that such influences are far less important than would ordinarily be supposed. This is recognized by the client in the early part of the next interview. The client's basic adjustment to life and its problems is something which is more fundamental than the new demands being made upon him, unless those demands are very extreme.

the sort of business that if I work hard at it, why I can make a very nice living.

*C*267. And do I gather, too, that things about your business that have been hard for you have been those that would take a good deal of initiative, and yet faced with the opposite situation where little or no initiative would be needed, that seems even worse, or seems much worse?

*S*268. Well, yes. I mean, I know that the plums are there, but that it takes actions which have been hard for me to do; even though I have forced myself to do them, the nervous toll has been such that it couldn't go on without an improvement in my psychology.

*C*268. But even that difficulty, as I get your feeling, doesn't make you want the lack of independence that you would find in army life?

*S*269. Oh, no. 'Cause there you'd have more than just a lack of independence. You'd be subject to the regimentation, and — well, to say nothing of the goal that it is directed towards — the same thing would be — well, the mass carnage which it would inevitably lead up to. The actual involvement in a battle I think, odd as it may seem, would be more agreeable to me than the army life in camp.

*C*269. M-hm. In other words, the thing that strikes you worst about it is the possible regimentation and having somebody else order your life.

*S*270. Yes. I'd feel there — I'd have a very abysmal feeling that all of the spirit of '76 was lost, as it were, and that I were just a puppet.

*C*270. M-hm.

*S*271. Outside of this thinking about the war, I feel that I have been definitely making progress. I find myself doing more, and at less of a sacrifice in nervous tension.

*C*271. You really felt that you were doing some things you hadn't done before?

---

*S*271–*S*274. Here are fresh indications of minor but important actions pointing toward a more mature handling of situations.

*S*272. Oh, yes.   Very definitely.

*C*272. What sort of things?

*S*273. Along the line of photography.   I've lined up a job for this evening.

*C*273. M-hm.

*S*274. I'm going to take photographs of a fraternity group. And I had to go through several obstacles to get the job, which required a great deal of sacrifice on my part.   I know that definite improvement has been made there.

*C*274. M-hm.

*S*275. The last time you left a final word with me that I was to ask myself when I felt my condition worsening and also when I felt it bettering — I was to ask myself, "Honestly now, what is this getting me?" and I find that the impression I have there is that the word *this* in there seems to have two very different meanings for me.   During the worsening condition, the *this* refers to the old trouble, and as it's leaving, the *this* has an upswing to — I mean, a new meaning.   I say to myself, "Now, what is this getting me — now that I'm becoming healthier — now that I feel it leaving me?   Why, this is getting me a more satisfying life."   So you see, the one word *this* there takes on two meanings, to my notion.

*C*275. M-hm.   And as a matter of fact, those two meanings of the word *this* are your whole struggle, aren't they?   I mean — whether to hang on to *this*, or whether to take the second *this*, that leads toward ——

---

*s*275. This statement and those which follow seem to be the result of the "homework" which the counselor suggested at the close of the preceding interview.   The outcome proves to have been definitely constructive in this instance.   This rather involved paragraph bears careful re-reading, since it contains much fundamental insight.   The client is recognizing that leaving his symptoms might well mean a more satisfying life, a view which he has never fundamentally held before.

*c*275. This is an excellent response, helping to clarify the complex attitudes just expressed.   It indicates that the counselor was genuinely concentrating upon the feelings the client was struggling to express.

*S*276. Yes, that's it right there, in a nutshell. I did a little analyzing on the neurotic *this* — I think I've got it pinned down very, very closely now. I think that has helped me. I seem to have two definite neurotic conditions — the one is when I'm in pain, when I find the rôle that I would like to adopt — that is, the manly, vigorous rôle — I find it blocked. Then my retreat, the release that seems to be most enjoyable for me, of going into the voyeuristic situation, which I have analyzed more, as I mentioned the other day — which seems to be a vicarious exhibitionism. That is, I take two rôles — I vicariously experience the girl as she exhibits to me and get a vicarious sexual enjoyment from that, so that I am both the exhibitor and the exhibitee. So what it seems to be is that, when my condition becomes worse, I find that my man rôle seems to be blocked, so I escape into what we might call a semi-feminine rôle, whereas I adopt vicariously the feminine enjoyment of exhibitionism to me.

*C*276. You feel that is a feminine rôle, or a more childish rôle, or something of both?

*S*277. Well, I think the origin came from the girl roomers that we had when I was a child, whom I am sure got an exhibitionistic enjoyment in exhibiting to me. I believe that my reactions were probably something like this: my parents were inhibiting my own life — my own particular pattern — so perhaps I felt that in order to get the forbidden enjoyments of sex I would have to slip into a feminine rôle, which was just

---

*S*276–*C*276. This kind of involved intellectual explanation can easily confuse the counselor, unless he is focusing on the feelings, rather than the content, of the client's remarks. Here the feeling seems to be, "When I am blocked from being a man, I tend to retreat." If the counselor could have responded to this fundamental feeling, it would have been better than the somewhat interpretive question raised in *C*276.

*S*277–*C*277. This is obviously another intellectual detour on the part of the client, discussing again the things that "perhaps I felt," or what "I believe my reactions were," rather than expressing actual attitudes. The cause of the detour is not clear. The counselor, at

at the same time, you see, presented to me by the exhibitionistic girls. So that the temporal juxtaposition of the two situations, you see — I wanted to retreat and escape young masculine activity, and searching about for a way to get the tabooed sex pleasures, I seized upon a vicarious enjoyment of the exhibitionistic girls.

C277. Let me see if I get what you're meaning there — in other words, when you're faced with something — I'm not quite sure whether the blocking is that there is something pretty difficult in this masculine rôle, or whether you're referring to other kinds of blocking — at any rate, when you're blocked in being a man, you tend to fall back into a possibly more feminine kind of satisfaction — certainly a more childish kind of satisfaction, in voyeurism.

S278. M-hm. Well, my young life there, you see, was subjected to a sexual puritanism, and I had a fear of masturbation, and a fear of playing with girls for fear that something might happen, and then I observed that girls had exhibitionistic tendencies which they seemed to enjoy, so I felt that in order to dodge my own taboo, I could get vicarious enjoyment, you see, from the feminine exhibitionism to me.

C278. Yes, I think I get your meaning there. I wasn't quite so sure that I did get your meaning in regard to the type of blocking that would throw you into that, as it were.

S279. Yes, m-hm. Well, I had very early sex puritanism imposed on me. Just about the time that I was beginning to have infantile sex feelings, anyway. So that the two things coincided so closely there that I believe it was a direct escape from the boy rôle to the vicarious girl rôle.

---

any rate, gives an excellent response in C277, which clarifies the feelings expressed in S276 and S277. The counselor is still intent upon interpreting the retreat as childish rather than feminine, but on the whole, his response catches the essentials of the client's viewpoint.

C278, C279, C280. These counselor statements are subtly directive and distinctly inferior in quality to C277. Obviously the counselor wants Mr. Bryan to discuss the present situations which prevent him

C 279. That is, you're now talking about it again back in — what it might have meant to you then.

S 280. Yes. But I don't think that that has changed. I still get the same voyeuristic enjoyment. I go through three phases. One is the blocked and painful feeling. Then I either go into the voyeuristic phantasy or actuality, whichever the situation may be. I'm able to have a release from the blocked and painful feeling and go on with my masculine rôle. By masculine rôle, I mean the healthy sex activities and healthy economic activities which we usually associate with that term. Being a man of the world — out making money, fighting economic battles successfully, and having successful sexual experiences. That's the rôle that I have — the rôle that I want.

C 280. The rôle that you have when you are successful, and the rôle that you want always. And — I don't want to push you on this — perhaps you didn't make it plain — perhaps it isn't plain in your own mind, but I'm not quite clear as to whether you felt some certain type of thing tended to block you in that masculine rôle, and therefore causes you to make use of these other satisfactions.

S 281. Yes. The type of thing was the sum total of my puritan conditioning there, that I received from my mother and my father and my old-maid aunt, and so forth. They were horrified at masturbation and whenever they would suspect that I was masturbating, why, they would immediately go up in the air and make all sorts of preachments about it. And so I was looking around for an avenue of sex expression which would not be fearful or which would not be painful and terrifying, and in my observation of the exhibitionistic girls, I found such a rôle would not be painful and terrifying to me, which I adopted.

---

from being masculine, and Mr. Bryan is plainly not ready to talk about this aspect of it. Directive approaches are almost uniformly unsuccessful when they are pointed toward significant emotionalized areas.

*C*281. And you feel pretty sure that it is still the fears and so on, engendered by puritanism, that tend to cause you to take these ——

*S*282. Yes, I feel very sure of that. And also, another interesting thing — the same puritanism, the same sort of a taboo, in a way, seems to be associated with money matters along my conditioning. I seem to have a religious conditioning there that runs along something like this: that money is the root of all evil — it's sordid and tainted, you see, just like sex is, and there seems to be a definite parallel there between money and sex, so that when I go out aggressively after money, I get the same sort of fear reaction, the same sort of a blocking as I get from going after sex.

*C*282. You could almost — as I get your description of these various things — you could almost say that any time that you endeavor to play a thoroughly masculine rôle in the economic world and in the sex area, then you draw back into other satisfactions.

*S*283. Yes, that's an excellent way of putting it. (*Pause.*)

*C*283. Perhaps you're not entirely sure, yourself — or haven't been in the past, how much you really wanted to play a masculine rôle.

*S*284. Well, yes, I believe that that's very obvious. That is, I think my young reasoning, although I didn't reason it out at the time — I think we might rationalize it this way now — that, well, here are the girls having a good time showing off, and they can have enjoyment without having fears and inhibitions, so I'm going to enjoy something like that myself. So that I definitely adopted the desire for a temporary playing of the feminine rôle. Now that urge only obtains, you see, during the voyeuristic excitation. Other times, I don't notice any feminine rôles about myself — or I've never heard anyone

---

*C*281, *C*282. Here the counselor returns to the more constructive clarification of attitudes.

*C*283–*S*284. After a pause, the counselor raises a question which is highly interpretive in its implications. It seems to be accepted, but drives the client into another intellectualistic excursion in *S*284.

refer to my actions as being that. Now, I don't know whether anyone else has ever referred to voyeurism itself as being necessarily a feminine rôle, but that's the way I have analyzed it. I haven't read any literature on that, but I feel that that's the origin, and that was my reaction at that time, and I don't believe that there has been any radical change in that. You asked me the other day now — about the ego connections. And I've been recalling some incidents on that. I believe that in certain fields where I have an egotistical desire to excel and cannot do so, I find a definite worsening of my pain — that is, if I find myself not up to my intellectual par when I'm among other intellectual fellows and that condition would happen to manifest itself to the others, I would feel a distinctly negative feeling there — that my intellectual life was handicapped there.

*C*284. That is — do I understand — your symptoms would be worsened and so on, in that kind of situation?

*S*285. Yes.

*C*285. M-hm.

*S*286. And in a realm of friendship, if I thought that a friend would betray me, I would get that same sort of a feeling. So it seems to operate in other lines than the economic and the sexual, even though the origin was such.

*C*286. In other words, anything that makes you feel somewhat insecure, or somewhat inadequate, could bring on or make worse those feelings?

*S*287. Yes, yes — exactly.

*C*287. M-hm.

*S*288. (*Pause.*) The other evening I thought that a friend of mine had left me in a situation which should have been handled by both of us, and I was very downcast, but when he returned to the situation — he only had a temporary absence — why, then I felt joyful again that he hadn't let me down.

*C*288. M-hm.

---

*C*284, *C*286. The counselor gives clear recognition to the feelings expressed, which leads to an expansion of expression running through *S*291.

*S*289. If I find that a good friend — this happens once in a while: I'll have a good friend and then the friend will get a steady girl friend who oftentimes takes a dislike to me, because she doesn't want me to lead him around night clubs and pick up other girls, so she forms a hostility. And then if I see him, perhaps ——

*C*289. That makes another comparison that's hard to ——

*S*290. Yes, I feel that — well, I take it out on my friend. I say, why should he be such a sentimentalist to give up a better value of friendship just for the sake of a girl who I know in the long run will not be so meaningful to him. I feel that he shouldn't make such a temporary aberration from the loyalties that are due me. But, of course, a great many of my friends are very susceptible to feminine charm, and every once in a while that occurs.

*C*290. M-hm.

*S*291. They think, well — they'll do more for the girl and be more thoughtful of her for the sake of her affection and her sex, and tend to — tend to depend on the expectation that I will overlook it and all will be forgiven when they return.

*C*291. Well, let me raise a question with you there, about some of the things you've been saying today. It would appear that the negative feelings you have — or these symptoms — tend to operate to give you more of a childish kind of satisfaction or feminine kind of satisfaction and they make it a little unnecessary to be fully responsible or fully masculine ——

*S*292. M-hm.

*C*292. Or fully adult.

*S*293. Well, they make it impossible — not only unnecessary, but impossible. Or at least it's easier to slide into the other, rather than to keep making a battle. But I've noticed I always do make a battle. I never go into voyeurism, or into

---

*C*291, *C*292. The counselor attempts an over-all interpretation which, while probably accurate, is a definite threat to the ego of the client. The client accepts it only partially, if at all, and defends himself in *S*293.

the infantile satisfactions or whatever you want to term them, without having made quite a battle with the negative feeling. Of course, I've never yet found a voluntary key to the relief of negative feelings, but of course I keep on struggling against them, and I always do put up a struggle before I lapse.

*C*293. Well, of course, one reason why it is a struggle — from some of the things you've said — is that you get satisfactions both ways — I mean, there is a good deal of satisfaction in battling the thing through, and there's also a satisfaction on the other side of the fence.

*S*294. Yes.   So that the neurotic satisfaction, of course, you see, could itself be a motivation to keep going back to it. I mean, the whole thing has a vicious downward spiral.

*C*294. Well, or put it this way — that if the neurotic satisfactions — if you want to call them that — were the only ones that you actually found, there'd be no reason for being ever anything but that.   But the fact that you do get satisfaction in working on your job, and in contacts with girls, and so on, even though you don't get those satisfactions all the time, they continually draw you out, and then when difficulty comes you drop back.

*S*295. Yes, I've often had the thought that if I had an independent income it would be much harder for me to cure myself.

*C*295. M-hm.   That would make it easier to slip back than to go forward.

*S*296. Oh, yes.   But then I don't — the way I am now

---

*C*293, *C*294. These are also interpretive statements, but are much more completely accepted and lead to the rather surprising degree of insight contained in *S*295.   What is the difference between the accepted interpretation given here, and the unacceptable interpretation given in the two preceding counselor statements?   The essential difference seems to be that *C*293 and *C*294 are based entirely upon what the client has already stated, and they do not imply a direct threat to his ego.   They truthfully interpret his real ambivalence. The risk in all interpretation is that it slides so easily from this successful type to the unsuccessful and sometimes damaging sort exemplified in *C*291–*C*292.

— even if I were to inherit a large sum of money and could indulge those activities, I wouldn't have my self-respect, and I think perhaps my money might even be a mockery to me — to know that I had the money, yet didn't have the fundamental soundness.

C296. That's one reason why your coming in here to see me and to see about this whole thing, I think, has a lot of significance, because — in other words, that was a part of your decision as to which way you wanted to go.

S297. Oh, very definitely. You see, look how long I put it off. I might have consulted a man of your profession, you see, any time, along the way.

C297. Surely. You had twenty-odd years that, theoretically at least, you might have ——

S298. M-hm. I did, a number of years ago, see Dr. D. at M—— University, but I found no satisfaction from his techniques. He attempted to impose certain romantic and monogamistic values upon me, so that I felt — well, we could never get anywhere.

C298. Even at that time you did have ——

S299. I was entering the University. I had just finished taking a course for my speech impediment, but I'm convinced now that the fellow was a quack. It cost me two hundred bucks and didn't do a damn bit of good. So I then resolved that the best way was to get at the root of the trouble, and I had a conviction that that avenue to the root of trouble lay in psychoanalysis. Well, I still have that conviction, but the person wasn't the right person for me. I don't know what success he has had or anything like that — I don't want to cast any aspersions on him, but it just didn't happen to work out in my case — I do know that. He went into my child-

---

C296. This is both directive and interpretive, but is successful because it correctly recognizes the constructive decision involved in seeking help.

S298-S301. It is extremely interesting to see the aftereffect of a strongly directive and interpretive approach, as viewed several years later by an intelligent and analytical client. The person mentioned

hood and seemed to have a notion that my mother was largely responsible — that my mother had an incestuous attachment for me, which, when it came out into the open, why my mother had been repressed and all that sort of thing — he was working on that. Then he wanted me to masturbate for my sex outlet till I fell in love, so that I wouldn't have a straight sexual experience. He felt that it had to be ennobled, you see, by love.

*C*299. M-hm.

*S*300. So I felt that we weren't getting anywhere. As a matter of fact, he was the one that broke off the interviews. I don't know whether he had the same feeling that I did or not.

*C*300. At any rate, enough antagonism developed, at least, that it just didn't work out.

*S*301. There wasn't any personal antagonism there. He was trying to mold me into what I think was the image that he wanted to be. That's my own impression of him.

*C*301. Well, I think the thing that is most significant to me about that whole experience is that there have been — at the present time, and also at certain times past — there have been instances when you felt, "I'm going to cast the balance in this direction."

*S*302. M-hm. I noticed a very interesting thing. Formerly, prior to ten years ago, I dwelt entirely upon the one symptom

---

is not a psychoanalyst. As we know from his previous use of the term, Mr. Bryan refers to any intensive series of counseling contacts as psychoanalysis.

*S*302, *S*303. This revealing statement raises significant questions about many specialized systems of training, whether in speech, reading skills, study skills, or other areas. If we do not recognize the purposive aspect of the individual's adjustive behavior, we are likely to suppose that it can be dealt with by superficial methods. Yet in many instances of educational disabilities, the individual is actually ambivalent about his educational symptoms, just as Mr. Bryan was ambivalent about his speech difficulty and his desire to overcome it.

*S*302–*S*311. In this section is contained an important part of the case history of the individual, but it is a case history in terms of dynamics. It is interesting to speculate about how some of these

there; that is, namely, the talking symptom — you see, the speech impediment symptom occupied my whole consciousness. Then, going out to this school for training in speech defect, I noticed a very curious reaction. After I had persuaded my parents, with a great deal of difficulty, to send me there, I found myself wondering there on the train whether I really wanted to be cured.

C302. M-hm.

S303. Then I began to ask myself — now there is no reason at all why a person with speech defect would not want to be cured. There must be something behind that outward speech symptom. And so I found myself not cooperating very wholeheartedly with the man's methods out there.

C303. That was one of the first realizations on your own part that this wasn't all something imposed on you. I mean, part of it was that you wished to hang on to some of these symptoms.

S304. Yes. That was back eleven years ago, not ten.

C304. M-hm.

S305. I went through a bunch of mechnical motions—purely superficial mechanical techniques, which didn't do me any good at all. Then that treatment continued. I was to adopt mechanical aid to my speech. A motion like this — a pendulum motion with my hand — for six months. So I adopted that for six months, all the time knowing that it wasn't doing me any good — but I went through with it. And then at the end of that time I experienced a feeling that I was not going to concentrate any more upon my speech. I was going to shove it completely out of my mind. And six months after the

---

facts would appear if obtained in the usual case-history fashion, in which the unsuccessful speech training, the counseling treatment at the University, the interest in night clubs, and the other facts related would be portrayed in descriptive rather than dynamic fashion. This section will help to explain the statement in Chapter III (p. 000) that "in a true counseling process, the individual is much more likely to reveal the genuinely dynamic forces in his experience, the crucial patterns of his life behavior, than in a formal history-taking process.'

speech treatment, I made the conscious shoving out of my mind of dwelling morbidly upon my speech.   Now, right at that time I had a peculiar reaction to that.   Or a different reaction, I should say, perhaps.   I found that after I shoved the worry about my speech out of my mind, I began to worry about everything else.

C 305.   M-hm.

S 306.   I would worry — well, things like this would run through my mind: I was very thin at the time and had acne. In order to get rid of the acne I thought that I had to diet, but that kept me thin, so I said, "Well now, which would I rather have — a good build or the acne?"   And I would very carefully weigh the pros and cons — perhaps meditate a whole day on that.   Then I would wonder whether — wonder about certain ethical things: like if I saw a man drop a wallet full of money, would I keep the money or return it to him?   And I began to wonder whether I should indulge in intercourse or be continent till what I thought would be a full maturity — I think I fixed the age of twenty-six, for some reason or other. And I had quite a health fetish.

C 306.   M-hm.   M-hm.

S 307.   So, you see, I had quite a number of romantic ideas and emotions surrounding ethics, sex, and health.

C 307.   And a good many uh — difficult choices.   I mean, evidently the situation has always been ——

S 308.   So then I sought my first psychoanalytic aid.   Uh — that was as I was entering M—— University.   I felt that the university was too important a thing for me to go through it as I had been going through high school.   Then after I received my letdown from psychoanalysis, then I just sort of — I tried to cure myself by self-psychoanalysis, and I'd dwell on my childhood experiences for hours at a time and try to experience them in terms of new values.   Well, I don't know what they call that — that's the old familiar Freudian technique.

C 308.   M-hm.

S 309.   But that didn't work, and then about a year later I tried to abandon all intellectual concepts and go in for self-generated euphoria — uh, that is, I'd walk down the street and deliberately try to make myself happy — pull myself up by the bootstraps.

*C*309. M-hm. M-hm.

*S*310. Say, "I'm not — not going to think about anything unpleasant. I'll whistle a happy tune that I happened to like at the time. I'll go to night clubs and so forth and so on." But I found that I couldn't rid myself from painful thinking about these things. So during recent years I've fluctuated between self-analysis — a futile attempt at therapy — and between leading a purely sensual life where no intellectual analysis takes place. Night clubs, swing music, and so on.

*C*310. That brings you up to the present, where you ——

*S*311. Yes, where I made the decision to come to you. As I mentioned to you before, I felt that the efforts on my part were not wholehearted, otherwise — otherwise they would have worked, and that what I was doing was just a sop to the minority, as it were. So I believed that a man such as yourself could point the way to a key whereby I could make my change.

*C*311. At least a part of that key, in what you're saying to-day, seems to lie in a pretty clear recognition of the choice that you are making. I mean, you certainly have brought out much more plainly the contrast between going ahead, which involves responsibility and involves both satisfactions and dissatisfactions, or slipping back into the easier possibility of simply living with your symptoms.

*S*312. In the last analysis, it comes down to this, that I enjoy the neurotic symptoms more but respect them less.

---

*S*312, *S*313. These statements represent the deepest insight thus far achieved. They may, in fact, be regarded as the high point in insight. One has only to glance back at Mr. Bryan's account of his problem, in *S*1–*S*9 in the first interview, to see the amazing progress which has been made. From looking at his problem as a "blocking," an "inhibition," a "pressure," an "excruciating" pain, "an axe pressing down on the whole abdomen" (*S*29), Mr. Bryan has come

*C*312. Yes, that's a good way of ——

*S*313. Or to use other words, I suppose I'm beginning to value self-respect more now, otherwise I wouldn't give a damn.

*C*313. That's right. That's — uh — you talked when you came in the first time about the fact that here was this picture, now, where could the motivation come from to change it? Well, a large measure of the motivation to change it comes from that much clearer recognition on your own part of what aspect of this whole situation you wish to preserve on a permanent basis.

*S*314. I have a subtle philosophic way of cheating myself on that, though, that I ought to mention. Of course, as a

---

to face the fact that he has enjoyed these symptoms because they have served his purpose, and that now he is wondering whether he will continue to choose the satisfactions they give, or whether he would prefer other satisfactions. To have achieved this radical alteration in self-understanding during four contacts, covering a period of ten days, is unusually rapid progress. Note that this insight has not been "given" to the client, but that it has been gradually achieved by a process of frank exploration of attitudes, of free expression of feelings, and a facing of self in an atmosphere in which defensiveness is unnecessary. The counselor has played as neutral a part as possible, serving only to reflect and clarify the client's motivating viewpoints as they are expressed.

*C*313. The counselor's handling of this insight, while satisfactory, is not the best. He must certainly have been pleased with the progress exhibited. Out of his pleasure he endeavors to hurry the client into a definite choice between the two alternatives which Mr. Bryan now sees so clearly. This is emphatically not the time for hurry. A better response would have been limited to acceptance and recognition of the insight achieved. The counselor might have said, "You're really beginning to feel that it's a choice between the satisfactions of your symptoms, and the satisfactions of self-respect." It is probably the subtle pressure implied in the counselor's response which causes Mr. Bryan in *S*314 to embark again on a philosophical analysis of his choice, which is, however, more profitable than some of his philosophical discussions.

*S*314–*S*324. It may be noted that throughout this portion of the interview, a subtle change is evident in the relationship between counselor and client. There is more evidence of "togetherness,"

philosopher, I know that there is no way of evaluating values. I know that any attempt to say that one set of values is superior to another set of values always resolves itself into one of two things. It either is a logical tautology, where you repeat the same idea in different words and say, "Well, these values are better because so-and-so and so-and-so," and what you're really saying is that they are better because they're better; or you come back to some sort of a fiat — either a divine fiat — "These values are better because God says they are," or some sort of a naturalistic fiat, which of course are philosophically not provable. So that when I find myself, uh — I find myself valuing the intellectually more desirable values, that is, when I find myself valuing the good rôle, another part of me says, "Well, you can't prove that that set of values is better." I have such a philosophical fetish that if I could prove — if there were some cosmic yardstick, some sort of a cosmic absolute, uh — comparable to the religious person's absolute trust in God, you see, uh — then I could have a philosophic proof that one set of values was definitely better than the other, but this way I know that I cannot have such a philosophic proof, or at least I haven't run across it. We can never prove values — we always have to assume them. I think as a philosopher you'll have to agree with me.

---

probably because both of them are for the first time seeing the situation from much the same viewpoint. For example, the counselor's responses in C314, C320, C322 not only accept the client's attitudes, but also agree with and approve of these attitudes. Is this necessary or wise? It is doubtful whether we can know the answer until more research has been done, but it is probable that this approach is not particularly helpful, and it is so easily overdone that the counselor would do well to avoid it. One of the main reasons to doubt its wisdom is that in the next interview Mr. Bryan retreats from some of his new insights, which makes the counselor's approval of them something of a barrier.

On the other hand, it is probable that a certain amount of encouragement, such as is contained in C319, is helpful. The straightforward way in which the client is facing the reality of his situation takes courage, and some applauding of his efforts seems sound. Too much approval of his conclusions, however, may "backfire."

*C*314. I don't know whether it's as a philosopher, but I certainly would agree with you that, in situations of this kind, I don't think there is any proof that could be advanced that would prove one set of values rather than the other.

*S*315. Nothing out in the universe. It all must lie within ourselves.

*C*315. It comes right back to the naked self pretty much, doesn't it? Here are two general roads; which do you prefer? It comes right down to a personal and probably quite un-philosophical choice.

*S*316. Yes. In other words, I can't — I can't look to the cosmos and say, "Now which of the two roads do you approve of?" I can't ——

*C*316. You can, and some people do, but it's doubtful if that is what really settles it.

*S*317. Yes, I imagine that when a person does make a change they oftentimes think that they're doing it for God, but they're really doing it for themselves. Well (*thoughtfully*), perhaps I don't need anything out in the cosmos, then.

*C*317. Well, there's just the chance that you've got enough within yourself.

*S*318. Yes, that's a good point there. The — uh, my philo-sophic searching for something in the cosmos to justify my taking one of the two roads was really searching for something that I knew I would never find.

*C*318. M-hm.

*S*319. Because I had the intellect to know that I would never find a cosmic command to take a certain path. And then I allowed myself to utilize the absence of such a cosmic command as a rationalization for my own lack of motiva-tion.

*C*319. Nothing wrong with your understanding of yourself when you let it loose.

*S*320. Well, I guess that's about the first thing — know thyself.

*C*320. Right.

*S*321. That's what I'm going to work on now — is, to not

seek a proof for my values, but go ahead and assume the ones that I can have the most self-respect and satisfaction for.

*C*321. The ones that you most deeply want. I think that it is a real choice, and different individuals take different roads. There are, as you know, certain satisfactions connected with, well, with evading life, with building up things that make it unnecessary to go out and fight some of these battles and assume some of these responsibilities and so on. Some people choose that road. On the other hand, there certainly are satisfactions connected with the tougher road too.

*S*322. I think that my religious conditioning has made me sort of dependent on some kind of a cosmic sign. Originally, I had to depend upon God's approval. As I lost a belief in a personalized sort of deity, then I sought signs from nature and other things like that. But I must learn to assume my values without the justification of the outside. That boils down to what I really want. (*Pause.*) I think it's a pretty close battle.

*C*322. I think so too. To be quite frank with you, I think so too.

*S*323. It isn't just a case of Rotarian optimism and saving, "Well, now my better judgment is going to have its way."

*C*323. No.

*S*324. I don't think it's that.

---

*C*321. This statement by the counselor is a rather satisfactory interpretation of the position reached by Mr. Bryan. It is doubtful whether it is necessary when the client is making such rapid progress. Certainly Mr. Bryan does not think so, for his next statement ignores it completely, and *S*322 is simply a continuation of *S*321.

*S*322. It is fascinating to see how Mr. Bryan reacts to his newly discovered insight. As the full realization strikes him, as he begins to see what this insight implies in terms of his own behavior, there is a significant pause and a recognition that the conflicting forces within himself are very evenly balanced. The counselor's response is good, in that it does not attempt to sway the balance, but merely to recognize that it is a close decision (how close becomes evident in the two succeeding interviews).

*C*324. No. I think — uh, I think your whole experience shows that it's a very close choice indeed, but probably with a number of indications in recent, uh — well recent elements of your experience that make it look as though you were deciding that balance. (*Pause.*)

*S*325. And, of course, I sometimes get somewhat pessimistic feelings too. I think I ought to reveal those. Perhaps anything could be a sop to the minority — perhaps even my walking in here, so that I mustn't let myself be beguiled by a false sense of progress. I must realize the utter and deep-seated seriousness of it.

*C*325. Yes, you might be just kidding yourself.

*S*326. I can see that while there is a certain psychological outlet about talking about one's self and revealing intimate things, that that in itself wouldn't necessarily work a therapy.

*C*326. No, there's no — there's no getting away from the fact that it — as you mentioned yourself, it is a very real battle.

*S*327. Then, too, I've been looking for a sign from the cosmos which would — in the last analysis, that would relieve me from the responsibility of a choice, wouldn't it?

---

*C*324. The first part of this response is satisfactory. When the counselor goes on to hint at the type of choice the client is probably making, he is handling the situation unwisely. Even this subtle hint as to the probable outcome is enough to drive Mr. Bryan into an evasion, where he presents the viewpoint that perhaps none of this progress is real. We are dealing here with the most crucial decision of the whole therapeutic experience — the decision whether the client will put his fundamental insight into effect. This decision cannot be made by the counselor, and if he even attempts to influence the decision, he will frighten the client into retreat.

*S*325–*S*326. Partly because of the counselor's statement in *C*324, partly because he sees how far-reaching his new insight may be, the client begins to retreat from its full implications. We shall see this retreat maintained during the next interview.

*S*327–*S*341. Throughout the remainder of the interview Mr. Bryan moves forward into fresh areas of insight, and the situation is well handled by the counselor, except for a somewhat excessive use of approval.

*C*327. M-hm. M-hm. That's right.

*S*328. I'd just look up in the heavens and see the handwriting and there would be no other choice, unless I weren't able to conform with the cosmic sign for some reason.

*C*328. Then if it didn't work out well, you could blame the cosmos too.

*S*329. Well, I could disbelieve. Of course, that's how my disbelief first arose, anyway. You see, God was interfering with certain desires, so I sought about for a destruction of the usual reasons which are given for God's existence — so forth and so on. Then I looked for naturalistic signs. Theories like the survival of the fittest and laws of the jungle, and so on. Animalistic pleasures. And I had a sort of mystical faith in psychoanalysis. I imagined I wanted the same there — in other words, I wanted the psychoanalyst to turn the key for me, rather than do it myself.

*C*329. M-hm. That's right.

*S*330. But I'm to the point now where if the analyst would flash the light upon a key I believe that I could turn it myself. Or maybe there isn't any key — maybe it's — that is, maybe the key and the turning are one psychologically. Maybe there is no division of labor there.

*C*330. You're getting to some real issues there, and I think

---

*S*331. Well, what is your theory of psychoanalysis? Are the key and the turning motivation one and the same or do you think there should be a division of labor, where the psychoanalysis flashes the light on the key and the subject turns the key — or shouldn't we talk about that this time?

*C*331. Well, certainly I don't want to get off in theories of psychoanalysis, but I think our experience together would be

---

*C*331 is an excellent handling of a difficult situation, where the counselor has been asked a direct question. He replies in a way which again defines the structure of the counseling relationship, but avoids an unprofitable intellectual discussion. The client's response in *S*332 is nothing short of amazing. For a person like Mr. Bryan, who places such enormous stress upon the intellect, to recognize that

somewhat typical — that the business of throwing light on the whole thing is somewhat mutual. But then the business of turning the key is up to you.

*S*332. Yes. Well, now, here's what I was wondering: is there any mysterious key? I mean, have I been looking for something that isn't necessarily there? I mean, would the key be nothing definite in the intellectual realm, but all in the emotional resolve?

*C*332. Right. That is, I think there isn't much doubt you've touched a key today — the key being that question of what do you really and deeply want most to do — not just the superficial statement of what you want to do, but what ——

*S*333. Well, I'd had the idea that there was some sort of a secret button that I had overlooked and that I would have to touch. I knew that it would take motivation and will-power to touch it, but I felt that first I had to find it — now I'm beginning to have the belief that there is no definite button as an ideological concept *per se* — that what it boils down to is looking at your present-day life, and saying, "Well, what are you going to do about it — which reaction are you going to have?" And that that emotional resolve which we term the act of will, will relieve the negative feelings without any hidden mystery or anything like that having to be exposed.

---

effective therapy rests upon the "emotional resolve" rather than upon intellectual understanding, is an important deepening of insight.

In *C*332 and *C*333 we find approval of ideas when recognition would have been preferable. In *C*334 and *C*336, on the other hand, one finds the type of response which gives general encouragement to the client in his progress, without specifically approving of his ideas. This seems helpful at this stage of therapy.

*S*333 and *S*337 are such excellent statements of a functioning individual psychology that it is hard to believe that they are made by the client and not by the counselor. Certainly the therapeutic experience has made a psychologist out of this client. To recognize that symptoms are retained because of their present significance and value, not because of their past origin, is a deeper insight into human behavior than has been attained by some psychologists. The point which is worth noting is that, although it is unusual to find this

C333. That's what I think too.

S334. I'm glad to hear that.

C334. Well, there's no doubt that you were right when you first came in that you had a lot to say today.

S335. Oh, I knew it. I mean — I know myself pretty well; I think I'm pretty honest with myselves.

C335. And growing increasingly honest, I would say.

S336. M-hm. Yes. I imagine that that's the true function of psychoanalysis — is to — well, to sort of force the issues, to make them clear-cut, and so that the resolve can take the right direction.

C336. Well, you raised the question last time whether I thought you were making much progress. I guess you wouldn't have to ask it today. (*Laugh.*)

S337. No. Well, I'm not going to search around any more for any mysterious event in my life or — I used to have the idea that there was perhaps one significant event which I had repressed to the subconscious which I needed to call up from the subconscious for my therapy. But I see now that the — no matter what the origin is, these things after all operate under present circumstances, and that it's the present operational function which is — which does have the true significance.

C337. I'm tempted to say — you're damn right. M-hm. I think so. Well ——

S338. Well, we'll assume that we want to value self-respect more and more, and we know what those values are — that we can respect.

---

understanding stated in such a clear-cut and well-worded fashion, it is very common for clients to recognize this fundamental truth in some more halting way.

In *C335* the curious slip "myselves" is clearly recorded. Probably it refers to the two conflicting selves which the client has begun to see more clearly.

S338. This rather final statement, which sounds as though the basic issues were all settled, probably has been induced by the approval of the counselor in *C337*, and previously. Actually the client

*C*338. It isn't the kind of decision that comes all at once, or that is just a matter of saying so, either. I mean, there are things to work out in regard to it. But, to see it clearly, as clearly as you've seen it today is a long way ——

*S*339. Well, I can look — we can say, "My revenge will fly on swift wings," or something like that, and then do nothing about it.

*C*339. That's right.

*S*340. We can work ourselves up into a very high fervor of high resolve and so forth, but there's the old — the real world right before us ——

*C*340. That's right. That's why it becomes ——

*S*341. There are only two roads fundamentally.

*C*341. M-hm. That's right. Well, let's see, did we — we didn't set a time, did we? Thursday afternoon is possible for me — at four.

*S*342. Fine.

*C*342. O.K. M-hm. All right.

*S*343. In case I'm working — now ——

*C*343. You can call in here any time to change the appointment.

*S*344. All right. Early evening then would be the time if we need to ——

*C*344. Yeah.

*S*345. I may take a defense job. I may be getting a job at the roller-bearing plant.

*C*345. Good.

---

has not fully made the choice, and the counselor attempts to point out this possibility in *C*338, which is a good response in the circumstances, but would probably have been unnecessary if the approvals had been omitted.

*S*345. It is interesting that the client saves this highly constructive decision to reveal at the last minute. The interview closes as it began, with proof that much has gone on in the interval between contacts.

General Comments

To understand the full measure of progress which this interview represents, the most important of the spontaneous attitudes expressed should be listed. These may be put as follows:

I am fearful of the draft and all it would do to me.

I feel that I'm making progress — meeting obstacles better.

I feel that when I'm blocked from being a man, I retreat into neurotic symptoms.

I blame my early conditioning for the blocking.

If my ego is deflated, it also brings on the symptoms.

Any thwarting or insecurity makes my symptoms worse.

I see satisfactions both in being neurotic and in being adult.

I have no use for systems of cure which were imposed on me.

I've tried everything to cure myself.

I feel that you have the key.

I enjoy being neurotic, but I don't respect myself that way.

I should like to have someone prove which is the right choice.

I realize that the choice lies within me.

I think it is a difficult decision — a very close battle.

I think that with help I could make the decision — turn the key.

I feel that the emotional resolve is the important thing.

I feel that it isn't something in my past which needs therapy, but the present.

It is possible for me to see all this and do nothing about it.

I may take a responsible job.

A comparison of these attitudes toward the self with those expressed in previous interviews indicates clearly the tremendous development in insight and the increasingly positive attitudes. The reader may recognize that almost all of the points raised in Chapter VII (pp. 174–216) are illustrated in this interview. The achievement of various types of insight, the counselor techniques for aiding in the development of insight, and the beginning phases of positive decisions are all evident here.

This fourth interview has, on the whole, been well handled by the counselor. He has served his function well, acting in such a way as to mirror the client's attitudes in order to bring them more clearly into consciousness. In this connection, it might be noted that Mr. Bryan has revealed many of his "unconscious" motivations during this contact. If we can create situations in which there is no need of being defensive, unconscious motivations come to the surface rather easily.

The one type of error which occurs with any frequency in this interview is the counselor's tendency to evaluate and approve the positive advances which the client is making. Such evaluations do not hinder progress at this point, but they probably are unwise, for they make it appear that the counselor is sharing the responsibility for these positive decisions and insights, when actually this responsibility can constructively be carried only by the client.

A further comment might be made on the series of interviews up to this point. We have seen a variety of blunders on the part of the counselor, and some such blunders are almost certain to occur. In the rapid flow of the interview situation, it is impossible that every response should be the most appropriate, or the one most consistent with the general view held in regard to counseling. The encouraging thing to notice is that very rapid progress has been made in spite of some blunders. We are dealing here with forces of such strength that perfect handling is not necessary to promote progress. We may say, indeed, that if the situation is not too badly mishandled, these constructive forces will be certain to operate. If the client is given some freedom to explore his situation without being made defensive; if the counselor remains relatively accepting and non-directive; if the counselor and client together achieve some clarification of the subject's attitudes and feelings; then a gradual growth of insight, a gradual recognition of choices which may be made and steps which may be taken, is almost sure to occur. This is the fascination of therapy, that the forces seem to be real and predictable, opening new vistas for psychological advance.

❧ FIFTH INTERVIEW ❧

*C*346. How's it today?

*S*346. Well, I'd say generally, since the last time, my main problem has been this: that I know intellectually that I should adopt one way of life and one way of acting and so forth, but I don't have yet an emotional persuasion to that effect. That is, it's — there's no feeling realization there like there is intellectual realization of which is the better way, as it were. I suppose that since — when a person has nothing but neurotic satisfactions, it's hard for him to feel that other satisfactions would be better. So, there was sort of a counterpart there, that is, the knowledge of which is better, without being able to fully realize it with all aspects of the personality. My self-respect motive seems to shift somewhat — sometimes I feel — well, that is, I get more hedonistic — I want to accept pleasures even though I know they're neurotic pleasures, from a hedonistic valuation. My self-respect seems to dwindle, as it were.

*C*347. M-hm. In other words, as you face the thing rather squarely, the neurotic pleasures, as you call them, seem fairly appealing.

*S*347. M-hm. Then, too, I think there might be some other motives in there. I would hate to say it was entirely a matter of neurotic pluses — I think that there are certain fears there,

---

*s*346. It is very evident from this whole conversation that the "emotional resolve," which Mr. Bryan recognized so clearly as being the basis of any progress, is still lacking.

*C*347. This is an excellent response to a complex statement, catching the basic feelings.

*s*347. Here, in a sentence, Mr. Bryan sums up all that we know of the dynamics of a neurosis. It provides certain pleasures, and it helps to avoid more painful experiences. This is the kind of deep insight which cannot be given to an individual, but which can be achieved only through a process of frankly facing the self.

too. I mean, I don't think I hang on to the neurosis just because it gives me pleasure, but I think I hang on to it because I also believe that it avoids me pain — I mean, there's both barrels there, in the urge to retain it, I think.

*C*348. Yes.

*S*348. The general war situation, I think, influences me something like this: I feel, well, why should I grow, as it were, only to be mowed down in the war machine. Of course, there could be two ways of looking at that — I mean, it might be better to be a fallen giant than a trampled-on worm, as it were.

*C*349. (*Laughs.*)

*S*349. But then there is the irony, too, there of just when you're on the verge of growing, as it were, to be sucked into some sort of a war destruction.

*C*350. Yes, I couldn't help but think of that. It seems as though just at the time when you're trying to decide a very difficult issue in your own life, the world pops up and makes the growth side of that decision very much more difficult, doesn't it?

*S*350. Well, I don't really — that's what I was wondering — whether the world situation actually makes it more difficult or whether I just seize on that. You see, that could be a possibility too — I mean, even if everything were rosy, I might find myself balking on the threshold, anyway. So, I imagine that's it — because in the last anlysis, no matter what the environment is, there can be no question that it's better to be a healthy organism, no matter what environment you're in. So ——

---

*C*350. The counselor responds so adequately to the attitudes being expressed that it enables Mr. Bryan to move significantly forward.

*S*350, *S*351. One could scarcely find a clearer statement of the place of environmental disturbances during therapy. They are only the backdrop, or at most minor incidents, in the much more fundamental drama which is being played. The situation is even more explicitly put in *S*357, *S*358, where Mr. Bryan points out that the greater environmental demands of wartime only heighten the dramatic intensity of the struggle.

*C*351. So you're inclined to feel that war situation or no war situation, the struggle is pretty much within you, after all.

*S*351. Yes, I believe it would be. I can imagine myself in a situation where I knew I wouldn't be in war, and where I had lots of money, where I'd still have to face the issue.

*C*352. M-hm. M-hm.

*S*352. And I'm trying now to get some motivations to feel a deep-seated want to make the change, in addition to my intellectual concepts. I'm looking for a way to have the emotional urge to change. That's just about the hardest nut to crack.

*C*353. M-hm. That is, you sound as though you had thought your way through fairly well to a decision, but the courage to take the initiative, that's pretty difficult.

*S*353. I don't know whether to call it courage — it's the — the evaluating emotion seems to be absent there. It's — you see, if I had the evaluating emotion, why, then it wouldn't take courage, but it's only in the absence of the evaluating emotion that we say we have a lack of courage, so — you're using a term, by its absence, when it wouldn't be there if the desired situation were present. In other words, if I really valued the new way of life emotionally, it wouldn't take any courage at all — just like I can handle any situation when I have a good day — I mean, courage, to my way of thinking, means that you go over some sort of a barrier — that you have a conflict there. Of course, I don't know what your definition of it might be, but that's what I've always thought of it as. (*Pause.*) I notice, even though I do have the blockings, I seem to have, nevertheless, more ambition, and I don't let the blockings make me so inert as I used to. I did a very difficult photographic job the other night, and — I photographed a fraternity group, and I went ahead and made a proposition with the treasurer that he give me a check from the

---

*C*353–*S*353. A bit of interpretation, of the sort which threatens the ego, is included in this statement by the counselor. Mr. Bryan responds in his usual way by a retreat into an intellectualistic discussion. He then returns to his own train of thought, telling of the positive new actions he has taken.

house, so I wouldn't have to go to each of the individual members. That perhaps takes somewhat of initiative — you know, to go to a strange fellow that way.

*C*354. M-hm.

*S*354. So he gave me a check from the house, and then put the charge on the individuals' house bills, so that that saved me the trouble of going to each of the individuals and wangling the money out of them.

*C*355. M-hm.

*S*355. I've got another idea for making money. I'm going to work with a photo-supply dealer, and whenever I photograph a group, I will also sell frames, cameras, and so forth, to the group that I photograph. I figured that one worked right along with the other, and I might as well get the added commission out of it too. It's a little more salesmanship.

*C*356. Those sound like very positive steps.

*S*356. Well, they were made at a great sacrifice of nervous energy, but they were made. I suppose it's better to go over the hurdle at a sacrifice than do nothing at all. I say it somewhat doubtfully — as you can gather from my tone, but I still perhaps feel a little bit more that I would rather work in a conflict than just to lie suppliant. (*Pause.*) I still want my ideal of effortless action there — I mean, I feel that there's enough in the environment — enough obstacles in the environment, that I don't want any within myself. And you get more of a joy of battle — I think you actually get a joy of battle when all the obstacles are in the environment, because then you're not fighting yourself.

*C*357. Yes. I think that's very true.

*S*357. And right now the environment is such that it's going to take every ounce of guts and brains to survive, so that gives me at once an added motivation, yet somehow an added dread, too, along with that. It sort of intensifies both sides. But if it intensifies them both equally, why, there won't be any net loss.

*C*358. Intensifies both sides? I don't know that I quite get that ——

*S*358. Well, if the crucial stage of the environment both intensifies my motive to be cured and my neurotic dread equally, why, then there won't be any net loss, due to the environmental situation. It'll make it a more gigantic conflict, but won't influence the balance. It'll just add more weight to both sides. Of course, that's all highly speculative — we don't know how to weigh those things, I suppose — they can't be reduced to mathematics, like some of the other sciences.

*C*359. No, but we can feel the forces of them, all right.

*S*359. Oh, yes. Even though I left the office with a very clear intellectual picture last time, I had quite a depressed feeling up until noon today — the usual thing that happens before I come in, so I try to take advantage of that period and do some business during that time, anyway.

*C*360. I should think you would have had a setback after our last talk.

*S*360. It'd be more or less normal, would it?

*C*361. Well, you looked at yourself more squarely than you have in any of our contacts so far, and — as you pointed out several times — I mean, it left you facing a pretty tough decision, and — I know I felt afterward, "Well, you'll have a worse time after this chat than you've had after any of the others."

*S*361. Well, I'm glad to know that that would be one of the symptoms rather than to be looked upon as a sign of marking time. I've sort of felt myself on a plateau — that intellect has sort of come to the end of the rope there. Perhaps I've been leaning on the intellect, hoping that my intellect would do the trick. But — (*pause*) — how to provide a motive. You see, we can't evaluate our values from the cosmos or any outward sign — we have to assume them, and then we evaluate them through our own nervous systems; that is, we say that one way of life is better. Of course, some people try to rationalize it by saying that it's better because the Bible says so, and so

---

*C*360, *C*361. This encouraging interpretation of the client's depressed mood is probably justified, though not entirely necessary.

forth and so on, but in the last analysis we evaluate different modes of life — they're good because they feel good to us, and that's all there is to it.

C362. That's right. If you didn't gain more satisfaction out of confronting the treasurer with this idea, it would be foolish to confront him.

S362. Confront who?

C363. The treasurer of the fraternity or whatever it was that you ——

S363. Oh, yes. M-hm.

C364. I was thinking of that incident. Certainly there's no use going through the painful aspects of that unless it was more satisfying to you.

S364. Yes, I was really on. I could use the money at the time, so I got an advance check. Rather an achievement, if you know treasurers. (*Both laugh.*)

C365. I think so.

S365. And I worked at it very thoroughly and conscientiously and made delivery within forty-eight hours and got the rest of the payment for the job. But it makes me nervous to work. It's rather a painstaking job — you have a lot of gadgets to work with. I find myself wishing that I could go through these necessary actions without the inward negativeness, which makes it so much more difficult. But although it's a rather discouraging thing in a way, I can remember my good days, but I can't remember the feeling fully. Of course, if I were able to remember the feeling fully, why that would mean that I was having a good time right at the moment of memory.

C366. M-hm.

S366. So that — I wonder why that is — why is it — this is what I've often wondered: now, why is it that when I have a splendid day and I'm very happy about it, why don't I retain

---

c362. The counselor is obviously endeavoring to have Mr. Bryan consider his problems in terms of specific issues. It appears to be a directive technique of doubtful value, leading only to a short detour.

s366–s370. The client raises questions and wants answers. A direct answer would be futile, and the counselor avoids this. The

it? I retain the bad days, so why shouldn't I retain the good ones?

C367. Doesn't seem as though our feelings are anything we can store up in a bank.

S367. Well, how did you mean ——

C368. Well, I think that's true of both bad and good, isn't it?

S368. Oh, you mean sort of build up a reserve so that it would last? Well, the bad feelings — of course, numerically speaking, there are more units of time that I feel bad than that I feel good, but after I am feeling good and I say to myself, "Now this is a far better way of life," I feel no doubt whatsoever that this is absolutely the tops and has it all over the other ways, then the other way creeps back into power. So I was wondering why that was. I can see how it would be very hard to get out of the bad way, but when it happens momentarily, why shouldn't it be just as easy to maintain the good way as it is to maintain the bad way? I mean, the dice seem to be loaded there.

C369. In other words, you have the feeling that you have more genuine preference perhaps for the bad days than the good.

S369. Well, not when I'm having a good day. When I'm actually having it, why, I'm very exuberant about it, and say

---

situation might have been better handled, however. For example, the response at *C367* might have been, "If the bad days stay with you, you think the good ones should too." At *C369*, a better statement would be, "You've found that even though the good days give satisfaction, the bad days regain control." At *C370* a more satisfactory remark would be, "You get so much satisfaction out of good days, you can't understand why they don't continue." In other words, the best handling of questions directed toward the counselor is simply to clarify the feelings which are expressed in the questions themselves.

Note that throughout this discussion of "good" and "bad" days Mr. Bryan never once mentions that he gets satisfactions out of the bad days as well as the good. The insight which he gained in the last contact is somewhat frightening, and he is retreating from it. It would certainly be damaging to progress to try to convince him that his previous insight was correct.

to myself how superior my feelings are, and how much in harmony every department of me is with the other one. The functioning is an integrated whole. I have more music appreciation, more business ability, more initiative — everything is functioning right. And I'm aware of that — and I get a great deal of self-satisfaction out of it. But why doesn't that law of inertia tend to operate there as well as operate when I'm in a bad condition?

*C*370. What's your own feeling as to the answer on that?

*S*370. Well, I just put it down as one of those things. You see, the laws of inertia say that matter in rest and matter in motion tend to remain so. Well, if I am in the good state, why don't the laws of inertia operate for me there? Of course — that again — that's trying to ride on a cosmic horse again, thinking that the laws should benefit me personally. But even so, I feel that there's an abstract element of justice there — that the dice are loaded there.

*C*371. You seem to be saying, too, that to maintain what you call the "good" state, that's an uphill struggle at all times, whereas ——

*S*371. Well, not when I'm in a good state. When I'm in a good state I have such a euphoria and such efficiency that — well, I'm not aware of any — of any sort of a struggle at all, and I go along perfectly — everything's all right — then I get a mysterious — for no apparent cause, the other mood returns. In other words, I don't mind fighting to gain ground, but after I have gained the ground involuntarily — I mean, the thing comes and goes very mysteriously — it comes and goes as an emotional absolute, and so when I have the euphoria, why, then I feel that I have gained — there is no more need to fight — no more desire to fight, because there isn't anything to fight. And so naturally I relax, because there's nothing to put me on my guard, and I go ahead and function very efficiently and very joyously, and then I have a return, so — it just sort of puzzles me.

*C*372. Can you tell of one of those times — I mean, any specific time when it happened?

*S*372. Well, I'll give you a typical example. I wake up, and right away as soon as I wake up, I notice my cramped feeling, and I don't want to get up — I just want to lie in bed and doze. Perhaps have pleasurable phantasies rather than to face reality. And then I get up, and maybe while I'm taking a shower, all of a sudden it'll leave me and I'll start to sing and be very happy. Everything will be all right. And just as suddenly the whole thing can happen — I mean, I can have a change — it wouldn't be an exaggeration to say that I could change in two or three seconds.

*C*373. M-hm. M-hm.

*S*373. It happens very, very suddenly and there's no regular ideological pattern along with the change. I mean, the thoughts don't seem to be a constant parallel factor there. I can be thinking almost about anything. I get the impression — my own impression of it is that the feelings — that they're operating independently of the ideational aspect.

*C*374. Then you feel quite strongly that you can't at any time put your finger on the thing that changes that feeling.

*S*374. Yes, I mean I don't know what to do to make a change. Sometimes I think I know — now, I have had several catchwords. One of my methods of self-therapy was to search around for some sort of a vivid slogan that I could repeat over and over again to myself — something that I felt would reach down into the emotions. And I remember one of my — oh, about two or three months ago I was feeling very, very badly and was trying to analyze myself, so I said, "Well, I don't think the intellectualizing is going to get me anywhere — I'll just try to think up some simple slogan that I can say to myself which might prove effective." So I boiled down some ideas

---

*S*372–*S*382. Throughout this section the client is painting a full picture of his helplessness and his hopelessness. He has tried everything, he has looked everywhere for motivation, he cannot make the change. The counselor, for the most part, clarifies these attitudes satisfactorily, particularly in *C*374, *C*378, *C*379. By means of this full and adequate acceptance of his discouraged feelings, Mr. Bryan is enabled to move ahead to admitting that he is not in complete

and they resolved themselves into a slogan, "There is a better way," — I kept saying over and over again to myself, and that worked, and I had a very good day.   But the next day the slogan didn't work.

C375. In other words, you feel that attempts to trick yourself out of one of those moods fall pretty flat.

S375. Well, why do you say "trick"?   I didn't get any notion of that.   It was rather I wanted to get a psychologically good slogan — one that would be vivid and penetrating enough to reach the emotions.   I didn't get an impression of trickery ——

C376. Perhaps that is a misstatement there.

S376. Sometimes I feel that I'm sort of dealing with a slippery eel — that it's pretty hard to spear, as it were.

C377. M-hm.

S377. So then I began to wonder whether slogans were any good, because after all, to be effective it would have to work every time, or there wasn't any use in doing it.   Then I got — I had another slogan that worked very well for me — that I shouldn't try to cast out my neurosis, as they cast out devils in Biblical times, because what I was really doing was casting out a part of myself, and there would naturally be a resistance to that, and so I said to myself that "This is all my will — I'm doing what I want to with my own will-power," and try to change it rather than cast it out, and I thought there wouldn't be so much resistance to the word "change" as there would be to the phrase "get rid of."   I felt that if I said "get rid of this" that there would be more resistance than if I said to myself "change this."   And that worked fine, but all those things that worked fine only worked once, and then I have to look

---

despair about himself (*S379, S380*).   It is worth noting that his reference here to the pain he is suffering is the only such reference since the first interview.   At other times he has spoken of pain as part of his past experience, but only here does it again become part of the present picture.   Obviously it is his need to gain sympathy and help at this point which brings it once more into the foreground. He paints it vividly in *S382.*

around for a new one, and, of course, it's a hopeless process, because you're always one step behind.

*C*378. That's it — you feel that you've just tried every means that you could discover or think up to do something about the alien within your borders.

*S*378. Well, I don't feel that I am out of means, as far as means exist, but I am out of means as far as I've been able to think them up. I mean, I know that there have been cures, or rather I have a faith in the data that I read and that I hear about, that there have been cures, so that gives me hope there. But I suppose my main element of discouragement is there, that when I do either voluntarily or involuntarily have a good day, it doesn't last. That the laws of momentum operate for the bad, but not for the good.

*C*379. And you're feeling quite discouraged today, aren't you, about your whole situation?

*S*379. Well, I feel on sort of a plateau. Uh — I'm having the pain itself, but there are not overtones of despair along with it. Now, sometimes I feel the neurosis itself, and then also a dejection about the neurosis. Other times I feel the neurosis itself, and feel an optimism that — well, I'll be out of it.

*C*380. M-hm.

*S*380. Now, the neurosis itself has been bad, but I haven't felt as dejected about it as I have before. Now, sometimes I feel not only the neurotic pain but a very overwhelming despair also. Other times I feel the neurotic pain just as badly, but — well, maybe I go on a party and act like I'm having a good time anyway, so that the overtones — I have a negative here (*abdomen*) and a rather cheerful feeling here (*head*). Other times I have negative here and negative here too — negative all over. And there doesn't seem to be any correlation there, except when the lower negative is very, very bad, why, then that just sort of blots everything out. And I even get to the point where I don't care what happens — I mean, I make no plans — just say, "Well, I'm just going to drift along, and let things happen to me what will — I'm not going to use any will power of my own — I'm just going to let the world act on me, and not give a damn about the outcome."

C381. You feel somewhat that way at the present time but not quite as strongly as that — is that ——

S381. M-hm.   I feel reasonably happy emotionally, but 'way down deep of course there's still a negative.   It's — I don't know, do most people feel it way down in the abdomen, or is that something peculiar in my instance?

C382. Yes, I suppose that different people experience their troubles in quite different ways.

S382. I used to feel it here (*chest*), but it's so definite, so real, so like an actual object — I think I mentioned it was like an axe, as it were.   Some kind of a sharp and hard and painful sort of a pressure.   It didn't use to be — it used to be more vague, and permeate my chest, and I'd notice that my wrists would tingle.   Very definitely a physical sensation.   And I imagine too that — I have the hope that after I sort of talk myself out, that you're going to pull some kind of a rabbit out of the hat; yet my better judgment tells me that you're going to keep throwing me on my own —— (*Both laugh.*)

C383. I don't think I'm the one that fundamentally throws

---

*S*382, *C*383. This is a most interesting bit.   After stating very fully all his discouraged attitudes, he suddenly breaks off and indicates the real reason for his discouragement.   He has been hoping that the counselor will solve his problems, yet knows that basically this cannot be.

The counselor handles this very well in *C*383.   Inexperienced counselors are frequently too blunt and direct in throwing the client on his own resources.   They may even create the impression that they *could* solve the situation, but feel that it would be better for the client to do so himself.   This invariably arouses hostility.   The deeper truth is that no matter how much the counselor may *know* about the situation, the client is the only one who can choose the satisfactions which he desires, and therefore the only one who can solve the problem.   No outsider can possibly choose for Mr. Bryan whether he wishes to become healthy or to continue to be neurotic. The counselor's response carries this meaning in its stress that the counselor *cannot* give a magic solution, even if he wished.

you on your own. It's that nobody *can* pull a rabbit out of a hat for each one of us, can they?

*S*383. That's right. In the end one experiences only one's self — as Nietzsche said. Experiences only one's self in the now. Life is a series of "nows." But have you found by experience any way to change emotions there — that is, whereby a person can help himself to reach a better state? I thought maybe you had come across some practical aids there in your experience.

*C*384. I think I have, and I think you have, too. That is, it interests me that, while you're feeling quite discouraged today, and I think that's quite understandable, yet at the same time you're telling of doing things that sound to me like real progress.

*S*384. Yes, well — that's — I think we can probably best describe it this way — although I have been feeling bad, I've refused to let it — even though it does interfere with my con-sciousness, I haven't let it interfere with my behavior, so that to the outside observer I would be up and doing, even though it was painful to me on the inside, which — but it leaves me so exhausted! I mean, I feel very weary ——

*C*385. You're raising very much the question with yourself, "Is it worth the battle?"

*S*385. I imagine it would be very hard to keep it up. That is, to go through a well man's behavior pattern when a person wasn't really well would be very exhausting. Of course, my work, and the number of jobs I do, is of course up to my own initiative. Now, when I have a regular job where I have to be on hand — I've had several of those, where I was working for a company and had to go through a certain routine — that gets very exhausting after a while. I come away from work and feel that the day has been so unsatisfactory that I have

---

*C*384. This is a clever response, which avoids intellectualism and answers the question out of the client's own experiences.

*C*385. This response gives real clarification to the discouraged attitudes being expressed. It is particularly important at such a time that the counselor should refrain from reassurance and simply should recognize with the client the depths of his depressed feeling.

to go out to some night clubs, and of course that keeps me up all night and makes it harder the next day.

*C*386. M-hm.

*S*386. You see where that would lead. I had thought this — of relaxing myself, that is, relaxing my conscious volition — just let myself get so miserable that I would change — change automatically from the very misery of it. But I don't know — that might make me worse. What do you think about that?

*C*387. Well, I think that's another——

*S*387. The thing might grow on me and make my condition worse. Of course, it's easy enough to say that if a person was so very miserable that they just had to change, why they would. But I don't know — there seems to be some sort of a countercheck there. Maybe I don't let myself get to that point.

*C*388. Well, and I think——

*S*388. Sort of like vomiting, I guess — you get so sick that something happens to give you relief.

*C*389. And again, you're feeling there that it's only by conscious struggle and battle that you win any ground. If you let yourself go, what you would really prefer to do would be to drop back into misery, to some extent.

*S*389. Well, I don't know whether it would make me so miserable that I would have a spontaneous change in —— You see, I get a psychological impression of two distinct kinds of will. One a conscious will — sort of a voluntary will — and the other, sort of a reflex. I don't draw any line of distinction philosophically, but I do psychologically, and sometimes I feel like using my voluntary will on myself. Then other times, when that doesn't work, I feel like completely relaxing that and seeing if the change won't occur involuntarily. I know that the neurosis is involuntary. That's the psychological

---

*C*389. Here the counselor seems either to have missed the attitude, or to be attempting an interpretation. A better response would have been, "If you gave up the struggle and let yourself get completely miserable, you hope you might change automatically; is that it?"

impression that I get of it, so that I reason — well, that the change would have to be on the same grounds, with involuntary will. And then every once in a while I have success with a voluntary technique and that leads me to try that. That is — by voluntary technique I mean such a thing as a slogan that I — yeah, I mentioned that.

*C*390. M-hm. Yes, you feel that the neurosis is nothing that you have any voluntary control over, and therefore ——

*S*390. I sometimes get — an intuition is the only thing that I can call it — that there is some sort of a key that I can voluntarily turn, but I don't know exactly what the key is. Sometimes I feel that it would be something very, very specific. Other times I feel that it would be something very general and very emotional. Other times I feel that it would be something very definite, with a very definite ideological pattern along with it, and other times I feel it would be a vague emotionalism, so, since there isn't any proof either way, it just happens to be the way I happen to believe at the time.

*C*391. M-hm.

*S*391. What do you find on these matters? Do you find that it's mostly generalized emotion, or do you ever find a definite key with an intellectual pattern to it?

*C*392. I think just as you felt last week — that it's not very often that the specific intellectual key is the primary factor — sometimes you find it.

*S*392. Well, by an intellectual key, of course I didn't mean that it would not have definite emotional roots.

*C*393. I realize that.

*S*393. But sometimes I feel that there isn't any one emotional root — that it's — oh, just sort of a vague — overwhelming, vague thing which has to do with one's general adaptation toward life.

*C*394. M-hm.

*S*394. The reason I don't think it would be any particular

---

*C*392. Again the counselor uses the client's own thinking to answer his question.

intellectual key is that I feel that I have examined my life pretty thoroughly and, as you may have noticed, I don't seem to mind facing socially tabooed things in my own life.

C 395. That's right.

S 395. So I imagine that my solution would be general, rather than any one specific thing.

C 396. Yes. You feel pretty confident that if it were in that specific realm, or some specific happening in the past, that sort of thing — that you would have found it by now.

S 396. But on the other hand, a person may examine the discrete elements in his own life — the different events — and at the same time be blind to the key one. I mean, that's entirely possible.

C 397. Yes. Yes.

S 397. It's actually a matter of self-deceit. You say to yourself, "See how willing I am to look back upon these episodes," and then you reassure yourself that since you are willing to see episodes A to Y, that you can sort of cover up episode Z that way.

C 398. That's right.

S 398. But my feeling operates in so many realms that I feel that the best approach would be a general change in reactional life rather than monkeying around with any little pigeonhole.

C 399. Yes, I'm inclined to be skeptical too that you can find the answer in a pigeonhole. I think it's more in the general realm.

S 399. What do you think about voluntary action? Do you think that I should maintain the fight along that realm, or —— Sometimes I look at it this way: that if I don't use up so much energy in my voluntary struggle, that I will have more energy to use down in the involuntary fields — I mean, down in the deeper-seated involuntary fields. And that has worked on me several times. I've absolutely relaxed the conscious struggle and let my energy seep down to deeper roots. Of course, allowing the energy to seep down to the deeper roots may mean that the energy may go over to the wrong side. There's always that danger.

*C*400. Yes, it comes back in either event, doesn't it, to the course of action that really gives you the greatest satisfactions of the deeper sort. That's the thing that's easier to follow, voluntarily or involuntarily.

*S*400. M-hm. That's right. In other words, whether the will is voluntary or involuntary doesn't particularly matter psychologically — the point is, where it gets what it believes to be the largest return on its investment, as it were.

*C*401. That's right. M-hm.

*S*401. And, of course, that's a somewhat appalling thought — according to that, a fellow could be neurotic all his life.

*C*402. M-hm. I think very definitely — I think your statement there is right. That if the greater satisfactions in the balance are the neurotic ones, we tend to stay neurotic.

*S*402. But however, though, I get so much more satisfaction when I'm not neurotic, so why don't I cling to that, then? I mean, why relapse — I mean, that seems to violate the laws there. I know that if you could ask me to outline my happiest days of my life, every one of those happiest days would be non-neurotic days.

*C*403. That's right. That's the thing you're building on, isn't it? That you do gain very real satisfactions that way. Just as ——

*S*403. But shouldn't that satisfaction tend to keep itself in power, though? That's a thing that puzzles me.

*C*404. Well, I think you've answered it yourself very well. I mean that if the votes are very evenly divided, first one party and then the other may be in power.

*S*404. M-hm. Yes, that's right.

---

*C*400. This is rather definitely interpretive, but undoubtedly productive.

*S*401, *C*402. This is the deepest new insight achieved in this interview, and it is well handled and clarified by the counselor.

*C*403, *C*404, *C*405. These responses tend to be interpretive, but since they contain nothing the client has not expressed, they are accepted. *C*405 is evidently the counselor's attempt to draw the interview to a close through a summary of the views brought out.

*C*405. And I think that that is one of the reasons for your feeling as you do this week. I mean — last time you took some awfully courageous steps. You looked at yourself very clearly, and saw very clearly some of the balance of power. Well, now if you do decide to follow one course of action, it tends to mean a giving up of the other. And this week you're saying, "My gosh, I don't know — that's giving up quite a lot."

*S*405. Well, we do what we will — we will what we will. That's why I was wondering ——

*C*406. Well, I expect we'll have to discuss that next time.

*S*406. Here's a thing that I thought was some — it just occurred to me now — non-neurotic satisfactions, while they are definitely satisfying, there must be some way in which they lack weight — in which they lack meat. In other words, the neurotic satisfactions must be of a more precious metal to me.

*C*407. Those may be the ones with the real meat to them, hm?

*S*407. M-hm. I think this might have something to do with it. I think that if I could have some good sexual experiences and good musical experiences when I was non-neurotic,

---

This is an unusually good statement of what has been occurring and contains no element of forcing. It is not often that such a satisfactory summary can be produced on the spot, and hence it is usually best not to make the attempt.

*s*406. Here is actually the acid test of the counselor's viewpoint. Is he willing that the client should make the choice which seems to him unwise and unhealthy? Does he genuinely believe in the right of the individual to self-determination? If not, it is doubtful whether he can carry on satisfactory therapy of the sort we are describing. The counselor should not suppose that it is an academic question. In many cases, as in this one, the client may hover, in somewhat agonizing suspense, between the constructive and the destructive choice. In rare instances the choice may be a regressive one, rather than a choice which makes for growth. The counselor needs to have a very real sense of his own limitations, a freedom from the need to play God, if he is to allow the client this most basic of all freedoms.

that that would give me the weight, but those things — we're limited by the environment there. I mean, if we could always have sex and always have music and other satisfying things right at our fingertips, why, then we could give weight to the situation that we wanted to maintain permanently. But since I am neurotic most of the time, it makes it harder for me to get into those situations before I have my relapse.

*C*408. In other words, if the environment would bolster you more, you perhaps could stay on the up side?

*S*408. Well, if it would give me opportunity. If I could — for example, hurry up and have an intercourse while I was feeling good, then I would realize that that was more satisfying than my neurotic sex.

*C*409. Well, let's think over some of these things next time.

*S*409. I don't like to depend on the environment. I realize that that's a bad psychology. But on the other hand, there is no doubt that opportunities are limited by the environment.

*C*410. Definitely. Now, I'm tied up next Monday. It would have to be either sometime Saturday, or Tuesday afternoon at four. Would that be a possible time for you?

*S*410. M-hm. I think I would like to drop in Saturday.

*C*411. Well, could you make it Saturday at one?

*S*411. Any time.

*C*412. All right. Saturday at one.

*S*412. We met at that time once before, didn't we?

*C*413. Yes, I guess we did.

*S*413. I guess it doesn't matter much. Voluntarily or involuntarily, the point is to weight the satisfactions differently. Make the healthy satisfactions outweigh the unhealthy ones, so we ——

*C*414. Yes, and to make the choice fairly deeply, perhaps, of the kind of satisfactions that you most want.

*S*414. Well, you take a jump of faith there. That is, you

---

*C*408. Again the counselor is successful in catching the essential meaning of a complex series of statements, with resulting clarification.

*S*414. Mr. Bryan sums up his situation beautifully. Dare he

take it on faith that you're going to have a better life, and
faith — it's pretty hard for faith to work against actual old
neurotic satisfactions.

*C*415. That's right. That's right. That's right at the spot
where you are at the moment.

*S*415. M-hm. I'll see you Saturday, sir, and —— (*They
both go out.*)

---

leave the satisfactions he has actually realized for those which seem
to be better but which he has not experienced so fully? This is the
dilemma of all growth. The counselor fortunately recognizes this
dilemma and makes no effort to settle it prematurely.

General Comments

Mr. Bryan well describes this interview as representing a plateau.
The full measure of his discouragement, as he faces the implications
of the insight achieved in the previous contact, is best shown by
listing, as before, the spontaneous sentiments voiced during the
interview.

I haven't any motivation to choose the better way.

When I have nothing but neurotic satisfactions, it is hard
to feel that other satisfactions would be better.

I should like to avoid the pain of growth.

If I grow I shall only be destroyed in the war.

But I should balk on the threshold of growth even if there
were no war.

I want a motivation for change.

I have gained satisfactions from taking more initiative in my
job but it has cost me much sacrifice.

I feel that the present world situation makes it more important
for me to be healthy, and more fearful for me to be healthy.

I feel myself depressed, on a plateau.

I feel that my "bad" days are somehow more powerful than
my "good" days.

I have no control over my changes in feeling.

I've tried every possible way to get motivation and to cure
myself.

I feel discouraged about myself.

I'm suffering real pain.

I should like to have you pull a rabbit out of a hat for me.

This whole struggle is very exhausting to me.

Perhaps I should let myself be miserable. Then I might change automatically.

If I do what is satisfying, I might be neurotic all my life.

Perhaps the neurotic satisfactions mean more to me than the healthy ones.

I want circumstances to help me.

I need faith to go ahead, but it's hard, because I enjoy the neurotic satisfactions.

The counselor has done very satisfactory work in this interview, helping the client to face fully and frankly his discouraged feelings. There seem to be no really serious counseling errors in this contact.

Mr. Bryan's situation at this point might be rather easily summarized. He has come to see himself clearly, but he cannot decide whether to take steps in the direction of growth or to continue in his neurotic satisfactions. He feels discouraged, and he would like to have the counselor work a miracle for him, or to have the environment bolster him. On the other hand, it is significant that the actions he reports are of a healthy sort, in the direction of maturity

❧ SIXTH INTERVIEW ❧

SATURDAY THE FIFTEENTH (*Ten minutes late for appointment*)
C416. Hello.
S416. Hello. I'm afraid I'm a little bit foggy — I got in bed at nine this morning — got up at a quarter of one.
C417. Got in bed at nine?
S417. Yeah.
C418. I think you might be a little foggy.
S418. At least I know that I have a very good motivation to come here, because I had a good excuse not to show up. (*Pause.*) Well, I haven't noticed any definite change. I sort of feel like I'm on a plateau, with one exception there —— Am I out of matches again? I know I have some here.
C419. Here is a match.
S419. Thanks. I developed quite a bit on our conclusion that the — that any change in personality, any radical change, is, in the final analysis, sort of a jump of faith. That is, you have faith that you're changing for the better, and — well, faith in your intelligence, I suppose it would be — not necessarily a blind faith, but at least a faith, and I sort of — I have a tendency to be sort of deprecating toward faith. It, I suppose, has a religious connotation for me. Above all, I realize that a great many things are faith — even a logical scientist, as he interprets his data, why, the final act of knowledge is an act of faith rather than an act of rationality, inasmuch as knowledge can merely mean — well, knowledge as I see it is a feeling of confidence to act in a certain way. Since we do have limited data on practically everything, why, that would make knowledge ultimately, I think, an act of faith. That is,

---

s418. Although Mr. Bryan points out his strong motivation for coming, it is probable that his lateness in arriving is an indication of his resistance to coming. Actually the appointment is only another symbol on which to focus his deep ambivalence in regard to going forward or remaining in his present state.

we'd have faith that we were going to interpret the data in a certain way. It seems reasonable that we'd have faith we had interpreted it rightly.

*C*420. Well, is it the knowledge that represents faith, or is it the action based on inadequate knowledge that's an act of faith?

*S*420. Well, it's the acting on the inadequate.

*C*421. Yes. I wasn't quite sure that I got your point.

*S*421. Of course, even when knowledge seems adequate, why, we can never know for sure but what there might be some more. Some other facts. I tend to be leery of faith. I seem to want more before I'm willing to act.

*C*422. M-hm.

*S*422. It seems like you have to have faith to have faith, and so on.

*C*423. In other words, it isn't any lack of knowledge that keeps you from going ahead, because you realize that would always be inadequate, but the not having quite sufficient faith, if you wish to call it that, to take the action, or the actions.

*S*423. Yes. M-hm. I believe that I want to take the action — well, it could be verbalized either that I want to but don't know how to generate myself, or I don't really want to. It may be two ways of saying the same thing.

*C*424. M-hm.

*S*424. I've often wondered about this — if I were in a hypothetical situation — let's say that there were some X-ray machine invented that could change a person just exactly the way they wanted to be changed, I believe that I would reach out and push the button to make the change. I don't think that there would be any doubt there. But ——

---

*C*423–*S*424. The counselor's discerning clarification in *C*423 brings out a statement of the client's underlying ambivalence in *S*423. This client has an uncanny way of predicting in some initial statement an outline of the whole interview. In the preceding contact, his remark that he was on a plateau characterized the whole hour. This interview, it will be seen, could be summed up in the statement, "I want to, but don't know how — or maybe I don't want to."

*C*425. If it could be done by a miracle or all of a sudden, you don't doubt that you'd want the change made.

*S*425. I've thought that that would be the — one of the tests of whether a person really wanted to be cured, if he could do it by some simple little act like that. Then if we could have some sort of a situation like that, then we could knew whether people *really* wanted to be changed.

*C*426. You feel that would be the truthful ——

*S*426. Well, it might. Of course, you get back to the problem of definition there again — I mean, the term "really" in the phrase "really want" may be defined by the amount of effort that would be necessary.

*C*427. Well, I was thinking of it in another way, too. A person might be willing to press the button to get from here to there, but I don't know that that necessarily means that he would be willing to go through the struggle to make the achievement of getting from here to there.

*S*427. M-hm. Well, I feel that a strong portion of me is willing at least, but that the whole thing is sort of vague to me. I don't know exactly where to begin. I can adopt certain behavior patterns — that is, sort of as if — rather to act as if I were cured. But that doesn't seem to work — it always makes it harder for me to act. And I feel sort of in the dark as to a method of making the change. Of course, that's another way of inviting a resistance.

*C*428. You feel, though, that you are pretty willing to take the necessary steps if you can discover what those steps are.

*S*428. M-hm. And I feel that it isn't just a matter of

---

*C*425, *C*427. Like *C*403 and *C*404 in the last interview, these responses are subtly interpretive. If the counselor had avoided interpretation and had simply clarified the attitudes, the result would probably have been better. If the counselor had fully accepted Mr. Bryan's insistence that he wanted to be changed, Mr. Bryan would then have been free to bring his real ambivalence into the picture.

*S*428. Mr. Bryan seems to be pleading for definite suggestions from the counselor. Only experience can teach the counselor that

difficulty. If I were to have a definite — let's say, the change involved doing a number of definite things — even if those things were very difficult, if I knew exactly what they were definitely, why, I believe that I would do it, but since I don't know definitely what to do — I feel that that's a part of the barrier there. In other words, if I were to climb a high mountain every day, or do something intellectually difficult, as long as it were definite, the difficultness of the action would not be a barrier, would it? But when I have both indefiniteness and difficulty, the combination of the two would be too much.

*C*429. Well, as you've thought about the changes that might be involved, what steps have you thought of, or what changes have you considered?

*S*429. Well, you mean what would be certain specific goals, you mean?

*C*430. I suppose.

*S*430. Well, the whole thing can be summed up in a change of feeling. My goal would be to get rid of my negative feeling, which tends to block me in all those different operational fields that we talked about. I know that just as soon as I get rid of that feeling that success will come in all of these different fields. So ——

*C*431. And you feel that it's ——

*S*431. I know from experience that when the feeling does leave me, that everything takes care of itself — I don't have to say to myself, "Well, am I going to have success in this or that?"

---

such a procedure would be futile. Every suggestion made at this point would be argued down in one manner or another. If the reader is in doubt on this point, let him reserve judgment until the following interview.

*c*429. It is unfortunate that the counselor did not continue to clarify attitudes, rather than becoming directive at this point. He might have responded, "If someone would only give you some definite steps, no matter how difficult, you would go ahead, but without these you are blocked."

*s*430. This is the keynote of much that follows — that he must be cured first, then he will find success.

*C*432. You feel that progress will come first by being rid of negative feelings, and then having success?

*S*432. No, the success will take care of itself, as soon as I have positive feelings. I know from previous experience that just as soon as the feeling leaves me, why — well, I'm so sure that I'm in good condition, that I can go into any situation with confidence. I don't have any doubts at all, when I am in good condition, because I have such a feeling that it gives me emotional confidence without requiring any sort of proof that I am all right. I feel all right, therefore I know that I am all right without having to prove it to myself by any acid test or anything.

*C*433. You think that perhaps it might — the change also might come in the reverse direction — that as you work for certain successes the negative feelings would disappear?

*S*433. You mean to alter consciousness by behavior — by altering the volitional behavior first?

*C*434. Well, I've been very much interested, for example, in the ——

*S*434. Along William James's angle there?

*C*435. Well, I've been interested in the steps you've taken in regard to your work, for example. I haven't gathered that all of those were easy, or that you always felt all right when you undertook them. But you have evidently felt quite good when you've achieved them.

*S*435. M-hm. The satisfaction that I feel is one of having gone ahead in spite of a barrier, but there hasn't been any lessening of the barrier itself. And I feel that although I can from time to time have actions in spite of the barrier, there's so much of the sacrifice involved there, that — well, it leaves me pretty exhausted.

*C*436. And that that type of satisfaction is hardly worth striving for.

---

*C*433. Here the counselor is definitely pushing the client to accept the idea that change might come from self-initiated, positive actions. This pressure is definitely not helpful.

*S*436. Well, it isn't a full satisfaction like complete cure would be. Now, to make it concrete: one time I had to be toastmaster at a banquet — there wasn't any way that I could wiggle out of it — and I got through it very well, without any speech impediments, but I was very nervous through the whole thing, although I didn't show it outwardly, and very worn out afterward. And while I got the satisfaction, my old negative, you see, kept it from being complete satisfaction. I mean, it's just such a terrific sacrifice — like driving with the brakes on — you can do it, but it's very hard to maneuver.

*C*437. And you feel that the goal for you is a life without that type of struggle.

*S*437. Oh, yes. M-hm. That is, I want the effortless ease and grace in all those situations — not necessarily a cinch, but I want the obstacles to be on the outside rather than on the inside. In other words, you don't mind environmental obstacles and problems, when you don't have any inside you — you can attack the outside ones without feeling so dejected about it. As a matter of fact, I get a kick out of overcoming obstacles when they're all on the outside, when I don't have anything blocking me inside — why, then I get sort of the joy of battle, you might say. A joy out of using my intellect and using forcefulness, but when I don't feel good inside, why it's just a painful process there — the only satisfaction is that that comes from the achievement itself; that is, the fact of having done something, even though it was very difficult. But that's tending to disappear now — I mean, I don't tend to praise myself so much any more, because I have lost that Horatio Alger praising of struggle. I say, "Well, it's a shame that I had to have a struggle, rather than a triumph." So the only satisfaction I can get is the pragmatic fruits of the labor. I don't know whether I'm making myself clear.

*C*438. Yes, I think so. And it looks as though it comes back to the notion again that if you could press a button and find yourself completely changed and cured, you would press that, but perhaps slower and struggling roads don't look so attractive.

S 438. Well, that's right. But I don't know just exactly what roads to take — that is, the only thing that I know to do is to go ahead and act as if I didn't have it, but that involves a tremendous struggle. I read a little article by William James one time. He said that most people think that feeling precedes action, but actually the two go hand in hand. If you act as if you had a certain feeling, why, soon you're going to find yourself having that feeling. He was working on a method of overcoming the blues. He said to go ahead and act as if you were happy, and pretty soon you'd find yourself being happy, even though it was difficult at first. So, I guess that's what I've been doing.

C 439. That's hardly adequate, is it?

S 439. M-hm. Yes, that's like — well, some of my teachers used to have the idea that if they forced me to talk, that that would cure my speech difficulty. But I never did have any confidence in that method. Just felt that I was knocking myself out for nothing.

C 440. That didn't particularly help your speech, and yet, somehow, you overcame your speech defect, pretty largely.

S 440. At certain times, yes. I could force myself into a situation and pull through it, but not always. I mean, I didn't have one hundred per cent success with that forcing-myself method. And always there was a terrific reaction set in. I mean, after I'd get through with a public speech, I would have a great deal of difficulty in talking to my friends even.

C 441. Do you imply that you still feel greatly bothered by a speech ——

S 441. Yes, but I'm not in situations any more where I have to make a lot of public speeches or anything like that. Oh, I talk to little groups and tell them the advantages of having group photographs and things like that, but — well, my out-

---

C 440. In the latter part of this statement, and in *C* 442, *C* 443, and *C* 444 the counselor is again trying to force the client to agree that his own choice has had something to do with overcoming his speech difficulty. This forcing is unprofitable. We see here some of the same impatience which characterized the second interview.

look has broadened in the last number of years. I used to single out the speech symptom, but I feel that for a number of years now, as I mentioned the other day, that that's just one tiny sector of the whole thing, so I don't dwell on that, to the exclusion of the others, but it still is an effort for me to talk — I'm on a definite strain.

C442. But you do it.

S442. But even if I didn't talk, I'd still have the feeling, so I go ahead and talk anyway.

C443. In other words, in that area, you have made a good bit of progress.

S443. Yes, that's right. I'm not such a bad speaker as I used to be.

C444. I presume that that progress was quite a struggle.

S444. Well, it just sort of happened. I mean, there were certain situations, that I wanted to do in order to achieve something, where speech was necessary, so I went ahead and did it.

C445. M-hm.

S445. If I hadn't done it, I would have avoided the struggle; then I would have lost some sort of fruits.

C446. That's right. So the total results ——

S446. — were more satisfying. But I feel this: that that takes a tremendous amount of vitality to live that way; and although I have had the vitality, I know that I'm not always going to have it. I mean — it's just a matter of age, if nothing else. I don't feel that I'm getting old or anything, but I know that in the late thirties or early forties there is a decline physically that shows up in a person's vitality.

C447. M-hm.

S447. Then the — well, my main gripe against my condition is just its very unpleasantness. It just makes me very dissatisfied with myself at harboring such a feeling.

C448. As I get it from what you're saying today, the other side of that picture also looks pretty unpleasant - I mean, that the struggle to achieve a different level of adjustment looks like a pretty tough climb.

*S*448. M-hm. Yes, many a time I have forced myself to go through difficult situations, and even though my behavior has been all right, my inward feelings haven't been. And I'm afraid that I tend to regard it as not being worth the candle so much any more. I mean — say — I've often had this thought: that even if I worked hard and made a lot of money, without a psychological cure it wouldn't be very satisfying — I mean, even though I had a lot of money, I couldn't lead a satisfying life till I had the psychological cure along with it. My money might — I think would tend to be a mockery to me.

*C*449. So to some extent it might be easier to remain with your present dissatisfaction in regard to your condition rather than to make the even harder struggle to get somewhere else.

*S*449. Yes, that's true as far as it goes, with this addition, that I want to change my methodology to curing myself before I go into the situation. In other words, I don't want to go into any more situations till I'm cured; because I have done that so much and it has been such a strain and such an exhaustion that I feel that I want to be cured first, then handle the situation. Of course, I don't know whether that's a bad method or not, but regardless of the merits of the method, that's what I would like.

*C*450. M-hm.

*S*450. That's the way I would like to handle it. Because I don't have any confidence that going into the situation uncured is going to help the cure. You get certain satisfactions, but they're not the satisfactions of a cure, at least they haven't been so far in my experience. But if going ahead and forcing myself to handle certain situations, perhaps in combination with something else, would be a good method and I had confidence that it would be a good method, why, I'd keep on going into the situations. But something new would have to be added there (*laugh*) before I could get confidence in that——

---

*C*449, *C*451, *C*453. Here the counselor redeems himself by very adequate recognition of Mr. Bryan's attitudes and feelings. *C*455 is also a good response, though more interpretive.

*C*451. M-hm. M-hm. And at the present time you don't see from your own experience anything new being added there.

*S*451. No. I don't know — as I see it, there are just two things that I can do. One is to lie back and get inertia dissatisfaction; the other is to go ahead and get a lot of nervous strain. Either way it's — I mean, well — it's a dilemma.

*C*452. M-hm.

*S*452. Either way is bad. What I want to do is to go ahead without the nervous strain, but I know from experience that if I go ahead, that in itself will not be a cure. Just going through the outward motions won't do me any — hasn't given me the desired cure. I don't have confidence that it would. (*Pause.*) So the ideal for me would be to — well, perhaps it's too yogi-istic or something, but I want to sort of effect a cure by myself, apart from the environmental problem. Then after the cure, why, I'll go out and tackle the problem.

*C*453. You feel that growth can sort of take place in a vacuum, and then once you have developed the growth, then you would be capable of dealing with the situation.

*S*453. Well, growth hasn't occurred in the environment, so perhaps it could occur by some sort of solitary meditation or whatever you'd want to call it. That doesn't sound so good, does it?

*C*454. Well, I don't know of growth taking place that way, but I can understand your feeling in regard to it.

*S*454. You know certain religious mystics will meditate in solitude for a long time. Then that seems to gird their loins, as it were. Then they go out and make achievements. So there must be some sort of a building up of power there while they're in their solitude.

*C*455. M-hm. And that seems also kind of tempting to you, doesn't it? To press a button, or to retreat from the situation and grow and develop away from it — any of those possibilities looks pretty good.

*S*455. Well, yes — I mean, it sounds like a retreat — perhaps it is. You should call a spade a spade. But anyway — even though I have gone through situations as if I were cured, it hasn't done a thing to the deep-seated neurosis itself, and so I've lost the confidence in that.

C456. Yes, I think that just pretending doesn't get one anywhere. I think that's true.

S456. I get a satisfaction out of the pragmatic fruits of such behavior, and to a certain extent a Horatio Alger sort of a pride in the — oh, the old sink-or-swim angle, and, well — *ad astra per aspera* sort of satisfaction, but that's tending to dwindle. I think more and more of the terrific nervous sacrifice involved, rather than regarding myself as a hero, which I used to. So I think we might list it this way: that I would first of all prefer to be cured, then go into situations; but if that were not possible, why, then I would want to go into situations with something more than the "as if." But so many times I have gone through situations outwardly seeming O.K., but inwardly not, and only to have a reaction after the situation was over, it — I'm discouraged by that method.

C457. So it probably wasn't worth it to make the unusual efforts that you did in getting the treasurer to advance you the money.

S457. I don't have a retrospective feeling that it wasn't worth it, but I feel that I'm about at the end of the rope where I would feel that it was worth it. In other words, the outward symbols of achievement are less and less satisfying to me as long as I don't have the inward satisfactions. The money that I made from the job wasn't nearly as satisfying to me as it would have been if I had been inwardly O.K., so ——

C458. So you feel that you got no inward satisfactions out of it?

S458. Yes, I got an inward satisfaction, but it was all up here and here — it didn't reach down to here where I want it to. It's — well, a superficial satisfaction, whereas I want a radical satisfaction. I enjoy making money and spending money, but it doesn't reach down to the roots of my trouble. I mean, that sort of satisfaction hasn't been nor do I think would be a means of therapy. But I don't know what a means of therapy would be. I suppose there might be some sort of self-psychology there; that is, if you could go ahead and tackle a situation and then at the same time say something to yourself while you were doing it — maybe that might be a means of getting therapy satisfactions rather than just the superficial satisfactions. Well, I don't know. As you can see, I'm just sort of groping around.

*C*459. Yes, you're very much teetering on the balance, aren't you, as to which direction gives you the greatest degree of satisfaction that you want. I think that the more you've considered this, the more plain it becomes that there are certain satisfactions which you know you can gain through the type of behavior that you've shown for a long time; that is, you tend to escape from some of the most difficult situations through such behavior. You know, too, from your experience that there are certain satisfactions in playing a more masculine rôle — a more adult rôle, but as you weigh those and you see that it would be a slow, step-by-step struggle to achieve satisfaction along that line, I think that makes you hang right in the balance as to which you'd most prefer.

*S*459. Well, there's one very, very important point that you've slightly misstated there. I don't feel that it's a step-by-step thing — I feel that I'm marking time. Even in the adult rôle, the satisfactions are superficial — they're not radical — they don't go deep enough down to the roots of my trouble. So that as far as any radical progress goes, there

---

*C*459, *S*459. The dangers of interpretation are clearly shown by this excerpt. The counselor's statement seems to be an accurate picture of the situation, and a statement which the client in some of his more constructive moods would accept. But at this time he cannot accept it, and consequently begins arguing against the counselor, when the real debate is within himself. Thus interpretation which is not accepted allows the client to use the counselor as a symbol and attack him, avoiding the fact that the real struggle is all within.

It is fascinating beyond words to see that Mr. Bryan himself recognizes that the real battle is the inner one. His slip of the tongue causes him to say that it is his progress which is disheartening, and this is the truth. It is the progress he has made which puts him

isn't any step-by-step thing to it — it's just a marking of time. And since my trouble is deep-seated, why, that's where the progress — the absence of progress — is more disheartening than anything else. That's an interesting lapse of words there.

*C*460. Hm?

*S*460. I said that since my trouble is deep-seated that's where the progress — then I changed it to lack of progress — is most disheartening.

*C*461. M-hm. (*Laugh.*)

*S*461. (*Long pause.*)   So pragmatic fruits — the satisfactions gained by the adult behavior — are not radical enough to give me complete satisfaction.   And as far as radical progress goes, I feel that I'm marking time.   I have the conviction that no matter what I achieve in the environment, if I don't get a radical cure, I'll never have any true satisfaction.   And, of course, that tends to lower my environmental ambition. Unless I would have a hope for a radical cure.

*C*462. Yes, you feel that the money you earn or that sort of thing, that certainly isn't the thing that would make the difference.   In other words, if the satisfactions you gain in doing a difficult photographic job or selling yourself to someone or getting across ideas — if those satisfactions aren't real to you apart from the money they bring in, then they do compare unfavorably with the satisfactions that you find in avoiding that sort of thing.

*S*462. M-hm. (*Pause.*)   Those environmental fruits — oh, you tend to sigh, "Vanity, vanity," if you have those without the inward satisfaction.

*C*463. Yes, certainly.   That isn't the aspect that's important — it's the way in which the ——

*S*463. I'd rather be a wealthy neurotic than a poor one, but

---

face to face with this overwhelmingly difficult decision.   It is evidence of the fundamental non-directiveness of the contact that he is free to point out his own slip, damaging as it is to the case he is making.

*c*462. This is a summarized recognition, with some flavor of interpretation, but it is accepted satisfactorily.

I would not go to any very great effort to be a wealthy neurotic.

*C*464. That's right.

*S*464. But I would go to a great effort to be a healthy, wealthy person. You know my idea. There's a certain reverse angle there, though, too. When I am healthy, then I don't need so much money. I find myself not requiring so many luxuries, and all that sort of thing.

*C*465. You're still hoping very, very much that someone can, first, make you healthy, and then achievements will follow.

*S*465. M-hm. I feel that with a fundamental change in my feelings, to get rid of this blocking feeling, everything else would take care of itself; because I know that when I have been free of it in any field that I could name, I have success and I have it spontaneously and effectively, without any sacrifice of nervous energy. When I'm feeling good I do an amazing amount of work — I mean, it's actually amazing to me. I look back and say, "Why, how did I ever do that?" I marvel at myself. It's just as if someone else did it. And it sort of appalls me to think of it. I say, "Well, how did I ever have nerve enough to do that?" or, "How did I ever think so clearly and quickly as to achieve that?"

*C*466. And if that state could come without effort, you'd accept it in a minute.

*S*466. Oh, sure. And if it would come with effort, I would work for it, if I had a confidence in the method I was using, and — well, if I had some sort of a definite pattern to follow — some sort of a prescription, shall we say, that I had a confidence in. It's just the marking time in the dark that's becoming more and more discouraging to me. I know that I can get satisfactions from these achievements, but the satisfactions don't cure the neurosis. In other words, the neurosis seems to be buried so deeply that these achievement satisfactions don't touch it. My heart feels happier, but ——

*C*467. At least they don't cure it immediately, do they?

---

*c*465. This is somewhat curious. The counselor breaks the train of thought to give another recognition to *S*452.

S 467. Well, my heart feels happier, but my guts still have the same old cramped pain. Of course, there might be a contagion there — I mean, it might eventually work down to the neurosis, but so far it hasn't.

C 468. Well, I think I can see quite clearly how you feel today, and I think that — I wish there were some easy, off-hand solution that could be given to that.

S 468. Well, I realize that I want a solution, but let's not say that I wouldn't work hard if I had a definite program to follow — I feel that I would work hard. But having run the gamut of all of these attempts to get my radical satisfaction has been the reason why I feel at the end of the rope, as it were. Of course —— (*Pause.*)

C 469. Well, you do. You feel at the end of your rope — several of these expressions you've used here are interesting and truthful, I think. You feel somewhat at the end of your rope — you feel also on a plateau. You feel as though you've come to the point where probably you've got to go forward or backward — one or the other. You can't stay indefinitely on the spot.

S 469. M-hm. Then too sometimes I get the feeling that this is the way I'm going to live all my life — just sort of on the fence — going along until some kind of economic pressure forces me to earn a little money and then going and spending that money in different sort of empty pleasures.

C 470. M-hm. Yes, probably that would be another possible outcome. You could avoid meeting the situation fully and just get along enough to get by.

S 470. M-hm. But that's a very distasteful prospect to me. I mean, that's a pessimistic dream — a sinister phantasy.

C 471. Yes, it looks kind of hard each way you look, doesn't it?

S 471. I really believe that I'm willing to work hard if I

---

*C*468–*C*471. In this section the counselor is highly successful in reflecting the attitudes expressed. His responses lead to a full exploration of all the pessimistic possibilities in the situation, and hence make it more possible for the client to leave these thoughts behind.

knew exactly how to apply my energies, but I feel that I don't know what would be good therapy. I know that it's sound to get into these situations that require and promote growth, but so far they haven't given me any deep-seated, radical growth — any deep-seated change.

C472. M-hm. Seems very slow and very dubious to you.

S472. Well — slow — it doesn't even seem slow as far as radical change goes. I feel that no matter how many — how many success situations I would have, 'way down deep it wouldn't alter the neurotic condition. And what I'm looking for now is something that will reach 'way down deep into me, and — even if it means a continuation of the environmental battle, I feel something new must be added to that environmental battle before there will be any radical change. And that's why I wish I knew definitely what that was.

C473. M-hm.

S473. Of course, I still have a preference for the yogi means of changing myself, but I don't mind another alternative too much, so that I would be willing to tackle it.

C474. Well, I think probably we'd better discuss some of that another time. If there was — if there were easy and quick answers — you do thus and so and you'll feel lots better — why, we could settle it now. But it's a matter of slowly working out the things that would give real satisfaction to you — noting your experience as you live it, and thinking in terms of what satisfactions you want to go on to repeat and so on — then you might be able to work out some kind of a road which — then you could decide whether or not you wanted to take that road.

S474. Well, I get these satisfactions from achievement. As you notice, I come in here cheered by these different experiences, but it doesn't change me deeply like I want it to. So that — well, this is the whole thing: my neurotic satisfactions

---

C474. This statement possibly helps to structure the situation. In a sense it is somewhat of a "homework assignment," but of a very general sort.

are deeper and weightier than my healthy satisfactions. Now, how can I make my healthy satisfactions deeper and weightier — how can I make the healthy satisfactions of more precious metal than the neurotic satisfactions? There are definitely two sets of satisfactions, but the neurotic satisfactions, I have a definite feeling, are much deeper — much more deeply rooted — much more radical than my healthy satisfactions — and how to change my evaluation there.

*C*475. If they are so much more satisfying, then why not work on that basis?

*S*475. Well, it's so painful to maintain that basis.

*C*476. It is a tough choice any direction you look, isn't it?

*S*476. Yes. It would seem that my neurosis is definitely a thorn, but there's such a nice rose along with it. And the healthy satisfactions seem to be more flimsy, not so much meat to them. And, of course, that's all a matter of evaluation. I know that I could evaluate — that if I changed I could evaluate the healthy satisfactions and be non-interested in the unhealthy satisfactions, but (*laugh*) that means a change in me — I'd have to have a change before I would evaluate them differently. In other words, new evaluation is change.

*C*477. Yes.

*S*477. It's change by definition.

*C*478. M-hm. Well, I think ——

*S*478. I have a very definite feeling of a clinging impulse — an impulse whereby I impulsively hug my neurosis to me.

*C*479. M-hm. M-hm. I was just going to say — I think that there is surely the possibility that you might wish to live by neurotic satisfactions rather than healthy ones.

---

*c*475. The rather challenging wording of this response may not be the most fortunate, but the full and complete recognition of the fact that the neurotic way does represent a real possibility, is very helpful indeed. It leads to *s*475 and *s*476, in which Mr. Bryan puts more clearly than ever before his ambivalent desires. In fact, he has given a classic definition of a neurosis in his statement, "My neurosis is definitely a thorn, but there's such a nice rose along with it."

*S*479. Yes, and my dissatisfaction with the neurosis doesn't seem to be deep-seated enough to overthrow it.

*C*480. You can't quite decide whether to hug it to you or to leave it behind. And ——

*S*480. Well, I think that I have decided to leave it behind, but I don't know what means to take.

*C*481. Now, suppose we consider that next time we get together and try and see what ways there are of developing that road.

*S*481. I wish we could do it now. I have a date with a beautiful chorus girl tonight.

*C*482. (*Laugh.*) Well, it would be — it would always be pleasant if our problems could be solved at one fell swoop.

*S*482. You know, an interesting thing about my inhibition — it's so deep-seated that even alcohol doesn't lower it at all. I have a lowering of certain inhibitions through alcohol, but not the deep-seated condition. Now, I've seen shy and retiring fellows get drunk and lose their inhibitions, but — and I lose certain of my inhibitions under alcohol, but not the deep-seated one that I never lose.

*C*483. M-hm. Yours stays with you at all times, hm?

*S*483. M-hm. Yes.

*C*484. Well, I know you feel that, my gosh, I ought to give you some pills, psychological or otherwise, but I don't know that that's ——

*S*484. Well, I realize that there's nothing magical — that

---

*C*484. This is a sound recognition of the client's underlying plea for help. It is probably based on the inflections of *S*482, in which his low mood is definitely reflected. Certainly the whole interview represents a plea for assistance, and the counselor does well to bring this fact fully into the open. *C*485 carries this clarification even further. This section represents perhaps as low a point in the client's mood as his first statement of his problem in the first contact. There is, however, this very striking difference. In the first interview he felt depressed and discouraged because of his problems. Now he sees clearly the cause of his problems and is depressed and discouraged because he is sure he does not have the resources to deal with this cause.

the whole thing is up to me — that it's going to be practical rather than magical. But I do notice very definitely two sets of inhibitions — that is, some inhibitions I can lose, and the main one I can't. I mean, there's — oh, you've seen fellows that were — well, that were bashful and restrained and all that, but I don't have any of those inhibitions. I do have a more deeply seated one. (*Pause.*) Yes, that's a very dismal experience to try to drink it away, you know — try to lose it by drink, and then have all of the inhibitions go but the one that is very deep, so that ——

C485. You feel that you can't lose it through alcohol, and you can't shake it off in constructive experiences, and, in fact, you're feeling quite discouraged about it today.

S485. I always have a hopefulness that — well, I want to know a means — I'd like to know something definite to do, even though it were very difficult.

C486. Well, let's talk over that whole angle of it. Now I have Tuesday at four or Friday at four.

S486. All right. Tuesday at four.

C487. Tuesday at four? O.K.

S487. O.K. (*Long pause.*)

C488. The weather today about fits the mood, hm?

S488. Well, you know mood is a funny thing with me. I can have a cheerful mood here, and yet have a bad mood down lower. That's a silly correlation.

C489. Another indication of the division within yourself.

S489. M-hm.

C490. O.K. Tuesday at four, then.

S490. Yes.

General Comments

The most important attitudes coming out in this interview are listed here. It will be noted that they are very similar to the attitudes of the preceding interview. There would seem to be less evident progress between these two interviews than between any others in the series. The attitudes are:

It is costing me much effort to come for this interview.

I still feel on a plateau.

I need more faith in order to take action.

Maybe I don't really want to take the action.

If I could change myself by pressing a button, I'd do it.

I need to know definite steps before I can go ahead.

I want to get rid of my negative feelings first, then meet situations.

The satisfactions of struggling ahead are hardly worth the candle.

I want to cure myself (or be cured) before I go into life situations.

Positive actions give me satisfactions, but they are not sufficiently deep-seated.

Progress is disheartening to me — lack of progress, I mean.

I want a prescription for cure. You must add something new.

I'm just marking time in the dark.

I'm at the end of my rope.

Perhaps I shall just drift along on a neurotic level all my life.

My neurotic satisfactions are more weighty than my healthy satisfactions.

It's painful to be neurotic, but it's pleasant, too.

I wish you would tell me what to do.

My problem is a very deep-seated one.

From the point of view of satisfactory counseling, there are in this interview some excellent instances of recognition of deep feeling, but also some tendency to hurry the client and to give interpretations for which he is not yet ready. The counselor is most successful in "staying with the client's feeling" when that feeling is discouraged and hopeless and when the client is pleading for help. The counselor sympathetically clarifies the struggle the client is going through, but does not try to make the choice for him or to influence the decision. The fact that the choice is his to make has become painfully clear to Mr. Bryan, yet without any feeling that the decision is being forced upon him by the counselor.   •

The attitudes in Interviews Five and Six show a real relapse from the insights gained in Interview Four. The self-understanding which was gained has proved so painful that the client retreats from the hard choice ahead of him and gives an indication that he may choose the course of immediate satisfaction, the neurotic road, rather than the course which is immediately painful but in the long run more satisfying.

A theoretical question might be raised here, which the writer will not attempt to answer. Is it possible that the heavy use of interpretation in the second interview, and the considerable use of approval in the fourth interview, hastened the client into insight somewhat more rapidly than he could face it?   Is it possible that if he had gone at his own speed throughout these two interviews, this plateau could have been avoided?   Or is it a normal aspect of the therapeutic process that the full light of insight tends to have a disheartening effect upon the client?   May this plateau of indecision be due to the fact that the reorientation involved is so fundamental?   Further study will be necessary to answer these and similar questions.   It might be noted, however, that such a rapid development of insight, and such a marked plateau following the development of insight, are not, in the experience of the writer, typical.   In this respect the progress in this case differs in its timing, though not in its fundamentals, from the sequence of therapeutic progress as it has been described in Chapters VI to VIII.

❧ SEVENTH INTERVIEW ❧

(Mr. Bryan was nearly half an hour late for this interview. Shortly after the hour of his appointment he telephoned, saying that he was delayed, but would arrive late and had "some interesting things to talk over.")

C491. Still puffing a bit, hm?

S491. Oh, yeah. I walked pretty fast. I'm sorry to be late. (*Pause.*) I was sitting at a bar last evening, having a few drinks and thinking about myself and psychology in general, so I jotted down some things here. (*Pulls out a paper.*)

C492. I see.

S492. I can interpret them now. We were talking about the speech situation the other day. One of the things that was brought up was that when I forced myself into such a speech situation — over a period of years, there does seem to be an improvement in that situation. I was wondering if I used the same technique for all the outward symptoms, what would happen to the fundamental negative that underlay all of those symptoms. I was wondering whether you can attack the fundamental behind all of the symptoms by attacking the symptoms one by one, or whether there's a constant jumping there which would make new symptoms crop up anyway.

C493. You're wondering whether trying to attack one aspect of it would just make it crop up somewhere else.

S493. M-hm. I thought maybe that technique would not be radical enough.

S491. This is the only apology Mr. Bryan makes for being late. He never explains the reasons for his tardiness, but the content of the interview is ample evidence of the fact that it was not caused this time by resistance or ambivalence. This statement also gives another example of the fact that if counseling is non-directive, and the initiative is left with the client, much of the real work of psychotherapy goes on in the intervals between contacts.

*C*494. I suppose it depends on what the fundamental thing is.

*S*494. M-hm. But we had noticed that although the speech had improved, the deep-seated negative feeling was still there and cropped up in other ways. Now, I got a feeling too — I think this was after the third shot — that I should force myself into any and every neurotically resistant situation, and if any improvement shows, to dwell on that improvement and value the satisfaction of it. I think that might be a gradual way of improving it, and — of course, I got a parallel thought with this — that I also might be worsened that way — that is, I might have defeat situations which would make me feel worse. Now, I was wondering, is this my healthy or my neurotic self advising me to force myself into situations? I mean, I don't know which self ——

*C*495. You feel you can't quite tell your selves apart.

*S*495. Well, you see it might improve and it might make me worse, so I don't know which — from whence that advice comes. Now, I got a conviction last night that I'm willing to do anything for the cure — I mean, I'm not asking for any easy way. I just don't know just exactly what to do. And then I was wondering ——

*C*496. What you're saying — what you said a moment ago is part of your thinking about what you might do.

*S*496. M-hm. Then I got to thinking about your technique. I was wondering whether your technique might not be to have every neurotic sort of prescribe for himself — that is — then I asked myself, does my prescription mean — does

---

*S*494. Here Mr. Bryan begins to map out for himself in constructive fashion the steps he could take. The latter half of this response seems to be charged with doubt. This and the statement in *S*511 represent the last negative and pessimistic attitudes voiced by the client, although of course the counselor could have no advance notice of this fact. It is as though, in moving forward, the client feels it necessary to make at least some gestures in the regressive directions which have been so much a part of his past.

*S*496–*S*497. This excerpt is an excellent justification of the course of therapy which has been followed. The full realization of the

that above prescription that I made — does that mean that
the technique would be generally the same for all people, or is
it that every neurotic who seeks to do something about it can
get an inkling of what to do in his own individual case, since
he has a budding healthy desire — does that budding desire
give each individual inklings of what to do for his own particular case, or is it sort of a generalized technique?

C497. I think it's both, and it seems to me that's a beautiful
statement of it. That is, that each person — I don't care
whether they're neurotic or not — essentially *has* to write
his own prescription. I mean, if anybody could write it for
him, why fine — why have him write it himself? But when
you get right down to it, who knows what steps you can take
and what steps would really improve your situation? Well,
you don't know off-hand, but no one else can tell you either.

S497. Well, I got a pretty definite conviction there that the
budding healthy desire has implicit in it means to its achievement for each of the individuals, and that the fact that they
do want to do something about it will give them inklings of
means to employ. I suppose that's perhaps largely intuitive,
yet not to be invalidated for that reason, necessarily. I
mean ——

C498. In fact, that's what you found happening in your
own case.

S498. Yeah. I got a definite feeling — I said, "Well, now
you know that you're not going to cure yourself in a vacuum.
You can only achieve growth by meeting real situations."
I said, "Now, that's just the bunk — what you were saying

---

fact that "the budding healthy desire" brings with it "inklings of
means to employ" to gain that desire, is a vital and fundamental
principle of sound treatment. The counselor handles this situation
nicely in C497, in a way which clarifies again the structure of the
therapeutic relationship.

S498. If there is any doubt as to the progress which has been
made between interviews, one has only to read S449–S452 in the
preceding interview, where Mr. Bryan was stating positively that
he must be cured before he could enter any new or difficult situations.

the other time.   What you're looking for there is a way of avoiding situations, not a way of cure."   So I jotted those notes there.

*C*499. M-hm.   You came to see pretty clearly that that kind of statement on your part last time was really another element in this balancing proposition, "Do you want to go forward or do you want to go back?"

*S*499. M-hm.   But as soon as I have a new goal, why, then I'm going to be able to prescribe means to myself, the same as I prescribe means to myself for the old goal.

*C*500. Sure.   Absolutely.   Absolutely.   We find ways of putting into effect the things that we most deeply want to do.

*S*500. My satisfactions, of course, suggest means of achieving them, whether it be voluntary or deep-seated involuntary. I mean ——

*C*501. That's right.

*S*501. Take eating a piece of beef.   The act of cutting it up would be voluntary, but the flow of juices, and so forth, would be involuntary; yet they both tend to get toward the same satisfaction — that of eating.

*C*502. Right.   M-hm.

*S*502. And then I went on: if one says to one's self, "I'll do anything to be healthy," and then sits home and does nothing, words and resolves are meaningless, because such words and feelings cannot pass the vital test of real activity. And to mean business about curing himself, one must enter

---

*S*499–*S*502. Here is a genuinely thrilling statement, involving the deepest type of insight and the prescription which Mr. Bryan has been seeking.   It is plain that the "emotional resolve" which he felt must be given to him in the fifth and sixth interviews he has at last been able to achieve for himself.   Once he has chosen a new goal, ordinary intelligence can find ways of achieving that goal.   But without the alteration in goal, suggestions as to ways of achieving it are futile.   This statement is the best answer to the question of whether or not suggestions should have been given in the last interview at *S*428. It is now clear that at that time he could not have accepted suggestions.   Now he does not need them, because he can make them himself.

into what his own self regards as healthy activity, and grow by achieving. And I had a parenthesis here — one may get worse this way too. (*Laugh.*)

C 503. (*Laugh.*) You gave yourself quite a lecture at the bar.

S 503. Yes. M-hm. Right. Yes. Let's see (*reading*) — "grow by achieving, and valuing this achievement." I think there ought to be some kind of — some sort of meditation on each little bit of achievement. Overvaluing it — one might say — of course, that's all a relative term. But at least ——

C 504. Well, perhaps merely seeing it in relation to the goal. I mean, take some of the things you've talked about before — one of the things that interested me — it really was pretty swell the way you handled that fraternity situation on the photographic job. But if you look at that merely as some isolated incident — well, what's its value? If you see the relationship of that to going forward — to meeting real situations in a better way, well, then it has some value.

S 504. M-hm. Of course, when I have a reaction, why, then I tend to forget all about that.

C 505. That's right.

S 505. It's just sort of lost and unimportant — that sort of thing, so I think a person should have a constant dose of actual situations.

C 506. M-hm.

S 506. And then I got to wondering what the technique should be in case of a setback. I guess it should just lead to more resolve and more determination rather than allowing one's self to get morbid about it.

C 504, *C* 507, *C* 508, *C* 509, *C* 510. The counselor succumbs to the temptation to give a little exposition of the implications of some of the things that are happening. He has placed so much restraint on himself throughout the critical aspects of therapy, enduring the suspense of "standing by" during the two preceding interviews while Mr. Bryan balanced on the brink of his decision, that we should not be too critical of some release on the counselor's part once the

C 507. Well — and one point that might be helpful there too; a setback doesn't occur without some reason. It may be a silly reason — it may be a very minor reason, but something hits you that tends to make you feel, "Oh, I'm no good — this isn't worth the struggle," and so on. And to ——

S 507. Well, to the person himself it wouldn't be silly or minor ——

C 508. No, that's right — but often you can — if your purpose is fairly clear-cut, then you can be objective enough to find what it was that set you off, I mean, what started this bad mood.

S 508. M-hm. It can usually be linked up — I mean, it's some egotistical setback, or some betrayal of loyalty perhaps that you had that you were counting on, or some slip magnified — anything like that.

C 509. M-hm. That's right.

S 509. Success breeds success and failure breeds failure — that sort of thing.

C 510. And if you can see it in terms of the specific incident that caused it, then it doesn't seem quite so overwhelming as if you just feel, "Well, nothing's worth trying." That's a general mood and feeling. But sometimes we can see it in terms of a specific incident, and it doesn't appear so important.

S 510. M-hm. (*Pause, studying his notes.*) Some of this stuff I can't reinterpret.

C 511. Well, if it's all as good as what you've given, you'd better take time to figure it out. (*Laugh.*)

---

crisis is past. Nevertheless, it is plain that while these statements do no harm, it is doubtful whether they accomplish much good. The counselor's personal dilemma might be summed up as follows: During the earlier aspects of therapy, when negative feelings and conflicts are being expressed, the counselor *must* refrain from interjecting his personal views because they can do damage and will certainly delay the process; in the later and constructive phases of therapy, he might as well refrain from intruding his personal point of view, because it is so unnecessary and because the situation will be so much better handled by the client himself.

*S*511. Well, I've got a pessimistic thought here — that maybe my majority goal is self-destruction. Since I haven't really done so much about avoiding the draft, I thought maybe I had some kind of a hidden motivation there to go to war, which might be on the morbid side — or perhaps was it that I would be influenced by the glamorous conditioning that has been attached to war? I made an application for a job at the roller-bearing plant, but I suppose I should have gone back and pestered them awhile — that seems to be the usual technique of getting a factory job — you have to show them that you want to work. Just signing the application doesn't seem to be enough.

*C*512. Well, it interests me that you made the application, and it also interests me that you don't seem nearly as overwhelmed by the thought of the draft as you did earlier.

*S*512. Well, I picked up a couple of techniques that I think can get me deferred that I have a lot of confidence in. I still have just as much objection to going.

*C*513. M-hm.

*S*513. I don't know how, though — I think they'll work out pretty well. Darned if I can make it out (*looking at his notes*). (*Pause.*) Oh, that had to do with a girl I got to talking to. She said she hoped that there would not be a strip-tease to the floor show, and I was trying to analyze why she objected to it. I guess maybe she didn't want any competition. Either she would feel that the girl would be superior to her, or she had secret desires in that direction which she could condemn in someone else, but not in herself.

*C*514. Doing a little evaluating of others' motives as well as your own, hm?

*S*514. Oh, yes. I've always done that. Well, I've always analyzed others perhaps a little bit more than myself. (*Pause.*) Well, then, to sum all this up: I think that I should seek out

---

*S*514. If the fourth interview represents the high point of insight in this case, here certainly is the high point of positive decision. Mr. Bryan has plainly and clearly made the decision to take the hard way of growth, rather than the weak way of neurotic evasion.

every and all healthy situations and enter into them. I noticed a curious thing. When I made the resolve that I would take the hard way, and even though it might be the long way too, although I made the resolve in a vacuum, I got a release (*laugh*), so that way back in the last analysis, one experiences only one's own nervous system, so that it seems to be the resolve that counts, but at the same time that resolve does have to be nourished by the outward situations. And I suppose once in a while a person can resolve in a vacuum when they really sincerely mean it, but it's too hard to keep meaning it in a vacuum.

C515. And also, as you pointed out before, perhaps your earlier notion of doing something in a vacuum was really not too much a desire to make a resolve, but more a desire to get away from making a resolve.

S515. M-hm. Well, there're all sorts of masks. (*Pause.*) Well, what do you think of my prescription? Do you care to add anything to that?

C516. No, I think that — well we might be able to add details to it, but I think that that is the prescription that really will count toward more long-time satisfactions. I think you're right — it may be a hard road, may be a long road. But ——

S516. At least it's the only road.

C517. It's a road that you feel pretty well convinced now offers more satisfactions in the long run than the other direction.

S517. M-hm. The other direction seems to be a series of brief satisfactions with long intervals of great dissatisfaction. Of course, a curious thing about the human mind — it can be motivated by very brief moments. Some fellow told me that he wanted to write a book — not so much to achieve academic

---

Having faced, fully and frankly, especially during the past two interviews, all the difficult and dangerous aspects of moving ahead, he has nevertheless chosen that road. The long-time satisfactions have won out over the more immediate satisfactions of the neurosis.

C516, C517. The counselor gives clear recognition of the crucial choice which has been made.

greatness, but to have a girl praise him for it — have a dream girl come and praise him for it. And he said that that one moment when his ideal girl would react to his book that way and praise him for it would be the sufficient satisfaction — I mean, that that was the real thing that he wanted. Just that one moment. Time seems to be weighted. I mean, some instants are very, very precious metal, and others are not.

C518. And it's quite evident that since our last talk there've been some fairly heavily weighted times.

S518. Yes, that's right. One practical element enters in here. Say I had my choice of two healthy situations. Should I attack the easier one first and work up to the harder, or attack the harder first? I was wondering whether to take more risk of a defeat and at the same time take a chance on greater satisfactions, or take the easier one and work up to the harder one, as it were?

C519. I suppose that's hard to say, and evidently you're wondering there how much defeat you could stand, for example.

S519. Yes.

C520. Where eventually, I suppose, your goal is to be able to take both success and defeat without being too much disturbed by either one.

S520. I think that would probably depend largely on mood. Sometimes you're in a gambling mood — all or nothing. Other times you say, "Well, right now failure in this particular instance might do me more long-run harm, and moderate success would do me moderate good, so the easier goal — I better choose that." I guess it becomes a rather flexible thing, after all.

C518. This is by no means a recognition of the feeling that has just been expressed. It is important to note that when the client is moving forward constructively, minor errors on the counselor's part are much less significant and do little or no damage.

S518–S525. Throughout this segment one again feels the same "togetherness" which was last noted in the fourth interview. Both client and counselor are less guarded, each supplements the thinking of the other, and each can fully accept the thinking of the other.

*C*521. I don't myself see any hard and fast rule that would settle it.

*S*521. M-hm. Sometimes a terrific success in one situation might shorten the cure by a month's time. I have the definite feeling that some outstanding success might — even though it took a lot of resolution — might pay big dividends in shortening the time for a permanent cure to be achieved.

*C*522. That might be true. You feel that the road to cure is all success?

*S*522. It depends on what you mean by success. If by success you mean completely mastering every situation — no. But if by success you mean the ability to take ups and downs, why — yes.

*C*523. That's right. Yes, I wasn't quite sure how you were defining it. Yes, I think that the right road ——

*S*523. If a person needed one hundred per cent environmental success, why, that would mean he had some sort of success mania there to cover up inadequate feelings. I mean, the ego should not need that much bolstering.

*C*524. No, and the real success, or the real feeling of success, probably comes from being willing to do our damnedest, no matter how it turns out objectively.

*S*524. Well, the feeling that you have a stout ship, as it were, that could take all sorts of weather, and not pay so much attention to the weather as to the ship itself.

*C*525. The storm may tatter the sails once in a while, but you could still have the feeling that it's a good sturdy craft.

*S*525. M-hm. I have a chance to go on a trip for a couple of weeks. Do you think that that intermission in our talks would be detrimental or ——

*C*526. No, I don't. As a matter of fact, one thing I was

In *S*524 Mr. Bryan gives a classic definition of the goal of this type of therapy, or the goal of all sound mental hygiene, for that matter. To have a stout ship, and to be able to take any kind of weather — that is indeed a constructive goal. Here is no desire to have problems solved or to avoid difficult problems — simply the desire to have enough internal strength to meet life's difficulties.

going to talk about was just what we would do in that regard, because I'm going to be gone probably part of the next two weeks, during vacation.

*S*526. M-hm. I'll leave Saturday morning — this coming Saturday morning, and get back, let's see — the thirtieth, I imagine. What is — do you know when you'll be ——

*C*527. Yes, or at least I know when you could come again. We could have an appointment — oh, in the first couple days of next month. We could have one more on Friday of this week, if you wish.

*S*527. All right, fine. I've got another photographic job today, and possibly two. I'm going to try to get a society man to let me take pictures of his wedding ceremony. (*He describes the details.*) I think that'd be a nice thing — I think that'll appeal to him.

*C*528. Very good.

*S*528. Charge him twenty-five bucks for a half hour's work.

*C*529. Well, this was no empty resolve, was it?

*S*529. No. Those empty resolves remind one of Hamlet, don't they? (*Laugh.*) Where he sits and soliloquizes for long paragraphs. Did you ever have a dream where you were very thirsty and kept on drinking and didn't get any satisfaction from drinking? I mean, you drink and drink and drink — I mean, drinking water ——

*C*530. M-hm.

*S*530. — and yet your thirst wasn't at all satisfied. That seems to me what resolving in a vacuum boils down to — sort of drinking in a dream.

*C*531. M-hm. And although you're determined to get a little of ——

*S*531. I did get that flash, but I think that that was an initial flash that would have to be kept nourished by the

---

*S*527. This is the sort of implementation of decision with positive action which forms such an important aspect of the closing phases of therapy. The counselor gives a very adequate recognition to its meaning in *C*529.

*S*531–*C*535. Here again we see the much more mutual aspect of actual situations. When I did resolve to go into actual situations, why, then I got a healthy feeling. But I felt that I would need to immediately follow that up by actually going into the situation, rather than keeping on resolving in a vacuum.

*C*532. Yes, and I think your earlier statement is right, too. There isn't anything wrong with thinking in a vacuum, but real growth is much more apt to take place in contact with real situations.

*S*532. Well, there's no sense in making it easier for you to kid yourself, which is what you'd be doing.

*C*533. That's it.

*S*533. Because resolves can be sincere, or they can seem sincere.

*C*534. It's pretty important——

*S*534. The vital test would be to go out and get in the situation.

*C*535. Well, I think that you've done a real job of writing your own prescription. I think you'd better save that paper. (*Laugh.*)

*S*535. M-hm. Well, I felt that I would be more satisfied if I relied on myself, and if your rôle was one of gentle suggestion and not too much revelation — let me find out for myself. And I imagine that's the rôle that you most like to adopt anyway. I suppose some people do lean on you more heavily than others.

*C*536. Well, the thing that one finds so much is that leaning on someone is such a deceptive support. I mean, it seems

---

therapy in its later stages. Client and counselor are working together in cooperative fashion.

*S*535. It is difficult to believe that this is the same client who three days earlier was saying that he was "in the dark as to the method of making the change" (*s*427), that "I don't know just exactly what roads to take" (*s*438), and that "I realize that I want a solution" (*s*468). Five days previous to this interview he was hoping that the counselor "would pull some kind of a rabbit out of the hat." Now he has arrived at the point where he is relying upon himself and is proud of it. This is indeed progress.

like a support only for a time, and eventually it comes back to the individual himself, just as he's ——

S 536. So you're just wasting time, in the last analysis. Yes, it comes right down to "dear Brutus," doesn't it?

C 537. That's a good one. "Dear Brutus" seems to have done a pretty good job. (*Laugh.*) Well, now, I've got some other things that I have to do — I mean, I haven't much time beyond our usual hour, but we can get together again on Friday, if you like, at four. Is that O.K.?

S 537. Fine.

C 538. And then at that time we'll set an appointment for early next month.

S 538. M-hm. Yes.

C 539. O.K.

S 539. Perhaps my trip will be a physical factor that will help — I mean, there's no sense in drawing a line between the mental and physical.

C 540. Surely. Those things don't do any harm anyway. Well, I think that ——

S 540. I think I can do some photographic work down there too, to keep myself in active situations.

C 541. So that it won't be entirely vacation, it'll be also ——

S 541. The equipment — it's a matter of persuading the owner of the equipment that I'll do some good for him with it.

C 542. M-hm.

S 542. Of course, it's a little disappointing to share the profits. Wish I had my own equipment. It's up in —— and it's too big to lug around anyway.

C 543. Your own equipment is up in ——?

S 543. M-hm. So I've been getting equipment here. I know several people — of course, they're using it somewhat heavily, so — I have to scurry around for it, but at least I can get ahold of it.

S 540, *S* 542, *S* 543. These positive practical steps are very different from any of his previous conversation. They are the statements of a man who is interested in what he is doing, and is no longer solely interested in himself.

*C*544. M-hm.

*S*544. It would be better, of course, to have my own cameras.

*C*545. I'm sure you would like that better.

*S*545. Well, see you Friday.

General Comments

Discussion of the progress shown in this interview can best be initiated by indicating the spontaneous feelings expressed throughout the hour. They are as follows:

I think it would be futile to attack one symptom at a time.

I want to force myself into every situation and value the satisfactions gained.

I'm not entirely sure whether this is a healthy or an unhealthy desire.

When I have a budding healthy desire, I can find the means for achieving it.

What I said about curing myself in a vacuum was the bunk.

I can only achieve growth by meeting real situations.

Perhaps all this courage will lead only to self-destruction.

I am going to enter all healthy situations and meet them.

I have made the resolve to choose the hard way.

It is the only road for me.

I want the feeling that I am a stout ship that can take all kinds of weather.

I'm planning to take initiative in regard to my job.

I'm going to solve this problem in actual situations, not in a vacuum.

I wish to rely on myself, not on you.

These attitudes show very vividly the fact that, after teetering for two interviews between neuroticism and growth, Mr. Bryan has chosen the pathway of growth with a clearness and vitality that is amazing. Between the sixth and seventh interviews the accumulated insight has been translated into a positive decision, which brings a decided feeling of release. The attitudes expressed are in sharp contrast to the weakness and helplessness which were evident in the two preceding interviews. The crisis is fully passed. The client has discovered resources within himself for making this crucial choice and moving ahead. The counselor has handled the situation rather adequately, although at one point taking a more active part than was necessary. There is no doubt that, because the client is definitely on the upgrade in his progress, minor aspects of counseling technique become less important.

Recalling Mr. Bryan's plea in the last interview for definite suggestions, for a prescription, it is well to note how unimportant that issue has become. He realizes now that once a goal is clearly chosen, it is a relatively simple problem to discover the steps to take to reach that goal. Furthermore, he has come to recognize that he does not want help in discovering such steps. He wishes to write his own prescription. Material of this sort is of the deepest significance if we would understand the alteration of human behavior. It is the alteration of motivation that is the core of the problem.

Some readers may ask whether the marked increase in self-confidence and the courageous decision which mark this contact may not be temporary. Is this only a sort of conversion experience? Will there be a relapse? Can anything permanent be achieved in such a short space of time? Two comments may be made on these questions. In the first place, this choice has not been made under pressure. It is not a choice which has been "sold" to the client. It is not a choice in which one pathway has artificially been made to seem more desirable than the other. It is a choice which has been made after facing fully all the black and difficult aspects of each decision The neurotic solution has been seen as a thorny and painful solution, "but there's such a nice rose along with it." The growth solution has been seen as impossibly difficult, as almost too much to face, but with the important values of self-respect, greater achievement, greater long-time satisfactions. Out of this clear vision of what is involved, the client has made an absolutely independent choice, without being swayed or influenced by the counselor. Hence there is reason to suppose that it may be permanent.

In the second place, it should be stressed that the choice, though a hard one, has been made precisely because it offers satisfactions more desired by the client. Hence it will be continually reinforced by those satisfactions, this being another guarantee of its permanence.

FRIDAY THE TWENTY-FIRST

C 546. Well, not very long till vacation now, is it?

S 546. Let's see, when is it, a week or so?

C 547. Just a week, I guess.

S 547. Well, I've been noticing something decidedly new. Rather than having fluctuations, I've been noticing a very gradual steady improvement. It's just as if I had become more stabilized and my growth had been one of the hard way and the sure way rather than the wavering and fluctuating way.

C 548. M-hm.

S 548. I go into situations, and even though it's an effort, why, I go ahead and make my progress, and I find that when you sort of seize the bull by the horns, as it were, why it isn't so bad as if you sort of deliberate and perhaps — well, think too long about it like I used to. I sort of say to myself, "Well, I know absolutely that avoiding the situation will leave me in the same old rut I've been taking," and I realize that I don't want to be in the same old rut, so I go ahead and go into the situation, and even when I have disappointments in the situation, I find that they don't bring me down as much as they used to.

C 549. That sounds like very real progress.

S 549. And what pleases me is that my feelings are on an even keel, steadily improving, which gives me much more of a feeling of security than if I had fluctuations. You see, fluctuations lead you from the peaks to the valleys, and you

---

S 547–*S* 551. These statements contain the full measure of progress which has been made. The gradual improvement, the client's full control over his life and progress, stand out in the sharpest contrast to his attitudes when he first came in. At that time he was a suffering, helpless person. Now he is a confident adult, in command of himself, and no longer fearful of reality.

can't get as much self-confidence as when you're having gradual improvement.

C550. M-hm.

S550. So that the harder way is really the more satisfactory way.

C551. Then you're really finding a step-by-step type of improvement that you hadn't found before.

S551. That's right. I never — I'd always had a fluctuating thing before. I would either be all released or all inhibited. Well, I feel that this is something that I'm earning rather than something that comes from my involuntary whim.

C552. And you have really earned it in more ways than one. I mean, you've earned it by making a pretty deep-seated choice, and then you go ahead and earn the different satisfactions that come along too.

S552. Well, that's the best way, and at the rate I'm going now, I realize it won't be over a month or two before I'll be completely fixed up.

C553. I think there's no doubt about that, and my only question about that statement is that probably you've made it longer than it ——

S553. Of course, I don't know much about estimating these things, but I can sense a real wave of progress. But I know what to do with myself now.

C554. Yes, you're almost at a point right now where you have changed your direction and you've discovered some new ways of tackling your situation, and that's almost — those are the fundamentals that you need.

S554. I had a very interesting acid — sort of an acid test

S552–C554. Here is the first occasion on which Mr. Bryan has ever mentioned the possibility of completing or leaving the contacts. Fortunately the counselor is quick to recognize and accept this feeling in *C553* and *C554.* If such attitudes are not accepted, the client still feels the desire to leave, but becomes conflicted about it, fearing that the counselor wishes him to continue.

S554–S558. These "tests" exhibit a degree of self-confidence which is greater than anything we have seen before.

that I think might interest you. I bumped into a former girl friend whom I hadn't seen in some months — well, it's been longer than that, over a year I guess — and I used to get very — a large number of neurotic satisfactions with her. She increased my neurotic pleasures and also gave me more neurotic pain. And we were very attracted to each other, but broke up, and I found myself making a resolve to see if I couldn't get her to go with me again. Of course, she's somewhat wary of me now. (*Laugh.*) But I wanted to — I found myself desiring to get new and healthier satisfactions with her, rather than go back to her on the old basis. I felt that that would be a very good acid test — I mean, since we usually think of going back to something as going back to it the way it was before, but I find myself reacting differently to her. Well, it's like any situation — it isn't so much the situation that counts, but how you react to it. I mean, you can react to it neurotically or you can react to it healthily.

*C*555. You wanted to sort of test out and see whether you really had changed as much as you thought you had.

*S*555. Well, no — it wasn't so much that — I felt the healthy desires first.

*C*556. I see.

*S*556. It wasn't a case of having a doubt, then wanting to test myself.

*C*557. Well, that's true. M-hm.

*S*557. Then I had another interesting acid test. I had two jobs lined up, and the fellow who was to help didn't show up with the camera. Ordinarily that would have disappointed me very much, but I handled it pretty satisfactorily, I thought. I had a special camera coming in from ——, but the fellow had some sort of delay and wasn't able to make it. Of course, I would have to watch myself in a situation like that — that is, that might be neurotic satisfaction that I wouldn't have to go through with the job, but ——

*C*558. Well, you're getting more ——

*S*558. Well, at any rate, it perhaps wouldn't be necessary to analyze the satisfactions on every occasion, since there is improvement anyway. After all, in the last analysis I don't suppose you can analyze it — you have to have other evidence besides the feeling itself. I mean, just a feeling of satisfaction — it's very hard to label whether it's neurotic or otherwise, unless you look at other data too.

C 559. M-hm. That's true.

S 559. I mean, just the feeling *per se*, without reference to your other behavior patterns, isn't going to give you any answer.

C 560. And you're the one that knows really whether or not this particular experience was more in the nature of growth or more in the nature of an avoidance, and I would feel very certain that you know that you are reacting quite differently from what you would have before.

S 560. Well, a thing like this doesn't happen overnight.

C 561. No.

S 561. There'll be a few neurotic satisfactions, but as long as they keep getting less and less and there aren't any wild fluctuations — well, I feel much more secure than I did before.

C 562. Yes, they're likely to be — I mean, you can find a certain amount of fluctuations, to be sure, but I don't think it's the kind of road on which there's any basic turning.

S 562. Well, you know where to roll up your sleeves and what to do about it if you do find yourself slipping.

C 563. M-hm.

S 563. My parents' reaction might interest you. I had my dad drive me down. He wondered why I had to make an appointment. I told them, and they got rather upset. They might put the pump on you. You see, they have a resistance to psychoanalysis for two reasons: one is, they feel a certain amount of guilt that they had something to do with my condition; and secondly, they value the religious way of cure, and so they want me to feel that I should pray and let God do it — that sort of thing.

---

s 560–*S* 562. Another instance of client and counselor thinking together more like one person than two. One can find nothing of this "togetherness" in early interviews.

C 564. And you've found it somewhat more satisfactory to do it yourself.

S 564. That's right.

C 565. Well, if they should get in touch with me, I'm afraid I shall just refer them to you.

S 565. Well, I didn't know what you'd do in a case like that. I wanted you to know that I had told them. I thought that would be the best thing, to tell them. They — it's rather amusing in a way — they — you see, they believe in a strictly free will, in the fullest sense of the word. Well, they have sort of a — rather a mixed up ideology there — that is, God rules things, but one of His gifts is free will, which you can even use to turn against God — that is, by his consent, in the larger sense of the word. So — yet at the same time they have a sneaking feeling that they didn't raise me right, which is one of the reasons that I — I mean, they look at me rather askance — like I'm a queer bird — yet they subconsciously blame themselves. But they don't extend that to blaming their own parents for what they did to me, see? (*Laugh.*)

C 566. M-hm.

S 566. So I have a hostility there. So they're praying, and when they see me more ambitious, why, they'll give credit to prayer, and so everything will be all right.

C 567. Well, you can take that. I mean, if that's the thing that's satisfying for them to believe ——

S 567. Why, it doesn't matter to me. I'm very tolerant of other persons' feelings. The main thing is, as long as I live at home, I keep things reasonably smooth.

C 568. And I suspect you feel that with some of the changes that you're making in yourself, probably things will go smoothly in relation to them.

S 568. M-hm. Well, they'll be pleased about me getting a defense job. You see, they don't like photography — they think it's sort of a loose way to live. Of course, I like it be-

---

S 568–*S* 574. Here is constructive planning of the most satisfactory sort. As in his last remarks in the seventh interview, Mr. Bryan is no longer thinking solely of himself and his problems, but has accause you don't have to work very many hours and make a good deal of money in relationship to the hours, but they have a puritan belief in work *per se*. But I want to get into an industrial plant anyway, because of the war, so it's working out all right for a different reason. My motive is different from theirs, but the results will be the same. And I've canvassed the town enough now — made my initial contacts in the photographic field so that I can do it part-time now — do it in the evening. When you first hit a town, you have to make the opening contacts to sell the idea of the thing. Then you make a follow-up contact to set a definite date. I've already made my initial canvasses to do in the evening, and I want to hook my way into the office out there at the plant — make myself very valuable to the program.

C 569. Do I gather that you have a pretty good chance of getting something there now?

S 569. Oh, yes, I can get on there. See, I worked at a similar job in ———. I went out there last summer and got a job.

C 570. I see.

S 570. But just being an ordinary workman's not enough. I've got some ideas about production efficiency — how the assembly lines can be speeded up, and something like that will make a person very valuable, so that I can serve my country and incidentally myself.

C 571. (*Laugh.*) What's more — you're getting into what will probably be a fairly challenging situation, but meeting it.

S 571. Yeah. M-hm. The — any kind of a job like that would be valuable just from the psychological viewpoint alone.

C 572. M-hm.

S 572. Of course, some work's awful monotonous — that's where I get pretty impatient that way. But the higher up you go, the more interesting it becomes. I don't like a lot of

quired a healthy and optimistic interest in things outside himself. The fact that he may be slightly overoptimistic does not alter the value of the attitude.

mechanical detail, but I'm going to keep all I get from out there, and in about a couple weeks I'm going to walk into the production office with an idea.

*C*573. That arouses my curiosity. You say in a couple of weeks — does that mean you're not going to take your trip, or after you come back from your trip?

*S*573. No, we aren't going to go after all. (*Explains his change of plans.*)

*C*574. Well, that sounds as though you'd made a good deal of progress, and you're laying quite a lot of sound plans for the future.

*S*574. Yes, what I want to do now is to be a valuable man in defense work, and do photography on the side, and work on my novel.

*C*575. You keep bringing these surprises in intentionally, I think. (*Laugh.*)

*S*575. Hm? Well, it's the way I feel. I mean, a lot of times I feel — well, not very ambitious, and then I don't get my ideas, but when I feel my growth like I have been, why, I get more and more ideas — more and more plans. What's that about intentionally — you think I ——

*C*576. No, I'm just curious. I mean, you hadn't mentioned any novel before. You're actually working on one, or just contemplating one?

*S*576. I have the idea well worked out.

*C*577. Good.

*S*577. It's along the *Hamlet* theme. (*He discusses the plot in some detail.*) I want it to be sort of a thoughtful tragedy — even though it does have a pessimistic theme, I want to bring out all of these social and psychological implications.

*C*578. Well, that sounds like — certainly like material for a novel.

---

*s*577. It seemed unwise to include the details of the plot, and two or three minutes of conversation have been omitted here. Mr. Bryan's discussion of the plot has more the quality of a social conversation than any segment of any interview up to this point. He discusses his plans, giving evidence of a serious purpose.

S 578. And — it might have a timely appeal.

C 579. M-hm.

S 579. You see, right now, the literature of today will reveal the dawn, but there'll be a blackout before the dawn. I mean, that's the movement of the times.

C 580. M-hm.

S 580. Take now — the work that has looked into the future has been of such a fantastical nature that it doesn't have any real meat. Such things as *Lost Horizon*, things like that, have all been very fantastical — a brave new world, that sort of thing. But I have a gift of expression with words, and I want to use it.

C 581. You're really going to try out this new self of yours, aren't you?

S 581. I've always felt that I could do two things; one, be satisfactory to myself, and I feel too that I could get a certain amount of social recognition, which will be an inevitable by-product of one's own self-satisfaction and self-achievement. I don't want to be famous *per se*. I believe my desire there is that it helps you to gain social goals and to have social prestige. I prefer to get the satisfaction from self-appraisal, and then public acclaim as a means of enabling you to achieve your social touchdowns, as it were.

C 582. Well, that all sounds good.

S 582. Well, I know that I'm a dynamo when I get started, and I have done some written work, and I've had some very different professors, and they all said that I had a knack of working with words, and expressing my ideas — my use of vivid metaphors, and so forth.

C 583. And now you're willing to take the chances that are involved in trying to really do something along that line.

---

s 580. Contrast this bold, confident self with the individual of the first interview, blocked by his neurosis from entering any field of activity.

C 583. The counselor cannot refrain, even at this point, from a mildly interpretive comment. His statement in *C* 585 is more satisfactory, and is accepted.

*S*583. Well, I don't know as it's exactly a gamble·— I mean——

*C*584. Well, I was thinking that perhaps before it was a little too much of a gamble for your self-esteem, and so on, and now you're more willing to enter into a lot of these things.

*S*584. Well, in case I had manuscripts rejected, you mean?

*C*585. Yes, I suppose that'd be one kind of thing. And even more than that, the willingness to make the actual attempt.

*S*585. Well, that's the main thing. You see, it had been awfully hard for me to sit down. When I'd sit down I'd find that I — I mean, I'd feel that I wasn't getting any pleasure and I'd get very restless and perhaps write a little bit — then I'd go out to a night club and try to get some sort of pleasures. But now — when you feel right inside, you don't mind spending a quiet evening at home — you don't have to go out and seek that sort of a pleasure. Of course, I'll always enjoy night life, but it won't be such a compulsion. It's interesting how the same behavior can mean such a vastly different thing inside.

*C*586. That's right. (*Pause.*) M-hm. Yes, the things that happen to you or some of the things you do may be the same things, but they can look very different when your own viewpoint is changed, or your direction is changed.

*S*586. Well, I'd like a night club to be something that I can take or leave — not something that I have to haunt night after night. I find myself losing the urge to drink, too. I mean — I have known that that's what would happen to me. I can predict pretty well those things, and I knew that my urge to drink would lessen as I got healthier. That's one of the things that made me feel so tragic, because I could see so

---

*S*585, *S*586. As Mr. Bryan says, "It's interesting how the same behavior can mean such a vastly different thing inside." It is the goal, the direction of his life, which has changed, and this change gives new meaning even to old actions. Note, too, how easily the "problems" — the drinking, the compulsion in regard to night clubs and voyeurism — are solved when the basic issue of direction is settled. Different behavior is adopted almost immediately when different goals become predominant.

clearly what I might be, and of course that added to my motivation to do something about it.

C 587. M-hm.

S 587. So I have a feeling that I may be rather famous
— at least, I'll be pleased if I do something important.

C 588. Yes, I think that's entirely possible, and I think too
that you could face the fact of not being too famous if it worked
out that way, because ——

S 588. My self-satisfaction comes first, and if you have self-
satisfaction and money, you don't need fame to achieve your
goals. I mean, fame helps — when your name — you can
move people around more. I mean, they're anxious to do
your bidding — anxious to please you, anxious to identify
themselves with you — that sort of thing. But the actual
applause itself would mean nothing to me if I didn't have my
own self-satisfaction. If I know I'm all right, and the world
boos, why, that's a lot better than my inward dissatisfaction
with the world's applause.

C 589. Yes, that's quite true.

S 589. But as long as a fellow has it in him, he might as well
play to the public, as there are some pretty nice plums there
and a certain amount of public recognition. But if you lean
on public applause alone, you're in for a lot of ups and downs
there. I mean — you've seen people that live entirely, you
know — for the spotlight, and while the public's applauding,
they're 'way up, but just let something happen, they aren't
able to weather it.

C 590. They live by extreme fluctuation. M-hm.

S 590. They're not able to take public criticism. So I feel
that that's a two-edged sword, to overvalue those social opinions.

C 591. Well, it sounds as though today you're feeling pretty
sure of your own progress and you certainly have taken a lot
of steps in the direction of progress.

S 591. Well, it isn't just only today — it's been — I mean
since our last meeting there's been a steady improvement.

S 591. The client will not let the counselor, even by unintentional
implication, give the notion that this change is temporary.

*C*592. Oh, yes.

*S*592. When I have felt the negatives coming on, I've done something about it.

*C*593. M-hm.

*S*593. And in the act of doing something about it, I've actually felt the improvement taking place. Even in the act of dialing a number to make a business contact, I can feel the surge of improvement that I wouldn't have felt if I hadn't actually done the act.

*C*594. M-hm.

*S*594. Does that sound pretty sound to you?

*C*595. Yes, it does.

*S*595. Well, I feel that this is a technique that can be depended upon. It isn't the involuntary sort of improvement that I used to have.

*C*596. And it can be depended upon in large measure because you're the one that selected the road and you're the one that decided that's where you're going to go.

*S*596. Yes. I feel good about that. I felt that I was working for myself, and you gave me some signposts, of course, but I feel that I made the decisions, and I don't think that you feel that I detract from you when I say that.

*C*597. No, not at all. Matter of fact, it's my deepest conviction that I can't help you — I can't help anybody, but I can sometimes create an atmosphere where the person can help themselves.

---

*s*596. This interesting statement constitutes strong justification for the type of structure which has been given throughout the counseling relationship. Here Mr. Bryan gives some inkling as to what the structure has meant to him. It is, of course, doubly interesting when one thinks of the earlier passages in regard to these same decisions. The reader has but to recall the way in which he has dreaded making these decisions, his feeling that he was too helpless to make them, his desire for the counselor to settle some of the issues for him. But all this is now in the past. The fact that the counselor has held firmly to a sound counseling relationship has enabled the client to make these choices himself. Now, having made them, he has a basis of self-confidence which no one can take away.

S 597. M-hm.

C 598. And the — you had gone a long ways in helping yourself when you — before you ever saw me, and decided, "By gosh, I'm going to do something about this!"

S 598. You're sort of a pioneer in this, aren't you? Is this largely your own technique?

C 599. Oh — I don't know. It seems to work, at any rate.

S 599. I haven't kept up so much with the latest psychoanalytic techniques.

C 600. Well, there certainly are many others. I think that a good many different people have been working toward somewhat the same point of view.

S 600. Well, perhaps some day I can bring you a copy of my novel.

C 601. (*Laugh.*) Right. I'd be delighted to get it. Well, now, you're feeling really pretty confident of your own ability to handle this. I would like to leave the notion of further contacts up to you. That is, do you want to come in again or ——

S 601. That's the thought I had — that — I felt that since you were so busy and that I had made this improvement, that

---

S 598–*S* 600. This is the first instance in which Mr. Bryan has expressed any interest in the counselor as a person, separate and distinct from his own needs. This kind of interest is very typical of the closing phases of therapy. (See Chapter VIII, pp. 222–23.) Notice, too, how the client responds in *s* 600 as a genuinely independent equal. He is saying in effect, "I respect you as a person, and I am interested in the things you have done. I too am a person worthy of respect, and I too shall do things."

C 601. The counselor has fortunately caught the attitude expressed in *s* 595–*s* 600, an attitude that the contacts are complete and that they have served their purpose. He wisely responds to this by letting the client see that as soon as he is ready, the relationship may be concluded.

s 601. Note how quickly the client responds, without waiting for the sentence to be completed. Obviously he has been thinking a great deal about the end of the relationship, but has hesitated to bring this thinking fully into the open.

if there would be any problems arise, I perhaps could call in and make an appointment. But I feel that in the main the regular appointments will no longer be needed.

C602. I would feel that, too. And I shall be doubtful if you need others. Though, if you find that you want to come in some time next month — all right, call me, and I'll be glad to have you come in, but my guess is that you've got this thing pretty well where you want it and ——

S602. I had a feeling — I had read some literature that these things took months and oftentimes years, and I got to thinking — mine has been amazingly short, but nevertheless, after all, that need not invalidate things — the fact of it being a relatively short period.

C603. Well, you see, there's been some progress along that line too.

S603. Speed is what counts.

C604. I think part of the reason is — I wouldn't pretend and you wouldn't pretend that your problems are all solved or anything of that kind — I think though that you have found the direction you want to move and the kind of approach that you can take to work toward that goal; and surely problems will come up — probably quite difficult problems, but I think that you're — you have the tools that you want to meet those problems now.

S604. Sure, that's the main thing.

C605. I think that sometimes people have felt that this sort of thing should solve an individual's problems, and consequently, if you're going to try to do that, that does take years.

---

s602. This statement has considerable theoretical interest. Here is a client who has been expecting that the therapeutic process would take months, at the very minimum. Yet he feels such an assurance that he is no longer in need of help that he is willing to act upon his own inner feeling of independence, in spite of the fact that only three weeks have elapsed.

c604. The counselor gives excellent expression to the feeling the client has been expressing in various ways from S553 on.

*S*605. Well, as I see it, it's giving a person a technique to help himself — letting him work things out on his own and — that one of the nice things about it is that it makes problems interesting rather than disheartening, and you have your growth, so that's better than life without obstacles and problems.

*C*606. That's right. That's right. There's ——

*S*606. There seems to be something deeper grained in the satisfactions. When you're healthy, why, you get a kick out of problem solving and finding a way of overcoming obstacles.

*C*607. That's right. If you have a fairly clear-cut notion of what you're working toward, then obstacles are just an interesting challenge to battle through or solve in one way or another. And life would be very empty without them, I think. Be like the old fashioned pictures of heaven — just golden streets and nothing to do.

*S*607. M-hm. I just — I was wondering about — (*There follow some personal questions asked of the counselor, which have been omitted because of their identifying nature.*) I've often thought lately if I weren't somewhat too old or had had a different kind of training, I might like to go in for psychological work myself. I can always do it in an amateur way.

*C*608. Yes. You have a good deal of insight into other people, I think, as it is.

*S*608. And I can work it into my writings too.

*C*609. Yes. I was interested in the account of your novel. It had a good many ——

*S*609. M-hm. I'm going to write a novel about a psycho-

---

*S*605, *S*606. These statements give so clearly the aims of therapy as expressed in this book, that the reader may suppose that in some way Mr. Bryan has absorbed them from the counselor. It may be pointed out that at no time in these contacts has the counselor advanced the notion that growth is the ideal, rather than life without problems. Yet through the therapeutic experience, Mr. Bryan has come to feel that this is true.

*S*607, *S*609. This indirect way of expressing warmth of feeling toward the counselor is quite typical of the final interviews in therapy.

analyst, too — I had that in mind. Maybe you might see a ghost of yourself in print some time.

C610. (*Laugh.*) Don't make it too identifying. (*Laugh.*)

S610. Well, we've got a bargain there.

C611. O.K. (*Pause.*) Well, it's been very nice to ——

S611. This has certainly been a fine experience for me.

C612. Well, I always feel that I get something out of it, too.

S612. Well, I hope that even though you have been very busy, you felt that finding time for me was worth while to you.

C613. Very much worth while. Very much.

S613. Fine.

C614. O.K. And good luck to you.

S614. The same to you.

---

s611–s614. This is a clean-cut ending of a cycle of experience which has definitely made for growth. Mr. Bryan is obviously ready to leave and to face life without the support which the counseling relationship has given him.

General Comments

The most vivid measure of what has been accomplished is contained in the list of attitudes expressed by Mr Bryan during this interview. The reader would do well to read first the feelings voiced by Mr. Bryan in the first interview (pp. 287–88), and then to contrast them with the following:

I'm steadily improving. I'm growing the hard and sure way.
I meet situations differently.
I'm finding more satisfactions in this hard way of growth.
I'm earning my satisfactions.
I'm nearly finished with our contacts.
I know what to do with myself now.
I've tested out the difference in myself and know that it is real.
I've told my parents what I'm doing.
I reject their attitudes, but I can let them think their own way.
I have many constructive plans in regard to my work.
I plan to work on my novel.
I am full of confidence.
I no longer feel the compulsion for night clubs or the need to drink excessively.

I expect to work for public recognition, but it's my own judgment of myself that counts.

I am able to control my own improvement.

I feel a personal interest in you.

I shall not need your help any longer.

I'm going to get a healthy satisfaction out of solving my problems.

I have a warm feeling toward you personally.

This has been a fine experience for me.

This is a highly satisfactory concluding interview. It belongs to Mr. Bryan from beginning to end. The extremely positive feelings and actions and the self-confidence expressed are in the most astonishing contrast to the first three interviews, or to Interviews Five and Six. He has completed the full cycle of therapy — expression, insight, positive decision, reoriented action in line with the newly chosen goals.

This final interview is very well handled by the counselor. There is good recognition of progress. Most important of all, the counselor is alert to the client's first faint expression of the fact that he feels ready to become independent of counseling help. It is not often that all aspects of the closing phases of therapy are condensed into one interview. In many respects this interview reads like a summary of Chapter VIII. To be sure, the closing was forecast in the preceding interview, but there has been no consideration of the issue until this contact. In spite of the fact that closing is more rapid than is usual, it is nevertheless complete, and Mr. Bryan leaves with full recognition of a process cleanly finished and left behind, with a new and more challenging vista opening ahead.

SOME CONCLUDING REMARKS

Readers who approach this series of therapeutic contacts from varying points of view, may differ in their interpretation of the material. Yet any thoughtful reader would find it difficult to deny that something significant has occurred. There may be criticisms of techniques, there may be disagreements as to viewpoint, but at least there must be agreement that a change has taken place. It is this that gives this phonographic account its significance and justifies its complete reproduction.

Before asking what has happened, let us point out some of the things which have not happened. The client has not achieved complete insight, complete understanding of the significance of all of his actions. He has not yet completely solved all his present problems, and certainly he has not solved all his future problems. It is unlikely that this therapeutic process has altered any basic physiological instability which he may possess, though so close is the interaction of the psychic with the organic that further study will be necessary to answer this question. It is unlikely that the counseling contacts have completely insured him against the need of help in the future. Weighty combinations of unfortunate circumstances might again drive him into regressive solutions, though therapy has made this possibility less likely. It is certain that the interviews have not made him conform to goals and attitudes which are acceptable to the counselor, nor the goals and attitudes of any specific group. What, then, has occurred? What is it that has taken place?

Considering this question solely from the client's point of view, and disregarding for the moment the counselor's part in making these steps possible, we may say that what has happened may be summarized in a few statements:

1. The client has come for help. Whether or not this initiative is absolutely necessary, there is no doubt that it has facilitated the process.

2. He has freely explored his problems and their bases in his confused and conflicting fundamental desires.

3. He has developed a working insight into those reaction patterns which were blocking his growth toward maturity.

4. He has faced the full implications of that insight and has freely and of his own choice selected the "more weighty satisfactions," around which he can integrate his activities.

5. He has implemented his new choice by means of positive plans carried out in action.

6. He has become independent of further help from the counselor and has acquired confidence in his ability to direct his own life.

These would seem to be the significant steps in the therapeutic process in this case. Whether one chooses to regard this as sufficient progress, whether one wishes to disagree with the means employed, this is, at least, a description of the predictable process of therapy, as it has been presented throughout this book.

This process acquires a deeper significance when we see that it operates in different types of cases — with maladjusted children and maladjusted parents, with failing students, with situations of marital maladjustment, with persons of ordinary ability or those with superior intellectual endowment. Its import is further deepened when we discover that it is a process which can be and is duplicated by workers of differing training — psychologists, psychiatrists, social workers, college counselors. We cannot help being impressed by the fact that it is a process which, whether carried on in Philadelphia, New York, Chicago, or Columbus, has nevertheless its typical phases. The fact that such therapy can be carried on (in somewhat halting fashion, to be sure) by those with little therapeutic experience as well as by those with years of work behind them, adds to our conviction that it is a genuine process, not an artistic accident. The realization is forced upon us that the therapeutic process under discussion may represent a highly significant social discovery in the field of motivation of human behavior. The possibilities of refinement and improvement of the process, of its application to groups as well as to individuals, challenge the imagination, and give constructive and realistic hope for the future.

Recent Trends in Therapy

✒ A SELECTED BIBLIOGRAPHY ✒

AN exhaustive bibliography on counseling and psychotherapy would be unwieldy, and much of the material is now
distinctly out of date. The following list of references was
chosen with several factors in mind. It was chosen, first of
all, to give representation to widely different points of view
which have enriched and advanced our understanding of the
therapeutic process. There was no attempt to list references
of historical importance; on the contrary, the list is limited
to recent references which reflect current attitudes. It was
also the purpose to represent a variety of authors, and for this
reason no individual is listed more than three times. Finally,
it was the intent of the writer to include only work dealing
with the *practice* of counseling and psychotherapy, thus omit-
ting many works which are primarily theoretical formulations.
A number of the references contain bibliographies which will
carry the serious student farther into this large topic.

A word should be said as to the major streams of thought
represented in this list. They might be classified in different
ways, but the following will help to guide the reader who
wishes to gain an understanding of both the diversity and the
unity of thinking in the field. Although labels are always
objectionable, each group is identified by a name which has
at least the virtue of common use.

(*a*) Relationship therapy is a point of view stemming originally from the thinking of Otto Rank, modified and expressed

by different workers. The concepts underlying this book are much influenced by the Rankian group. This viewpoint is represented on the following list by such references as numbers 1, 19, 31, 42, 44d, 44f.

(*b*) Modern Freudian psychoanalysis has had an important influence on the development of therapeutic thinking. In general this group has not been bound by classical techniques, but has advanced beyond them. References 14, 15, 21, and 23 are examples of this viewpoint, though some of these authors differ sharply with each other.

(*c*) Student and marital counseling is a field which has grown up largely independently of the two previous groups. Within this field there are many variations of approach, of which examples would be numbers 8, 13, 25, 28, 41, 45.

(*d*) Industrial counseling has played very little part in our understanding of the counseling process. It is primarily because it is a highly independent development that reference 33 is of vital interest.

(*e*) Play therapy with children has grown into a separate field with a literature all its own. References 5, 6, 9, 11, 17, 18, 29 and 36 cover some of the developments which have taken place. For a general orientation, references 29 or 36 are most satisfactory.

(*f*) Group therapy is the name given to the attempt to translate the principles of individual treatment into procedures for groups, drawing heavily upon play techniques. See numbers 12 and 40.

(*g*) Therapy through drama is a field which has been little developed. It is noted here because it is a stimulating attempt to utilize the principles of therapy in fresh ways. See numbers 10 and 27.

(*h*) Supportive therapy, in which the worker plays a parental rôle, is a significant grouping, because it is undoubtedly rather widely used. It has been too little described. See number 3.

(*i*) In a last grouping, probably the largest of all, might be placed the eclectic writers, whose practice is influenced by many streams of thought. Here too should be listed those symposia which endeavor to present a variety of viewpoints to the eclectic reader. Examples are numbers 2, 22, 24, 30, 34, 37, 39, and 44. It is hoped that this rough classification, while not including all of the references, may serve as a helpful guide to the reader in selecting the avenues he wishes to follow in becoming acquainted with the following writers.

1. Allen, Frederick H. *Psychotherapy with Children.* New York: W. W. Norton Company, 1942. This is the most complete exposition of relationship therapy as practiced with children at the Philadelphia Child Guidance Clinic.

2. "Areas of Agreement in Psychotherapy," a symposium in the *American Journal of Orthopsychiatry,* vol. 10, number 4 (October, 1940), pp. 698–709, containing contributions by Goodwin Watson, chairman, Alexandra Adler, Frederick H. Allen, Eleanor Bertine, J. O. Chassell, Carl R. Rogers, Saul Rosenzweig, Robert Waelder. A symposium representing a variety of points of view.

3. Axelrode, Jeanette. "Some Indications for Supportive Therapy," *American Journal of Orthopsychiatry,* vol. 10 (April, 1940), pp. 264–271. Discussion of cases in which the worker plays a parental rôle.

4. Baruch, Dorothy W. *Parents and Children Go to School.* Chicago: Scott, Foresman and Company, 1939. Chap. 6, "In Conference." A case account of the treatment of parental attitudes.

5. Baruch, Dorothy W. "Therapeutic Procedures as Part of the Educative Process," *Journal of Consulting Psychology,* vol. 4 (September–October, 1940), pp. 165–172. An account of play therapy incorporated into a nursery school program.

6. Bender, Lauretta, and Woltmann, A. G. "The Use of Plastic Material as a Psychiatric Approach to Emotional Problems in Children," *American Journal of Orthopsychiatry,* vol. 7 (July, 1937), pp. 283–300.

7. Blanchard, Phyllis. "1937 Case for Symposium, and Symposium," *American Journal of Orthopsychiatry,* vol. 7 (July, 1937), pp. 383–422. Presentation of the therapeutic work carried on with one case.

8. Chassell, Joseph O. "Individual Counseling of College Students," *Journal of Consulting Psychology,* vol. 4 (November–December, 1940), pp. 205–209.

9. Conn, J. H.   "The Child Reveals Himself Through Play,"
Mental Hygiene, vol. 23 (January, 1939), pp. 49–69.   A discussion
of a directive type of play therapy.

10. Curran, F. J.   "The Drama as a Therapeutic Measure in Adolescents," *American Journal of Orthopsychiatry*, vol. 9 (April,
1939), pp. 215–231.

11. Despert, J. Louise, *Emotional Problems in Children*.   Utica,
New York: State Hospital Press, 1938.   An account of various
expressive play techniques used with children.

12. Durkin, Helen E.   "Dr. John Levy's Relationship Therapy
Applied to a Play Group," *American Journal of Orthopsychiatry*,
vol. 9 (July, 1939), pp. 583–598.

13. Elliott, H. S. and Elliott, G. L.   *Solving Personal Problems*.
New York: Henry Holt and Company, 1936, chaps. 11–14,
inclusive.   A book focused on an understanding of student
counseling.

14. Fenichel, Otto.   *Problems of Psychoanalytic Techniques*.   (Trans.
by David Brunswick.)   Albany, New York: Psychoanalytic
Quarterly, Inc., 1941.   130 pp.   A discussion of therapeutic
problems from the Freudian point of view.

15. Gerard, Margaret W.   "Case for Discussion at the 1938 Symposium," *American Journal of Orthopsychiatry*, vol. 8 (January,
1938), pp. 1–18.

16. Gerard, Margaret W. "The 1938 Symposium," *American Journal
of Orthopsychiatry*, vol. 8 (July, 1938), pp. 409–435.   Discussion
of a treatment case presented by Dr. Gerard.

17. Gitelson, M. and collaborators.   "Clinical Experience with
Play Therapy," *American Journal of Orthopsychiatry*, vol. 8
(July, 1938), pp. 466–478.

18. Gitelson, M.   "Direct Psychotherapy with Children," *Archives
of Neurology and Psychiatry*, vol. 43 (June, 1940), pp. 1208–1223.
A discussion of play therapy from a modified Freudian point of
view.

19. Hankins, Dorothy.   "A Psychology of Helping in Work with
Adolescents," *Journal of Social Work Process*, vol. 1 (November,
1937), pp. 85–103.

20. Hollis, Florence.   *Social Case Work in Practice*, New York:
Family Welfare Association, 1939.   Case records of treatment.

21. Horney, Karen.   *New Ways in Psychoanalysis*, New York:
W. W. Norton Company, 1939.   Especially Chap. 16, "Psycho-

analytic Therapy." This book is a critical re-evaluation of the Freudian point of view.

22. Lewis, Virginia W. "Intensive Treatment with Adolescent Girls," *Journal of Consulting Psychology*, vol. 4 (September–October, 1940), pp. 181–184. A preliminary analysis of various phases of psychotherapy.

23. Lippman, H. S. "Direct Treatment Work with Children," *American Journal of Orthopsychiatry*, vol. 4 (July, 1934), pp. 374–381. A discussion of child analysis.

24. Maslow, A. H. and Mittelmann, B. *Principles of Abnormal Psychology*. New York: Harper and Brothers, 1941. Part IV, "Psychotherapy," pp. 273–362.

25. May, Rollo. *The Art of Counseling*. Nashville, Tennessee: The Cokesbury Press, 1939. 247 pp. A somewhat popular presentation.

26. Mills, Harriet J. "The Prognostic Value of the First Interview," *Smith College Studies in Social Work*, vol. 8, number 1 (September, 1937), pp. 1–33. A research study of the criteria which determine treatability of parental attitudes through psychotherapy.

27. Moreno, J. L. "Psychodramatic Shock Therapy," *Sociometry*, vol. 2 (January, 1939), pp. 1–30.

28. Mowrer, Harriet R. *Personality Adjustment and Domestic Discord*. New York: American Book Company, 1935. Techniques used in the adjustment of marital problems.

29. Newell, H. W. "Play Therapy in Child Psychiatry," *American Journal of Orthopsychiatry*, vol. 11 (April, 1941), pp. 245–251. A review of current points of view, with a selected bibliography of 36 titles.

30. Potter, Howard W. "Psychotherapy in Children," *Psychiatric Quarterly*, vol. 9 (July, 1935), pp. 335–348. A psychiatrist presents an eclectic point of view.

31. Rank, Otto. *Will Therapy*. New York: Alfred A. Knopf, 1936, 291 pp. Rank's own statement of his point of view.

32. Ritterskampf, Louise. "The First Interview as a Guide to Treatment," *Smith College Studies in Social Work*, vol. 8, number 1 (September, 1937), pp. 34–84. A companion study to number 26 on this list.

33. Roethlisberger, F. J., and Dickson, W. J. *Management and the Worker*. Cambridge, Mass.: Harvard University Press, 1939, chap. 13, "The Interviewing Method"; chap. 14, "Complaints

and Personal Equilibrium"; and chap. 26, "Implications for Personnel Practice." Presents the counseling program based on research studies at the Western Electric Company.

34. Rogers, Carl R. *The Clinical Treatment of the Problem Child.* Boston: Houghton Mifflin Company, 1939, chaps. 7, 10, 11. These chapters discuss treatment interviews with parents and children.

35. Rogers, Carl R. "The Processes of Therapy," *Journal of Consulting Psychology*, vol. 4 (September–October, 1940), pp. 161–164. A brief statement of basic elements.

36. Rogerson, C. H. *Play Therapy in Childhood.* London: Oxford University Press, 1939. 63 pp. An account of play therapy in a British guidance clinic.

37. Rosenzweig, Saul. "Some Implicit Common Factors in Diverse Methods of Psychotherapy," *American Journal of Orthopsychiatry*, vol. 6 (July, 1936), pp. 412–415.

38. Schilder, Paul. *Psychotherapy*, New York: W. W. Norton Company, 1938, chapters 8, 9, 10. An eclectic account of various approaches to psychotherapy.

39. Shaffer, L. F. *The Psychology of Adjustment.* Boston: Houghton Mifflin Company, 1936, chap. 16. A general discussion of treatment techniques.

40. Slavson, S. R. "Group Therapy," *Mental Hygiene*, vol. 24 (January, 1940), pp. 36–49.

41. Stogdill, E. L. "Techniques of Student Counseling," *Journal of Consulting Psychology*, vol. 4 (September–October, 1940), pp. 176–180. An outline of various techniques used in this field.

42. Taft, Jessie. *The Dynamics of Therapy.* New York: The Macmillan Company, 1933. A presentation and discussion of two cases of children treated from a Rankian point of view.

43. Towle, Charlotte, *Social Case Records from Psychiatric Clinics.* Chicago: University of Chicago Press, 1941. A detailed presentation of twelve case records involving treatment.

44. "Trends in Therapy," Symposium in the *American Journal of Orthopsychiatry*, vol. 9 (October, 1939), pp. 669–760, containing the following seven articles:

    a. L. G. Lowrey, "Evolution, Status, and Trends."
    b. H. S. Lippman, "Child Analysis."
    c. David M. Levy, "Release Therapy."
    d. Frederick H. Allen, "Participation in Therapy."

e. George H. Reeves, "A Method of Coordinated Treatment."
f. Almena Dawley, "Interrelated Movement of Parent and Child in Therapy with Children."
g. A. T. Poffenberger, "Specific Psychological Therapies."
45. Wrenn, Gilbert, "Counseling with Students," chap. IV, pp. 119–143, in *Guidance in Educational Institutions*, part I of the 37th Yearbook of the National Society for the Study of Education. Bloomington, Illinois: Public School Publishing Company, 1938
A modern point of view in college counseling.

Index